Karen E. Lovaas, PhD
John P. Elia, PhD
Gust A. Yep, PhD
Editors

LGBT Studies and Queer Theory: New Conflicts, Collaborations, and Contested Terrain

LGBT Studies and Queer Theory: New Conflicts, Collaborations, and Contested Terrain has been co-published simultaneously as *Journal of Homosexuality*, Volume 52, Numbers 1/2 2006.

Pre-publication
REVIEWS,
COMMENTARIES,
EVALUATIONS . . .

"MOST USEFUL FOR READERS WHO DO NOT KNOW MUCH ABOUT THESE DISCIPLINES. The more specific articles focus on how the tensions between lesbian and gay studies and queer theory translate into various arenas of life. The reader can choose all or specific areas of interest to explore how they are enlightened by the views of these disciplines and the critiques of queer theory."

Ski Hunter, MSW, PhD
Professor, School of Social Work
University of Texas at Arlington

Harrington Park Press

LGBT Studies and Queer Theory: New Conflicts, Collaborations, and Contested Terrain

LGBT Studies and Queer Theory: New Conflicts, Collaborations, and Contested Terrain has been co-published simultaneously as *Journal of Homosexuality*, Volume 52, Numbers 1/2 2006.

Monographs from the *Journal of Homosexuality*®

For additional information on these and other Haworth Press titles, including descriptions, tables of contents, reviews, and prices, use the QuickSearch catalog at http://www.HaworthPress.com.

1. *Homosexuality and the Law,* edtied by Donald C. Knutson, JD (Vol. 5, No. 1/2, 1979). *Leading law professors and practicing lawyers address the important legal issues and court decisions relevant to male and female homosexuality–criminal punishment for gay sex acts, employment discrimination, child custody, gay organizational rights, and more.*

2. *The Gay Past: A Collection of Historical Essays,* edited by Salvatore J. Licata, PhD, and Robert P. Petersen (Vol. 6, No. 1/2, 1980). *"Scholarly and excellent. Its authority is impeccable, and its treatment of this neglected area exemplary." (Choice)*

3. *Philosophy and Homosexuality,* edtied by Noretta Koertge, PhD (Vol. 6, No. 4, 1981). *"An interesting, thought-provoking book, well worth reading as a corrective to much of the research literature on homosexuality." (Australian Journal of Sex, Marriage & Family)*

4. *A Guide to Psychotherapy with Gay and Lesbian Clients,* edited by John C. Gonsiorek, PhD (Vol. 7, No. 2/3, 1982). *"A book that seeks to create affirmative psychotherapeutic models.... The contributors' credentials and experiences are impressive and extensive.... To say this book is needed by all doing therapy with gay or lesbian clients is an understatement." (The Advocate)*

5. *Gay and Sober: Directions for Counseling and Therapy,* edited by Thomas O. Ziebold, PhD, and John E. Mongeon (d. 1994) (Vol. 7, No. 4, 1982). *"A good book, easy to read, and free from jargon and prejudices. It is a research-oriented, academic work which deals with special problems posed by being an alcoholic and at the same time being gay. Even those whose work does not involve specifically working with the gay population will find this an interesting book." (Alcohol & Alcoholism)*

6. *Literary Visions of Homosexuality,* edited by Stuart Kellogg, PhD (Vol. 8, No. 3/4, 1983). *"An important book. Gay sensibility has never been given such a boost." (The Advocate)*

7. *Homosexuality, Masculinity, and Femininity,* edited by Michael W. Ross, PhD (Vol. 9, No. 1, 1983). *"A useful addition to the literature in both gender roles and sexual preference . . . it raises a number of questions which deserve further exploration." (Family Relations)*

8. *Origins of Sexuality and Homosexuality,* edited by John P. DeCecco, PhD, and Michael G. Shively, MA (Vol. 9, No. 2/3, 1984). *"Raises fundamentally important questions about the variable usage of the concept 'identity' in theory development and research. It is important reading for scholars who use that concept, regardless of any interest they may have in the specific topic of homosexuality." (The Journal of Nerves and Mental Disease)*

9. *Gay Personality and Sexual Labeling,* edited by John P. DeCecco, PhD (Vol. 9, No. 4, 1984). *Some of the best minds in sexual liberation take a hard look at how homosexuality is still defined and viewed by established schools of thought and propose fascinating and often controversial ideas on the true nature of the gay personality and identity.*

10. *Bashers, Baiters, and Bigots: Homophobia in America Society,* edited by John P. De Cecco, PhD (Vol. 10, No. 1/2, 1984). *"Breaks ground in helping to make the study of homophobia a science." (Contemporary Psychiatry)*

11. *Two Lives to Lead: Bisexuality in Men and Women,* edited by Fritz Klein, MD, and Timothy J. Wolf, PhD (Vol. 11, No. 1/2, 1985). *"The editors have brought together a formidable array of new data challenging old stereotypes about a very important human phenomenon.... A milestone in furthering our knowledge about sexual orientation." (David P. McWhirter, Co-author, The Male Couple)*

12. ***The Many Faces of Homosexuality: Anthropological Approaches to Homosexual Behavior,*** edited by Evelyn Blackwood, PhD (cand.) (Vol. 11, No. 3/4, 1986). *"A fascinating account of homosexuality during various historical periods and in non-Western cultures." (SIECUS Report)*

13. ***Historical, Literary, and Erotic Aspects of Lesbianism,*** edited by Monika Kehoe, PhD (Vol. 12, No. 3/4, 1986). *"Fascinating. . . . Even though this entire volume is serious scholarship penned by degreed writers, most of it is vital, accessible, and thoroughly readable even to the casual student of lesbian history." (Lambda Rising)*

14. ***Gay Life in Dutch Society,*** edited by A. X. van Naerssen, PhD (Vol. 13, No. 2/3, 1987). *"Valuable not just for its insightful analysis of the evolution of gay rights in The Netherlands, but also for the lessons that can be extracted by our own society from the Dutch tradition of tolerance for homosexuals." (The San Francisco Chronicle)*

15. ***Integrated Identity for Gay Men and Lesbians: Psychotherapeutic Approaches for Emotional Well-Being,*** edited by Eli Coleman, PhD (Vol. 14, No. 1/2, 1987). *"An invaluable tool. . . . This is an extremely useful book for the clinician seeking better ways to understand gay and lesbian patients." (Hospital and Community Psychiatry)*

16. ***The Treatment of Homosexuals with Mental Disorders,*** edited by Michael W. Ross, PhD (Vol. 15, No. 1/2, 1988). *"One of the more objective, scientific collections of articles concerning the mental health of gays and lesbians. . . . Extraordinarily thoughtful. . . . New thoughts about treatments. Vital viewpoints." (The Book Reader)*

17. ***The Pursuit of Sodomy: Male Homosexuality in Renaissance and Enlightenment Europe,*** edited by Kent Gerard, PhD, and Gert Hekma, PhD (Vol. 16, No. 1/2, 1989). *"Presenting a wealth of information in a compact form, this book should be welcomed by anyone with an interest in this period in European history or in the precursors to modern concepts of homosexuality." (The Canadian Journal of Human Sexuality)*

18. ***Lesbians Over 60 Speak for Themselves,*** edited by Monika Kehoe, PhD (Vol. 16, No. 3/4, 1989). *"A pioneering book examining the social, economical, physical, sexual, and emotional lives of aging lesbians." (Feminist Bookstore News)*

19. ***Gay and Lesbian Youth,*** edited by Gilbert Herdt, PhD (Vol. 17, No. 1/2/3/4, 1989). *"Provides a much-needed compilation of research dealing with homosexuality and adolescents." (GLTF Newsletter)*

20. ***Homosexuality and the Family,*** edited by Frederick W. Bozett, PhD (Vol. 18, No. 1/2, 1989). *"Enlightening and answers a host of questions about the effects of homosexuality upon family members and the family as a unit." (Ambush Magazine)*

21. ***Homosexuality and Religion,*** edited by Richard Hasbany, PhD (Vol. 18, No. 3/4, 1990). *"A welcome resource that provides historical and contemporary views on many issues involving religious life and homosexuality." (Journal of Sex Education and Therapy)*

22. ***Love Letters Between a Certain Late Nobleman and the Famous Mr. Wilson,*** edited by Michael S. Kimmel, PhD (Vol. 19, No. 2, 1990). *"An intriguing book about homosexuality in 18th-Century England. Many details of the period, such as meeting places, coded language, and 'camping' are all covered in the book. If you're a history buff, you'll enjoy this one." (Prime Timers)*

23. ***Male Intergenerational Intimacy: Historical, Socio-Psychological, and Legal Perspectives,*** edited by Theo G. M. Sandfort, PhD, Edward Brongersma, JD, and A. X. van Naerssen, PhD (Vol. 20, No. 1/2, 1991). *"The most important book on the subject since Tom O'Carroll's 1980 Paedophilia: The Radical Case." (The North American Man/Boy Love Association Bulletin, May 1991)*

24. ***Gay Midlife and Maturity: Crises, Opportunities, and Fulfillment,*** edited by John Alan Lee, PhD (Vol. 20, No. 3/4, 1991). *"The insight into gay aging is amazing, accurate, and much-needed. . . . A real contribution to the older gay community." (Prime Timers)*

25. ***Gay People, Sex, and the Media,*** edited by Michelle A. Wolf, PhD, and Alfred P. Kielwasser, MA (Vol. 21, No. 1/2, 1991). *"Altogether, the kind of research anthology which is useful to many disciplines in gay studies. Good stuff!" (Communique)*

26. *Homosexuality and Male Bonding in Pre-Nazi Germany: The Youth Movement, the Gay Movement, and Male Bonding Before Hitler's Rise: Original Transcripts from Der Eigene, the First Gay Journal in the World,* edited by Harry Oosterhuis, PhD, and Hubert Kennedy, PhD (Vol. 22, No. 1/2, 1992). *"Provide[s] insight into the early gay movement, particularly in its relation to the various political currents in pre-World War II Germany." (Lambda Book Report)*

27. *Coming Out of the Classroom Closet: Gay and Lesbian Students, Teachers, and Curricula,* edited by Karen M. Harbeck, PhD, JD, Recipient of Lesbian and Gay Educators Award by the American Educational Research Association's Lesbian and Gay Studies Special Interest Group (AREA) (Vol. 22, No. 3/4, 1992). *"Presents recent research about gay and lesbian students and teachers and the school system in which they function." (Contemporary Psychology)*

28. *Homosexuality in Renaissance and Enlightenment England: Literary Representations in Historical Context,* edited by Claude J. Summers, PhD (Vol. 23, No. 1/2, 1992). *"It is remarkable among studies in this field in its depth of scholarship and variety of approaches and is accessible." (Chronique)*

29. *Gay and Lesbian Studies,* edited by Henry L. Minton, PhD (Vol. 24, No. 1/2, 1993). *"The volume's essays provide insight into the field's remarkable accomplishments and future goals." (Lambda Book Report)*

30. *If You Seduce a Straight Person, Can You Make Them Gay? Issues in Biological Essentialism versus Social Constructionism in Gay and Lesbian Identities,* edited by John P. DeCecco, PhD, and John P. Elia, MA, PhD (cand.) (Vol. 24, No. 3/4, 1993). *"You'll find this alternative view of the age old question to be one that will become the subject of many conversations to come. Thought-provoking to say the least!" (Prime Timers)*

31. *Gay Studies from the French Cultures: Voices from France, Belgium, Brazil, Canada, and the Netherlands,* edited by Rommel Mendès-Leite, PhD, and Pierre-Olivier de Busscher, PhD (cand.) (Vol. 25, No. 1/2/3, 1993). *"The first book that allows an English-speaking world to have a comprehensive look at the principal trends in gay studies in France and French-speaking countries." (André Bèjin, PhD, Directeur, de Recherche au Centre National de la Recherche Scientifique [CNRS], Paris)*

32. *Critical Essays: Gay and Lesbian Writers of Color,* edited by Emmanuel S. Nelson, PhD (Vol. 26, No. 2/3, 1993). *"A much-needed book, sparkling with stirring perceptions and resonating with depth. . . . The anthology not only breaks new ground, it also attempts to heal wounds inflicted by our oppressed pasts." (Lambda)*

33. *Gay and Lesbian Studies in Art History,* edited by Whitney Davis, PhD (Vol. 27, No. 1/2, 1994). *"Informed, challenging . . . never dull. . . . Contributors take risks and, within the restrictions of scholarly publishing, find new ways to use materials already available or examine topics never previously explored." (Lambda Book Report)*

34. *Gay Ethics: Controversies in Outing, Civil Rights, and Sexual Science,* edited by Timothy F. Murphy, PhD (Vol. 27, No. 3/4, 1994). *"The contributors bring the traditional tools of ethics and political philosophy to bear in a clear and forceful way on issues surrounding the rights of homosexuals." (David L. Hull, Dressler Professor in the Humanities, Department of Philosophy, Northwestern University)*

35. *Sex, Cells, and Same-Sex Desire: The Biology of Sexual Preference,* edited by John P. DeCecco, PhD, and David Allen Parker, MA (Vol. 28, No. 1/2/3/4, 1995). *"A stellar compilation of chapters examining the most important evidence underlying theories on the biological basis of human sexual orientation." (MGW)*

36. *Gay Men and the Sexual History of the Political Left,* edited by Gert Hekma, PhD, Harry Oosterhuis, PhD, and James Steakley, PhD (Vol. 29, No. 2/3/4, 1995). *"Contributors delve into the contours of a long-forgotten history, bringing to light new historical data and fresh insight. . . . An excellent account of the tense historical relationship between the political left and gay liberation." (People's Voice)*

37. *Gays, Lesbians, and Consumer Behavior: Theory, Practice, and Research Issues in Marketing,* edited by Daniel L. Wardlow, PhD (Vol. 31, No. 1/2, 1996). *"For those scholars,*

market researchers, and marketing managers who are considering marketing to the gay and lesbian community, this book should be on their required reading list." (Mississippi Voice)

38. **Activism and Marginalization in the AIDS Crisis,** edited by Michael A. Hallett, PhD (Vol. 32, No. 3/4, 1997). *Shows readers how the advent of HIV-disease has brought into question the utility of certain forms of "activism" as they relate to understanding and fighting the social impacts of disease.*

39. **Reclaiming the Sacred: The Bible in Gay and Lesbian Culture,** edited by Raymond-Jean Frontain, PhD (Vol. 33, No. 3/4, 1997). *"Finely wrought, sharply focused, daring, and always dignified. . . . In chapter after chapter, the Bible is shown to be a more sympathetic and humane book in its attitudes toward homosexuality than usually thought and a challenge equally to the straight and gay moral imagination." (Joseph Wittreich, PhD, Distinguished Professor of English, The Graduate School, The City University of New York)*

40. **Gay and Lesbian Literature Since World War II: History and Memory,** edited by Sonya L. Jones, PhD (Vol. 34, No. 3/4, 1998). *"The authors of these essays manage to gracefully incorporate the latest insights of feminist, postmodernist, and queer theory into solidly grounded readings . . . challenging and moving, informed by the passion that prompts both readers and critics into deeper inquiry." (Diane Griffin Growder, PhD, Professor of French and Women's Studies, Cornell College, Mt. Vernon, Iowa)*

41. **Scandinavian Homosexualities: Essays on Gay and Lesbian Studies,** edited by Jan Löfström, PhD (Vol. 35, No. 3/4, 1998). *"Everybody interested in the formation of lesbian and gay identities and their interaction with the sociopolitical can find something to suit their taste in this volume." (Judith Schuyf, PhD, Assistant Professor of Lesbian and Gay Studies, Center for Gay and Lesbian Studies, Utrecht University, The Netherlands)*

42. **Multicultural Queer: Australian Narratives,** edited by Peter A. Jackson, PhD, and Gerard Sullivan, PhD (Vol. 36, No. 3/4, 1999). *Shares the way that people from ethnic minorities in Australia (those who are not of Anglo-Celtic background) view homosexuality, their experiences as homosexual men and women, and their feelings about the lesbian and gay community.*

43. **The Ideal Gay Man: The Story of Der Kreis,** by Hubert Kennedy, PhD (Vol. 38, No. 1/2, 1999). *"Very profound. . . . Excellent insight into the problems of the early fight for homosexual emancipation in Europe and in the USA. . . . The ideal gay man (high-mindedness, purity, cleanness), as he was imagined by the editor of 'Der Kreis,' is delineated by the fascinating quotations out of the published erotic stories." (Wolfgang Breidert, PhD, Academic Director, Institute of Philosophy, University Karlsruhe, Germany)*

44. **Gay Community Survival in the New Millennium,** edited by Michael R. Botnick, PhD (cand.) (Vol. 38, No. 4, 2000). *Examines the notion of community from several different perspectives focusing on the imagined, the structural, and the emotive. You will explore a theoretical overview and you will peek into the moral discourses that frame "gay community," the rift between HIV-positive and HIV-negative gay men, and how Israeli gays seek their place in the public sphere.*

45. **Queer Asian Cinema: Shadows in the Shade,** edited by Andrew Grossman, MA (Vol. 39, No. 3/4, 2000). *"An extremely rich tapestry of detailed ethnographies and state-of-the-art theorizing. . . . Not only is this a landmark record of queer Asia, but it will certainly also be a seminal, contributive challenge to gender and sexuality studies in general." (Dédé Oetomo, PhD, Coordinator of the Indonesian organization GAYa NUSANTARA: Adjunct Reader in Linguistics and Anthropology, School of Social Sciences, Universitas Airlangga, Surabaya, Indonesia)*

46. **Gay and Lesbian Asia: Culture, Identity, Community,** edited by Gerard Sullivan, PhD, and Peter A. Jackson, PhD (Vol. 40, No. 3/4, 2001). *"Superb. . . . Covers a happily wide range of styles . . . will appeal to both students and educated fans." (Gary Morris, Editor/Publisher, Bright Lights Film Journal)*

47. **Homosexuality in French History and Culture,** edited by Jeffrey Merrick and Michael Sibalis (Vol. 41, No. 3/4, 2001). *"Fascinating. . . . Merrick and Sibalis bring together historians, literary scholars, and political activists from both sides of the Atlantic to examine same-sex sexuality in the past and present." (Bryant T. Ragan, PhD, Associate Professor of History, Fordham University, New York City)*

48. **The Drag King Anthology,** edited by Donna Jean Troka, PhD (cand.), Kathleen LeBesco, PhD, and Jean Bobby Noble, PhD (Vol. 43, No. 3/4, 2002). *"All university courses on masculinity*

should use this book . . . challenges preconceptions through the empirical richness of direct experience. The contributors and editors have worked together to produce cultural analysis that enhances our perception of the dynamic uncertainty of gendered experience." (Sally R. Munt. DPhil. Subject Chair, Media Studies, University of Sussex)

49. **Icelandic Lives: The Queer Experience,** edited by Voon Chin Phua (Vol. 44, No. 2, 2002). *"The first of its kind, this book shows the emergence of gay and lesbian visibility through the biographical narratives of a dozen Icelanders. Through their lives can be seen a small nation's transition, in just a few decades, from a pervasive silence concealing its queer citizens to widespread acknowledgment characterized by some of the most progressive laws in the world." (Barry D. Adam, PhD, University Professor, Department of Sociology & Anthropology, University of Windsor, Ontario, Canada)*

50. **Gay Bathhouses and Public Health Policy,** edited by William J. Woods, PhD, and Diane Binson, PhD (Vol. 44, No. 3/4, 2003). *"Important. . . . Long overdue. . . . A unique and valuable contribution to the social science and public health literature. The inclusion of detailed historical descriptions of public policy debates about the place of bathhouses in urban gay communities, together with summaries of the legal controversies about bathhouses, insightful examinations of patrons' behaviors and reviews of successful programs for HIV/STD education and testing programs in bathhouses provides. A well rounded and informative overview." (Richard Tewksbury, PhD, Professor of Justice Administration, University of Louisville)*

51. **Queer Theory and Communication: From Disciplining Queers to Queering the Discipline(s),** edited by Gust A. Yep, PhD, Karen E. Lovaas, PhD, and John P. Elia, PhD (Vol. 45, No. 2/3/4, 2003). *"Sheds light on how sexual orientation and identity are socially produced–and how they can be challenged and changed–through everyday practices and institutional activities, as well as academic research and teaching. . . . Illuminates the theoretical and practical significance of queer theory–not only as a specific area of inquiry, but also as a productive challenge to the heteronormativity of mainstream communication theory, research, and pedagogy." (Julia T. Wood, PhD, Lineberger Professor of Humanities, Professor of Communication Studies, The University of North Carolina at Chapel Hill)*

52. **The Drag Queen Anthology: The Absolutely Fabulous but Flawlessly Customary World of Female Impersonators,** edited by Steven P. Schacht, PhD, with Lisa Underwood (Vol. 46, No. 3/4, 2004). *"Indispensable. . . . For more than a decade, Steven P. Schacht has been one of the social sciences' most reliable guides to the world of drag queens and female impersonators. . . . This book assembles an impressive cast of scholars who are as theoretically astute, methodologically careful, and conceptually playful as the drag queens themselves." (Michael Kimmel, author of* The Gendered Society; *Professor of Sociology, SUNY Stony Brook)*

53. **Eclectic Views on Gay Male Pornography: Pornucopia,** edited by Todd G. Morrison, PhD (Vol. 47, No. 3/4, 2004). *"An instant classic. . . . Lively and readable." (Jerry Zientara, EdD, Librarian, Institute for Advanced Study of Human Sexuality)*

54. **Sexuality and Human Rights: A Global Overview,** edited by Helmut Graupner, JD, and Philip Tahmindjis, BA, LLB, LLM, SJD (Vol. 48, No. 3/4, 2005). *"An important resource for anybody concerned about the status of legal protection for the human rights of sexual minorities, especially for those concerned with attaining a comparative perspective. The chapters are all of high quality and are written in a straightforward manner that will be accessible to the non-specialist while containing much detail of interest to specialists in the area." (Arthur S. Leonard, JD, Professor of Law, New York Law School)*

55. **Same-Sex Desire and Love in Greco-Roman Antiquity and in the Classical Tradition of the West,** edited by Beert C. Verstraete and Vernon Provencal (Vol. 49, No. 3/4, 2005). *"This wide-ranging collection engages with the existing scholarship in the history of sexuality and the uses of the classical tradition and opens up exciting new areas of study. The book is an important addition to queer theory." (Stephen Guy-Bray, PhD, Associate Professor, University of British Columbia)*

56. **Sadomasochism: Powerful Pleasures,** edited by Peggy J. Kleinplatz, PhD, and Charles Moser, PhD, MD (Vol. 50, No. 2/3, 2006). *"I would advise anyone interested in doing research on this topic or trying to understand this severely stigmatized behavior to begin with this collection." (Vern L. Bullough, PhD, DSci, RN, Visiting Professor Emeritus, State University of New York; Editor of* Before Stonewall: Activists for Gay and Lesbian Rights in Historical Context*)*

57. *Current Issues in Lesbian, Gay, Bisexual, and Transgender Health,* edited by Jay Harcourt, MPH (Vol. 51, No. 1, 2006). *"A fine addition to our knowledge of LGBT youth adults. The chapter by Dr. Case and her colleagues gives us a wonderful study that supports the addition of sexual orientation to the demographic questions within research studies. Dr. Koh and Dr. Ross's work exploring mental health issues by sexual orientation is also very important." (Suzanne L. Dibble, RN, DNSc, Professor and Co-Director, Lesbian Health Research Center, University of California at San Francisco)*

58. *Sodomites and Urnings: Homosexual Representations in Classic German Journals,* edited and translated by Michael A. Lombardi-Nash, PhD (Vol. 51 Suppl. 1, 2006). *"These classic articles are a reminder that the homosexual liberation movement existed long before Stonewall. Especially interesting to me was Karoly Maria Kertbeny's 1868 letter to Karl Heinrich Ulrichs, which raises theoretical and tactical questions that are still pertinent. A 1909 poem by Magnus Hirschfeld,* Three German Graves in a Distant Land, *is informative and moving." (John Lauritsen, Independent Scholar, Author of* A Freethinker's Primer of Male Love, *and co-author of* The Early Homosexual Rights Movement (1864-1935), *(1974/ Revised Second Edition 1995)*

59. *LGBT Studies and Queer Theory: New Conflicts, Collaborations, and Contested Terrain,* edited by Karen E. Lovaas, PhD, John P. Elia, PhD, and Gust A. Yep, PhD (Vol. 52, No. 1/2, 2006). *"Most useful for readers who do not know much about these disciplines. The more specific articles focus on how the tensions between lesbian and gay studies and queer theory translate into various arenas of life. The reader can choose all or specific areas of interest to explore how they are enlightened by the views of these disciplines and the critiques of queer theory." (Ski Hunter, MSW, PhD, Professor, School of Social Work, University of Texas at Arlington)*

LGBT Studies
and Queer Theory:
New Conflicts, Collaborations,
and Contested Terrain

Karen E. Lovaas, PhD
John P. Elia, PhD
Gust A. Yep, PhD
Editors

LGBT Studies and Queer Theory: New Conflicts, Collaborations, and Contested Terrain has been co-published simultaneously as *Journal of Homosexuality*, Volume 52, Numbers 1/2 2006.

HPP

Harrington Park Press®
An Imprint of The Haworth Press, Inc.

New York • London • Victoria (AU)
www.HaworthPress.com

Published by

Harrington Park Press®, 10 Alice Street, Binghamton, NY 13904-1580 USA

Harrington Park Press® is an imprint of The Haworth Press, Inc., 10 Alice Street, Binghamton, NY 13904-1580 USA.

LGBT Studies and Queer Theory: New Conflicts, Collaborations, and Contested Terrain has been co-published simultaneously as *Journal of Homosexuality*, Volume 52, Numbers 1/2 2006.

The development, preparation, and publication of this work has been undertaken with great care. However, the publisher, employees, editors, and agents of The Haworth Press and all imprints of The Haworth Press, Inc., including The Haworth Medical Press® and Pharmaceutical Products Press®, are not responsible for any errors contained herein or for consequences that may ensue from use of materials or information contained in this work. With regard to case studies, identities and circumstances of individuals discussed herein have been changed to protect confidentiality. Any resemblance to actual persons, living or dead, is entirely coincidental.

The Haworth Press is committed to the dissemination of ideas and information according to the highest standards of intellectual freedom and the free exchange of ideas. Statements made and opinions expressed in this publication do not necessarily reflect the views of the Publisher, Directors, management, or staff of The Haworth Press, Inc., or an endorsement by them.

Cover design by Jennifer M. Gaska

Library of Congress Cataloging-in-Publication Data

LGBT studies and queer theory : new conflicts, collaborations, and contested terrain / Karen E. Lovaas, John P. Elia, Gust A. Yep, editors.
     p. cm.
     "[C]o-published simultaneously as Journal of Homosexuality, Volume 52, Numbers 1/2 2006."
     Includes bibliographical references and index.
     ISBN-13: 978-1-56023-316-9 (hard cover : alk. paper)
     ISBN-10: 1-56023-316-8 (hard cover : alk. paper)
     ISBN-13: 978-1-56023-317-6 (soft cover : alk. paper)
     ISBN-10: 1-56023-317-6 (soft cover : alk. paper)
     1. Homosexuality. 2. Gays. 3. Bisexuals. 4. Transsexuals. 5. Queer theory. I. Lovaas, Karen. II. Elia, John P. III. Yep, Gust A. IV. Journal of homosexuality. V. Title: Lesbian, gay, bisexual, and transgender studies and queer theory.
     HQ76.25.L5 2007
     306.76'601–dc22
                                                  2006039108

The HAWORTH PRESS, Inc.

Abstracting, Indexing & Outward Linking

PRINT *and* ELECTRONIC BOOKS & JOURNALS

This section provides you with a list of major indexing & abstracting services and other tools for bibliographic access. That is to say, each service began covering this periodical during the the year noted in the right column. Most Websites which are listed below have indicated that they will either post, disseminate, compile, archive, cite or alert their own Website users with research-based content from this work. (This list is as current as the copyright date of this publication.)

Abstracting, Website/Indexing Coverage . . . . Year When Coverage Began

- *(IBR) International Bibliography of Book Reviews on the Humanities and Social Sciences (Thomson)* <http://www.saur.de> **2006**

- *(IBZ) International Bibliography of Periodical Literature on the Humanities and Social Sciences (Thomson)* <http://www.saur.de> **1996**

- *Abstracts in Anthropology* <http://www.baywood.com/Journals/PreviewJournals.asp?id=0001-3455> **1982**

- *Academic ASAP (Thomson Gale)* **2000**

- *Alternative Press Index (print, online & CD-ROM from NISC)* <http://www.altpress.org> **1996**

- *Applied Social Sciences Index & Abstracts (ASSIA) (Cambridge Scientific Abstracts)* <http://www.csa.com> **1987**

- *Biological Sciences Database (Cambridge Scientific Abstracts)* <http://www.csa.com> **2006**

- *Book Review Index (Thomson Gale)* **1996**

- *British Library Inside (The British Library)* <http://www.bl.uk/services/current/inside.html> **2006**

- *Cambridge Scientific Abstracts (A leading publisher of scientific information in print journals, online databases, CD-ROM and via the Internet)* <http://www.csa.com> **1993**

(continued)

- *Contemporary Women's Issues (Thomson Gale)* **1998**
- *Criminal Justice Abstracts (Sage)* **1982**
- *Current Contents/Social & Behavioral Sciences (Thomson Scientific) <http://www.isinet.com>* **1985**
- *EBSCOhost Electronic Journals Service (EJS) <http://ejournals.ebsco.com>* **2001**
- *Elsevier Eflow-I* **2006**
- *Elsevier Scopus <http://www.info.scopus.com>* **2005**
- *EMBASE.com (The Power of EMBASE + MEDLINE Combined) (Elsevier) <http://www.embase.com>* **2006**
- *EMBASE/Excerpta Medica (Elsevier) <http://www.elsevier.nl>* . . **1974**
- *Environmental Sciences and Pollution Management (Cambridge Scientific Abstracts) <http://www.csa.com>* **2006**
- *Expanded Academic ASAP (Thomson Gale) <http://www.galegroup.com>* **1989**
- *Expanded Academic Index (Thomson Gale)* **1992**
- *Family & Society Studies Worldwide (NISC USA) <http://www.nisc.com>* **1996**
- *Family Index Database <http://www.familyscholar.com>* **2002**
- *Family Violence & Sexual Assault Bulletin* **1992**
- *GenderWatch (ProQuest) http://www.proquest.com>* **1999**
- *GLBT Life Product Family, (EBSCO) <http://www.epnet.com/academic/glbt.asp>* **2004**
- *Google <http://www.google.com>* **2004**
- *Google Scholar <http://scholar.google.com>* **2004**
- *Haworth Document Delivery Center <http://www.HaworthPress.com/journals/dds.asp>* **1974**
- *Health & Psychosocial Instruments (HaPI) Database (available through online and as a CD-ROM from OVID Technologies)* . **1986**
- *Health & Safety Science Abstracts (Cambridge Scientific Abstracts) <http://www.csa.com>* **2006**
- *HEALTHLIT (NISC SA) <http://www.nisc.co.za>* **2006**
- *Higher Education Abstracts, providing the latest in research and theory in more than 140 major topics* **1997**
- *IHLIA/Homodok-LAA <http://www.ihlia.nl/>* **1995**

(continued)

- *Index Copernicus <http://www.indexcopernicus.com>* **2006**
- *Index Guide to College Journals (core list compiled by integrating 48 indexes frequently used to support undergraduate programs in small to medium sized libraries)* **1999**
- *Index to Periodical Articles Related to Law <http://www.law.utexas.edu>* **1986**
- *InfoTrac Custom (Thomson Gale)* **1996**
- *InfoTrac OneFile (Thomson Gale)* **1996**
- *International Bibliography of the Social Sciences (IBSS) <http://www.ibss.ac.uk>* **2003**
- *Internationale Bibliographie der geistes- und sozialwissenschaftlichen Zeitschriftenliteratur . . . See IBZ <http://www.saur.de>* **1996**
- *Journal Citation Reports/Social Sciences Edition (Thomson Scientific) <http://www.insinet.com>* **2005**
- *Lesbian Information Service <http://www.lesbianinformationservice.org>* **1991**
- *Links@Ovid (via CrossRef targeted DOI links) <http://www.ovid.com>* **2005**
- *MEDLINE (National Library of Medicine) <http://www.nlm.nih.gov>* **1992**
- *Men's Studies Database (NISC USA) <http://www.nisc.com>* **2006**
- *MLA International Bibliography (Thomson Gale)* **1995**
- *National Child Support Research Clearinghouse <http://www.spea.indiana.edu/ncsea/>* **1998**
- *NewJour (Electronic Journals & Newsletters) <http://gort.ucsd.edu/newjour/* **2006**
- *OmniFile Full Text: Mega Edition (H. W. Wilson) <http://www.hwwilson.com>* **1987**
- *Omni V Full Text (H. W. Wilson) <http://www.hwwilson.com>* . . . **2006**
- *Ovid Linksolver (OpenURL link resolver via CrossRef targeted DOI links) <http://www.linksolver.com>* **2005**
- *ProQuest 5000 <http://www.proquest.com>* **1974**
- *ProQuest Discovery <http://www.proquest.com>* **2006**

(continued)

- *ProQuest Platinum <http://www.proquest.com>* 2006
- *ProQuest Research Library <http://www.proquest.com>* 2006
- *ProQuest Social Science Journals <http://www.proquest.com>* . . . 2006
- *Psychological Abstracts (PsycINFO) <http://www.apa.org>* 1995
- *PSYCLINE <http://www.psycline.org>* 2006
- *Public Affairs Information Service (PAIS) International (Cambridge Scientific Abstracts) <http://www.pais.org/www.csa.com>* 1982
- *PubMed <http://www.ncbi.nlm.nih.gov/pubmed/>* 2003
- *Risk Abstracts (Cambridge Scientific Abstracts) <http://www.csa.com>* 2006
- *Sage Family Studies Abstracts* 1986
- *Scopus (See instead Elsevier Scopus) <http://www.info.scopus.com>* 2005
- *Social Sciences Citation Index (Thomson Scientific) <http://www.isinet.com>* 1985
- *Social Sciences Index / Abstracts / Full Text (H.W. Wilson) <http://www.hwwilson.com>* 1991
- *Social Scisearch (Thomson Scientific) http://www.isinet.com>* 1985
- *Social Services Abstracts (Cambridge Scientific Abstracts) <http://www.csa.com>* 1982
- *Social Work Abstracts (NASW) <http://www.silverplatter.com/catalog/swab.htm>* 1994
- *Sociological Abstracts (Cambridge Scientific Abstracts) <http://www.csa.com>* 1982
- *Studies on Women and Gender Abstracts <http://www.tandf.co.uk/swa>* 1987
- *SwetsWise <http://www.swets.com>* 2001
- *Violence and Abuse Abstracts (Sage)* 1995
- *Web of Science (Thomson Scientific) <http://www.isinet.com>* . . . 2003
- *WilsonWeb <http://vnweb.hwwilsonweb.com/hww/Journals>* 2005
- *zetoc (The British Library) <http://www.bl.uk>* 2004

Bibliographic Access

- ***Cabell's Directory of Publishing Opportunities in Psychology***
  <http://www.cabells.com>

- ***Magazines for Libraries (Katz)***

- ***Ulrich's Periodicals Directory: International***
  Periodicals Information Since 1932
  <http://www.Bowkerlink.com>

Special Bibliographic Notes related to special journal issues
(separates) and indexing/abstracting:

- indexing/abstracting services in this list will also cover material in any "separate" that is co-published simultaneously with Haworth's special thematic journal issue or DocuSerial. Indexing/abstracting usually covers material at the article/chapter level.
- monographic co-editions are intended for either non-subscribers or libraries which intend to purchase a second copy for their circulating collections.
- monographic co-editions are reported to all jobbers/wholesalers/approval plans. The source journal is listed as the "series" to assist the prevention of duplicate purchasing in the same manner utilized for books-in-series.
- to facilitate user/access services all indexing/abstracting services are encouraged to utilize the co-indexing entry note indicated at the bottom of the first page of each article/chapter/contribution.
- this is intended to assist a library user of any reference tool (whether print, electronic, online, or CD-ROM) to locate the monographic version if the library has purchased this version but not a subscription to the source journal.
- individual articles/chapters in any Haworth publication are also available through the Haworth Document Delivery Service (HDDS).

As part of Haworth's continuing committment to better serve our library patrons, we are proud to be working with the following electronic services:

AGGREGATOR SERVICES

EBSCOhost

Ingenta

J-Gate

Minerva

OCLC FirstSearch

Oxmill

SwetsWise

FirstSearch

Oxmill Publishing

SwetsWise

LINK RESOLVER SERVICES

1Cate (Openly Informatics)

CrossRef

Gold Rush (Coalliance)

LinkOut (PubMed)

LINKplus (Atypon)

LinkSolver (Ovid)

LinkSource with A-to-Z (EBSCO)

Resource Linker (Ulrich)

SerialsSolutions (ProQuest)

SFX (Ex Libris)

Sirsi Resolver (SirsiDynix)

Tour (TDnet)

Vlink (Extensity, *formerly Geac*)

WebBridge (Innovative Interfaces)

1cate

CrossRef MEMBER

Gold Rush

LinkOut. LINKING TO A WORLD OF RESOURCES

atypon

OVID LinkSolver

ULRICH'S RESOURCE LINKER

S·F·X

SerialsSolutions

SirsiDynix

TOUR

extensity

WebBridge

ABOUT THE GUEST EDITORS

Karen E. Lovaas (PhD in American Studies, University of Hawai'i at Manoa, 1993) is Associate Professor of Communication Studies at San Francisco State University. Her teaching, research, and consulting work are in the areas of gender, sexuality, culture, conflict, and communication, with an emphasis on critical theory. She co-edited *Sexualities and Communication in Everyday Life* (Sage, 2006) with Mercilee Jenkins. She was co-editor, with Gust Yep and John Elia, of the predecessor to this volume, *Queer Theory and Communication: From Disciplining Queers to Queering the Discipline(s)* (Harrington Park Press, 2003). Other publications underscore her interest in queer theory, queer communities, and queer pedagogy. She authored encyclopedia entries on "gender roles" and "sexism" for *The International Encyclopedia of [Homo] sexualities, Education, and Cultures* (2005), and glossary entries on "cross-dressing," "free love," "liberation," and "sexual assault" for *Sexuality: The essential glossary* (2004), "A Critical Appraisal of Assimilationist and Radical Ideologies Underlying Same-Sex Marriage in LGBT Communities in the United States," written with Gust Yep and John Elia, was published in 2003. "Sexual Practices, Identification, and the Paradoxes of Identity in the Era of AIDS: The Case of 'Riding Bareback,'" was co-authored with Gust Yep and Alex Pagonis in 2002. She is the lead author of an article written with two former students, entitled "*Trans*cending Heteronormativity in the Classroom: Using Queer and Critical Pedagogies to Alleviate Trans-Anxieties," in *Journal of Lesbian Studies* (2002), which was simultaneously published as a chapter in E. P. Cramer (Ed.), *Addressing homophobia and heterosexism on college campuses*. A book chapter entitled, "Communication in 'Asian American' Families with Queer Members: A Relational Dialectics Perspective," co-authored with Gust Yep and Philip Ho, is in the anthology, *Queer Families, Queer Politics: Challenging Culture and the State* (2001). Dr. Lovaas is on the editorial board of the *Journal of Homosexuality*. She is active in the National Communication and Western States Communication Associations and a regular presenter at their annual conferences. Ongoing projects utilize critical, queer, and feminist approaches to communication research and pedagogy.

John P. Elia (PhD, University of California, Davis, 1997) is Associate Professor of Health Education, and has been on the faculty at San Francisco State University for two decades. Besides teaching over a dozen courses on the undergraduate and graduate levels, he has served as Interim Chair and Associate Chair of the Department of Health Education, and is Co-Graduate Coordinator of the Masters of Public Health Program. His recent scholarship has focused on democracy and sexuality education in public schools, and he has published numerous articles and book reviews in *The Educational Forum*, *The Journal of Sex Education and Therapy*, the *Journal of the History of Sexuality*, and the *Journal of Homosexuality*. The books he has co-edited include: *Sex and Relationships*, 2nd edition (2005), *Readings in Contemporary Sexuality*, 2nd edition (2005), *Queer Theory and Communication: From Disciplining the Queers to Queering the Disciplines* (2003), and *If You Seduce a Straight Person Can You Make Him Gay?: Issues in Biological Essentialism and Social Constructionism in Gay and Lesbian Identities* (1993). Currently, he is co-editing a volume on sexual minority youth and school culture. Recently, he was interviewed as an expert on school-based sexuality education for a PBS video series on sociology. Most recently, he has authored encyclopedia entries on "homophobia" and "sexuality education" for *The International Encyclopedia of [Homo]sexualities, Education, and Cultures* (2005), as well as serving on the international advisory board of this publication. His areas of expertise are: school-based sexuality education, school health education, health promotion of sexual minority youth, youth development, history and philosophy of American education, critical pedagogy, and queer studies. He is on the editorial boards of two international peer reviewed journals, *The Educational Forum* and the *Journal of Gay and Lesbian Issues in Education*. Additionally, after many years, he continues to serve as the Associate Editor and Book Review Editor of the *Journal of Homosexuality*, an internationally renowned peer-reviewed journal.

Gust A. Yep (PhD, University of Southern California, 1990) is Professor of Communication Studies and Human Sexuality Studies at San Francisco State University. He is also Director of Graduate Studies in Communication Studies. He is the lead editor of *Queer Theory and Communication: From Disciplining Queers to Queering the Discipline(s)* (Harrington Park Press, 2003) and co-author of *Privacy and Disclosure of HIV in Interpersonal Relationships: A Sourcebook for Researchers and Practitioners* (Lawrence Erlbaum, 2003). The latter was nominated for the 2004 International Communication Association (ICA) "Book of the Year" award and the 2004 National Communication

Association (NCA) Applied Communication Division "Book of the Year" award. His research has been published in numerous interdisciplinary journals and anthologies. His work has appeared in a number of scholarly journals: *AIDS Education and Prevention*; *CATESOL Journal*; *Communication Quarterly*; *Feminist Media Studies*; *Hispanic Journal of Behavioral Sciences*; *International and Intercultural Communication Annual*; *International Quarterly of Community Health Education*; *Journal of American College Health*; *Journal of Gay, Lesbian, and Bisexual Identity*; *Journal of Health Communication*; *Journal of Homosexuality*; *Journal of Lesbian Studies*, and *Journal of Social Behavior and Personality*, among others. Dr. Yep's work has appeared as chapters in books such as *Queer Families, Queer Politics: Challenging Culture and the State* (Columbia University Press); *Overcoming Heterosexism and Homophobia: Strategies that Work* (Columbia University Press); *Balancing the Secrets of Private Disclosures* (Lawrence Erlbaum); *Readings in Intercultural Communication: Experiences and Contexts* (McGraw-Hill); *Explaining Illness: Theory, Research, and Strategies* (Lawrence Erlbaum); *Power in the Blood: A Handbook on AIDS, Politics and Communication* (Lawrence Erlbaum); *Progress in Preventing AIDS? Dogma, Dissent, and Innovation: Global Perspectives* (Baywood Publications); *Communicating about Communicable Diseases* (Human Resource Development Press); *Confronting the AIDS Epidemic: Cross-cultural Perspectives in HIV/AIDS Education* (Africa World Press); *Women and AIDS: Negotiating Safer Practices, Care, and Representation* (Harrington Park Press); *Hispanic Psychology: Critical Issues in Theory and Research* (Sage Publications); *Communicating Ethnic and Cultural Identity* (Rowman & Littlefield); *Group Communication in Context: Studies of Natural Groups* (Lawrence Erlbaum); *Handbook of Health Communication* (Lawrence Erlbaum); *Race/Gender/Media: Considering Diversity across Audiences, Content, and Producers* (Longman); *Media-Mediated AIDS* (Hampton Press), and *National Days/National Ways* (Greenwood Press), among others. He received over a dozen research grants and several teaching, mentorship, advisement, and community service awards in the past decade. Dr. Yep was nominated for "Outstanding Professor Award" in 1992-93, 1993-94, and 1994-95 at California State University, Los Angeles before joining the faculty at San Francisco State. He was named "Outstanding American Educator" in *Who's Who Among America's Teachers* (1994), nationally recognized for his teaching and mentoring in the "Teachers on Teaching" Series at the Annual Meeting of the National Communication Association (1997), and honored as a founding member of the Gamma Psi Chapter of Phi Beta Delta, an Honor Society for International Scholars. In 1999, he was the university-wide nominee for the Carnegie Foundation "U.S. Professors of the Year" Award. Dr. Yep is a past chair of the Gay, Lesbian, Bisexual, and Transgender (GLBT) Communication Studies Division of the National Communication Association. He currently serves on several disciplinary and interdisciplinary editorial boards.

LGBT Studies
and Queer Theory:
New Conflicts, Collaborations,
and Contested Terrain

CONTENTS

Foreword   xxiii
Steven Seidman, PhD

Acknowledgements   xxvii

INTRODUCTION

Shifting Ground(s): Surveying the Contested Terrain
    of LGBT Studies and Queer Theory   1
Karen E. Lovaas, PhD
John P. Elia, PhD
Gust A. Yep, PhD

THEORETICAL DEBATES AND INTERVENTIONS

Queer Theory, Late Capitalism, and Internalized Homophobia   19
Max Kirsch, PhD

Anti-Homosexual Prejudice . . . as Opposed to What?
    Queer Theory and the Social Psychology
    of Anti-Homosexual Attitudes   47
Peter Hegarty, PhD
Sean Massey, PhD

Outlaws or In-Laws? Queer Theory, LGBT Studies,
    and Religious Studies   73
Melissa M. Wilcox, PhD

A Queer Anxiety: Assimilation Politics and Cinematic Hedonics
in *Relax . . . It's Just Sex*   101
Jeff Bennett, PhD

INTERSECTIONS

Historicizing (Bi)Sexuality: A Rejoinder for Gay/Lesbian Studies,
Feminism, and Queer Theory   125
Steven Angelides, PhD

Troubling the Canon: Bisexuality and Queer Theory   159
Mark A. Gammon, ABD
Kirsten L. Isgro, PhD

Cape Queer? A Case Study of Provincetown, Massachusetts   185
Karen Christel Krahulik, PhD

Jewish Disappearing Acts and the Construction of Gender   213
Ruth D. Johnston, PhD

Desiring Mates   237
Dean Durber, PhD

CONTEXTS

Teaching Queer Theory at a *Normal* School   257
Jen Bacon, PhD

Containing Uncertainty: Sexual Values and Citizenship   285
Claudia Schippert, PhD

Ferment in LGBT Studies and Queer Theory:
Personal Ruminations on Contested Terrain   309
R. Anthony Slagle, PhD

Index   329

Foreword

Ideas about same-sex sexuality would seem to be a part of all societies. However, it was only in the 19th century in Europe and the United States that specific ideas about homosexuality first appeared. At least, scholars seem to agree that the idea of the homosexual as a personage or human type appears to date from the late nineteenth to the early 20th century. Through World War II, the discussion around of homosexuality was confined to small sectors of the medical-psychiatric-scientific community, and was overwhelmingly dominated by a biological or psychological model. Homosexuality was seen as an illness or abnormality and the questions researchers asked were about its origin, essential meaning [gender inversion or sexual perversion], and its cause.

It was not until the 1960s and 1970s that homosexuality was understood as a fundamentally social phenomenon. It was only when scholars were able to imagine that homosexuality as a behavior may very well be natural or universal, while homosexuality as an identity or social status is historical, that the idea of the social study of homosexuality was made possible. New questions were asked: How and under what sociohistorical conditions did this desire become an identity? What social factors shaped the meaning and social role of this desire or identity? What explains the subordinate social status of homosexuality in different societies? This breakthrough to a "social constructionist" or sociological view of homosexuality occurred in the 1970s and 1980s among scholars, many of whom were connected to the rise of a lesbian and gay movement in America and in Europe. In other words, the intellectual challenge to the notion of the natural (and inferior) status of homosexuality

[Haworth co-indexing entry note]: "Foreword." Seidman, Steven. Co-published simultaneously in *Journal of Homosexuality* (Harrington Park Press, an imprint of The Haworth Press, Inc.) Vol. 52, No. 1/2, 2006, pp. xxxv-xxxviii; and: *LGBT Studies and Queer Theory: New Conflicts, Collaborations, and Contested Terrain* (ed: Karen E. Lovaas, John P. Elia, and Gust A. Yep) Harrington Park Press, an imprint of The Haworth Press, Inc., 2006, pp. xxiii-xxvi. Single or multiple copies of this article are available for a fee from The Haworth Document Delivery Service [1-800-HAWORTH, 9:00 a.m. - 5:00 p.m. (EST). E-mail address: docdelivery@ haworthpress.com].

Available online at http://jh.haworthpress.com

was in part made possible by, and connected to, a social movement challenging the inferior social status of homosexuality.

By the 1980s, an impressive body of research and scholarship accumulated that took shape around the theme of the origins of the homosexual and the making of a homosexual minority. Historians, social scientists and other scholars researched the origin and development of lesbian and gay identities, dynamics of coming out, community building, the formation of lesbian and gay cultures, and so on. By the 1990s, lesbian and gay studies were recognized as a legitimate scholarly field and were integrated into colleges and universities.

However, just as the lesbian and gay movement, and lesbian and gay studies, was beginning to be mainstreamed, intellectual and political challenges emerged from friendly critics. In particular, the core assumption of lesbian and gay studies came under scrutiny and criticism: The idea of a common homosexual identity. Critics argued that it was misleading to speak in general terms, without considerable qualification, of the homosexual self or identity. Individuals experience being gay or lesbian, and having gender, race, and class in specific ways. In short, there is no gay self in general but only multiple lesbian and gay identities.

The idea of multiple, intersecting identities proved enormously fruitful in terms of opening up new lines of research and social thinking. However, for some thinkers the very plasticity or fluidness of the idea of homosexuality, the very idea that homosexual experiences could be multiplied virtually endlessly, posed a bigger challenge to the tradition of lesbian and gay studies. Does the idea of a lesbian and gay identity have any common reference and is it intellectually coherent? If gay identities or experiences can be multiplied ad infinitum because the combination of factors shaping such experiences are without limit, what sense does it make to speak of a gay self or identity? While a notion of a lesbian self might prove effective and necessary as a political strategy, it would seem to lack a defensible epistemological rationale.

While many scholars were reluctant to follow the logic of this critique of identity to this epistemological conclusion, a new type of thinking stepped forward, so-called queer theory, which embraced this logic as both a critique of lesbian and gay studies and as potentially opening up the field of sexuality studies. Queer theory broke from the tradition of lesbian and gay studies by framing identity in consistently relational terms. The meaning of homosexuality is to be grasped within a discourse that positions homosexuality and heterosexuality as contrasting ideas. The key point is that sexual meanings are not fixed or determined by the nature of desire or behavior but by understanding such concepts in a network of texts and discourses. And, to the extent that societies are composed of multiple discursive networks, sexual meanings will be varied, somewhat fluid, and the subject of social conflict. Queer theory shifted the focus of the scholarly gaze from the making of the homosexual self and community to the relationship between heterosexuality and homosexuality and to the broader culture of sexuality. Instead of centering inquiry on the making of a homosexual self, queer theorists would broaden inquiry to the making of a culture of sexuality, a culture that creates sexual selves, that establishes sexual identities, and that sets up a sexual hierarchy around notions of sexual normality and abnormality.

Although the idea of multiple and intersecting identities is now conventional wisdom, many students and scholars of lesbian and gay studies continue to question the intellectual and political value of queer theory. In the last decade this field of scholarship has been divided between a lesbian and gay studies approach and queer theory. This division is often a disciplinary division, as queer theory has been concentrated in the humanities, especially among English or comparative literature departments, whereas lesbian and gay studies has been concentrated in the social sciences and history. Of course, this disciplinary division also means that these two approaches tend to operate with different analytical languages and intellectual conventions.

Through the 1990s, the discussion between gay and lesbian studies and queer theory has occurred in highly theoretical terms and often removed from the disciplinary cultures that many of us work within. This has begun to change, in part because queer theory is itself being incorporated into the social sciences and history. Accordingly, this is a particularly fruitful time to address this discussion.

LGBT Studies and Queer Theory: New Conflicts, Collaborations, and Contested Terrain, a collection of original essays, addresses the challenge that queer theory presents to the study and the politics of gay and lesbian studies. What is especially noteworthy and useful is that these essays aim to take up this discussion less as an abstract theoretical debate than as an empirical and political issue. The reader will find essays that attempt to understand queer theory by situating it socially and historically, for example, by linking queer theory to the development of capitalism and to the evolution of the lesbian and gay movement. There are essays that critically examine queer theory in relation to the study and politics of bisexuality and gender. In particular, this volume contributes a series of original essays that examines what queer theory has to offer to the existing academic disciplines. Students and scholars from different disciplines will learn much from essays that explore the implications of queer theory for social psychology, religious studies, film studies, and women's studies.

Steven Seidman
University at Albany

Acknowledgements

This volume was only possible with the tremendous help of many colleagues, partners, and friends. In addition to the contributors to this volume, we express our profound gratitude to:

John DeCecco, Editor-in-Chief of the *Journal of Homosexuality,* for his inspiring leadership in the field and graciousness throughout this project;

Paul Sherwin, Dean of the College of Humanities at San Francisco State University, for his institutional assistance and encouragement;

Gerianne Merrigan, Chair of the Department of Communication Studies, for her support; and,

Our reviewers, Bryant Alexander, James Chesebro, Fred Corey, John Erni, Craig Gingrich-Philbrook, Larry Gross, Judith Halberstam, Lisa Henderson, E. Patrick Johnson, Kevin Kumashiro, Jackie Martinez, Tony Slagle, Ralph Smith, and Jacqueline Taylor, for their superb work.

Karen again thanks Erich for his patience, faith, and love, and her feline companion, Kobo, for his very dear presence everyday. She also acknowledges her long time circle of women friends who love, among other things, to gather every month in each other's homes to discuss a good book, catch up on our lives, and share a randomly assembled potluck that always turns out to be scrumptious; thank you Lin, Elizabeth, Kathleen, Sharon, Terry, Trina, Gayl, Mandy, and Nancy.

John is grateful to Gina and Brian for being such positive, powerful, and comforting forces in his life. Also, he is indebted to his sister, Debbie, who has been not only extremely supportive of his academic work, but also she has been an exemplary friend and confidant.

Gust says: I thank Emma Negrón whose loving support, gentle ear, and personal wisdom have taught me that life is a wonderful spiritual, emotional, and intellectual journey. Our ongoing dialogue continues to enrich and touch me deeply. I also thank Tyler and Dino, my faithful and fluffy companions, who continue to teach me about living and appreciating the present moment and accepting and experiencing their unconditional love.

The three of us dedicate this volume to those individuals inside and outside of the academy who have the courage to continue to struggle with the debates originating from the contested terrain between LGBT studies and Queer studies. In part, such struggles have been in the service of pushing the scholarship in these areas further, and to liberate people in their everyday lives–both valuable by-products of the tensions.

INTRODUCTION

Shifting Ground(s):
Surveying the Contested Terrain
of LGBT Studies and Queer Theory

Karen E. Lovaas, PhD

San Francisco State University

John P. Elia, PhD

San Francisco State University

Gust A. Yep, PhD

San Francisco State University

SUMMARY. While queer theory initially grew out of lesbian, gay, bisexual, and transgender (LGBT) studies, there are numerous points of

Correspondence may be addressed: Karen E. Lovaas, San Francisco University, Department of Communication Studies, 1600 Holloway Avenue, San Francisco, CA 94132 (E-mail: klovaas@sfsu.edu).

[Haworth co-indexing entry note]: "Shifting Ground(s): Surveying the Contested Terrain of LGBT Studies and Queer Theory." Lovaas, Karen E., John P. Elia, and Gust A. Yep. Co-published simultaneously in *Journal of Homosexuality* (Harrington Park Press, an imprint of The Haworth Press, Inc.) Vol. 52, No. 1/2, 2006, pp. 1-18; and: *LGBT Studies and Queer Theory: New Conflicts, Collaborations, and Contested Terrain* (ed: Karen E. Lovaas, John P. Elia, and Gust A. Yep) Harrington Park Press, an imprint of The Haworth Press, Inc., 2006, pp. 1-18. Single or multiple copies of this article are available for a fee from The Haworth Document Delivery Service [1-800-HAWORTH, 9:00 a.m. - 5:00 p.m. (EST). E-mail address: docdelivery@haworthpress.com].

contestation between these two approaches, originating mostly from their disparate positions on (sexual) identity politics. To describe, analyze, and contextualize this *contested terrain*, we begin this piece by providing some historical notes on LGBT studies and queer theory. Next, we turn to an explication of some enduring tensions to identify the criticisms generated by LGBT scholars toward queer theory approaches and vice versa. What follows is our rationale for producing *LGBT Studies and Queer Theory: New Conflicts, Collaborations, and Contested Terrain*. In this section we discuss how this project originated and the specific objectives we hope this volume will meet. The contributions of the individual articles in this volume are identified and summarized next. Finally, in the context of LGBT studies' and queer theory's similar qualities and points of difference, we offer ideas for potential directions of scholarship in the future that would explore three major areas: identity and difference; community and community organizing; and political engagement and social change.

doi:10.1300/J082v52n01_01 *[Article copies available for a fee from The Haworth Document Delivery Service: 1-800-HAWORTH. E-mail address: <docdelivery@haworthpress.com> Website: <http://www.HaworthPress.com>* © 2006 by The Haworth Press, Inc. All rights reserved.]

KEYWORDS. Gay and lesbian community, heteronormativity, identity politics, lesbian and gay studies, queer theory, sexual identity, sexual oppression, sexual politics

Queer, as a political theory and practice, has been viewed as the "radical" face of the lesbian and gay movement. Yet in a surprisingly short time, it has become respectable. The popular media has lapped up the language and imagery of queer. Queer cultural theory now abounds in academic books and courses. Queer [theory] claims to be a more "inclusive" politics, but inclusive of whom and of what? . . . Queer is far from the revolutionary movement it would like itself to be, it is little more than a liberal/libertarian alliance . . . [Q]ueer offers us [feminists] nothing. It is yet one more face of the backlash, trying to pass itself off as something new–we will not be fooled!

–Julia Parnaby (1996, pp. 3, 10)

"Queer" acknowledges ongoing debates over the question of essentialism versus constructionism in both gay and lesbian studies, and in feminist theory, and recognizes the inadequate current knowledge of differences between and among various gay men and women.

–John C. Hawley (2001, p. 6)

[O]ne of the great failings of queer theory and especially queer politics has been their inability to incorporate into analysis of the world and strategies for political mobilization the roles that race, class, and gender play in defining people's differing relations to dominant and normalizing power.

–Cathy J. Cohen (1997, p. 457)

Queerness provides a positionality from which differences, such as class, race, gender, and sexual style, can be further theorized and reevaluated . . . I see some hope in the healthy tensions and contradictions of a lesbian and gay intellectual endeavor: namely the possibility of reopening a wider discussion on gender, sexuality, class, race, and other differences in the context of queer experience . . . "Queer" like "woman" or "subaltern" is a pragmatically generic and diffuse category, outlining an area for legitimate condensation and contestation.

–Jacqueline N. Zita (1994, pp. 258, 268)

The tensions produced by LGBT and queer approaches to studying sexuality exemplified in the quotes above indicate just how significant the contested terrain is between those scholars using LGBT Studies and queer theory. Such a contested terrain may be seen in a variety of arenas, including scholarship, the classroom, politics, and in our communities and relationships. Studying these tensions from a variety of disciplinary and inter/transdisciplinary contexts sheds light on the magnitude of influence these approaches have had on scholars studying sexual identity politics and sexuality and gender, more generally.

In this introduction to *LGBT Studies and Queer Theory: New Conflicts, Collaborations, and Contested Terrain*, we establish a context for this volume by: (1) offering some historical notes on LGBT studies and queer theory; (2) outlining some enduring tensions between these two approaches; (3) describing our rationale for undertaking this project at this particular moment and delineating our specific objectives; (4) summarizing the contributions of the individual articles in this volume; and (5) suggesting possibilities for future work utilizing the productive potentials of these areas of contestation. The overarching hopes for this volume are to articulate some enduring points of contestation from multiple points of view and from a variety of disciplinary and inter/transdisciplinary perspectives, and to provide ideas–and possibly incentive–for future research and/or teaching in this arena. We begin with a discussion of some historical notes on LGBT studies and queer theory.

SOME HISTORICAL NOTES ON LGBT STUDIES AND QUEER THEORY

Lesbian and gay studies in the U.S. are generally discussed as having emerged from the homophile movements of the 1950s and 1960s and the gay and lesbian liberation movements. They largely followed the early stages of the civil rights and women's movements of the 1960s and 1970s that led to the incursion of ethnic and women's studies in the academy (D'Emilio, 1992). The primary goal of lesbian and gay studies has been "to express and advance the interests of lesbians, bisexuals, and gay men, and to contribute culturally and intellectually to the contemporary lesbian/gay movement" (Abelove, Barale, & Halperin, 1993, p. xvi). Queer theory is a more recent theoretical development dating from the early 1990s spurred on by Queer Nation, and is frequently described as an outgrowth of LGBT and feminist studies and politics (Duggan, 1995; Jagose, 1996; Stein, 1999).

It may be useful to remind ourselves briefly of the larger frame within which these approaches arose and continue to develop, i.e., to view them in the context of ongoing intellectual movements of modernism and postmodernism. Modernist approaches, associated with much traditional work in the social sciences, including LGBT studies, are likely to involve a search for knowable meanings via rational and scientific methods (Seidman, 1993). For example, within this worldview, history is seen as a linear process of progressive development. From the modernist perspective, historical records and artifacts provide us with a window through which we may come to understand the past. Modernism is undergirded by the notion that there is significant consensus in the West about history, identities, and values, allowing the telling of metanarratives of the origins and identity development of the sexual self. This is the logic of much of the "coming out" literature, which presumes a process of uncovering an essential homosexuality; one's past may be read and re-read as having always contained the "true self."

Queer theory is conceptually aligned with the postmodernism and poststructuralism of literature, the arts, and the humanities more generally. In particular, it employs a postmodernist critique of biological determinism, or essentialism, and emphasizes a self-reflexive understanding of gender and sexuality. Seidman (1993) notes that "[q]ueers are not united by any unitary identity but only to their opposition to disciplining, normalizing social forces" (p. 133). Subjectivities are multiple, fluid, and include agency, the ability to act, as opposed to a static, unified, view of the self, an object controlled by the dominant society. Master narratives are deconstructed to expose the falsely unified stories they tell about subjects and countered by local narratives. The postmodernist take on subjects highlights the necessity of situating or contextualizing subjects, past and present, with as much specificity as possible. "Queer theory," says Plummer, "is really poststructuralism (and postmodernism) applied to sexualities and genders" (2003, p. 520). Gamson (2000) concisely summed up the recent history of ideas regarding various thoughts about sexual subjectivity. He avers,

> . . . we have gone from unreflective confidence in the existence of sexual subjects—who only needed to be found and documented—to a boom in lesbian and gay studies filled with subjects speaking and writing about their own lives, to a suspicion that sexual subjects do not exactly exist to be studied, an ongoing deconstruction of sexual subjectivity. (p. 348)

The chronology Gamson suggests certainly helps us understand one of the major, if not the most significant, clashes between LGBT studies and queer theory, viz., their respective positions on sexual identity politics. This will be explored in more detail later. Now, we turn to an examination of some tensions between LGBT studies and queer theory.

SOME ENDURING TENSIONS

Although we recognize that LGBT studies and queer theory share moments of historical emergence and growth that have profoundly influenced the other's theoretical development, academic expansion and political engagement (de Lauretis, 1991; Gamson, 2000), we chose the title of this volume, *LGBT Studies and Queer Theory: New Conflicts, Collaborations, and Contested Terrain*, to highlight areas of disputation and competition between these two lines of inquiry. Holding LGBT studies and queer theory apart, at arms' length, is an intentional device that we hope will serve to acknowledge real areas of tension. However, the danger in this strategy is that it may appear to polarize, or at least accentuate the divide. Thus, we have titled this introductory essay, "Shifting Ground(s): Surveying the Contested Terrain of LGBT Studies and Queer Theory," purposefully. Though there is considerable critique of the existing research coming from both of these approaches to understanding sexualities within the pages of this volume, we do not want to lose sight of the shared, overlapping, frequently complementary grounds on which they stand. In terms of commonalities, both LGBT studies and queer theory are modes of inquiry whose focal point is gender and sexuality. Both are linked to significant social movements of the mid-late 20th century, particularly the 2nd wave of feminism and the gay liberation movement. Both have made significant use of qualitative approaches to how meanings are subjectively constructed. Both seek to link research with politics and liberate sexual and gender "minorities" from oppressive forms of heteronormativity and sexual and gender prejudice that have been, and continue to be, harmful to those who do not fit gender and sexual norms.

But there are also significant differences in LGBT's and queer theory's assumptions about the nature of individual and collective realities and the appropriate modes of inquiry for describing and transforming them. As summarized above, some of these have included, respectively: disciplinary distinctions (e.g., the social sciences and the humanities); disciplinary and inter/transdisciplinary modes of research; and, questions of stability and fluidity of sexual and gender identities. On this last point, it is our sense that gay and lesbian studies have tended to emphasize the stability of gay and lesbian sexual identities, while queer theory, though growing out of LGBT studies, *primarily* aims to continuously destabilize and deconstruct the notion of fixed sexual and gender identities. LGBT studies is generally criticized for taking a minoritizing view (see Sedgwick, 1990), that maintains rather than disrupts the homosexual/heterosexual binary (Gamson, 1995/1998; Sedgwick, 1990). Akin to an ethnic identity model, the minoritizing view has been challenged both in the critique of compulsory heterosexuality made by lesbian feminists that highlights differences between women's and men's life choices, and by scholars and activists of color who argue that this is predominately studied through the lens of white, middle-class males. This charge has been appropriately leveled against both approaches. While some scholars describe queer theory as more radical and inclusive than gay and lesbian studies (Stein, 1999; Warner, 1993), many queer theorists' penchant for overlooking race has also been demonstrated (see, for example, Alexander, 2003; Barnard, 2003; Johnson, 2001). Additionally, Hennessy (2000), Jackson (2003), Kirsch (2000, and in this volume), and Morton (1996) are among those who critique queer theory for its inattention to material conditions and practices.

Disciplinary struggles between the two approaches are played out in the academy where queer theory has been perceived by some as a "mixed blessing" in that, on the positive side, it "has produced an enormous amount of publishing activity among lesbian, gay, bisexual and transgender scholars, invigorating the field and helping to usher in a new visibility for the study of gender and sexuality" (Brookey & Miller, 2001, p. 139). Alternately, Halperin asserts that queer theory's ascendancy in institutions of higher education has had "the undesirable and misleading effect of portraying all previous work in lesbian and gay studies as under-theorized, as laboring under the delusion of identity politics" (2003, p. 341).

Identity politics are a recurring theme of the contested terrain. There is much heated discussion about the political utility of queer theory: "some critics have portrayed queer theory as an esoteric and politically bankrupt approach that contributes little to social change" (Brookey & Miller, 2001, p. 139). Queer theory is accused of compromising, if not abandoning, its subversive origins and questions are raised as to whether or not it has the wherewithal to sustain effective political alliances. For example, Medhurst and Munt (1997), co-editors of *Lesbian and Gay Studies: A Critical Introduction*, protest "[W]hilst Queer Theory seems to have suspended Lesbian and Gay Studies nomenclature in the academy, we are disturbed by the elitism which has come to be associated with it, in spite of its originally inclusive political agenda" (p. xi). Parnaby (1996) argues that queer theory fails to address the ways in which men oppress women and Jeffreys (2003) observes that queer theory has yet to supply sufficiently specific channels of tackling heteropatriarchal power. Similarly, Namaste (2000, p. 23) notes that queer theory shows "remarkable insensitivity" to the lives and experiences of transgendered people. This position is countered by those who argue that it is the identity politics associated with LGBT approaches have been primarily fueled by assimilationist impulses that are unable to adequately deal with contemporary exigencies. The social implications of our theories matter a great deal, for "[t]here is much at stake here, not just for research and theory but for everyday politics: Collective action . . . requires sophisticated inquiry into the simultaneous, and linked, processes by which the experiences of sexual desire are given institutional, textual, and experiential shape" (Gamson, 2000, p. 360). We propose that we cannot afford to be more engaged in undermining each other's efforts than in vigorous discussions and constructive dialogues.

RATIONALE AND OBJECTIVES FOR THIS VOLUME

This project flows from a series of conversations begun almost six years ago about the possibilities for queering communication and other related fields of study. The book *Queer Theory and Communication: From Disciplining Queers to Queering the Discipline(s)* (Yep, Lovaas, & Elia, 2003) was a tangible product of those talks and spurred our interest in the subject of this volume. We were intrigued with the strength of feeling evinced by many contributors to the prior collection regarding queer theory's real and promised achievements, evidence of its failings, and its sometimes antagonistic relationship with LGBT studies.

As we stated in the introduction to the previous volume, we believe that LGBT studies and queer theory need "to coexist in an ongoing productive tension" in which neither holds nor pursues "theoretical hegemony" (Yep, Lovaas, & Elia, 2003, pp. 4-5). This volume critically explores a variety of facets of the evolving debates over the ground of sexuality and gender studies and politics, highlighting their academic, social, and personal implications. Its objectives are: (1) to extend the conversation begun in the previous volume (Yep, Lovaas, & Elia, 2003) to more disciplines and interdisciplinary contexts; (2) to create a vehicle for disseminating current work grappling with the "contested terrain" of LGBT studies and queer theory; (3) to consider the implications of this research for scholars, teachers, and political activists; and (4) to galvanize further research related to engaging tensions of multiple approaches to research and political action.

This volume contains 12 articles from a variety of disciplinary and interdisciplinary fields, and each one in its own way offers a description of the contested relationship between lesbian, gay, bisexual, and transgender (LGBT) studies and queer theory. Although both of these approaches were born in the service of liberating sexual and gendered *others*–and have been important theoretically and have served as the basis for much needed activism–from the injustices and harm inherent in heteronormativity, in many instances scholars who have endorsed the LGBT studies perspective have been at odds with the theoretical positions employed by queer theorists and vice versa. Many of the pieces contained in this work articulate the tensions between these two theoretical positions, and the implications these various points of contestation have on academic, community, and personal life. This volume has been divided into three sections, viz., theoretical debates and interventions, intersections, and contexts.

CONTRIBUTIONS OF THE ARTICLES

We begin with "Theoretical Debates and Interventions," a grouping of four essays that address some of the current theoretical issues in research on sexualities and offer ways to push the work in a few specific disciplines to move in new directions. First comes Max Kirsch's "Queer Theory, Late Capitalism and Internalized Homophobia." Kirsch points out that while queer theory offers a different approach than LGBT studies and cultural theory in an attempt to liberate lesbian, gay, bisexual, and transgender individuals, it is actually dubious in terms of whether or not it can create positive social change. He contends that queer theory's erasure of identity feeds into late capitalism and perpetuates internalized homophobia. He concludes that queer theory would be more useful if it shifted from the critique of identities to an acknowledgement of the value of *identifying with* social movements. Then, Kirsch believes, more effective coalition building can occur and greater focus on matters of importance to promoting social change.

Next, the volume turns to Peter Hegarty and Sean Massey's article, "Anti-Homosexual Prejudice . . . as Opposed to What? Queer Theory and the Social Psychology of Anti-Homosexual Attitudes." Using Sedgwick's observations about minoritizing and universalizing theories of sexuality as a backdrop, this piece includes a critical examination about how anti-homosexual prejudice has been framed and studied by social psychologists. After offering a comprehensive summary and analysis of the prominent recent research that has focused on the minoritizing approach, Hegarty and Massey conclude that queer theory has the potential of revolutionizing social psychological research and could foster an enhanced understanding of anti-homosexual prejudice.

Following this piece, Melissa M. Wilcox's "Outlaws or In-Laws? Queer Theory, LGBT studies, and Religious Studies" reveals how religious studies have been either overlooked or superficially treated in both LGBT studies and queer theory. In some cases, Wilcox contends, religious studies are treated disparagingly within these canons. Her work assesses LGBT studies and queer studies in religion and suggests ways that both approaches can provide productive new avenues for the future in terms of infusing LGBT studies and queer theory in religious studies.

The final article in this section is Jeff Bennett's "A Queer Anxiety: Assimilation Politics and Cinematic Hedonics in *Relax . . . It's Just Sex*," which provides a rigorous analysis of how queerness is commodified in independent cinema. Specifically, this piece uses the film, *Relax . . . It's Just Sex* to show the tensions of trying to maintain gay and lesbian sexual politics while trying to appeal to a wide audience with a variety of sexual tastes and sexual politics. Bennett points out that while this film defies sexual norms, it ultimately falls back on hegemonic and "essentialized understandings of identity closely aligned to liberation rhetoric." Bennett urges queer activists to be more attentive to discourses that shape everyday life.

"Intersections" is the second section of the volume. These five essays examine how LGBT studies and queer theory explore the interplays and collisions between sexuality and other vectors of difference, such as race, class, and gender, in both U.S. and international contexts.

This section begins with an article by Steven Angelides entitled, "Historicizing (Bi)Sexuality: A Rejoinder for Gay/Lesbian Studies, Feminism, and Queer Theory." His article begins by discussing the irony—misfortune—that while queer theory promises to interrogate heteronormativity and ". . . work the hetero/homosexual opposition to the point of collapse," bisexuality has been virtually ignored within queer theory. Angelides points out that no one has ever attempted to explain this phenomenon, and therefore he sets out, in part, to offer an historical account of bisexuality's erasure within the canons of queer theory. This study clarifies the tensions between LGBT studies, feminism, and queer theory. In the end, Angelides contends that many queer theorists have had a misguided theoretical approach to sexuality and gender. Angelides concludes by asserting that ignoring the history of bisexuality and the conflict within these theoretical paradigms has created problems in terms of deconstructing the hetero/homosexual binary.

Also examining the territory of bisexuality, Mark A. Gammon and Kirsten L. Isgro's "Troubling the Canon: Bisexuality and Queer Theory" is an historical account about how bisexuality has been theorized, and an analysis of how such theorizing has shaped its relationship to queer theory. Like Angelides, these scholars note bisexuality's absence in Queer theory and research, an absence with serious consequences on a few fronts. Gammon and Isgro address bisexual epistemologies and their significant implications for queer theory, politics and daily life.

Moving from explorations of bisexuality to other vectors of difference, this section continues with Karen Krahulik's Cape Queer? A Case Study of Provincetown, Massachusetts. This article examines how sexuality intersects with race, gender, and class in the development of Provincetown, a gay and lesbian resort community. In the process, Krahulik finds how this community was affected by the global mechanics of capitalism that eventually led to a rearticulation of race, class, and gender inequities.

In the next essay "Jewish Disappearing Acts and the Construction of Gender," Ruth Johnston focuses on the interarticulation of race/ethnicity and gender. She investigates this interarticulation by examining the conceptualization of the Oedipus complex at the turn of the 20th century and the conceptualization of gender performativity in contemporary queer theory. More specifically, Johnston registers a contradiction as well as a historical shift in the representations of Jewish identity that is implicated in the construction of sexual categories in the last century.

Our final essay in this section is Dean Durber's "Desiring Mates." In this piece, Durber examines the relationships between male friends ("mates") in Australia. In his historically situated, and culturally specific analysis, Durber challenges the discourse of gay liberation and the notion of the closet by positioning "mateship" unions within a queer theoretical framework. He argues that through silence and the refusal to be labeled as either homosexual or heterosexual, mates can claim a space of deep emotional bond and pleasure that may or may not include sexual contact. Through this process, Durber maintains that mates resist normalized constructions of sexual identities.

"Contexts" is the third section of this volume. It consists of two essays by authors embodying, practicing, and reflecting on LGBT studies and queer theory in different institutional arrangements and contexts.

This section starts with Jen Bacon's "Teaching Queer Theory at a *Normal* School." It is a case study of the ongoing struggle to queer an institution of higher learning. In the essay, Bacon identifies and reflects on the attempts to introduce sexual diversity at the level of the institution, the curriculum, and the classroom. She notes that the process of sexual diversification is full of tensions and contradictions that are manifested in debates over free speech on campus, departmental jurisdiction for a queer studies minor, and curricular content for a lesbian studies course.

The second article in this section is Claudia Schippert's "Containing Uncertainty: Sexual Values and Citizenship." In the essay, the author reflects on one of the challenges of being a queer ethicist. Drawing from the writings by Weeks, Richardson, Bell and Binnie, and Phelan, Schippert engages the debate of citizenship and the ongoing tensions between LGBT and queer positions. Based on her analysis, she concludes that these debates suggest that political morality and sexual ethics need not be conceptualized according to a particular constructive engagement of citizenship in order to "count" as politically effective.

To close our volume, we offer R. Anthony Slagle's "Ferment in LGBT Studies and Queer Theory: Personal Ruminations on Contested Terrain." In this self-reflexive essay, Slagle examines the personal struggles, relational investments, and disciplinary politics that characterize the ongoing effort to address issues of theory and praxis related to human sexual diversity in a highly charged social and intellectual landscape.

PRODUCTIVE POSSIBILITIES ON CONTESTED TERRAIN

As stated earlier, LGBT studies and queer theory exhibit paths of on-going convergence and divergence. The essays in this collection attempt to bring together and make explicit these topics of continuing consensus and agreement as well as contestation and debate in a singular volume. Although some individuals are calling for the moment of the "post-queer," we argue that there are a number of potentially productive venues for theory, research, and praxis as LGBT studies and queer theory continue to evolve and engage in the production of sexual knowledges on this contested terrain. In this final section, we make speculations about some of these productive possibilities.

We believe that there are three general areas that appear to be productive for future work. The first focuses on issues of identity and difference. Although both LGBT studies and queer theory engage these concepts differently, the notion of a sexual identity–whether fixed and permanent or fluid and eternally changing–is central in theory and praxis. However, sexuality is always already intersecting with other vectors of identity and difference. For example, the concept of a "gay identity" tends to generally refer to U.S. middle-class white men (Bérubé, 2001), or to put it another way, sexuality intersects with race, class, gender, and nationality. Writing about sexual oppression, Blasius (1997) observes that "we are oppressed because of our sexuality, our gender, and our sexed corporeality" and "this sexual oppression is mediated, subjectified, and enacted through the categories and relations of racism, of class exploitation and economic advantage or deprivation, and of cultural hegemony" (p. 350). Although this intersectional approach to sexual identity is now widely accepted and recognized, neither LGBT studies nor queer theory has adequately embraced it as a theoretical lens or as a tool for activism (Cohen, 1997). This situation becomes even more complex if we examine how sexual desires, practices, and expressions are embodied by individuals and groups who challenge the homosexual/heterosexual binary such as bisexuals (e.g., Fox, 2004; Storr, 1999; Tucker, 1995) and the gender binary system such as "genderqueers" (e.g., Nestle, Howell, & Wilchins, 2002) and trans-identified persons (e.g., Green, 2004; Namaste, 2000; Rubin, 2003). Finally, these intersections become further complicated if we consider how sexuality is lived and experienced in diasporic, transnational, and global contexts (e.g., Altman, 2001; Cruz-Malavé & Manalansan, 2002; Lee, 2003). But can we afford to think about sexuality without attending to how it intersects with gender, race, class, nation, and ability/disability?[1] While many salute the inclusive potential of the term *queer*, it is still the case that there is far more literature about middle class white males than about dykes of color, "genderqueers," or trans immigrants, for example. Wherever we go and whatever contexts we work and play in, how does the homosexual/heterosexual binary figure in those arenas and with what material effects? What transpires and what can be transformed when LGBT and queer viewpoints meet in a classroom, a boardroom, a playroom? How do we go about constructing unconventional, alternative, queer relationships in the face of hostile institutions and discourses (see Elia, 2003)? How do the forces of globalization and transnationalism operate in constructing and deconstructing sexual identities?

The second area focuses on community and community organizing. To maintain itself as the universal standard of normality, heterosexuality–as an identity, institution, practice, and experience–desperately needs an "abnormal and pathological other" (e.g., sexual deviants) and this process created an entire class of abject and abominable bodies, souls, and persons (Yep, 2003). The "abnormality" of sexual deviants serves to authenticate the "normality" of heterosexuality. However, an unforeseen consequence occurred as these sexual deviants started organizing around their assigned pathological status: their sexual identity. A sexual minority community was formed and this gave them strength in numbers and resources to combat their own oppression and sexuality became the basis for a political movement. But should the notion of community as a site for cooperation, equality, and communion be unquestioned and unexamined (Joseph, 2002)? As gender, class, and racial diversity became more and more apparent, multiple sexual communities started developing and the question of organizing across these constituencies has become increasingly important for effective political action (Blasius, 1997). How do LGBT studies and queer theory imagine, construct, and enact community? How do they mobilize these groups for social change?

The third area focuses on political engagement and social change. Questions such as "what constitutes political engagement?" and "what constitutes social change?" become important ones to clarify, debate, and operationalize. Should change be at the level of individual psyches and interpersonal relations and/or at the level of the social structure? Which ones should receive higher priority given limited resources? Should change be immediately "measurable" such as modification of current legislation or implementation of new ones? What about changes in individual consciousness such as awareness of the harms of homophobia and heterosexism and the violence of heteronormativity? Should change occur from within the current social system or should change mean an overhaul of the existing system? What ideologies drive these actions? Should sexual minorities assimilate into heteronormative culture? Should sexual minorities challenge the structure and dynamics of current social and cultural arrangements? These ideological struggles have given rise to what Paul Robinson (2005) calls the "queer wars"– the debates about the politics of sexuality in contemporary U.S. culture. How do LGBT studies and queer theory conceive social change and how it could be enacted? How do LGBT studies and queer theory frame the current debates over sexuality, sexual oppression, and sexual liberation and with what personal, collective, and material consequences? Engaging these questions has the potential to change the quality of life for many individuals. It could also produce different social worlds.

To conclude, LGBT studies and queer theory need not be viewed as locked in a competition from which only one will inevitably emerge, as the modernist mythology of history as linear progression urges us to believe. Post-feminism was also prematurely announced, as feminism gave way–under some duress–to womanism and feminisms. Judith Butler has said that she approaches feminism

> with the presumption that no undisputed premises are to be agreed upon in the global context. And so, for practical and political reasons, there is no value to be derived in silencing disputes. The

questions are: how best to have them, how most productively to stage them, and how to act in ways that acknowledge the irreversible complexity of who we are? (2004, p. 176)

The terrain of sexuality and gender studies will continue to be contested rather than permanently settled, leaving ample spaces for intellectual growth and new political moves. Scholars, activists, and scholar/activists have the option and the responsibility to work to make the tensions productive and complex. Together, we are shifting the grounds on which these debates and dialogues are taking place. Collectively the articles in this volume integrate institutional, cultural, and discursive facets of sexualities; individually the articles explore, integrate, and push current conceptions of LGBT studies and queer theory across and within a variety of disciplines. As such, we hope it is a powerful example of this direction. There is always new ground to break, new ground to stand on.

NOTE

1. As we write this introduction, we are particularly mindful of the power of whiteness to re-center itself whenever and wherever we allow our attention to stray for even a moment, despite intentions and commitments to the contrary. We had hoped that this volume would, in the end, include more voices of people of color, and address issues of race and nation more forcefully.

REFERENCES

Abelove, H., Barale, M. A., & Halperin, D. H. (Eds.). (1993). *The lesbian and gay studies reader.* New York and London: Routledge.

Alexander, B. (2003). Querying queer theory again (or, queer theory as drag performance). In G. A. Yep, K. E. Lovaas, & J. P. Elia (Eds.), *Queer theory and communication: From disciplining queers to queering the discipline(s)* (pp. 349-352). New York: Harrington Park Press.

Altman, D. (1971). *Homosexual: Oppression and liberation.* New York: Outerbridge & Dienstfrey.

Altman, D. (2001). *Global sex.* Chicago: University of Chicago Press.

Barnard, I. (2003). *Queer race: Cultural interventions in the racial politics of queer theory.* New York: Peter Lang.

Bérubé, A. (2001). How gay stays white and what kind of white it stays. In B. R. Rasmussen, E. Klinenberg, I. J. Nexica, & M. Wray (Eds.), *The making and unmaking of whiteness* (pp. 234-265). Durham, NC: Duke University Press.

Blasius, M. (1997). Introduction. *GLQ: A Journal of Lesbian and Gay Studies, 3*, 337-356.

Brookey, R. A., & Miller, D. H. (2001). Changing signs: The political pragmatism of poststructuralism. *International Journal of Sexuality and Gender Studies, 6*(1/2), 139-153.

Butler, J. (2004). *Undoing gender.* New York and London: Routledge.

Cohen, C. J. (1997). Punks, bulldaggers, and welfare queens: The radical potential of queer politics? *GLQ: A Journal of Lesbian and Gay Studies, 3*, 437-465.

Cruz-Malavé, A., & Manalansan, M. F. (Eds.). (2002). *Queer globalizations: Citizenship and the afterlife of colonialism.* New York: New York University Press.

de Lauretis, T. (1991). Queer theory: Lesbian and gay sexualities–An introduction. *differences: A Journal of Feminist Cultural Studies, 3*(2), iii-xviii.

D'Emilio, J. (1992). Gay and lesbian studies: New kid on the block? In J. D'Emilio (Ed.), *Making trouble: Essays on gay history, politics, and the university* (pp. 160-175). New York and London: Routledge.

Duggan, L. (1995). Making it perfectly queer. In L. Duggan & N. D. Hunter (Eds.), *Sex wars: Sexual dissent and political culture* (pp. 155-172). New York: Routledge.

Elia, J. P. (2003). Queering relationships: Toward a paradigmatic shift. In G. A. Yep, K. E. Lovaas, & J. P. Elia (Eds.), *Queer theory and communication: From disciplining queers to queering the discipline(s)* (pp. 61-86). New York: Harrington Park Press.

Fox, R. C. (Ed.). (2004). *Current research on bisexuality.* Binghamton, NY: Harrington Park Press.

Gamson, J. (1995/1998). Must identity movements self-destruct? A queer dilemma. In P. M. Nardi & B. E. Schneider (Eds.), *Social perspectives in lesbian and gay studies: A reader* (pp. 589-604). London: Routledge.

Gamson, J. (2000). Sexualities, queer theory, and qualitative research. In N. K. Denzin & Y. S. Lincoln (Eds.), *Handbook of qualitative research* (pp. 347-365). Thousand Oaks, CA: Sage.

Green, J. (2004). *Becoming a visible man.* Nashville, TN: Vanderbilt University Press.

Halperin, D. M. The normalization of queer theory. In G. A. Yep, K. E. Lovaas, & J. P. Elia (Eds.), *Queer theory and communication: From disciplining queers to queering the discipline(s)* (pp. 339-343). New York: Harrington Park Press.

Hawley, J. C. (Ed.). (2001). *Post-colonial queer: Theoretical intersections.* Albany, NY: State University of New York Press,

Hennessy, R. (2000). *Profit and pleasure: Sexual identities in late capitalism.* New York and London: Routledge.

Jackson, S. (2003). Heterosexuality, heteronormativity and gender hierarchy: Some reflections on recent debates. In J. Weeks, J. Holland, & M. Waites (Eds.), *Sexualities and society: A reader* (pp. 69-83). Malden, MA: Blackwell.

Jagose, A. (1996). *Queer theory: An introduction.* New York: New York University Press.

Jeffreys, S. (2003). *Unpacking queer politics: A lesbian feminist perspective.* Cambridge: Polity Press.

Johnson, E. P. (2001). "Quare" studies, or (almost) everything I know about queer studies I learned from my grandmother. *Text and Performance Quarterly, 21*, 1-25.

Joseph, M. (2002). *Against the romance of community*. Minneapolis, MN: University of Minnesota Press.

Kirsch, M. H. (2000). *Queer theory and social change*. London: Routledge.

Lee, W. (2003). *Kuaering* queer theory: My autocritography and a race-conscious, womanist, transnational turn. In G. A. Yep, K. E. Lovaas, & J. P. Elia (Eds.), *Queer theory and communication: From disciplining queers to queering the discipline(s)* (pp. 147-170). New York: Harrington Park Press.

Medhurst, A., & Munt, S. R. (Eds.). (1997). *Lesbian and gay studies: A critical introduction*. London and Washington: Cassell Publishers.

Morton, D. (Ed.). (1996). *The material queer: A lesbigay cultural studies reader*. Boulder, CO: Westview Press.

Namaste, V. K. (2000). *Invisible lives: The erasure of transsexual and transgendered people*. Chicago: University of Chicago Press.

Nestle, J., Howell, C., & Wilchins, R. (Eds.). (2002). *GenderQueer: Voices from beyond the sexual binary*. Los Angeles: Alyson.

Parnaby, J. (1996). Queer straits. In L. Harne & E. Miller (Eds.), *All the rage: Reasserting radical lesbian feminism* (pp. 3-10). New York: Teachers College Press.

Plummer, K. (2003). Queers, bodies and postmodern sexualities: A note on revisiting the "sexual" in symbolic interactionism. *Qualitative Sociology, 25*(4), 515-528.

Robinson, P. (2005). *Queer wars: The new gay right and its critics*. Chicago: University of Chicago Press.

Rubin, H. (2003). *Self-made men: Identity and embodiment among transsexual men*. Nashville, TN: Vanderbilt University Press.

Sedgwick, E. K. (1990). *Epistemology of the closet*. Berkeley, CA: University of California Press.

Seidman, S. (1993). Identity and politics in a "postmodern" gay culture: Some historical and conceptual notes. In M. Warner (Ed.), *Fear of a queer planet: Queer politics and social theory* (pp. 105-142). Minneapolis: University of Minnesota Press.

Stein, E. (1999). *The mismeasure of desire: The science, theory, and ethics of sexual orientation*. Oxford and New York: Oxford University Press.

Storr, M. (Ed.). (1999). *Bisexuality: A critical reader*. London: Routledge.

Tucker, N. (Ed.). (1995). *Bisexual politics: Theories, queries, and visions*. New York: Harrington Park Press.

Warner, M. (Ed.). (1993). *Fear of a queer planet: Queer politics and social theory*. Minneapolis: University of Minnesota Press.

Yep, G. A. (2003). The violence of heteronormativity in communication studies: Notes on injury, healing, and queer world-making. In G. A. Yep, K. E. Lovaas, & J. P. Elia (Eds.), *Queer theory and communication: From disciplining queers to queering the discipline(s)* (pp. 11-59). New York: Harrington Park Press.

Yep, G. A., Lovaas, K. E., & Elia, J. P. (2003). Introduction: Queering communication: Starting the conversation. In G. A. Yep, K. E. Lovaas, & J. P. Elia (Eds.), *Queer theory and communication: From disciplining queers to queering the discipline(s)* (pp. 1-10). New York: Harrington Park Press.

Yep, G. A., Lovaas, K. E., & Elia, J. P. (Eds.). (2003). *Queer theory and communica-
    tion: From disciplining queers to queering the discipline(s).* New York: Harrington
    Park Press.
Zita, J. N. (1994). Gay and lesbian studies: Yet another unhappy marriage. In L.
    Garber (Ed.), *Tilting the Tower* (pp. 258-276). New York and London: Rout-
    ledge.

doi:10.1300/J082v52n01_01

Queer Theory, Late Capitalism, and Internalized Homophobia

Max Kirsch, PhD

Florida Atlantic University

SUMMARY. The emergence of queer theory represents a transformation in the approach to lesbian, gay, bisexual and transgendered peoples. It has claimed new ground for treating sexuality and gender as worthy subjects in their own rights, rather than offshoots of gay and lesbian studies or of general cultural theory. The author contends, however, that it is doubtful that this approach can lead to social change. Queer theory has dismissed the usefulness of the disciplines that were the foundation of the social movements that initiated gay and lesbian studies, such as political economy, and in doing so, it has surreptitiously mirrored the so-

Correspondence may be addressed: UNESCO Chair in Human and Cultural Rights, Ph.D. Program in Comparative Studies, Florida Atlantic University, 777 Glades Road, Boca Raton, FL 33431 (E-mail: Mkirsch@fau.edu).

[Haworth co-indexing entry note]: "Queer Theory, Late Capitalism, and Internalized Homophobia." Kirsch, Max. Co-published simultaneously in *Journal of Homosexuality* (Harrington Park Press, an imprint of The Haworth Press, Inc.) Vol. 52, No. 1/2, 2006, pp. 19-45; and: *LGBT Studies and Queer Theory: New Conflicts, Collaborations, and Contested Terrain* (ed: Karen E. Lovaas, John P. Elia, and Gust A. Yep) Harrington Park Press, an imprint of The Haworth Press, Inc., 2006, pp. 19-45. Single or multiple copies of this article are available for a fee from The Haworth Document Delivery Service [1-800-HAWORTH, 9:00 a.m. - 5:00 p.m. (EST). E-mail address: docdelivery@haworthpress.com].

cial relations of reproduction that constitute late capitalism. This mirroring has had unseen consequences for the individual in society, and with queer theory's insistence on the relativity of experience and the dismissal of identity, has set the stage for a benign reinforcement of internalized homophobia. The author argues that this approach can be mediated by recognizing that identity is fluid, and that by focusing on identifying with social movements rather than centering analyses on the problems associated with identifying as a particular category of status and being, we can refocus our energies on the building and maintenance of mutual support and collective recognition that can lead to resolving the stagnation now dominating attempts to develop coalitions around issues that matter. doi:10.1300/J082v52n01_02 *[Article copies available for a fee from The Haworth Document Delivery Service: 1-800-HAWORTH. E-mail address: <docdelivery@ haworthpress.com> Website: <http://www.HaworthPress.com> © 2006 by The Haworth Press, Inc. All rights reserved.]*

KEYWORDS. Queer theory, late capitalism, gender, homophobia, identity, gender politics, social change

    The emergence of queer theory during the past decade represents a transformation in our approaches to lesbian, gay, bisexual and transgendered peoples. It has claimed new avenues for treating sexuality and gender as worthy subjects in their own right, rather than as offshoots of lesbian and gay studies or of general cultural theory. Queer theory asserts that inclusiveness requires relativity, and that it is with this perspective that we can free our analyses from fixed, if hidden, meanings and structures of power. I will suggest here, however, that it is doubtful that this framing alone can initiate social change. While gay and lesbian studies developed from the new social movements of the 1960s, queer theory has dismissed the usefulness of the disciplines that they drew on, such as political economy, for analyzing exploitation and inclusion. I will also suggest that the ontology of queer theory, through postmodernism and poststructuralism, surreptitiously mirrors the development of late capitalism and the concurrent ideology of the ego-centered individual. The highlighting of the impossibility (and undesirability) of identification and the relativity of experience closely follows current capitalist relations of production, where the self-contained individual is central to the economic goal of creating profit through production and its by-product, consuming. It is thus my view that the tenets of queer theory closely pattern those characteristics of late capitalism that it claims to reject.[1]

This mirroring of late capitalism in queer theory has unforeseen consequences for the individual in society and has hindered its practioners from engaging important ways of envisioning collective action. Queer theory promotes the "self" of the individual as an alternative to wider social interaction, disassembling the social ties that bind. Recognizing that oppression and violence, symbolic and physical, are part of the daily reality for those of us who do not correspond to dominant standards is compromised by queer theory's rejection of the category of identity, and indeed, categories as a whole. The stance that it is limiting to pose categories of behavior and belief, even if those constructs are fluid and changing, puts the individual subject in the position of internalizing thoughts and feelings without the benefit of peer feedback. Too, this aspect of marginality can itself become an identity: if one recognizes and embraces the fact that one is marginalized, there is no need to seek support or to engage social action. It declares that the only way to prevent being overwhelmed by power is to "disclaim" (Butler, 1993, p. 308). But to simply disclaim creates isolation, and, as I will maintain, reinforces internalized homophobia.

Finally, I will propose that a means of mediating the positions asserted by many queer theorists is to conceptualize methods of identifying *with* rather than identifying *as*. In this way, identity can maintain its importance in providing a vehicle for mutual support and as a basis for initiating and maintaining social action, while recognizing that the category of identity is fluid and changes with the consequences of the social world.

THE CROSSROADS OF LESBIAN AND GAY STUDIES AND QUEER THEORY

In their Introduction to the influential *Lesbian and Gay Studies Reader* (Abelove, Barale and Halperin, 1993), the editors acknowledge that their collection conflates gay and lesbian and queer studies, preferring the later but yielding to the then current usage of gay and lesbian as the institutionalized form of study most often recognized by scholars (1993, p. vii). Since the publication of that volume, much has changed. Queer studies and its most influential mode of inquiry, queer theory, has become the institutionalized norm within colleges and universities in the United States, and the discourse of study has refocused attention from the identity-centered character of gay and lesbian studies to the more reflexive and possibly more inclusive term, queer.

This change has not been accidental. In academic circles in particular, there has evolved a change in direction from the identity arenas in which gay and lesbian studies are based to the postmodern and poststructuralist bases of queer theory, which more often contends that identity is an essentialist category constraining rather than opening up possibilities for the analysis of gender and sexuality. [12] In short–gay and lesbian studies categorize, Queer theory does not.

I have argued (Kirsch, 2000) that this difference between gay and lesbian studies and queer theory is, in part, generational. Gay and lesbian studies developed from the movements for voice and identity that were prominent during the 1960s and 1970s, when many oppressed and de-valued sectors of the population were rising up to claim their place and their validity in society. These assertions corresponded with worldwide movements for independence, where the logic of colonialism was debunked and new regimes demanded that policy and governance be derived from indigenous sources rather than from the dominant powers of colonial mechanisms. Some of these movements, of course, were disappointing. Just as freedom from colonial powers did not automatically dissolve the relationships of power that oppressed groups as well as whole populations, the movements for voice and recognition in the (primarily) Western capitalized countries were not as inclusive as the intentions that drove their growth. It became clear that the dominant social relations of the society-at-large were also in play inside social movements. Women, people of color and those with sexual orientations other than heterosexual ones were often closed out of decision-making processes in organizations that were overwhelmingly dominated by a white and male leadership. Reacting to these differences in recognition, many dissident factions declared these movements invalid. The history of the Students for Democratic Society is but one poignant example of an organization that ultimately dissolved because of struggles over inclusion, voice and direction. Queer theory, while developed by a generation of academics who experienced the tumultuous movements of this period, has primarily been trumpeted by a generation of students that has not witnessed a social movement. Perhaps, too, their attraction is due in part to the queer theory's insistence on the impossibility of identity, and to the reality that our versions of ourselves change regularly and for younger students even more often. The pull of queer theory is often its declaration of independence and of a unique position, what Castells (1997) has referred to as "a resistance identity." These students have not yet formulated a "project identity," where, as Castells notes, "social actors, on the basis of whatever cultural materials are available to them, build a new identity that redefines their position in society, and by doing so, seek the transformation of the social structure" (Castells, 1997, 43; Kirsch, 2000, p. 7). Queer theory, then, is a combination of social influences that have taken shape over time by representatives of the academy and a generation that has not actively engaged in social struggle is central to its development. That it has been presented as a radical alternative to gay and lesbian studies is a paradox that will be further explored here in an attempt to elucidate the challenges we now face in countering the recent depoliticalization of the gay and lesbian rights movement.

THE DEVELOPMENT OF GAY AND LESBIAN STUDIES

The tumultuous relations that characterized the movements of the 1960s and 1970s were reflected in the academic disciplines. As Wolf (1972) so aptly noted, academic disciplines and the theory developed within them reflect wider social relations of society, providing modes of analysis that encompass and mirror the existing contradictions and relationships of power. So it was and continues to be in the halls of colleges and universities. During the 1960s and 1970s, discussions of social issues began to encompass the concerns of constituencies that had been excluded from academic theory building. Feminist writers, in particular, changed the landscape of disciplinary directions, reinterpreting classic texts and documenting observations about women in society that had been previously ignored, and in the process forging new ground. Race, sex and class also became central issues as new paradigms were built that included the many categories omitted or secondary in the standard analyses of social life. Fueled by the sexual revolution of the 1960s, and with the Stonewall uprising as the symbolic designation of the beginning of the gay and lesbian rights movement, the attention paid to differences in sexual desire, gender and the cultural construction of gender and sexuality gained prominence in the public sphere and in the academy.

Gay and lesbian studies grew out of the nexus of these movements. The theory building that highlighted devalued populations in the 1970s and 1980s, provided substance for the institutionalization of programs in American colleges and universities. What fueled gay and lesbian studies, as Annamarie Jagose (1998) suggests, was the constructionist view proffered by Foucault that homosexuality is a social, or constructed phenomenon. Positing through his *History of Sexuality* (1981) that there were homosexual acts before there were homosexual identities, the position of gay and lesbians became an issue of society and the medicalization of behavior rather than a universalist category of being. This concurred, in approach at least, with the many writings of feminists of the 1970s, particularly those anthropologists who were arguing that concepts of the universality of male dominance needed to be challenged and reevaluated, along with the position of women in the workforce and their role in the maintenance of communities (cf. Leacock, 1972, 1981; Etienne and Leacock, 1980; Nash and Safa 1980; Nash, 1978, 1981; Reiter, 1975; Ross and Rapp, 1997, and Safa, 1981, among others).

While the development of gay and lesbian studies provided a framework for the social basis of categories and their uses in dominant power relations, they also provided a space for the development of *identity* for many faculty, students and others who had previously been bereft of a place in academia to voice their interests and concerns. Identity became a topic that united those that had been isolated and enabled individuals to find comfort and strength in both feelings and numbers. No longer were solitary faculty or confused students left to negotiate their place in their own psychological realm; the structural availability of institutionalized forums lessened the isolation that had been felt by many. Importantly, this recognition made available arenas where individuals could discuss and organize around similar needs and demands. Like the consciousness-raising groups of the feminist movement, programs in gay and lesbian studies were more than academic correlates to discipline-based departments. They were safe-spaces for the personal growth of students and faculty. Academic scholarship also flourished. The demand for gay and lesbian studies grew exponentially during the 1980s, evidenced by the sheer volume of writing represented in Abelove, Barale's and Halperin's reader (1993). But with this productivity in scholarship came new questions about inclusiveness and representation, and thus the story continues.

MAKING QUEER THEORY

Like its predecessor, queer theory was born from the idea that more inclusiveness is better than less. But it holds that the categories presented by gay and lesbian studies are too narrow to encompass the range of behavior and sexuality that is presented by a wide range of preferences. It was also, however, a product of a development of theory in the academy that rejected modernist notions of identity and representation. Thus, gay and lesbian studies are an area of inquiry, while queer theory is an approach to that inquiry. Gay and lesbian studies have encompassed a variety of approaches, from Marxist and neo-Marxist to mainstream sociology and political inquiry. Queer theory favors the deconstruction of those approaches and the categories that have been developed within them. It is thus a particular perspective on the place of social construction in gay, lesbian, bisexual, transsexual–in short, those who profess other than heterosexual–norms, and it is this fact of categorical deconstruction that defines its approach.

Queer theory blossomed as a mode of inquiry during the past decade. It is anchored in the post-1960s disengagement with organizational left politics, which arguably did not encompass the concerns of gender and sexuality in their complexities. The failure of the movements of the 1960s and 1970s to significantly include the voices of all of its constituents led to arguments about theory and its representation, and, most significantly, the place of political economy and Marxist theory in the analysis of social conditions. This followed in the footsteps of the European academy, where Marxism lost its prominence in the defeats of 1968. Many of the writers prominent in the postmodernist and post-structuralist movements that are the foundations for queer theory–Foucault, Baudrillard, Derrida, Barthes, Deleuze and Lacan–had been active in the social movements of the 1960s, only to become demoralized by the failure of these attempts to restructure the institutions of social life. The theories of Marx became equated with the reality of the so-called "socialism" of the Soviet bloc and its social oppression. It also became identified with the "meta-narratives"–as Lyotard (1984) called them–of the modernist period as produced by Marx and other writers of the Enlightenment whose theories came to be judged as false, crude and ultimately oppressive. One of the consequences of this perception was the questioning of Marxism as a tool for change that united theory and practice and the social with the individual. Thus, there was a widespread belief that the left had been defeated as a result of the theories that it had engaged.[3] With this contention came the concurrent claim that bounded categories of gender and sexuality could not be inclusive, a position, as we have stated, that was fueled by dynamics within the now-rejected left organizations.[4]

Shadowing this development was the questioning of *labor* as the starting point of analysis for social reproduction. Labor movements had failed to make significant differences in the inclusion of suppressed voices, both in their internal organizations and on a societal level. This failure began to be conceived as a problem not only with labor movements but also with analyses that posited labor as the strategic vehicle for social change. If theory, in the name of the "modern," had failed to provide adequate methodologies for solving the problems of inequality and exploitation, it was reasoned, then the basis of individual experience and social reproduction needed to be reconceptualized.[5]

With the rejection of Marxist renderings of the social, and more generally, political economy, also came the dismissal of all universalist theory as essentializing human interaction. When the collective as political did not suffice, the personal as political took hold. Class, in particular, became a contested category (cf. Laclau and Mouffe. 1985). It was replaced by *discourse,* which was seen to have a more reflective awareness of the nature of human interaction. Thus Foucault, in his *Archeology of Knowledge* (1972), presented the concept of discourse as a way of describing social interaction and regulation, posing *language* rather than labor as the grounds by which processes of thought and knowledge are derived, the way in which *discursive formations* order human experience. The subject, say "tradition" (1972, p. 21), is dismissed as an object of analysis; for the subject, or subjectivity, itself is a result of discursive formation, embodied by individuals but which includes aspects of individual experience as well as excludes them.

Foucault did not create new categories, for discourses themselves are a result of other discourses. In his words:

> . . . these divisions–whether our own, or those contemporary with the discourse under examination–are always themselves reflexive categories, principles of classification, normative rules, institutionalized types: they, in turn, are facts of discourse that deserve to be analyzed beside others; of course, they also have complex relations with each other, but they are not intrinsic, autochthonous, and universally recognizable characteristics. (1972, p. 22)

As further example, Baudrillard discarded the category of labor for the analysis of social reproduction. He referred to a "fetishism of labor" in his *Mirror of Production* (1975), and he dismissed historical materialism and the analyses it creates as both universalist and false. Specifically enjoining the experience of the Soviet Union in the twentieth century, he tells us that "When the structure is reversed and the proletarian class triumphs, as in the East, nothing changes profoundly, as we know, in social relations" (1975, p. 168). Baudrillard instead finds the bases for subversion in the "codes" that are superimposed by the relationships of power onto the individual. Collective action, we then would assume, would come from the mass rejection of these codes, although how this is accomplished is never elaborated.

For those dissatisfied with the categories of gay and lesbian studies, the introduction of postmodernist and poststructuralist writers were a welcome addition to the debate. What demarcates queer theory from its postmodern and poststructuralist foundations is its referral to a range of work "that seeks to place the question of sexuality as the centre of concern, and as the key category through which other social, political, and cultural phenomena are to be understood" (Edgar and Sedgwick, 1999, p. 321). Hogan and Hudson (1998) place the beginnings of a queer theory with Teresa de Laurentis's use of the term for a 1989 conference at the University of California, Santa Cruz, and cite Eve Kosofsky Sedgwick's *Between Men* (1985) and *Epistemology of the Closet* (1990) as the scholarly works most closely associated with its acceptance into academia (1998, p. 491). Certainly the publication of Judith Butler's *Gender Trouble* (1990) signaled the beginnings of an era that questioned many of the analyses provided by gay and lesbian studies, and the magnitude of her following, complete with dedicated web sites, testifies to the power of her philosophical queries into the nature of gender and its role in present day cultural phenomena.

Queer theory has evolved to encompass any analytic strategy that can be used to destabilize and to deconstruct. We know that queer theorists object to statements that would denote boundaries of any kind. All would seem to agree that the traditional heterosexual/homosexual dichotomy should be abandoned, and that a third or more ways of describing and analyzing sex and gender should be proposed. As Annamarie Jagose puts it, "queer is very much in the process of formation . . . it is not simply that queer has yet to solidify and take on a more consistent profile, but rather that its definitional indeterminacy, its elasticity, is one of its constituent characteristics"(1998, pp. 2-3). Other writers have gone further in emphasizing a refusal to take definitional stands. David Halperin suggests that even its designation is suspect, for "Once conjoined with 'theory' . . . 'queer' loses its offensive, vilifying tonality and subsides into a harmless generic qualifier, designating one of the multiple departments of academic theory" (1995, p. 32). There are also some that take the notion of queer outside of the limiting realm of gender and sexuality. Aaron Betsky, for one, explores "queer space" as a "misuse or deformation of a place, an appropriation of the buildings and codes of the city for perverse purposes" (1997, p. 5). The *principle* of queer, then, is the dissembling of common beliefs about categories in general, from the representation of gender and sexuality in film, literature and music to their placement in the social and physical sciences, to the queering of space. The *activity* of queer is the "queering" of culture, ranging from the reinterpretation of characters in novels and cinema to the deconstruction of historical analyses. As activity, we have seen the assertion of "queer" identity, notably held as lesbian, gay, transgender, bisexual, and transsexual, as variants of human behavior that have rights on their own terms. As *theory*, queer's derivation from postmodernism and poststructuralism leads to the rejection of all categorizations as necessarily produced by dominant 'regulatory regimes.' It situates the individual as the unfettered *self*, separate from circumstances that would limit its definition.

If the beginnings of queer theory are to be found in the perceived limitations of institutionalized gay and lesbian studies, its momentum has produced a paradoxical effect. While claiming to be more inclusive than its more general area of analyses, it has narrowed the focus of inquiry to the individual self rather than the social field, thus mirroring the development of late capitalism as it has developed during the last fifty years.

QUEER THEORY AND LATE CAPITALISM

As we have suggested, queer theory stems from movements in academic theory that developed after 1968, specifically, postmodernism and poststructuralism. The "post" of postmodernism presupposes something after, beyond what has already been experienced or accomplished. It is both a theoretical and an historical category.

As Eagleton has so succinctly put it, "postmodernity"

> . . . has real material conditions: it springs from an historical, ephemeral, decentralized world of technology, consumerism and the culture industry, in which the service, finance, and information industries triumph over traditional manufacture, and classical class politics yield ground to a diffuse range of "identity politics." Postmodernism is a style of culture which reflects something of this epochal change, in a depthless, decentered, ungrounded, self-reflexive, playful, derivative, eclectic pluralistic art which blurs the boundaries between "high" and "popular" culture, as well as between art and every-day experience. (Eagleton, 1997, p. vii)

In short, then, "postmodernity" is part of what Mandel (1972) has referred to as "late capitalism," while postmodernism is a reflection of this era. It has destabilized everyday experience and with it the identity politics that characterizes much of gay and lesbian studies. In doing so, it has projected a view of experience and change that is very much in sync with the realities of the dominant ideologies of the present period.

We know that in capitalist societies those in power are in control over the means and rewards of production. They are the same individuals and classes that effect the production of what we call the dominant culture, the nexus of relationships and ideas that condition the way that members of society act in accordance with the rules and structure that govern social functioning. Capitalism has produced the ideal of the individual as separate and self-sustaining, a position that enhances the role of the self in determining consciousness and action.

Mandel (1972) argued that late capitalism is a period where advances in the attempt to increase profit are centered on the use of technology to automate the labor that has historically prevented the unfettered flow of capital accumulation through class struggle. In late capitalist terms, the individual is presented as the basic unit of production, consumption, and indeed, being.

This focus on the individual as labor source and physical unit has produced an ideology in which individuals are viewed, in cultural terms, as successful when they are able to obtain the goods and services that distinguish them from their peers and those with lesser status (Bourdieu, 1982). But ideas do not operate as contained entities any more than individuals do; their genesis is elsewhere, in the social relations of society that provide the foundation for their development. The ideology that rationalizes capital is experienced by the individual as the necessity of furthering personal status. The ability to contribute and to reap the rewards of capitalist relations are dependent on class position and location; the *ideal* that capital presents is the achievement of those marks of status that define the successful individual. Capitalism has focused on the individual as seller of labor power and late capitalism has intensified that focus in both the realms of production and consumption. In turn, sexuality and desire have become massively consumerized. Roland Barthes (1990) showed us that "The Look" is more important than the act itself. But what does this mean on a cultural and on a strictly economic level? The creation of ideal behavior in capitalist societies is basic to social control. Striving to *obtain* commodities fixes energy on the acquisition of things as perceived needs. This of course, does not rule out a rejection of the creation of need; but it does lead to inequalities that are reinforced by that very act of striving.

The integration of advertising and consumerism into the psyche is a multi-layered process, mediated by a dominant "culture-ideology" (Sklair, 1998, p. 297). The seeding of the unconscious by social processes such as advertising acts to mask the etiology of desire, sexual or otherwise, which underpins consumer culture.

Queer theory has not addressed the attempts at the creation of uniformity in needs and desires. What the history of advertising shows is that you can appeal to the queer community without condoning its behavior. While the human need for community enhances the drive for conformity, the realization of the generalized non-acceptance and "otherness" of queerness fuels arguments for difference as an expression of resistance while, at the same time, it extols the desire to "normalize" and consume, evoking courses of action that often result in the buying of uniforms rather than the celebrating of difference.

Communities, both geographic and spatial, have historically acted as agents of resistance to exogenous forces that would transform their role as centers of daily physical and emotional maintenance for individuals, kinship units and groups. The aim of the capitalist engagement of the social realm, then, is the creation of the ego-centered individual and the destruction of communities as places of mutual support and resistance. In more recent times, transnational corporations have responded to the ability of communities to resist outside domination by actively fighting their influence on social life, and indeed, their very existence. In the face of conflict, they have moved their production to other areas where communities and unions are less organized. In the 1970s, the mass movement of factories around the world to areas where communities did not exist forced wage-seekers to travel to the worksite. The movement of corporations offshore serves to provide, at least initially, resistance-free factories. These are calculated strategies to counter incipient organization.

This separation of worker from both product and community affects every aspect of daily living and emotional life. But there *is* resistance to attempts to destroy solidarity on the part of global forces. *Geographic* communities can even act as barricades against the attempt to enforce hegemony. *Emotional* communities, whether they be produced by similarities based on sex, gender, race, or class, serve as centers of identification, spaces where individuals realize that there are others like themselves and which provide a counter to the alienation caused by rejection and discrimination. Communities can thus provide alternatives to the goals of capitalist production.

Jameson has proposed that the concept of alienation in late capitalism has been replaced with fragmentation (1991, p. 14). Fragmentation highlights the increased separation of people from one another and from place that is now occurring. It is located in a generalized and growing lack of cultural affect that distinguishes our present period from our past. Which is not to say, in Jameson's words, that "the cultural products of the postmodern era are utterly devoid of feeling, but rather that such feelings–which it may be better and more accurate, following J.F. Lyotard, to call 'intensities,"–are particularly free flowing and impersonal" (1991, p. 16). Here, many postmodernists and poststructuralists argue, is the disappearance of the individual as subject. Yet what is really completed with this disappearance is the *objectification* of the individual as alone and incomparable. As the *idea* of difference becomes embedded in culture it also becomes more abstract:

> What we must now ask ourselves is whether it is precisely this semi-autonomy of the cultural sphere that has been destroyed by the logic of late capitalism. Yet to argue that culture is today no longer endowed with the relative autonomy is once enjoyed as one level among others in earlier moments of capitalism (let alone in precapitalist societies) is not necessarily to imply its disappearance or extinction. Quite the contrary; we must go on to affirm that the autonomous sphere of culture throughout the social realm, to the point at which everything in our social life–from economic value and state power to practices and to the very structure of the psyche itself–can be said to have become 'cultural' in some original and yet untheorized sense. This proposition is, however, substantially quite consistent with the previous diagnosis of a society of the image or simulacrum and a transformation of the "real" into so many pseudoevents. (Jameson, 1991, p. 48)

The fragmentation of social life repeats itself in the proposal that sexuality and gender are separate and autonomous from bureaucratic state organization. If, as in Jameson's terms, differences can be *equated*, then this should not pose a problem for the mobilization of resistance to inequality. However, as postmodernist and poststructuralist writers assume a position that this equation is impossible and undesirable, then the dominant modes of power will prevail without analysis or opposition. The danger, of course, is that while we concentrate on decentering identity, we succeed in promoting the very goals of global capitalism that work against the formation of communities or provide the means to destroy those that already exist, and with them, any hope for political action.

For those who are not included in traditional sources of community building–in particular, kinship based groupings–the building of an "affectional community . . . must be as much a part of our political movement as are campaigns for civil rights" (Weeks, 1985, p. 176). This building of communities requires identification. If we cannot recognize traits that form the bases of our relationships with others, how then can communities be built? The preoccupation of Lyotard and Foucault, as examples, with the overwhelming power of "master narratives," posits a conclusion that emphasizes individual resistance and that ironically, ends up reinforcing the "narrative" itself.

As Ellen Wood (1986) asserts, the production of postmodernist and poststructuralist theory is based on unacknowledged but specific class interests. A class analysis means "a comprehensive analysis of social relations and power . . . based on a historical/materialist principle which places the relations of production at the center of social life and regards their exploitative character as the root of social and political oppression" (Wood, 1986, p. 14). Such an analysis does not mean overlooking "the differences which express the social formation" as Marx put it, nor a mechanistic materialism, but it maintains that oppression finds its most extreme and violent expression through economic exploitation and alienation (Marx, 1978, p. 247; Stabile, 1994, p. 48). Stabile further critiques postmodernist theory as

> . . . those forms of critical theory that rely upon an uncritical and idealist focus on the discursive constitution of "the real," a positivistic approach to the notion of "difference," and a marked lack of critical attention to the context of capitalism and their own locations within processes of production and reproduction. (1994, p. 52)

> She continues, "against the Marxist centrality of class struggle, and in an ironic if unintentional mirroring of the mercurial nature of capitalism, Michel Foucault argues: 'But if it is against *power* that one struggles, then all those who acknowledge it as intolerable can begin the struggle wherever they find themselves and in terms of their own activity (or passivity).'" (1994, p. 49)

Resistance to capitalism, then, involves practical struggle on issues that affect all of us on an everyday basis. We cannot pretend to disengage from the reality of discrimination or oppression and claim that we are fulfilling a task of resistance by refusing to engage the domination that exists.[6]

The Consequences of Queer Theory

If the tenets of queer theory reject strategies of mobilization for fear of essentializing identity, what then, are its politics? The historical and ethnographic fallacies in defense of postmodernist and poststructuralist critique aside, it is doubtful that queer theory would exist at all without new political juncture that Rorty (1991) and Jameson (1991) both note is being produced in late capitalism, and which Haraway (1985), Eagleton (1986) point to as having led to a new stage of politics.

Be that as it may, "queer" as put forward by queer theorists, has no inherent historical or social context. We continually return to the following question: to whom does it belong and what does it represent? These advocates of "queer" do not acknowledge that *queer* is produced by social relations, and therefore contains the attributes of existing relationships of power.

Legitimization in queer theory means the right to be as one is, a kind of free activity that incorporates gender, sexuality, and individual variants in thought and speech. The problem, of course, lies in the fact that this process of legitimization does not create equality: dominance still exists; ideals still rule the day.

The problem we thus encounter is that the collective level is deemed impossible: the legitimating function is purely personal, the ultimate statement of "the personal as political." Indeed, when Judith Butler was asked for suggestions on how to proceed in the political arena, she answered:

> I actually believe that politics has a character of contingency and context to it that cannot be predicted at the level of theory. And that when theory starts being programmatic, such as "here are my five prescriptions." And I set up my typology, and my final chapter is called "What is to be Done?", it pre-empts the whole problem of context and contingency, and I do think that political decisions are made in that lived moment and that they can't be predicted from the level of theory–they can be prepared for but I suppose I'm with

Foucault on this . . . It seems like a noble tradition." (Bell, 1999, p. 167)

But context and contingency, and the "lived moment," are aspects of personal recognition, and a failure to specify leads nowhere. Simply reflection on the success of *movements* around the world and throughout modern history tells us otherwise.

I have argued here that this turn towards the individual, acknowledged or disputed, has led to a disengagement of coalition building and social movements, and the mirroring of the current social conditions of late capitalism, including the renouncing of identity. Indeed, As Butler (1993) has stated, "the prospect of *being* anything, even for pay, has always produced in me a certain anxiety, for 'to be' gay, 'to be' lesbian seems to be more than a simple injunction to become who or what I already am." She is therefore

> . . . not at ease with lesbian theories, gay theories, for as I've argued elsewhere, identity categories tend to be instruments of regulatory regimes, whether as normalizing categories or oppressive structures or as the rallying points for a liberatory contestation of that very oppression. (1993, pp. 307-308)

In contrast to the currents in the development of gay and lesbian studies, the anxiety with categorical identification has been a main current in queer theory, from its beginnings in sex and gender studies to its expansion into the wider cultural realm. The concern is not unfounded. Labeling can become a constricting structure that limits the possibilities of being or becoming, as many queer writers have shown. But one has to wonder, if we do not have rallying points, from where do we fight prejudice and exploitation? Foucault has argued that participating in a homosexual perspective admits a homophobic discourse; yet how do we deny homophobia? Social movements and politics are necessary to counter dominant ideologies and power structures. A perception that we can reject static systems of identity without rejecting all bases for identity, however temporary they may be, is necessary for true resistance and social change. Thus, we can identify *with* social movements rather than simply identifying *as* a particular category.

The recognition of common goals can give rise to an identification based on common purpose. One need not have the same sexual orientation or the same taste in fashion to understand that discrimination exists and therefore to embark on a fight against it together. In a culture where variants on the norms of gender and sexuality are not fully accepted, those identities constitute a precondition for political action. As Weeks notes,

> To argue that 'anything goes' is to fall back on an easy libertarianism which ignores questions of power and the quality of relationships. . . . There exists a plurality of sexual desires, or potential ways of life, and of relationships. A radical sexual politics affirms a freedom to be able to choose between them . . . . Identity, may, in the end, be no more than a game, a ploy to enjoy particular types of relationships and pleasures. But without it, it seems, the possibilities of political choice are not increased but diminished. The recognition of "sexual identities," in all their ambivalence, seems to be the precondition for the realization of sexual diversity. (1985, p. 210)

Contrary to the fear that identity limits choice, then, *it is* a choice.

If our goal is to produce a society that accepts difference, welcomes diversity, and champions human rights, how do we get there? Working towards structural change requires strategies for social change, which is what answering the question "what is to be done" entails. We can learn from past successes and analytical mistakes. Just as Oscar Lewis's (1963) belief that the "culture of poverty" could only be broken through intensive psychotherapy ignored the structures that created it, so we too must recognize that the conditions of oppression are not self-generated. Anything else is blaming the victim.

Politics, Theory and Internalized Homophobia

The politics and focus on the self and individual status that queer theory creates has consequences for those who are not in a privileged position and who are able to weather or ignore the acts of physical and emotional abuse that many in de-valued positions experience. Symbolic violence–the sideward glance, the judged interaction–as Patricia Williams (1991) has called it, affects us all. It is mediated by the social position in which one finds oneself (1991, p. 134), and thus to the degree to which it effects the maintenance and experience of every-day life.

If we accept the presumption that alienation and fragmentation are parts of the individual's structural experience in capitalist relations, then the human essence is an abstraction in any individual. In reality, the individual is made up of the ensemble of human relations in which he or she is a part. If, as Judith Butler contends, "Gender is a norm that can never be fully internalized; 'the 'internal' is a surface signification, and gender norms are finally phantasmatic, impossible to embody" (1991, p. 141), then the reality of alienated gender is impossible to ignore. Gender becomes an unconnected aspect of existence within present-day society, a place that can be designated, but which cannot be fully experienced. We are all then, by definition, marginalized. This marginalization is presented in many ways–but more importantly, it is experienced differentially by class position, race, *and* gender. It is also reinforced by prejudice, stigmatization, and violence. The enormous burden of this position is enacted by the dis-eases of society: economic instability, psychological trauma, and "cures" that blame the victim. In this reality, gender is not performed but real, and, certainly, a queer reality is different from a heterosexual one.

The dominant culture is more than an abstract idea that posits the forces of oppression. It also causes pain. Hate crimes, the high rate of teenage suicide among queers, and job and economic discrimination all lead to psychological states that overshadow any discussion of differences, exclusion, parody and imitation. Further, the exclusion of this reality posits an uncomfortable question about queer theory, and in particular, performativity theory.[7] If resistance is located in the self, if parody and imitation are deemed subversive, and if this is viewed as more pre-emptive than active community-based resistance, what are the consequences? Consider Butler's remarks about "coming out":

> The discourse of "coming out" has clearly served its purposes, but what are its risks? And here I am not speaking of unemployment or public attack or violence, which are quite clearly and widely on the increase against those who are perceived as "out" whether or not by their own design. Is the "subject" who is "out" free of its subjection and finally in the clear? Or could it be that the subjection that subjectivates the gay or lesbian subject in some ways continues to oppress, or oppresses most insidiously, once, "outness" is claimed? What or who is it that is "out," made manifest and fully disclosed, when and if I reveal myself as a lesbian? What is it that is now known, anything? What remains permanently concealed by the very linguistic act that offers of the promise of a transparent revelation of sexuality? Can sexuality even remain sexuality once it submits to a criterion of transparency and disclosure, or does it perhaps cease to be sexuality precisely when the semblance of full explicitness is achieved? Is sexuality of any kind even possible

without the opacity designed by the unconsciousness, which means simply that the conscious "I" who would reveal its sexuality is perhaps the last to know the meaning of what it says? (1993, p. 309)

This statement by Butler, centrally representative of queer theory, begs the question of coming out, while arguing against identity. It also, oddly, makes a case for sexuality as a private affair, fully known only to the self. But what do we know about coming out? Does coming out in New York City or San Francisco have the same consequences as coming out in Kansas City or Paris, Tennessee? Does the coming out process differ by class, race, gender, and status? Does Butler's contention that coming out continues conceptual problems for the designation of linguistic, unconscious acts have any possible reality for the high school student who is accused of being a fairy and beat up in Nebraska (or anywhere else)? Can queer theory, in this form, be taken seriously anywhere except the most elitist of academic institutions, which by their very existence and nature, represent the arenas of power in American society? Certainly there has been a wide range of popular and scientific writing about coming out that supports the necessity of identity formation for emotional well being. As recent examples of a much larger literature, Rowen and Malcolm (2002) tell us "Typically, the earlier stages of gay/lesbian identity formation (HIF) are fraught with confusion and despair, marked by low self-acceptance and low self-esteem" (Ross and Rosser, 1996). Citing Cass's (1983) work on identity formation, they make the important point that children in industrialized societies are socialized through the "promotion of an ideal heterosexual image" (Cass, 1983, p. 145), and that therefore, "the process of HIF (homosexual identity formation) is one of change" (2002, p. 79). Importantly, they note that feelings and thoughts of homosexuality occur inwardly, and therefore are significantly prone to the harmful effects of social stigma and prejudice. Likewise, Huebner, Davis, Nemeroff and Aiken (2002) point out that "homosexual identities are formed in the context of extreme cultural stigma towards homosexual behavior" (Troiden, 1989), thus working against standard HIV prevention strategies. It is even possible that unsafe sexual practices are the result of resistance strategies to the normative practices of sexual acts (Kirsch, n.d.). The process of coming out is one of unlearning negative attitudes towards homosexuality. Frable, Wortman and Joseph (1997), show the importance of cultural stigma, personal visibility and community networks on predicting self-esteem and distress in gay men, and Williamson (2000), McGregor, Carver et al. (2001), and Boatwright, Gilbert, Forrest, and Ketzenberger (1996) review the effects of internalized homophobia on health issues and career trajectories for lesbians and gay men.

Queerness as a deviant form of heterosexuality results in oppression. When this fact is not confronted, it can lead to maladaptive responses that include the markings of internalized homophobia: depression, psychosis, resignation, and apathy. These are very much reactions to the ways in which we view ourselves, which in turn are, at least in part, due to the ways in which we are constantly told to view ourselves. Here, the production of consciousness takes a very concrete form. Those enduring this form of structural violence cannot, even in the academy, simply decide to disengage. We cannot simply refuse to acknowledge these facts of social life in our present society, and hope that our circumstances will change. Although the lack of definition is what has inspired the use of "queer," it cannot, as Butler herself asserts, "overcome its constituent history of injury" (1993, p. 223).

Butler's claim attempts to dissolve sexuality and annuls the basis for sexual identity, precluding a confrontation with a cultural morality that dictates sexual correctness, affirming some practices while stigmatizing others. What is forgotten is that "coming out" identifies our sexuality and gender in the sense of knowing who we are, and to whom we can relate in the larger society. This knowing is impossible without identifying with others engaged in a similar struggle. Since it is, in fact, impossible to constitute a movement for social change without this recognition, we must ask whom this aspect of queer theory benefits. To see one's gender identity as imitation or parody, as, following Butler, queer theory often does, is to view the self as unreal. It distances the actor from a confrontation with the objects of oppression and thwarts any resistance that matters. Individual difference is reified to the exclusion of community. Certainly denying a label or an identity is far easier than a fight for equity that might fail, thus rendering the individual even more isolated. To have a label that is not accepted as equal to others is to be "less-than," producing marginalization and *shame* for those desiring equal status. By denying the identification and the material fact of labeling, it is assumed that shame is avoided and no real resistance is needed. But in fact the individual becomes even more alone. The result is a fear of engagement, a true manifestation of an internalized homophobia that is masked by the individual's refusal to identify and to engage social constructions of power.

Huebner, Davis, Nemeroff, and Ailen (2002) remind us that given the powerful forces of the dominant culture that see homosexuality as deviant, "internalized homophobia may continue to affect individuals in varying degrees throughout their lives" (2002. p. 330). Given late capitalism's drive towards individuation and the creation of ideals for consumption, including desire, it becomes even more important that identity, however fluid, act to break the isolation of the individual that the "right to be oneself" engenders.

Community, identity and self-actualization are indeed complementary. Social and emotional health is promoted by active participation with others. Power in numbers has been the call of resistance movements world wide, from anti-colonial movements to calls for better working conditions. Such struggles have larger outcomes. The community is a forum for debate for the construction of strategy. Separatist movements have proven unproductive as the group becomes isolated and involutes with disagreement. Assimilationist movements cannot work towards sustained social change because there is no confrontation with the basis of oppression. The call for individuality, for "self," is the most harmful strategy of all, for it separates every person from any concrete sense of identity and collective opposition.

CONCLUSION:
IDENTIFYING WITH/IDENTIFYING AS

The sense of our own identity is fluid and tolerant, whereas our sense of the identity of others is always more fixed and often edges towards caricature. We know within ourselves that we can be twenty different persons in a single day and that the attempt to explain our personality is doomed to become a falsehood after only a few words. To every remark made about our own personal characteristics, we would want, in the interest of truth, quite disregarding vanity, to say, "yes, but . . .", or "that may have been true once but it is true no longer" . . . (Wilson, 1990)

The promise of queer theory–and its imagined advance over previous approaches in gay and lesbian studies–is inclusiveness. The paradox of queer theory is that while it strives for this inclusiveness in a manner that identity politics cannot–a laudable goal–the reliance by its practioners on postmodern and poststructuralist theory, the epistemology of which is the negation of political action and the reification of the individual 'self,' has made this strategy untenable.

Identifying with social movements in an era of global capitalist accumulation presupposes a recognition that exploitation, prejudice, and violence are facts of everyday life that many experience. It is not necessary to agree with all of the beliefs of your neighbor to establish a mutually supportive alliance. Nor it is necessary to *experience* the reality of your cohorts to identify with common causes. In other words, it is necessary to refocus on practice–unifying and practice–generating principles (Bourdieu, 1977, p. 101). The ability to create a true political movement assumes identification with the struggles and projected outcomes of that movement while recognizing the differences between members that need to be accommodated. The process is liberatory. The characters that Duberman documents in this exposition of Stonewall (1993) all differ in their backgrounds and in their understanding of the world at large. The movement generated by Stonewall cut across class and status, but its general demands were the same for all: an end to discrimination and persecution.

Castells' (1997) notion of project identity is again helpful here in defining the parameters of social movements. The struggles for colonial independence were specifically geared towards the rights of indigenous peoples and gaining freedom from exploitation. The anti-war movement, however much divisiveness it generated, was still focused on the right to self-determination. Past feminist struggles, despite incidents that threatened to destroy basic alliances, pulled together women of differing class, status, race, and sexual orientation. While it has not always been possible for these segments to productively work with each together, there has at least been a common understanding of the goals of liberation.

Hennessy (1994) reasons that true incorporation entails more than the granting of civil rights: "It also requires eliminating the inequities between the haves and the have-nots that allows the tolerance of 'minorities' necessary" (1994, p. 89). The focus on individual and local realities supports a negation of the discussion of larger systemic issues, the "grand narratives" that the postmodernists and poststructuralists would have us dismiss. But as O'Laughlin reminds, a "vulgar materialism" is not the same as a general theory through which to interpret social representations and organization (O'Laughlin, 1975, p. 348). The fact, as Hennessy notices, that any analysis of capitalism is notoriously absent from new social criticism in the postmodernist mode is reason enough to view it with a critical eye. Reflecting on his own participation in gay and lesbian politics, Duberman reflects

> It is true that political involvement requires some detachment from self-obsession. But . . . [p]articipation in common struggle with other opens up opportunities that feed the self in unexpected ways. Though political work does demand that we concentrate on the public purpose at hand, it simultaneously provides the individual with the comfort of community and newfound security and confidence. (1996, p. 89)

It is in communities that we *identify with*, support, and build connections, geographic and emotional, with each other. Communities act to connect individuals with the social. They provide the avenues for human social reproduction and serve as the basis for mutual support. Moreover, communities can be sanctuaries for people needing to recover from oppression, and they can provide for collective strategies against those who attempt to destroy and to subjugate their members. Weeks notes that the causes of class struggle, feminism, socialism, and gay and lesbian rights all have their own rhythms that make agreement difficult. Engels' assertion that "in all times of great agitation, the traditional bonds of sexual relations, like all other fetters, are shaken off" (in Weeks, 1985, p. 252) is scarcely borne out in a period in which that agitation is more *between* groups than *against* objects of oppression. This agitation is a choice too. And again, it follows a logic that divides and conquers rather than includes.

The tension between gay and lesbian studies and queer theory represents wider differences in the approach to the analysis of the social, and the individual's relationship to society, including the strategies that derive from those differences. But it should be clear that we cannot struggle alone against a global system of military power and the ever-present threat of economic and physical destruction. If "all things queer," then, is to become anything more than a novel digestion of difference, it must include the individual as more than the self as text. It must accommodate the individual in society. *Identifying with* social movements on the basis of the recognition of exploitation and devaluation, rather than mechanistically deconstructing the identities that comprise subjugated positions, can begin to resolve the stagnation that has dominated attempts to develop coalitions around issues that matter.

NOTES

1. Parts of the present paper were presented in *Queer Theory and Social Change* (Routledge, 2000). While I have sometimes borrowed from my previous introduction of these issues, the debate, of course, is ongoing.

2. Although the use of the terms postmodern and poststructuralism are sometimes differentiated by time, in this paper I combine the use of these descriptors, as is common in much of the writing in queer theory. The differences between postmodern and poststructuralist theories are more methodological than interpretive, Rosenau notes, writing that they are "not identical, they overlap considerably and are sometimes considered synonymous. Few efforts have been made to distinguish between the two, probably because the differences appear to be of little consequence . . . the major difference is one of emphasis more than substance. Postmodernists are more oriented towards cultural critique while the poststructuralists emphasize method and epistemological matters" (Rosenau, 1992, p. 13).

3. Terry Eagleton has made an interesting observation on the conclusions of many European academics during this period. In his words, " . . . *what if this defeat never really happened in the first place?* What if it were less a matter of the left rising up and being forced back, then of a steady disintegration, a gradual failure of nerve, a creeping paralysis? What if the confrontation never quite took place, but people *behaved* as if it did?" (1997, p. 19).

4. Lancaster and Di Leonardo (1997), in their excellent *Gender and Sexuality Reader* (Routledge, 1997), note, "In the course of the 1980s, a substantial current of gender and sexuality studies withdrew to a narrow, disengaged, and frequently idealistic conception of social constructionism. Postmodernism habitually and synecdochically misidentified Marxism and political economy with older, reductionist, mechanistic schools of thought . . . and thus often simply ignored political-economic contexts in their writing. Ironically, it was in the same decade that work in political economy became increasingly historically sophisticated . . . and took on culture, language, race and gender as key analytic categories" (1997, p. 4).

5. Interestingly, Mark Lilla has argued that the beleaguering fact of the holocaust, the failure of post-colonial experiments in Africa and Asia, the collapse of the Soviet bloc, and the aftermath of the struggles of 1968 left French radicals seriously doubting their premises. On the other hand, "These same events have had no appreciable effect on American intellectual life, for the simple reason that they pose no challenge to our own self-understanding. . . . That the anti-humanism and politics of pure will latent in structuralism and deconstruction . . . are philosophically and practically incompatible with liberal principles sounds like an annoying prejudice" (Lilla, 1998, p. 41).

6. See my Chapter Five of *Queer Theory and Social Change*. The preoccupation of poststructuralists with disengagement as an act of resistance, of parody as re-description (cf. Butler, 1993), works against the formation of community just as it (falsely) presents to world *towards* self-actualization. That we are members of a society *should* be self-evident. How power and domination are actualized and maintained through capitalist control is both an empirical and a political question.

7. For a full discussion of performativity, imitation and gender theory, see Butler, 1993, Kirsch, 2000.

REFERENCES

Abelove, H., Barale, M.A., & Halperin, D.M. (Eds). (1993). *The lesbian and gay studies reader.* New York: Routledge.

Barthes, R. (1990). *The fashion system.* Berkeley: University of California Press

Baudrillard, J. (1975). *The mirror of production.* St. Louis: Telos Press.

Bell, I. On speech, race, and melancholia: An interview with Judith Butler. *Theory, Culture, Society, 16*(2), 163-174.

Betsky, A. (1997). *Queer space: Architecture and same-sex desire.* New York: William Morrow.

Boatwright, K.J., Gilbert, M.S., Forrest, L., & Ketzenberger, K. (1996). Impact of identity development upon career trajectory: Listening to the voices of lesbian women. *Journal of Vocational Behavior, 48,* 210-228.

Bourdeiu, P. (1977). *Outline of a theory of practice.* Cambridge: Cambridge University Press.

Bourdieu, P. (1982). *Distinction.* Cambridge, MA: Harvard University Press.

Butler, J. (1990). *Gender trouble.* New York: Routledge.

Butler, J. (1993). Imitation and gender insubordination. In H. Abelove, M.A. Barale, & D. Halperin (Eds.), *The lesbian and gay studies reader* (pp. 3-21). New York: Routledge.

Castells, M. (1997). *The power of identity.* Malden, MA: Blackwell.

Duberman, M. (1993). *Stonewall.* New York: Dutton.

Duberman, M. (1996). *Midlife queer: Autobiography of a decade, 1971-1981.* Madison: University of Wisconsin Press.

Eagleton, T. (1986). *Against the grain: Essays 1975-1985.* London: Verso.

Eagleton, T. (1997). *The illusions of postmodernism.* Oxford: Blackwell.

Edgar, A., & Sedgwick, P. (Eds.). (1999). *Key concepts in cultural theory.* New York: Routledge.

Etienne, M., & Leacock, E. (1980). *Women and colonialization: Anthropological perspectives.* New York: Praeger.

Foucault, M. (1972). *The archaeology of knowledge and the discourse on language.* New York: Pantheon Books.

Foucault, M. (1990). *The history of sexuality, 3 vols.* New York: Vintage.

Frable, D.E.S., Wortman, C., & Joseph, J. (1997). Predicting self-esteem, well-being, and distress in a cohort of gay men: The importance of cultural stigma, personal visibility, community networks and positive identity. *Journal of Personality, 65*(3), 601-624.

Halperin, D. (1995). *Saint Foucault: Toward a gay hagiography.* New York: Oxford University Press.

Haraway, D. (1985). Situated knowledge. *Feminist Studies, 14*(3), 575-599.

Hennessy R. (1994). Queer theory, left politics. *Rethinking Marxism, 7*(3), 85-111.

Huebner, D.M., Davis, M.C., Nemeroff, C.J., & Aiken, L.S. (2002). The impact of internalized homophobia on HIV prevention interventions. *American Journal of Community Psychology, 30 (3)*, 327-348.

Jagose, A. (1998). *Queer theory: An introduction.* New York: New York University Press.

Jameson, F. (1991). *Postmodernism or the cultural logic of late capitalism.* London: Verso.

Kirsch, M. (2000). *Queer theory and social change.* London: Routledge.

Kirsch, M. (n.d.) (manuscript). "AIDS, structural violence and verticality in the Florida Everglades" *Manuscript.*

Laclau, E., & Mouffe, C. (1985). *Hegemony and socialist strategy: Towards a radical democratic politics.* London: Verso.

Lancaster, R.N., & di Leonardo, M. (Eds.). (1997). *The gender/sexuality reader: Culture, history, political economy.* New York: Routledge.

Leacock, E. (1972). Introduction and ed., Engels, Fredrich, *Origin of the family, private property and the state.* New York: International.

Leacock. E. (1981). *Myths of male dominance.* New York: Monthly Review.

Lewis, Oscar (1963). *The children of Sanchez.* New York: Vintage.

Lilla, M. (1998). The politics of Jacques Derrida. *New York Review of Books, 45*(11), June 25.

Lyotard, J-F. (1984). *The postmodern condition: A report on knowledge.* Minneapolis: University of Minnesota Press.

Mandel, E. (1972). *Late capitalism.* London: Verso

Marx, K. (1978). *Grundrisse,* in *The Marx-Engels reader,* ed. R.C. Tucker, New York: W.W. Norton.

McGregor, B.A., Carver, C.S., Antoni, M.H., Weiss, S., Yount, S.E., & Ironson, G. (2001). Distress and internalized homophobia among lesbian women treated for early stage breast cancer. *Psychology of Women Quarterly, 25*, 1-9.

Nash, J. (1978). The Aztecs and the ideology of male dominance. *Signs, 4*(2), 349-362.

Nash, J. (1981). Ethnographic aspects of the world capitalist system. *Annual Reviews in Anthropology, 10*, 393-423.

Nash, J., & Safa, H. (Eds.). (1980). *Sex and class in Latin America.* South Hadley, MA: Bergin and Garvey.

O'Laughlin, B. (1975). Marxist approaches to anthropology. *Annual Reviews in Anthropology, 4*, 341-370.

Reiter, R. (Ed.). (1975). *Toward an anthropology of women.* New York: Monthly Review Press.

Rorty, R. (1991). *Objectivity, relativism and trust.* Cambridge: Cambridge University Press.

Rosenau, P.M. (1992). *Postmodernism and the social sciences.* Princeton, N.J.: Princeton University Press.

Ross, M.W., & Rosser, B.R.S. (1996). Measurements and correlated of internalized homophobia: A factor analytic study. *Journal of Clinical Psychology, 52*, 15-21.

Ross, E., & Rapp, R. (1997). Sex and society: A research note from social history and anthropology. In R.N. Lancaster & M. di Leonardo (Eds.), *The gender/sexuality reader* (pp. 153-168). New York: Routledge.

Rowen, C.J., & J.P. Malcolm (2002). Correlates of internalized homophobia and homosexual identity formation in sample of gay men. *Journal of Homosexuality*, *43*(2), 77-92.

Safa, H. (1981). Runaway shops and female employment: The search for cheap labor. *Signs*, *7*(2), 418-433.

Sedgwick, E.K. (1985). *Between men: English literature and male homosexual desire.* New York: Columbia University Press.

Sedgwick, E. K. (1990). *Epistemology of the closet.* Berkeley: University of California Press.

Sklair, L. (1998). Social movements and global capitalism. In F. Jameson and M. Miyoshi (Eds.), *The cultures of globalization* (pp. 291-311). Durham: Duke University Press.

Stabile, C.A. (1994). Feminism without guarantees: The misalliances and missed alliances of postmodern social theory. *Rethinking Marxism*, *7*(1), 48-61.

Troiden, R.R. (1989). The formation of homosexual identities. *Journal of Homosexuality*, *17*, 43-73.

Weeks, J. (1985). *Sexuality and its discontents.* London: Routledge and Kegan Paul.

Williams, P. (1991). *The alchemy of race and rights.* Cambridge: Harvard University Press.

Williamson, I.R. (2000). Internalized homophobia and health issues affecting lesbians and gay men. *Health Education Research*, *15*(1), 97-107.

Wilson, A.N. (1990). *Incline our hearts.* London: Penguin.

Wolf, E. (1972). *Anthropology.* Englewood Cliffs, N.J.: Prentice Hall.

Wood, E. (1986). *The retreat from class: A new "true" socialism.* London: Verso.

doi:10.1300/J082v52n01_02

Anti-Homosexual Prejudice . . .
as Opposed to What?
Queer Theory and the Social Psychology
of Anti-Homosexual Attitudes

Peter Hegarty, PhD

University of Surrey

Sean Massey, PhD

Binghamton University

SUMMARY. This article uses Sedgwick's distinction between *minoritizing* and *universalizing* theories of sexuality to analyze variability in social psychologists' studies of anti-homosexual prejudice, focusing on studies of attitudes. Anti-homosexual prejudice was initially defined in conversation with gay liberationists and presumed, among other things, that fear of homoerotic potential was present in all persons. Later social psychologists theorized anti-homosexual prejudice in strict minoritizing

Correspondence may be addressed: Peter Hegarty, Department of Psychology, University of Surrey, Guildford, Surrey, GU2 7 XH, United Kingdom, or Sean Massey, Department of Human Development, College of Community and Public Affairs, Binghamton University, P.O. Box 6000, Binghamton, NY 13902-6000 (E-mail: smassey@binghamton.edu).

[Haworth co-indexing entry note]: "Anti-Homosexual Prejudice . . . as Opposed to What? Queer Theory and the Social Psychology of Anti-Homosexual Attitudes." Hegarty, Peter, and Sean Massey. Co-published simultaneously in *Journal of Homosexuality* (Harrington Park Press, an imprint of The Haworth Press, Inc.) Vol. 52, No. 1/2, 2006, pp. 47-71; and: *LGBT Studies and Queer Theory: New Conflicts, Collaborations, and Contested Terrain* (ed: Karen E. Lovaas, John P. Elia, and Gust A. Yep) Harrington Park Press, an imprint of The Haworth Press, Inc., 2006, pp. 47-71. Single or multiple copies of this article are available for a fee from The Haworth Document Delivery Service [1-800-HAWORTH, 9:00 a.m. - 5:00 p.m. (EST). E-mail address: docdelivery@haworthpress.com].

terms: as prejudice towards a distinct out-group. In the first section of this paper we discuss corresponding shifts in the conceptualization of anti-homosexual attitudes. Next, using a universalizing framework, we re-interpret experiments on behavioral aspects of anti-homosexual attitudes which were originally conceptualized using a minoritizing framework, and suggest avenues for future research. Finally, we examine how queer theory might enrich this area of social psychological inquiry by challenging assumptions about the politics of doing scientific work and the utility of identity-based sexual politics. doi:10.1300/J082v52n01_03 *[Article copies available for a fee from The Haworth Document Delivery Service: 1-800-HAWORTH. E-mail address: <docdelivery@haworthpress.com> Website: <http://www.HaworthPress. com> © 2006 by The Haworth Press, Inc. All rights reserved.]*

KEYWORDS. Attitudes, homophobia, LGBT studies, queer theory, sexual prejudice, social construction, social psychology

This volume concerns tensions between queer theory and lesbian, gay, bisexual, and transgender studies, and the present article explores this tension with regard to social psychological studies of anti-homosexual prejudice.[1] The early 1970s paradigm-shift away from disease models towards stigmatization models of homosexuality in psychology produced many attempts to measure individual differences in anti-homosexual prejudice among heterosexual-identified people (many of which were published in *Journal of Homosexuality*). This research drew conceptually on lesbian and gay liberationist thought and methodologically on the positivist tradition of attitude measurement in psychology. Since the 1970s, the study of anti-homosexual attitudes has become one of the most prolific areas of lesbian and gay research within psychology. However, studies of anti-bisexual and anti-transgender prejudice remain far rarer (although, see Spalding & Peplau, 1997; Tee, 2003). Both of us research anti-homosexual attitudes (see Hegarty, 2002; Hegarty & Pratto, 2001; Massey, 2004) and this paper aims to open the question of how the writings that have become known as *queer theory* lead to a reinterpretation of this area of social psychological research.

ANTI-HOMOSEXUAL ATTITUDES
AND SOCIAL CONSTRUCTIONISM

Although attitudes have long been dignified as a central concern of social psychology (Allport, 1935), interest in attitudes has waxed and waned over the decades (Eagly, 1992). An attitude is typically defined as an internally located value judgment; as "a tendency or state that is internal to the person" (Eagly, 1992, p. 694) that "is expressed by evaluating a particular entity with some degree of favor or disfavor" (Eagly & Chaiken, 1993, p. 1). Psychologists commonly measure individuals' attitudes by eliciting their level of agreement or disagreement with various opinion statements, and psychologists increasingly measure *implicit* attitudes via participants' speed of reaction to attitude relevant stimuli (Greenwald et al., 2002).

Social constructionist scholars have repeatedly critiqued the essentialist assumption that internal psychological constructs such as "attitudes" can be known by available scientific methods (see Potter and Wetherell, 1987 on explicit attitudes and Steele and Morawski, 2002 on implicit attitudes). Within social constructionism, Kitzinger's (1987, 1989) radical feminist social constructionist analysis of measures of anti-homosexual prejudice is most germane to the current discussion. By attending to the content of the questionnaire items selected to measure anti-homosexual prejudice, Kitzinger showed how psychologists had conflated pro-lesbian/gay attitudes with liberal humanist ideologies. For example, opinions that minimized differences between lesbians and straight women were defined as pro-lesbian attitudes. Kitzinger noted that this framework neglected political differences among lesbians and might even paradoxically cast radical lesbians as homophobic by virtue of their disagreement with liberal humanist assumptions.

Like Kitzinger's analyses, this paper unpacks the implicit sexual politics of anti-homosexual attitudes research. However, unlike Kitzinger (1987) we do not consider this research to be a misplaced rhetorical exercise devoid of epistemic value. Moreover, while Kitzinger forwarded a radical feminist alternative to liberal humanism, our suggestions are developed from the problems raised by queer theory. For Kitzinger, sexual politics remains a question of inter-group conflict between differentially powerful, clearly defined groups. For example, she writes:

> Central to radical feminism is the belief that the patriarchy (not capitalism or sex roles or socialization or individual sexist men) is the root of all forms of oppression; that all men benefit from and maintain it and are, therefore, our political enemies. (Kitzinger, 1987, p. 64)

In contrast, we seek to trouble the assumption that sexual politics operates exclusively, or even predominantly, through intergroup power contests. Rather we start with the observation that social psychologists have studied attitudes on just about everything: individuals, social groups, the self, objects, activities, policies, and ideologies. To what, then, are the anti-homosexual attitudes which social psychologists have measured opposed? Is the homosexuality in question a minority group, a form of sexual practice, an identity performance, or a political movement? One of the central points of this paper is that in spite of over thirty years of published research on this topic, we do not yet have the data to answer this seemingly basic question.

Our analysis is framed by Sedgwick's (1990) claim that modern epistemologies are founded on problematic definitions of the homo/heterosexual binary. Specifically Sedgwick (1990, p. 1) juxtaposed the assumptions that sexual definition is either "an issue of active importance primarily for a small, distinct, relatively fixed homosexual minority" (the minoritizing view) or "an issue of continuing, determinative importance in the lives of people across the spectrum of sexualities" (the universalizing view). Sedgwick proposed this binary to render essentialist/constructivist debates about sexuality redundant, privileged neither assumption over the other, and called for their use to further anti-homophobic inquiry rather than to resolve epistemological tensions between them.

In developing this analysis, we have leaned closer to the universalizing view. This is because current social psychological approaches to anti-homosexual attitudes are framed within an implicit minoritizing approach that is heavily focused on sexual *identity* rather than sexual *practice*, and which understands anti-homosexual prejudice as an exemplar of minority group oppression (see Kitzinger & Coyle, 2002; Herek, 2000; Sanford, 2000). Below we trace how and when attitude measurement techniques began to assume the minoritizing position, and show how the results of experiments on behavioral effects of attitudes can be re-interpreted from within the universalizing view. Although we look at attitude measurement in close detail in this paper, our broader aim is to stimulate a conversation between social psychology and queer theory. In the conclusion of the paper we suggest some reasons for the absence of such a conversation, and offer some possible starting points for discussion.

MEASURING ANTI-HOMOSEXUAL PREJUDICE I: GAY LIBERATION AND UNIVERSALIZING MODELS

One of the greatest successes of the gay and lesbian liberationist movements was the removal of homosexuality from its minoritizing psychiatric definition as a mental illness in 1973 (Bayer, 1981). Since World War II, American mental health professionals had increasingly defined homosexuality in psychoanalytic terms, while simultaneously overwriting Freud's (1923) universalizing–albeit heteronormative (Butler, 1990)–theory of primary bisexuality (Abelove, 1993; Lewes, 1989; Ryan & O Connor, 1998). This paradigm shift bore an uncanny resemblance to the earlier shift away from Eugenic models of race toward the study of anti-Black prejudice in post World War II American psychology (Richards, 1997; Samelson, 1978). The depathologizing of homosexuality occasioned new interest in the empirical study of anti-homosexual prejudice. Liberationist writings relied on both universalizing and minoritizing approaches to sexuality. Calls for rights for lesbians and gay men were central, but heterosexuality itself was also understood as a limited erotic choice and one that was socially enforced (see Altman, 1972; Hocquenghem, 1972, 1978; Radicalesbians, 1969; Rich, 1980; Whitman, 1969-70, 1997; and, the later writings of Ellis, 1976).

The term *homophobia* is most commonly attributed to clinical psychologist George Weinberg (Oxford English Dictionary), who described it as an irrational fear or "dread of being in close quarters with homosexuals" (Weinberg, 1972, p. 4). However, Weinberg's work was deeply indebted to sexual liberationism. Weinberg acknowledged the influence of many gay and lesbian liberationists including Arthur Evans of the Gay Activist Alliance of New York, Randy Wicker, the founder of the Homosexual League of New York, Kay Tobin and Franklin Kameny, (Weinberg, 1972 and Ayyar, 2002). Chapters of Weinberg's book *Society and the Healthy Homosexual* were first published in *Gay*, a magazine edited by gay liberation pioneers Jack Nichols and Lige Clarke. Weinberg also served as a spokesperson for some of the *homophile* organizations during their challenge to the APA's inclusion of homosexuality as a diagnostic category in the DSM (Lewes, 1988).

Weinberg's concept aimed to shift attention away from questions of homosexuals' mental (ill)health towards questioning the mental health of homophobes. Weinberg (1972) argued that he "would never consider a patient healthy unless he had overcome his prejudice of homosexuality" (p. 1). In a universalizing move, he suggested that homophobia not only limited self-identified heterosexuals' social relationships, it also inhibited their erotic potentiality–a point also made, but somewhat ambivalently, by psychologist and *sexual* liberationist Albert Ellis (1976).[2] Articulating a "new sexual culture," Weinberg (1972) wrote, "Gay liberation implies freedom from having to align oneself in sexual preference with dictates from anywhere" (p. 127). Positioning the sexual outsider as exemplary, he later stated that, "all love is conspiratorial and deviant and magical" (Ayyar, 2002). Other theorists, such as psychoanalyst Wainwright Churchill (1967) offered similar conceptualizations of anti-homosexual prejudice, locating its origins in *erotophobic* society.

Many of the social psychologists who developed technologies for measuring anti-homosexual attitudes favorably cited Churchill's and Weinberg's theories (e.g., McDonald & Moore, 1978; Larsen, Reed & Hoffman, 1980; Hudson & Ricketts, 1980). Even Smith's (1971) Homophobia Scale, which was published prior to *Society and the Healthy Homosexual* and before the depathologizing of homosexuality, was informed by Weinberg's writings (see Weinberg, 1972, p. 133; personal communication, June 25, 2003). Attempts to measure anti-homosexual prejudice explicitly located the source of discomfort around homosexuality in societal prejudice rather than in homosexuals themselves. Thus, Smith (1971) called for the study of the "social milieu" (p. 1089) in which the homosexual person lives and MacDonald, Huggins Young, and Swanson (1973, p. 10) argued for movement from an "organism deficiency" to a "social deficiency" explanation for discrimination. Such arguments occasionally drew on minoritizing frameworks by making analogies between anti-homosexual prejudice and anti-Black racism. For example, MacDonald and Games (1974) suggested that approaches to psychological inquiry that were "almost exclusively restricted to blacks [sic] and the poor . . . should be extended to include other discriminated against groups" (p. 10). In other words, anti-racist work provided an available model for understanding homophobia as a form of intergroup prejudice.

The "society" which was understood to be the origin of *homophobia* was to be assessed via correlations between measures of anti-homosexual prejudice and the endorsement of relevant ideologies. Weinberg (1972) had theorized that homophobia was derived from such motives as religion, fear of being homosexual, repressed envy, a threat to values, and fear of death. Attitude researchers correspondingly gathered data showing correlational relationships that were germane to these claims. Smith (1971) found evidence of correlations between anti-gay prejudice and the need for conventionality, conformity, and the need to maintain traditional sex and gender roles. Dunbar, Brown and Amoroso (1973) found that anti-homosexual participants were significantly more conservative and negative regarding sexual practices in general, expressed significantly more sex guilt, and were significantly more rigid in terms of their view of "appropriate" sex-roles. Yet, even as anti-homosexual prejudice was becoming understood as partially comprised of sex-role rigidity, feminists were transforming social psychologists' definitions of sex roles. Until the 1970s psychologists had assumed *masculinity* and *femininity* to be logical opposites, and often conflating *masculinity-femininity* with psychological differences between straight and gay men (Constantinople, 1973; Hegarty, 2003a; Lewin, 1982a, b). Feminist researchers re-theorized masculinity and femininity as constraining roles, and posited psychologically healthy *androgynous* individuals who could flexibly adopt either role as the situation dictated (e.g., Bem, 1974; Bem & Lenney, 1978). Research on androgyny and on anti-homosexual attitudes similarly presumed that individuals who could transgress overly rigid sexual and gender roles were psychologically healthy. Several researchers worked to correlate new measures of gender roles and new measures of anti-homosexual prejudice (e.g., Minnigerode, 1976; Storms, 1978).

Societal homophobia, in line with liberationists' universalizing notions and psychodynamic theory, was understood to shape individuals' emotions. Both Weinberg's and Churchill's works were frequently cited as the theoretical justifications for these hypotheses (e.g., Smith, 1971, p. 1091; Dunbar, Brown & Amoroso, 1973, pp. 271-272; Hudson & Ricketts, 1980, p. 357). Attitude researchers predicted affective responses within the parlance of ego defense. Anti-homosexual prejudice was thought to derive from *personal anxiety* (Millham, San Miguel, & Kellogg, 1976), *sex guilt* (Dunbar, Brown, & Amoroso, 1973), and *fear and denial of personal homosexual tendencies* (Mosher & O'Grady, 1979).

Sociological theories that cast sexual orientations as learned or *socially constructed* provided a further theoretical basis for universalizing approaches to the measurement of anti-homosexual prejudice. Citing constructionist theories which located male sex socialization in the context of sex guilt (i.e., Gagnon & Simon 1973; Simon & Gagnon, 1969), Mosher and O'Grady's (1979) measure of *homosexual threat* included heterosexuals' relationship to their own erotic responses in their empirical measure of anti-homosexual prejudice. *Fear and denial of homoerotic tendencies* became a component of their *Homosexual Threat Inventory*, originally conceptualized as agreement or disagreement with items referring to same-sex eroticism and desire, such as "to love another man is to know the heights of the human soul" and "I could never bring myself to suck another man's cock."

In short, there was *heterogeneity* of measures of anti-homosexual prejudice in the 1970s variously indebted to psychoanalysis, liberationist thinking, social constructionism, second wave feminism and the civil rights movement. The new scales typically included items that measured attitudes towards lesbians or gay men as a distinct minority group. For example, Smith's (1971) *H-Scale* included the item "Homosexuals should be locked up to protect society" and the item "A homosexual could be a good president of the United States" (p. 1094). Millham, San Miguel, and Kellogg's *Homosexuality Attitude Scale* included the item "Most male homosexuals dislike women" (p. 5), and Mosher and O'Grady's *Homosexual Threat Inventory* included the item "Homosexuals should stay in their own gay bars and not flaunt their deviance" (p. 864). However, universalizing ideas about universal bisexual potentiality were also commonly cited. For example, Smith's scale included the item "If laws against homosexuality were eliminated, the proportion of homosexuals in the population would probably remain the same" (suggesting, when reversed, the need for social control of a universal homosexual potential). Millham, San Miguel and Kellogg's scale included the item "Male homosexuality is a choice of lifestyles." Finally, Mosher and O'Grady's scale included the item "I am frightened that I might have homosexual tendencies." Indeed, to the extent that it drew on such universalizing themes, the work of the 1970s represented measurement of *bi*phobic attitudes as much as the measurement of *homo*phobic attitudes.

MEASURING ANTI-HOMOSEXUAL PREJUDICE II: SOCIAL REFORM AND MINORITIZING MODELS

Towards the end of the 1970s, gay and lesbian politics became organized less around the goal of sexual liberation and more around the assimilationist goal of achieving civil rights (see D'Emilio, 1983; Kitzinger, 1987; Weeks, 1985). The utopian call for sexual revolution was supplanted by the more moderate (and arguably more achievable) goal of social reform. Reactionary figures such as Anita Bryant who cast gay men and lesbians as a threat to the American family played a lethally important part in defining the terms of this cultural conflict. Radical theories of sexuality, perceived by some as fulfilling stereotypes of the promiscuous, predatory and anti-family homosexual (and perhaps aggravating unreconciled sex-guilt within gay people themselves) became more difficult to articulate. The increasing engagement of mainstream institutions with lesbian and gay right agendas occasioned new sexuality hierarchies within lesbian and gay subcultures. For example, in 1980 the National Organization of Women (NOW) codified its support for lesbian rights while signaling its condemnation of pederasty, sadomasochism, and pornography (National Organization of Women, 1980). As Rubin (1984) put it, several seemingly liberal institutions such as NOW still attempted to draw an "imaginary line between good and bad sex." Such sexual politics were motivated as much by fear of the unknown as by concern with liberation or fairness, as such a line was imagined to:

> ... stand between sexual order and chaos. It expresses the fear that if anything is permitted to cross this erotic DMZ, the barrier against scary sex will crumble and something unspeakable will skitter across. (p. 14)

Psychologists' definitions of anti-homosexual prejudice also became increasingly focused on minoritizing concerns during the early 1980s (e.g., Herek, 1984, Kite & Deaux, 1986; Larsen, Reed, & Hoffman, 1980). Earlier scales were vulnerable to several criticisms; those who scored high on homophobia scales did not manifest the typical physiological reactions that accompany a clinical "phobia" (see Millham & Weinberger, 1977; Shields & Harriman, 1984). Also, the predicted link between anti-homosexual prejudice and gender roles failed to materialize (see Whitley, 2001). Finally, the earlier scales had also been implicitly *androcentric*; by asking questions about homosexuals they probably elicited attitudes towards male homosexuality only (see Black & Stevenson, 1984). Thus the development of new scales for attitude measurement was easily positioned as a scientific advance rather than as a shift in the implicit politics that informed the concept of anti-homosexual prejudice.

However, consider Herek's (1984) *Attitudes Toward Lesbians and Gay Men* (ATLG) scale, which is now a standard in the field. Herek defined *heterosexism* in explicitly minoritizing terms as "a term analogous to sexism and racism, describing an ideological system that denies, denigrates, and stigmatizes any non-heterosexual form of behavior, identity relationship, or community" (Herek, 1990). Several of the earlier scales that drew on universalizing views were *multi-factorial*, and measured several distinct components of anti-homosexual prejudice allowing liberal notions of tolerance and civil rights to coexist with ego-defensive aspects of anti-homosexual prejudice. Herek (1984) questioned the necessity of multifactorial scales, and ultimately concluded that only a single factor was required to conceptualize heterosexism.

Herek (1984) reported four studies which drew on both earlier attitude measures (Levitt & Klassen, 1974; MacDonald et al., 1973; Millham et al., 1976; Smith, 1971) and some original items. Notably, Herek excluded items from Mosher and O'Grady (1979) arguing that the "locker room" language of these behavioral items would offend participants instead of tapping into feelings of personal threat. This empirically unsupported supposition was ironically made during the early days of the HIV/AIDS crisis when anti-homosexual prejudice operated most forcefully through heterosexuals' feelings of personal threat. The omission of Mosher and O'Grady's items demonstrates how social psychologists technologies are shaped as much by implicit sexual politics as much as the empirical results they gather.

Exploratory factor analysis revealed a variety of factors, including: *condemnation/repression, personal revulsion/threat and the desire to avoid contact, desire to keep away from children, beliefs about homosexuals, denial of similarities between heterosexuals and homosexuals,* and *comparing of heterosexual and homosexual relationships.* In each study, however, the condemnation/tolerance factor explained a much larger portion of the variance among items than the other factors, allowing Herek to argue that a unidimensional model was most "appropriate" and that all other factors were of trivial importance. Herek's resulting *Attitudes Toward Lesbians and Gay Men* (ATLG) scale examines attitudes along a single continuum from *tolerance* to *condemnation* via items which assess emotional reactions to lesbians and gay men and support for civil rights issues. Although Herek's definition refers to stigmatization of non-heterosexual *behavior*, questions concerning respondents own construction of their same-sex desires or behaviors are absent from the ATLG.

As Sedgwick notes, however, minoritizing and universalizing views of sexuality are never completely stable or separate in modern epistemologies. While developing the ATLG, Herek (1987) also began to assess the *functions* of anti-homosexual attitudes (and later, in articles related to AIDS, Herek, 2000). The study of attitude functions is indebted to psychoanalytic theorizing (see Katz, 1960), and had been critiqued on the grounds that attitude functions could not be empirically detected or measured. Herek's (1987) work argued that heterosexism served a variety of functions for different individuals including the expression of core values, reflecting cognitive beliefs, *and* defending against threats to the ego. In this last regard, Herek has explicitly argued that for a minority of heterosexual-identified persons, heterosexism is a result of displaced fear of their own homoerotic potential. Thus, Herek has operationalized universalizing ideas in his attitudes work, even though they have been excluded from his operational definition of anti-homosexual prejudice.

EXPERIMENTING WITH IDENTITY: LINKING ATTITUDES TO BEHAVIORS

Implicit in the study of attitudes is the promise that these internal constructs will in some way affect social behavior. However, the attitude-behavior link has often been shown to be absent (LaPiere, 1934) and during the 1970s social psychological research increasingly examined factors that might affect the strength of this link (Azjen & Fishbein, 1980). Thus, demonstrations of behavioral effects of anti-homosexual attitudes also became a topic of research, and such demonstrations were typically made with experimental studies. As in most other areas of social psychology, the experimental participants were typically college undergraduates, (Sears, 1986). These participants made a judgment about, or interacted with, a *target* individual, whose perceived sexual orientation was experimentally manipulated. Such experimental studies have varied in their realism. Some have involved the presentation of written information about individuals identified as gay, lesbian, or straight (see Laner & Laner, 1979, 1980; Sigelman, Howell, Cornell, Cutright, & Dewey, 1990; Snyder & Uranowitz, 1978; Storms, Stivers, Lambers, & Hill, 1981; Weissbach & Zagon, 1975). In others, participants encountered flesh-and-blood individuals who enacted particular sexual orientations (see Clark & Maass, 1988; Kite, 1992; Kite & Deaux, 1986, Study 2; Kruwelitz & Nash, 1980; San Miguel & Milham, 1976). In both cases, differences between the actions of participants with high and low levels of heterosexism to lesbian/gay and straight targets have been used to ground inferences about the behavioral consequences of anti-homosexual attitudes. For example, Kite and Deaux (1986) report that *intolerant* heterosexual males and *tolerant* heterosexual males differed in their liking of gay male targets, the information that they elicited from him, the information they presented about themselves and their memories of the interaction.

While these experiments have presumed to assess behavioral reactions to lesbians and gay men as a distinct minority group, they owe an unacknowledged debt to universalizing theories of homo/heterosexual definition. The experiments require that target individuals manipulate the presentation of their sexual identities, and typically, the same individuals have played the roles of both lesbian (or gay) target and of straight target in these experiments. Thus, targets have "done" straightness by direct disclosure (Clark & Maass, 1988), mention of an intention to marry (Kruwelitz & Nash, 1980), or, most frequently, by saying nothing about sexuality at all and allowing assumptions of compulsory heterosexuality (Rich, 1980) to go untroubled (see Cuenot & Fugita, 1982; Kite, 1992; Kite & Deaux, 1986; Gurwitz & Markus; San Miguel & Milham). Lesbian and gay identities have been "done" in the laboratory through direct verbal (Clark & Maass, 1988) or written (Kruwelitz & Nash, 1980) disclosure, expressions of interest in ongoing experiments about homosexuality (San Miguel & Millham, 1976), suggestions of homosexuality as a topic for discussion (Kite, 1992; Kite & Deaux, 1986), buttons that says "gay and proud" (Cuenot & Fugita, 1982), and mention of involvement in gay student organizations (Gurwitz & Marcus, 1978).

As Sedgwick (1990, p. 4) notes the wearing of a gay-positive t-shirt not only reports an identity, it also constitutes it. Participants' differential reactions to the targets in these experiments have been theorized as discriminatory reactions to lesbian/gay and straight individuals. However, the actions through which gay/lesbian identities are enacted are scripted to be highly volitional, and people who do not engage in such actions are not necessarily always straight. These experiments may just as readily be understood as assessing differential responses to *out* and *passing* lesbian/gay individuals, as to straight and (out) lesbian/gay individuals. In other words, the experiments may be assessing differential reactions to ways of enacting minority sexual identities, rather than differential reactions to members of separate discrete social groups.

Following Sedgwick and Butler (1990, 1991; Osborne & Segal, 1994) we might understand these targets identity enactments as *performative* of identity. If the targets' methods of performing identity are understood as *constituting* identity in different ways rather than simply *reporting* the same underlying identity, then it is less clear that these experiments are all examining the same social psychological processes. Explicit declaration of one's homosexuality, mention of involvement in a gay student group, and the wearing of a gay-positive button are not equivalent speech acts, and each accomplishes something more than the revelation of a presumed underlying identity (as readers who have negotiated disclosure dynamics will probably recognize). Butler argues against presumed unity among those represented by political signifiers (i.e., *women, lesbians* and *gay men*) and argues for a mode of politics that intervenes in the moments when such identities are thrown into question. This leads us to think differently about the empirical claims that are made from experimental results, and the need to theorize and examine social psychological experimental practice. On the first point, future experiments that acknowledged the performativity of identity could begin to examine if different performances of sexual identities moderates the relationship between research participants' anti-homosexual attitudes and their anti-homosexual behavior. On the second, the doing of experiments represents a particular kind of constructivist work; ironically, the positivist space of the psychological laboratory is perhaps the location where the postmodern fantasy that identities can be put on and taken off as easily as clothing has some legitimacy. An ethnographic study of psychological laboratories could greatly inform the politics of universalizing theories by illuminating a concrete set of practices where social identities are designed to be highly mutable (Hegarty, 2001).

QUEER THEORY AND ATTITUDES RESEARCH: WORKING THE TENSIONS

Compared to the early 1970s heterogeneous alliances between liberationist, psychoanalytic, and social constructionist thought and positivist technologies of attitude measurement, the intellectual work now known as *queer theory* (e.g., Abelove, Barale, & Halperin, 1993; Butler, 1990; DeLauretis, 1991; Fuss, 1991; Sedgwick, 1990; Warner, 1993) has, for better or worse, been considerably less engaged with academic psychology. Contrast, for example, the plethora of empirical articles on anti-homosexual prejudice published in the early volumes of *Journal of Homosexuality* with the almost complete lack of quantitative social science research in the more recent *GLQ: A Journal of Gay and Lesbian Studies.* Clearly, queer theory emerged in a way that was less bound up with the quantitative social sciences than did its liberationist forerunner. Below we examine why this might be so, and theorize where productive intersections might emerge in future work.

Of course, queer theory differs radically from liberationist thought in its conception of the individual subject. Liberationist work proposed that societal repression of individualized sexual natures was the primary mode of sexual politics. Foucault's *History of Sexuality: Volume 1* (1978), arguably the most influential book within queer theory, theorized power as operating through the *production* of sexuality and sexual categories as much as by their repression. Foucault called for heightened critique of ostensibly liberating breaks with the repressive past and seemingly rational advancements in the human sciences. As in much of Foucault's writing, his theory of sexuality describes the sciences of the human subject as originating in political attempts to control and order human bodies (see also Foucault, 1977). As such Foucault's work provides grounds for extreme skepticism about any project focused on individual differences or the measurement of mental states such as attitudes research.

Second, when queer theorists did turn to a theory of the individual subject, they tended to alight on psychoanalysis. Warner (1993, p. xi), for one, described psychoanalysis as "the most rigorous and sophisticated language about sexuality." As Kitzinger (1998) notes, imperatives to think the psychological subject as a psychoanalytic subject within sexuality and gender studies substantially limit engagement with academic psychology. Relationships between quantitative psychologists and psychoanalysts have never been easy in American psychology (Hornstein, 1992), and by the late 1980s, cognitive psychology, and not psychoanalysis, was the dominant truth regime in psychology (Friman, Allen, Kirwin, & Larzelere, 1992). By comparison with queer engagements with psychoanalytic assumptions, critiques of the heteronormativity of cognitive theories of the subject were slow to emerge (although see Curtain, 1997 and Helmreich, 1998 for notable exceptions). Thus queer theory became interested mostly in a theory of the subject which was peripheral to the interests of most social psychologists by the early 1990s.

Finally, lesbian and gay psychology has been a more cautious disciplinary project than queer theory. North American lesbian and gay psychologists positioned their work as empirical disciplinary work, often leading to a dismissal of the counter-disciplinary projects ongoing in lesbian, gay and queer studies. Most obviously, psychologist John Gonsierek (1993, viii-ix) in the foreword to a historical volume described lesbian and gay studies as an "inward looking," "self-absorbed" domain where "dogma is substituted for critical thinking." Lesbian and gay studies, for Gonsierek, was both "intellectually rigid and irrelevant both to the lives of gay and lesbian citizens and to honest intellectual inquiry." This caution has also limited the degree to which lesbian and gay psychologists discuss sex. Lesbian and gay psychologists, however, have typically been less willing to challenge the stigmatization of gay and lesbian sex than have their colleagues in the humanities. Sex research has always been stigmatized, and an explicit affirmative study of gay and lesbian sexualities has been read as constituting an infraction against implicit norms for scientific objectivity (Hegarty, 2003b; Irvine, 1990). While many queer theorists focused their approach on sex, rather than sexual identity (Sedgwick, 1990; Warner, 1993), lesbian and gay psychology has tended to privilege identity over behavior as the object of inquiry (Kitzinger & Coyle, 2002).

In spite of these differences, we agree with the editors of this volume that useful theory can be made from tensions between *lesbian, gay, bisexual, and transgender studies* and *queer theory*. Unlike Kitzinger (1987) we are not content to dismiss social psychology as purely rhetorical practice. Rather, we believe there are clear grounds for re-thinking the empirical record on anti-homosexual prejudice in light of the conceptual developments made by queer theorists.

Consider first the politics of knowledge production. Within social psychology, researchers have historically understood themselves to be accumulating empirical facts and developing an ever-growing body of knowledge about social behavior (Farr, 1996). However, even as gay liberationist ideas were being translated into attitude scales, Gergen (1973) suggested that both the findings of social psychological studies and the methods used to achieve those findings were bound by history. As Kitzinger and Coyle (2002) note, contemporary lesbian and gay psychologists have tended to either adopt traditional quantitative methods (Herek, 1998) or to embrace qualitative methods that eschew the reality of internal psychological processes (Gough, 2002; Speers & Potter, 2000). Queer theory might suggest how social psychologists could have their attitude technologies and deconstruct them, too. In the context of HIV/AIDS from which queer theory largely emerged, it became necessary to critically read the biomedical discourse through which "facts" about AIDS were being produced and to develop strategies for living with the virus. As Paula Treichler noted, this involves a kind of double consciousness:

> Of course, where AIDS is concerned, science can usefully perform its interpretive part: we can learn to live–indeed, *must* learn to live–as though there are such things as viruses. The virus–a constructed scientific object–is also a historical subject, a "human immunodeficiency virus," a real source of illness and death that can be passed from one person to another under certain conditions that we can apparently–individually and collectively–influence. The trick is to learn to live with this disjunction, but the lesson is imperative. (1991, p. 69)

We would like to encourage the learning of such a trick in regard to the psychological category of anti-homosexual prejudice. We need to theorize by acknowledging the interpretive work that attitude scales can perform with regard to social prejudices, while also recognizing their historicity, contingency, and limitations. In concert with Sedgwick's (1990) approach this may involve nurturing anti-homophobic inquiry within mutually incompatible epistemologies and a suspension of the Platonic desire to immediately resolve their inconsistencies.

One benefit of learning the trick to which Treichler (1991) refers would be the ability to see earlier modes of knowledge production as different from, but not necessarily inferior to, current paradigms. We might revisit the liberationist work of the 1970s as grounds for re-theorizing the complexity of heterosexism. Ironically, even work within the minoritizing perspective consistently shows relationships between anti-homosexual prejudice and authoritarianism, traditional gender role beliefs, and affective reactions (Pettigrew & Tropp, 2000; Whitley, 1999). Herek's shift away from *homophobia* to terms such as *sexual prejudice* and *heterosexism* may have obscured some persistent ways that anti-homosexual prejudice is bound up with affect and ego-defense. Consideration of the historicity of the psychological knowledge, coupled with a willingness to continue to work with that knowledge, might create new lines of inquiry within social psychology (see Massey, 2004).

The second productive "tension" concerns the position of identity categories in lesbian and gay psychology. Anti-heterosexual attitudes have been increasingly researched from within a minoritizing frame, and this frame limits our theorizing of the ways that different kinds of identity performances elicit different kinds of prejudicial responses. Queer theorists argued that the available political categories for thinking about sexual politics were insufficient, and prioritized a kind of *social reflection* in the doing of queerness (Warner, 1993). There were many reasons for this skepticism in addition to Foucault's skepticism about the ontology of the human subject. Jagose (1993) describes *queer* as originating within gay and lesbian communities' responses to the AIDS epidemic. Initially considered a *gay* disease, AIDS affected many who did not identify with this group, forcing researchers and activists to admit the obvious inconsistency between homosexual identity and homosexual behavior. Queer identity was then based on affinity rather than some essential quality, and attempts to analogize gay communities and gay and lesbian communities along ethnic lines (Epstein, 1985) were attacked as queer theory emerged (Cohen, 1991).

A queer approach would lead us to question the assumption that homosexual behavior and identity can be collapsed, or that one can serve as a valid ontology for the other. Butler (1993, pp. 1-23) has been careful to distinguish her account of performativity from the notion that identities can be constructed whole cloth, volitionally, as social psychologists report doing with their *targets* in their experiments. Her work then provides grounds for a critique, not only of lesbian and gay psychology, but of experimental psychologists' more general nature/nurture debates which nominate *learned* or *social* behaviors as those which can be changed in laboratory settings, and *natural* or *hardwired* behavior as those which can not. Butler's work would lead us to question the particulars through which social psychological variables are operationalized, rather than to assume that all operationalizations are equivalent (see also Cherry, 1995). What does the wearing of a button accomplish? Does it have the same performative effect as signaling a desire to take part in a psychology experiment pertaining to homosexuality?

Experiments using *multiple* performances of gay/lesbian or straight identities suggest that such an approach might produce useful theory. For example, Sigelman, Howell, Cornell, Cutright, and Dewey's (1990) participants read about a straight male target who acquired a gay male roommate either by choice or by accident, and assigned the former target more homosexual tendencies, "gay-stereotyped" traits, lower mental health, and rated him to be less likeable. Experiments have increasingly shown that gay male targets are derogated only when they enact their identities in particular ways. Moreno and Bodenhausen's (2001) participants only discriminated against an openly gay target (making a pro-gay speech) when his presentation was riddled with errors. Hegarty, Pratto, and Lemieux (2004) have since used vignette studies to show that gay male targets who express discomfort about straight environments are derogated in ways that equivalent targets who stifle their discomfort are not. Such experiments suggest that not all performances of sexual identities are equivalent, leading us to question whether or not experimental studies of gay identity represent a unified literature at all.

Finally, queer theory points to the need for a re-thinking of the relationship between racism and anti-homosexual prejudice in social psychology. Several of the key texts of queer theory linked their anti-essentialist claims to anti-racist scholarship (Duggan, 1990; Warner, 1993). As we have noted above, anti-homosexual inquiry has often looked to anti-racist work for ways of understanding both minority identities and majority prejudices. However, for queer theorists such analogies run the risk of raising one dimension of difference at the risk of obscuring others (Lorde, 1984), overlooking the effects of hetero-normativity on the lives of ethnic minority heterosexuals (Cohen, 1997), and ignoring the co-construction of racial and sexual categories (Sommerville, 2000). Such analogies confuse two very different forms of prejudice which social psychologists also argue are organized by different ideologies and motivations (Biernat, Vescio, & Theno, 1996; Whitley, 1999). At worst, the metaphor can imply that the two forms of prejudice are mutually exclusive, obscuring the ways that some lives are shaped by both. Such political commitments require that social psychologists do not simply position heterosexism as analogous to racism, but begin to use traditional technologies such as surveys and experiments to understand their intersections (see Battle et al., 2002; Clausell & Hegarty, 2003a).

CONCLUSION

Many of the now canonical queer theory writings cautiously position themselves as supplementary to, rather than in opposition to, scientific epistemologies (Treichler, 1991) and civil rights politics based on identity categories (Butler, 1990; de Lauretis, 1991; Warner, 1993). Similarly, our goal here is not to rehash social constructionist critiques of empirical social psychology that describes such work as meaningless, or simply as the operations of power (Gergen, 1973; Kitzinger, 1987). Rather it seems to us that empirical research on heterosexism constitutes a relatively new mode of creating knowledge, and that those of us who do that work would be well to attend to the sexual politics involved in carrying it out (Hegarty, 2001). Empiricist narratives lead us away from this kind of theorizing, diminish the contributions of our liberationist forerunners, and must be supplemented by the kind of reflection that queer theory engenders. Queer theory does not require the abolition of scientific epistemology. Rather, as Triechler (1991) notes, the trick is to have science play its interpretive part, while also remaining conscious of the distinction between the part and the whole of anti-prejudicial inquiry and action.

NOTES

1. The terms used to describe antipathy towards homosexuality have varied within the social psychological literature over the time period that we describe here. *Heterosexism* and *homophobia* have been the most commonly used terms but *homosexism, homonegativism,* and others have also been used. We use this somewhat

cumbersome term *anti-homosexual prejudice* in this paper to gain some distance from the more familiar terms, as one of our goals is to bring to light the implicit theoretical commitments that often pass unnoticed in the use of such terms.

2. Although Ellis was a sexual liberationist, activist, and a proponent of decriminalizing homosexuality, his views on the mental health of homosexuals changed over his long career. In earlier writings, while he argued from a universalizing perspective for a radical sexual humanism, Ellis also claimed that exclusive homosexuality was, "wrong—meaning inefficient, self-defeating, and emotionally disturbed" (1965, p. 78). Later, in the context of the gay liberation movement, he modified his theory. No longer singling out exclusive homosexuality as a problem, Ellis (1976) suggested instead that all fixed modes of (compulsive) sexual behavior, both homosexual and heterosexual, were potentially neurotic, and that these "standards of emotional disturbance" (p. 298) must be applied equally to both gay and straight people. In other words, Ellis' commitment to universalizing theory eventually took precedent over any commitment that he might have voiced towards anti-homosexual theory.

REFERENCES

Abelove, H. (1993). Freud, male homosexuality, and the Americans. In H. Abelove, M. A. Barale, & D. M. Halperin (Eds.), *The lesbian and gay studies reader* (pp. 381-393). New York: Routledge.

Abelove, H., Barale, M. A., & Halperin, D. M. (Eds.). (1993). *The lesbian and gay studies reader.* New York: Routledge.

Allport, G.W. (1935). Attitudes. In C. Murchison (Ed.), *Handbook of social psychology* (pp. 798-844). Worchester, MA: Clark University Press.

Altman, D. (1972). *Homosexual oppression and liberation.* Sydney: Angus and Robertson.

Ayyar, R. (November 1, 2002). George Weinberg: Love is conspiratorial, deviant, and magical. *GayToday.* http://gaytoday.com/interview/110102in.asp.

Azjen, I., & Fishbein, M. (1980). *Understanding attitudes and predicting social behavior.* Englewood Cliffs, NJ: Prentice Hall.

Battle, J., Cohen, C., Warren, D., Fergerson, G., & Audum, S. (2002). *Say it loud. I'm Black and I'm proud: Pride Survey 2000.* National Gay and Lesbian Task Force: New York.

Bayer, R. (1981). *Homosexuality and American psychiatry.* Princeton, NJ: Princeton University Press.

Bem, S. L. (1974). On the measurement of psychological androgyny. *Journal of Clinical and Consulting Psychology, 42,* 155-162.

Bem, S. L., & Lenney, E. (1978). Sex typing and the avoidance of cross-sex behavior. *Journal of Personality and Social Psychology, 33,* 48-54.

Biernat, M., Vescio, T. K., & Theno, S. A. (1996). Violating American values: A 'value congruence' approach to understanding outgroup attitudes. *Journal of Experimental Social Psychology, 32,* 387-410.

Black, K. N., & Stevenson, M. R. (1984). The relationship of self-reported sex-role characteristics and attitudes toward homosexuality. *Journal of Homosexuality, 10,* 83-93.

Butler, J. (1990). *Gender trouble.* New York, NY: Routledge.

Butler, J. (1991). Imitation and gender insubordination. In D. Fuss (Ed.), *Inside/Out: Lesbian theories, gay theories* (pp. 13-31). New York: Routledge.

Butler, J. (1993). *Bodies that matter.* New York, NY: Routledge.

Cherry, F. (1995). *The stubborn particulars of social psychology: Essays on the research process.* London: Routledge.

Churchill, W. (1967). *Homosexual behavior among males: A cross-cultural and cross-species investigation.* New York, NY: Hawthorn Books.

Clark, R. D., III, & Maass, A. (1988). Social categorization in minority influence: The case of homosexuality. *European Journal of Social Psychology, 18*, 347-364.

Clausell, E., & Hegarty, P. (2003). Prejduice and Attractiveness Attributions: Intersecting effects of target and participant ethnicity on stereotypes of gay and straight men. Manuscript under review.

Cohen, C. J. (1997). Punks, bulldaggers, and welfare queens: The radical potential of queer politics? *GLQ: A Journal of Gay and Lesbian Studies, 3*, 437-465.

Cohen, E. (1991). Who are "we"? Gay "identity" as political (e)motion (a theoretical rumination). In D. Fuss (Ed.), *Inside/Out: Lesbian theories, gay theories* (pp. 71-92). New York: Routledge.

Constantinople, A. (1973). Masculinity-femininity: An exception to a famous dictum? *Psychological Bulletin, 80*, 389-407.

Cuenot, R. G., & Fugita, S. S. (1982). Perceived homosexuality: Measuring heterosexual attitudinal and nonverbal reactions. *Personality and Social Psychology Bulletin, 8*, 100-106.

Curtain, T. (1997). The 'sinister fruitiness' of machines: *Neuromancer*, internet sexuality, and the Turing test. In E.K. Sedgwick (Ed.), *Novel gazing: Queer readings in fiction* (pp. 128-148*).* Durham, NC: Duke University Press.

D'Emilio, J. (1983). *Sexual politics, sexual communities: The making of a homosexual minority in the United States, 1940-1970.* Chicago: University of Chicago Press.

De Lauretis, T. (1991). Queer theory: Lesbian and gay sexualities, an introduction. *differences, 3*(2), iii-xviii.

Duggan, L. (1995). Making it perfectly queer. Reprinted in L. Duggan & N. Hunter (Eds.), *Sex wars: Sexual dissent and political culture* (pp. 155-172). New York: Routledge.

Dunbar, J., Brown, M., & Amoroso, D. M. (1973). Some correlates of attitudes toward homosexuality. *The Journal of Social Psychology, 89*, 271-279.

Eagly, A.H. (1992). Uneven progress: Social psychology and the study of attitudes. *Journal of Personality and Social Psychology, 63*, 693-710.

Eagly, A.H., & Chaiken, S. (1993). *The psychology of attitudes.* Fort Worth, TX: Harcourt Brace Javonovich.

Ellis, A. (1965). *Homosexuality: Its causes and cure.* New York, NY: Lyle Stuart.

Ellis, A. (1976). *Sex and the liberated man.* Secaucus, NJ: Lyle Stuart.

Epstein, S. (1987). Gay poliics, ethnic identity: The limits of social constructionism. *Socialist Review, 17*, 9-54.

Farr, R.M. (1996). *The roots of modern social psychology.* Oxford: Blackwell.

Foucault, M. (1977). *Discipline and punish: The birth of the prison.* Random House: New York.

Foucault, M. (1978). *The history of sexuality, Vol I*. Translated by R. Hurley. New York: Vintage Books.

Freud, S. (1923). *The ego and the id*. In J. Stratchey (Ed.), Standard edition of the complete works of Sigmund Freud, Volume 19, 3-66. London: Hogarth.

Friman, P. C., Allen, K. D., Kerwin, M. L., & Larzelere, R. (1993). Changes in modern psychology: A citation analysis of the Kuhnian displacement thesis. *American Psychologist, 48*, 658-664.

Fuss, D. (Ed.). (1991). *Inside/out: Lesbian theories/gay theories*. New York: Routledge.

Gagnon, J. H., & Simon, W. (1973). *Sexual conduct*. Chicago, IL: Aldine.

Gergen, K. J. (1973). Social psychology as history. *Journal of Personality and Social Psychology, 26*, 309-320.

Gonsierek, J. (1993). Foreward. In G. M. Herek & B. Greene (Eds.), *Lesbian and gay psychology: Theory, research and clinical applications. Psychological perspectives on lesbian and gay issues, Volume 1* (vii-ix). Thousand Oaks, CA: Sage.

Gough, B. (2002). 'I've always tolerated it but . . .': Heterosexual masculinity and the discursive reproduction of homophobia. In A. Coyle & C. Kitzinger (Eds.), *Lesbian and gay psychology: New perspectives* (pp. 219-238). Oxford: BPS Blackwell.

Greenwald, A. G., Banaji, M. R., Rudman, L. A., Farnham, S. D., Nosek, B. A., & Mellott, D. S. (2002). A unified theory of implicit attitudes, stereotypes, self-esteem, and self-concept. *Psychological Review, 109*, 3-25.

Gurwitz, S.B., & Markus, M. (1978). Effects of aticipated interaction, sex, and homosexaul stereotypes on first impressions. *Journal of Applied Social Psychology, 8*, 47-56.

Hegarty, P. (2002). "It's not a choice, it's the way we're built:" Symbolic beliefs about sexual orientation in the United States and in Britain. *Journal of Community and Applied Social Psychology, 12*, 1-14.

Hegarty, P. (2003a). "More feminine than 999 men out of 1,000:" The construction of sex roles in psychology. In T. Lester (Ed.), *Gender nonconformity, race and sexuality: Charting the connections* (pp. 62-83). Madison, WI: University of Wisconsin Press.

Hegarty, P. (2003b). Homosexual signs and heterosexual silences: Rorschach studies of male homosexuality from 1921 to 1967. *Journal of the History of Sexuality, 12*, 400-423.

Hegarty, P., & Pratto, F. (2001). Sexual orientation beliefs: Their relationship to anti-gay attitudes and biological determinist arguments. *Journal of Homosexuality, 41*, 121-135.

Hegarty, P., Pratto, F., & Lemieux, A. (2004). Heterosexist norms and heterosexist ambivalences: Drinking in intergroup discomfort. *Group Processes and Intergroup Processes, 7*, 119-130.

Helmreich, S. (1998). *Silicon second nature: Culturing artificial life in a digital world* (pp. 205-250). Berkeley, CA: University of California Press.

Herek, G. M. (1984). Attitudes toward lesbians and gay men: A factor analytic study. *Journal of Homosexuality, 10*, 39-51.

Herek, G. M (1986). The instrumentality of attitudes: Toward a neofunctional theory. *Journal of Social Issues, 42*, 99-114.

Herek, G. M. (1990). The context of anti-gay violence: Notes on cultural and psychological heterosexism. *Journal of Interpersonal Violence, 5*, 316-333.

Herek, G. M. (1994). Assessing heterosexuals' attitude toward lesbians and gay men: A review of empirical research with the ATLG scale. In B. Green and G. M. Herek (Eds.), *Lesbian and gay psychology: Theory, research and clinical applications. Psychological perspectives on lesbian and gay issues, Volume 1* (pp. 206-228). Thousand Oaks, CA: Sage.

Herek, G. M. (2000). The social construction of attitudes: Functional consensus and divergence in the U.S. public's reactions to AIDS. In G. R. Miao & J. M. Olson (Eds.), *Why we evaluate: Functions of attitudes* (pp. 325-364). Mahwah, NJ: Lawrence Erlbaum.

Herek, G. M. (2000). The psychology of sexual prejudice. *Current Directions in Psychological Science, 9*, 19-22.

Hocquenghem, G. (1972/1978). *Homosexual desire*. Translated by D. Dongoor. London: Alyson & Busby.

Hornstein, G. A. (1992). The return of the repressed: Psychology's problematic relationship with psychoanalysis, 1909-1960. *American Psychologist, 47*, 254-263.

Hudson, W. W., & Ricketts, W. A. (1980). A strategy for the measurement of homophobia. *Journal of Homosexuality, 5*, 357-372.

Irvine, J. (1990). *Disorders of desire: Sex and gender in modern American sexology*. Philadelphia, PA: Temple University Press.

Jagose, A. (1996). *Queer theory: An introduction*. New York: New York University Press.

Katz, D. (1960). The functional approach to the study of attitudes. *Public Opinion Quarterly, 24*, 163-204.

Kite, M. E. (1992). Individual differences in males' reaction to gay males and lesbians. *Journal of Applied Social Psychology, 22*, 1222-1239.

Kite, M. E., & Deaux, K. (1986). Attitudes toward homosexuality: Assessment and behavioral consequences. *Basic and Applied Social Psychology, 7*, 137-162.

Kitzinger, C. (1987). *The social construction of lesbianism*. Beverly Hills, CA: Sage Publications.

Kitzinger, C. (1989). Liberal humanism as an ideology of social control: The regulation of lesbian identities. In J. Shotter & K. Gergen (Eds.), *Texts of identity*. London: Sage.

Kitzinger, C. (1998). Feminist psychology in an interdisciplinary context. *Journal of Gender Studies, 7*, 199-209.

Kitzinger, C., & Coyle, A. (2002). Introducing lesbian and gay psychology. In A. Coyle & C. Kitzinger (Eds.), *Lesbian and gay psychology: New perspectives* (pp. 1-29). Oxford: BPS Blackwell.

Krulewitz, J. E., & Nash, J. E. (1980). Effects of sex role attitudes and similarity on men's rejection of male homosexuals. *Journal of Personality and Social Psychology, 38*, 67-74.

Laner, M. R., & Laner, R. H. (1979). Personal style or sexual preference? Why gay men are disliked. *International Review of Modern Sociology, 9*, 215-228.

Laner, M. R., & Laner, R. H. (1980). Sexual preference or personal style? Why lesbians are disliked. *Journal of Homosexuality, 5*, 339-356.

La Piere, R. T. (1934). Attitudes vs. actions. *Social Forces, 13,* 230-237.

Larsen, K. S., Reed, M., & Hoffman, S. (1980). Attitudes of heterosexuals toward homosexuality: A Likert-type scale and construct validity. *Journal of Sex Research, 16,* 245-257.

Lewes, K. (1988). *The psychoanalytic theory of male homosexuality.* New York: Simon and Schuster.

Lewin, M. (1984a). 'Rather worse than folly?' Psychology measures femininity and masculinity, 1. In M. Lewin (Ed.), *In the shadow of the past: Psychology portrays the sexes* (pp. 135-178). New York: Columbia University Press.

Lewin, M. (1984b). Psychology measures femininity and masculinity 2: From '13 gay men' to the instrumental-expressive distinction. In M. Lewin (Ed.), *In the shadow of the past: Psychology portrays the sexes* (pp. 179-204). New York: Columbia University Press.

Lorde, A. (1984). *Sister outsider.* Freedom, CA: Crossing Press.

Massey, S. (2004). Polymorphous prejudice: Liberating the measurement of heterosexuals' attitudes toward lesbians and gay men. Unpublished Ph.D. dissertation. City University of New York: University Center and Graduate School.

MacDonald, A. P., Huggins, J., Young, S., & Swanson, R. A. (1973). Attitudes toward homosexuality: Preservation of sex morality or the double standard? *Journal of Consulting and Clinical Psychology, 40,* 161.

MacDonald, A. P., & Games, R. G. (1974). Some characteristics of those who hold positive and negative attitudes toward homosexuals. *Journal of Homosexuality, 1,* 9-27.

Millham, J., & Weinberger, L. E. (1977). Sexual preference, sex role appropriateness, and restriction of social access. *Journal of Homosexuality, 2,* 343-357.

Millham, J., San Miguel, C. L., & Kellogg, R. (1976). A factor-analytic conceptualization of attitudes toward male and female homosexuals. *Journal of Homosexuality, 2,* 3-10.

Minnigerode, F. A. (1976). Attitudes toward homosexuality: Feminist attitudes and sexual conservatism. *Sex Roles, 2,* 347-352.

Moreno, K. N., & Bodenhausen, G. V. (2001). Intergroup affect and social judgment: Feelings as inadmissible information. *Group Processes and Intergroup Relations, 4,* 21-29.

Mosher, D. L., & O'Grady, K. E. (1979). Homosexual threat, negative attitudes toward masturbation, sex guilt, and males' sexual and affective reactions to explicit sexual films. *Journal of Consulting and Clinical Psychology, 47,* 860-873.

National Organization of Women. (1980/1997). Resolution on lesbian and gay rights. Reprinted in M. Blasius & S. Phelan (Eds.), *We are everywhere: A historical sourcebook of gay and lesbian politics* (pp. 468-469). New York: Routledge.

Osborne, P., & Segal, L. (1994). Gender as performance: An interview with Judith Butler. *Radical Philosophy, 67,* 32-39.

Pettigrew, T. F., & Tropp, L. R. (2000). Does intergroup contact reduce prejudice: Recent meta-analytic findings. In S. Oskamp (Ed.), *Reducing prejudice and discrimination: 'The Claremont Symposium on Applied Social Psychology'* (pp. 93-114). Mahwah, NJ: Lawrence Erlbaum.

Potter, J., & Wetherell, M. (1987). *Discourse and social psychology: Beyond attitudes and behavior.* Newbury Park, CA: Sage.

Radicalesbians. (1969). *Woman-identified woman.* Somerville, MA: New England Free Press.

Rich, A. (1980). Compulsory heterosexuality and lesbian existence. *Signs: A Journal of Women in Culture and Society, 5,* 631-660.

Richards, G. (1997). *'Race', racism and psychology: Towards a reflexive history.* London: Routledge.

Rubin, G. S. (1984). Thinking sex: Notes for a radical theory of the politics of sexuality. In C. S. Vance (Ed.), *Pleasure and danger: Exploring female sexuality* (pp. 157-210). Boston: Routledge & Kegan Paul.

O Connor, N., & Ryan, J. (1998). *Wild desires and mistaken identities.* New York: Columbia University Press.

Samelson, F. (1978). From 'race psychology' to 'studies of prejudice': Some observations on thematic reversals in social psychology. *Journal of the History of the Behavioral Sciences, 127,* 147-154.

San Miguel, C.J., & Milham, J. (1976). The role of cognitive and situational variables in aggression toward homosexauls. *Journal of Homosexuality, 2,* 11-27.

Sanford, T. (2000). Homosexuality, psychology, and gay and lesbian studies. In. T. Sandfort, J. Duvyendak, J. Weeks, & J. Schuyf (Eds.), *Lesbian and gay studies: An introductory interdisciplinary approach* (pp. 14-45). London: Sage.

Sears, D. (1986). College sophomores in the laboratory: Influences of a narrow data base on social psychology's view of human nature. *Journal of Personality and Social Psychology, 51,* 515-530.

Sedgwick, E. K. (1990). *Epistemology of the closet.* Berkeley, CA: University of California Press.

Shields, S. A., & Harriman, R. E. (1984). Fear of male homosexuality: Cardiac responses of low and high homonegative males. *Journal of Homosexuality, 10,* 53-67.

Sigelman, C. K., Howell, J. L., Cornell, D. P., Cutright, J. D., & Dewey, J. C. (1990). Courtesy stigma: The social implications of associating with a gay person. *The Journal of Social Psychology, 131,* 45-56.

Simon, W., & Gagnon, J. H. (1969). On psychosexual development. In D. A. Goslin (Ed.), *Handbook of socialization theory and research.* Chicago, IL: Rand McNally.

Smith, K. T. (1971). Homophobia: A tentative personality profile. *Psychological Reports, 29,* 1091-1094.

Snyder, M., & Uranowitz, S.W. (1978). Reconstructing the past: Some cognitive consequences of person perception. *Journal of Personality and Social Psychology, 36,* 941-950.

Somerville, S. (2000). *Queering the color line.* Durham, NC: Duke University Press.

Spalding, L., & Peplau, L.A. (1997). The unfaithful lover: Heterosexuals' perceptions of bisexuals and their relationships. *Psychology of Women Quarterly, 21,* 611-625.

Speer, S. A., & Potter, J. (2000). The management of heterosexist talk: Conversational resources and prejudiced claims. *Discourse and Society, 11,* 543-572.

Steele, R. S., & Morawski, J.G. (2002). Implicit cognition and the social unconscious. *Theory and Psychology, 12,* 37-54.

Storms, M. D. (1978). Attitudes toward homosexuality and femininity in men. *Journal of Homosexuality, 3,* 257-263.

Storms, M. D., Stivers, M. L., Lambers, S. M., & Hill, C. A. (1981). Sexual scripts for women. *Sex Roles, 7,* 699-707.

Tee, N. (2003). Transphobia. A neglected prejudice in social psychology? Unpublished Masters of Science Dissertation. University of Surrey.

Treichler, P. A. (1991). AIDS, homophobia, and biomedical discourse: An epidemic of signification. In D. Crimp (Ed.) *AIDS: Cultural analysis, cultural activism* (pp. 31-70). Boston, MA: MIT Press.

Warner, M. (1993). Introduction. In M. Warner (Ed.), *Fear of a queer planet* (vii-xxxi). Minneapolis: University of Minnesota Press.

Weeks, J. (1985). *Sexuality and its discontents.* New York, NY: Routledge.

Weinberg, G. (1972). *Society and the healthy homosexual.* New York, NY: St. Martin's Press.

Weissbach, T. A., & Zagon, G. (1975). The effect of deviant group membership upon impressions of personality. *Journal of Social Psychology, 95,* 263-266.

Whitley, B. E. (1999). Right-wing authoritarianism, social dominance orientation, and prejudice. *Journal of Personality and Social Psychology, 77,* 126-134.

Whitley, B. E. (2001). Gender-role variables and attitudes toward homosexuality. *Sex Roles, 45,* 691-721.

Whitman, C. (1969-70/1997). A gay manifesto. Reprinted in M. Blasius & S. Phelan (Eds.) *We are everywhere: A historical sourcebook of gay and lesbian politics* (pp. 380-388). New York: Routledge.

doi:10.1300/J082v52n01_03

Outlaws or In-Laws?
Queer Theory, LGBT Studies,
and Religious Studies

Melissa M. Wilcox, PhD

Whitman College

SUMMARY. Many queer theorists, like many queer activists and perhaps many LGBT people in general, regard religion as so inimical to their purposes and lives that it is not even worthy of critique; references to religion in queer theory, queer studies, and even LGBT studies are usually sparse, brief, and generally derogatory. Likewise, within most of the field of religious studies, queerness is rarely an issue of concern or even consciousness except in the context of organizational tensions over the proper roles of "homosexuals." While there is a growing body of work that brings these two fields together, the study of religion seems to be adapting only haltingly and partially to contemporary developments in LGBT studies and queer theory. This essay assesses the current state of the "proto-fields" of LGBT studies and queer studies in religion, offers suggestions for new directions in the future, and considers the potential benefits of the interaction of these fields. doi:10.1300/J082v52n01_04 *[Article copies available for a fee from The Haworth Document Delivery Service: 1-800-HAWORTH. E-mail address: <docdelivery@haworthpress.com> Website: <http://www. HaworthPress.com> © 2006 by The Haworth Press, Inc. All rights reserved.]*

Correspondence may be addressed: Department of Religion, 345 Boyer Avenue, Walla Walla, WA 99362 (E-mail: wilcoxmm@whitman.edu).

[Haworth co-indexing entry note]: "Outlaws or In-Laws? Queer Theory, LGBT Studies, and Religious Studies." Wilcox, Melissa M. Co-published simultaneously in *Journal of Homosexuality* (Harrington Park Press, an imprint of The Haworth Press, Inc.) Vol. 52, No. 1/2, 2006, pp. 73-100; and: *LGBT Studies and Queer Theory: New Conflicts, Collaborations, and Contested Terrain* (ed: Karen E. Lovaas, John P. Elia, and Gust A. Yep) Harrington Park Press, an imprint of The Haworth Press, Inc., 2006, pp. 73-100. Single or multiple copies of this article are available for a fee from The Haworth Document Delivery Service [1-800-HAWORTH, 9:00 a.m. - 5:00 p.m. (EST). E-mail address: docdelivery@haworthpress.com].

Available online at http://jh.haworthpress.com
© 2006 by The Haworth Press, Inc. All rights reserved.
doi:10.1300/J082v52n01_04

KEYWORDS. Comparative religion, homosexuality, LGBT studies, queer theory, religion, religious studies, spirituality

In their introduction to an anthology entitled *Que(e)rying Religion*, co-editors Gary David Comstock and Susan E. Henking note that "for many," queer identities and religious identities "are so dissimilar as to have no continuity at all" (1997, p. 11). Indeed, a brief survey of the foundational and recently influential works in queer theory yields no more than a small handful of passing references to religion. Generally, these address only Christianity and brand religion as a stultifying, oppressive institution of a heteronormative, sexist social order. This perspective is common among LGBT people, as well; O'Brien (2004) recalls attending several Pride parades in the late 1990s at which members of Affirmation (a group for LGBT Mormons and their allies) and Dignity (a similar group for Catholics) were met with silence and boos from the audience. It is notable, then, given this supposed agreement on the oppressive role of religion, that analysis of religion's discursive power and the potential for performative resistance to that power has not been of interest in queer theory to date.

On the opposite side of this apparent divide lies the discipline of religious studies. Despite the development of numerous LGBT religious groups and the growth of LGBT-centered theology and even queer theology, all too often when the topic of "homosexuality" is taken up by religion scholars, the discussion is heterosexist or downright homophobic–and bisexuals and transgender people are written out entirely. It is not uncommon to find conference panels and special journal issues dedicated to organizational analysis of the "homosexuality debates" in Protestant churches, or to debates over the "proper role" of gays and lesbians in a particular religious body. In some cases (e.g., Wellman, 1999) such work is still of high quality, but it is far from being LGBT studies in religion, not only because it rarely discusses queer folk (focusing instead on the pronouncements of heterosexuals) but also because the authors are often neither conversant with LGBT studies nor queer theory (for a particularly egregious example wherein the author resurrects the invert, see Sherkat, 2002).

If queer theorists are fond of seeing themselves as "academic outlaws," to quote William Tierny (1997), religion scholars (even those of us who are queer) all too often have appeared as queer theory's academic in-laws: claiming to be "family," barging in at inopportune moments, always managing to mess up the guest room. As someone with a foot in both camps, I wish to argue here that both fields stand to learn far more from each other than either one realizes, and that the roots of that potential are already in existence. This essay begins with a discourse on definitions, as I attempt to hold constant for just a few moments the elusive definitions of lesbian/gay studies, LGBT studies, queer studies, queer theory, religion, and religious studies. It then turns to an evaluation of existing works in LGBT and queer religious studies, and offers challenges for the future as we pull these works and others together into a visible and audible subfield of study. The final section considers the ways in which religious studies and queer theory might benefit from a closer association than they have had to date.

DEFINITIONS

Gay, Lesbian/Gay, Lesbian/Gay/Bisexual, LGBT, Queer

The history of the terminological shifts from "gay" through "lesbian/gay," "lesbian/gay/bisexual," and "LGBT" to (sometimes) "queer" is both convoluted and fairly well-known; for both reasons, I will not cover it in depth here. A few points are worth mentioning, however, in order to illuminate the use of terminology in the study of LGBT religiosities. First, this is a history of struggles over inclusion and exclusion, as shifts from "gay" through to "LGBT" and "queer" came about in part in an attempt to be more fully inclusive of the diversity in our communities. Second, each of these shifting terms is also contested. Sometimes this contestation leads to the creation of new terms, but it is also a function of the diversity of opinions within our communities. Third, and most important, simply changing the terms has repeatedly proven insufficient to bring about the desired inclusion.

Queer theorists, for instance, laud the radical inclusivity of "queer," even to the point of refusing to restrict the term to a fixed definition (c.f. de Lauretis, 1991; Garber 2001; Jagose, 1996; Warner, 1993). On the other hand, de Lauretis, who is credited with coining the term, dropped it within a few years, claiming that it had failed to live up to its promise of inclusion (de Lauretis, 1994). As a result of these tensions, not only do LGBT studies and queer theory often regard each other with suspicion, but feminist scholars accuse both of being androcentric, bisexuals and transgender people charge that they are included in name only, sex radicals object that sex itself is rarely mentioned, working class scholars and activists (as well as anti-capitalists) insist that both perspectives ignore class, and scholars and activists of color–both Western and Third-World–seem resigned to the idea that once again, a movement founded by primarily by whites has become a movement primarily of, and for, whites. And yet, none of these accusations stands entirely un-challenged, for gender, race, class, sexual and gender diversity, and even postcolonial theory (Hawley, 2001a, 2001b) have been ably and productively integrated into queer studies and queer theory.

Given this fraught and contested history, as well as the value that queer theorists place on fluidity, I dare not attempt a single definition of any of the above categories. However, at least a rough distinction must be made to evaluate the ways these areas of study have intersected with the study of religion. For that purpose, I propose the following working definitions, which are intended to congeal the centers of these fluid cat-egories only until the end of this essay. First, for the sake of simplicity, I will assume a chronological continuity between "gay studies," "les-bian/gay studies," "lesbian/gay/bisexual studies," and "LGBT" studies, with the difference being an increasing sensitivity (or at least an increas-ing intent to be sensitive) to sexual and gender diversity over time. As a result, while I will make clear which identities are included in the stud-ies I discuss, I will include older "gay," "lesbian," "lesbian/gay," and "lesbian/gay/bisexual" studies under the rubric of "LGBT." I will fol-low what seems to be the most common, current usage of this term; con-sequently, in the sections that follow, "LGBT studies" refers to scholarly works that attempt to add the experiences of lesbians, gay men, bisexuals, and/or transgender people to existing disciplines or schools of thought.

Secondly, I will use the term "queer theory" to refer to analytical ap-proaches that radically challenge societal norms and assumptions re-garding gender and sexuality. Again here, I attempt to follow current usage as much as possible. The term "queer studies" is also common, but it has been used variously to refer to LGBT studies, to applications of queer theory, or to both. While I agree with Garber (2001) that the two fields are far closer than they may wish to admit, and while I am personally fond of confusing these categories by using "queer studies" as a blanket term, for the sake of this essay I instead frame LGBT stud-ies and queer theory as separate, ideal types.

Religious Studies

Although some would argue that religious studies has its own unique, singular perspective as a field, in the end there is simply too much methodological diversity for this to be true outside of particular departments or conferences. As I will use it here, "religious studies" refers to scholars and scholarly works (some, like some LGBT studies, produced outside the academy but still by those with significant post-graduate academic training) that focus primarily on religion. This includes the work of people trained and employed in religious studies or religion departments; the work of those trained in such departments but employed in the practice of religion; and the work of those trained and perhaps employed in other fields such as sociology, art history, anthropology, history, literature, ethnic studies, women's studies, and the like, whose work focuses on the analysis of religion. Religious studies scholars thus include a wide range of people, from theologians and archaeologists to sociologists and literary critics.

Furthermore, the word "religion" is itself perhaps the most-discussed and least-defined term within religious studies. Despite earlier attempts at imposing a substantive definition on the term, many religionists now tend toward what is often termed a "functional" definition. In effect, this means that the proper objects of religious studies include not only those institutions, texts, traditions, beliefs, and practices that are commonly understood to be religious, but also those that *function similarly* to religion in terms of their ability to confer ultimate meaning and in terms of their centrality in the lives of their followers. This loose definition, which I will follow here, implies that not only are such obvious candidates as Judaism, Buddhism, and indigenous African traditions within the sphere of religious studies, but so too are communism (under certain circumstances; c.f. Lincoln 1989) and the nebulous phenomenon often referred to in the U.S. as "spirituality." This perspective opens interesting avenues for exploring the intersections of LGBT studies, queer theory, and religious studies.

LGBT STUDIES, QUEER THEORY, AND THE STUDY OF RELIGION

Although a few mid-century authors had discussed the intersection of "homosexuality" and religion, a larger body of scholarly works on the issue began to appear in the early 1970s. These were clearly influenced by the rise of LGBT religious organizations, which had begun to appear in the mid-twentieth century (see Comstock, 1996) and had mushroomed in the late 1960s and early 1970s. Scholarly writings in turn, however, also influenced both organizations and individuals. Early sociological studies of MCC (e.g., Bauer, 1976; Enroth & Jamison, 1974), while disturbingly simplistic in their rather pathological representation of "homosexuals," may have served to inform LGBT readers that a "gay church" existed. And as LGBT Christians and Jews struggled to make theological sense of their lives, John J. McNeill's enormously influential book, *The Church and the Homosexual,* appeared in 1976. Responding to the growth in LGBT participation in Catholicism, McNeill's book proved foundational not only for Catholic LGBT theology, but also for Protestant and Jewish reinterpretations of Biblical tradition.

Since these early and interrelated developments, the literature on LGBT issues in religion has grown exponentially (along with LGBT religious organizations). What was a trickle in the 1970s increased through the 1980s, and became a steady stream in the 1990s. In 2003, this trend shows no sign of diminishing, or even of leveling out. For a number of possible reasons (worthy of a study in themselves), the most common type of literature is first-person narrative. Several prominent autobiographies are in this class, written by such figures as Troy Perry, Mel White, Malcolm Boyd, and Chris Glaser (White & White, 2004). Far more common, however, are anthologies of personal reflections; in many cases, these have preceded scholarly studies in any given area or have included the earliest articles along with autobiography (c.f. Beck, 1982; Kolodny, 2000; Leyland, 1998). While these narratives deserve far more study than they have received to date, because this article focuses on secondary works I will not explore them in more depth here. This leaves four general areas of scholarly production within the intersection of LGBT studies, queer theory, and religion: theology and the study of sacred texts, historical studies, comparative approaches, and social scientific studies.

Theology and Sacred Texts

Overall, the goal of LGBT-focused theological and sacred text studies has been to reclaim or create religious traditions for lesbians, gay men, and (only more recently) bisexuals and transgender people. This has taken place through a number of methods, which have varied both over time and across religious traditions. However, the field was founded and has been dominated by Catholic and Protestant writers, whose approaches have also influenced those in other religious traditions.

While the earliest theological works argued for sympathetic treatment (Bailey, 1955; Fosdick, 1943) or limited tolerance of Christian homosexuals (see Comstock, 1996 for an overview), the first phase of concerted theological development by LGBT people can be said to stretch roughly from the publication of McNeill's *The Church and the Homosexual* (1976) to the appearance of Goss' *Jesus Acted Up* (1993). During this period, LGBT Christian theology was marked by a defensive form of theology, or what Goss (2002, p. 241) terms "an apologetic mode." Responding to an increasingly vociferous Christian conservatism that labeled homosexuality flatly sinful or even demonic, these theologians turned to the queer "texts of terror" (as Wilson [1995] terms them: the story of Sodom and Gomorrah, the Levitical injunctions, and so on) or to theological classics such as the Catholic tradition of natural theology to disprove homophobic interpretations of these traditions. Developing both theological sophistication and a certain inter-referentiality, authors such as McNeill, Mollenkott and Scanzoni (1978), Nugent (1983), Gramick and Furey (1988), and Countryman (1988) "fought fire with fire" against the onslaught of Christian homophobia.

In other areas, however, some LGBT people were already working on "constructive" rather than "defensive" forms of religious commentary-works that explored ways to claim or create religious traditions for LGBT people rather than defending LGBT people against the homophobia of existing traditions. Such an approach is implicit in some of the personal stories collected in such volumes as Beck's *Nice Jewish Girls* (1982) and in the autobiographical writings of some Christian theologians (e.g., Perry, 1972; Glaser, 1988). However, it is also evident in the work of lesbian theologians and theologians (a word coined by feminists to reflect their focus on the feminine divine). While feminist religious commentary has also relied on defensive theology, women within the feminist spirituality movement began in the early 1970s to focus on developing new rituals and images of the divine for women, rather than refuting existing, sexist theology, and Christian and Jewish feminists followed on their heels (c.f. Plaskow & Christ, 1979). Given the strong presence of lesbians in the feminist movement, it is unsurprising that lesbian writers (especially Daly, 1973, 1978, 1984; Heyward, 1984) were some of the earliest producers of constructive LGBT theology. Also important for feminists has been a re-working of religious ritual as well as religious thought; this impulse has retained its importance in LGBT religious commentary (possibly especially within Judaism; c.f. Alpert, 1997), but has been underdeveloped to date.

The most recent developments within constructive LGBT theology have been attempts to "queer" Christian theology–not just by making queer Christians visible, but by "spoil[ing]" or "interfer[ing]" with the tradition (Goss 2002, pp. xiv, 228-229). While this approach has met with varying degrees of success, as discussed below, it has come the closest to applying current trends in queer theory to the theological or textual study of religion.

Theologies and studies of sacred texts are extant but few and far between in Buddhism (c.f. Cabezon, 1992; Corless, 2004; and the first section of Leyland, 1998), Hinduism (Pattanaik, 2002; Wilhelm, n.d.), and Islam (al-Hajj Kugle, 2003; a few articles in Murray & Roscoe, 1997), but the fact that these areas are being explored at all holds great promise for broadening LGBT studies of sacred texts and traditions. As with theology and textual studies in Christianity and Judaism, the few works on Hinduism, Buddhism, and Islam are generally written by practitioners of those traditions and employ both defensive and constructive approaches. However, there is some indication, logically enough, that defensive approaches are more attractive when the author's religious context is explicitly homophobic and bases that homophobia in theological or textual arguments. Thus, at this point it appears that among these three religions, Muslims are more likely to argue *against* a basis for homophobia in Islam, while Hindus and Buddhists have expended more effort in arguing *for* the presence of homoeroticism and gender crossing in their traditions.

Historical Studies

In general, LGBT religious history has focused on excavating evidence of homoeroticism and gender-crossing in traditional religions to argue for the acceptance of LGBT people in contemporary religious groups. The groundbreaking scholar in this area was John Boswell, whose *Christianity, Social Tolerance, and Homosexuality* (1980) and *Same-Sex Unions in Premodern Europe* (1994) were both controversial and widely read. In the first book, Boswell argues that, contrary to Catholic and Protestant claims today, Western Christian attitudes toward homoeroticism have fluctuated considerably over the course of Christian history. In the second book, he claims to have unearthed a series of medieval rituals from both the Eastern and Western branches of Christianity that celebrated the union of two men or two women. Despite the controversy surrounding them, both books have served as an important base for claiming the right of gays and lesbians to full participation in the Christian tradition.

Much of Boswell's work focused on male homoeroticism and occasionally on male cross-dressing. In part this was from necessity, because of the dearth of texts on women's homoerotic activities or cross-dressing. However, in the mid-1980s and 1990s a few women scholars began to fill in some of these gaps by researching the lives of nuns who had "special friendships" or were particularly close to other women (e.g., Brooten, 1996; Brown, 1986; Matter, 1986). And in recent years, some of the most significant developments in LGBT Catholic history have come from Mark Jordan, whose *The Silence of Sodom* (2000; see also Jordan 1997, 2003) combines historical, theological, literary, and cultural-critical approaches to present a searing and insightful analysis of male homosexuality in the Church today.

While it is clearly in the context of Catholicism that historical studies of LGBT people in traditional religions have been most developed, in other religious contexts theological works have often delved into history, tradition, and culture as well as sacred text (e.g., Alpert, 1997). Daniel Boyarin's queer, feminist reinterpretations of the Talmudic tradition in Judaism (c.f. Boyarin, 1997) emphasize gender roles, but in so doing they also challenge traditional understandings of male homoeroticism in the Talmud. A few scholars have also unearthed evidence of homoeroticism in particular regions and historical periods in Buddhism (c.f. Ihara, 1990; Jackson, 1998) and Islam (Murray & Roscoe, 1997); again, in part because of limitations in the primary source material, this work is predominantly male-focused.

Increasingly, historical studies of gender systems in pre-colonial Native American cultures have been important sources of affirmation and identity for the Gay American Indian and Two-Spirit movements. Most important in these cases are the living sources of history: elders. In addition, some Native and white scholars, often combining interviews with critical readings of early anthropological texts, have outlined the structures of several of these quite varied systems (c.f. Jacobs, Thomas, & Lang, 1997). More than anything else, the growing breadth of historical work in LGBT religious studies is emphasizing that, just as in secular histories, religious understandings of gender-crossing, gender multiplicity, and homoeroticism are highly varied across religions, regions, and historical periods. In light of such historical work, it has become more difficult for either queer activists or anti-queer religious groups to claim that homophobia, biphobia, and transphobia are intrinsic and "natural" to any given religious tradition.

The newest histories to be written are those of LGBT religious movements themselves. With the growth of queer religious organizations beginning nearly a year before Stonewall, these histories are not only timely but critical, as they can serve to question our understanding of LGBT history as a whole in the twentieth century. Such histories are rare as yet, however (but see Gill, 1998; Wilcox, 2001), although at least two book-length histories are in process and an online database has been founded to encourage further work (the Lesbian, Gay, Bisexual, and Transgender Religious Archives Network, or LGBT-RAN, housed at the Chicago Theological Seminary). A great deal more work is needed in this area, especially in oral history as some of the founders and early leaders of these movements approach their later years.

Comparative Collections

Aside from the theological enterprises mentioned above, there have been no single-author attempts at broadly comparative studies of religious approaches to homoeroticism or gender-crossing. This may be for the best, as on the one hand religion scholars have increasingly recognized the difficulty of conducting nuanced, accurate, and responsible comparative studies, while on the other hand LGBT studies and especially queer theorists have emphasized the challenges of cross-cultural and transhistorical studies of sexuality and gender. This is not to say that studies of this sort could not be useful, but rather that the scholar undertaking such work would need to be meticulously precise in order to avoid the twin pitfalls associated with the cross-cultural comparison of two socially constructed sets of categories.

In the meantime, two useful sources exist for those who wish to undertake limited comparison on their own. The first is a collection of official religious statements (mostly Christian) on "homosexuals," "homosexuality," or occasionally "gays, lesbians, and bisexuals," primarily from the 1970s and 1980s (Melton, 1991). Though extremely useful, Melton's work is in dire need of a supplement that covers changes in the 1990s and the early twenty-first century. The second collection, also not updated since its 1993 publication, is Arlene Swidler's *Homosexuality and World Religions*. Each chapter of this volume covers a major world tradition or set of traditions, and is authored by a scholar whose work focuses on that tradition (though not always on LGBT issues); the chapters are not analytical but rather seek simply to detail general attitudes toward homoeroticism and gender-crossing in each religion or group of religions. While the book's "world religions" paradigm becomes somewhat awkward in the chapter on "traditional religions of the Americas and Africa" (over-generalized to say the least), it serves as a useful overview source in the absence of other resources.

Although both editors and all of Swidler's authors appear to be supportive of LGBT people, more often than not these two books focus on official and thus non- (or closeted) LGBT opinions of LGBT people in the tradition. Useful as such information may be, it may also perpetuate the silencing of religious LGBT people in favor of the pronouncements of heterosexuals and the mono-gendered. Perhaps the time is not yet ripe for a collection that focuses solely on LGBT, homoerotic, cross-gender, and Two-Spirit activism within world religions, but such a collection should be an important goal for the future.

Social Scientific Studies

Despite their frequent tendency to accord only passing attention to religion, the social sciences have in fact been quite productive on the topic of religion and LGBT studies. Most notable in this area is anthropology, which was perhaps the earliest field to take homoeroticism seriously and to acknowledge the global diversity of homoerotic practices and definitions of gender. That LGBT studies in religion have not sufficiently incorporated this work is most probably due to the typical focus of anthropology on small-scale, traditional societies. Because religion is not a distinct social institution in many of these societies, and because of the "whole-culture" approach that is typical of at least classical anthropology, studies involving homoeroticism and gender-crossing rarely focus on religion. However, it would be fruitful for scholars to seek in these works the possible intersections between religious beliefs and practices, homoeroticism, and gender-crossing. One potential source for such an undertaking is Blackwood and Wieringa's edited volume, *Female Desires* (1999).

There are three important exceptions to anthropology's lack of focus on religion and LGBT issues: all are studies of LGBT congregations in the United States. The earliest, and still to date the best planned, was well ahead of its time and sadly remains as an unpublished dissertation; it compares an MCC congregation, a Dignity chapter, and a synagogue in "Lake City" (Gorman, 1980). Leonard Norman Primiano's *Intrinsically Catholic* (1993a), a dissertation on Philadelphia's Dignity chapter, also has remained unpublished to date, but Primiano has published articles based on the study (Primiano, 1993b, 1995). However, the first book-length study of an LGBT congregation to reach publication is

Moshe Shokeid's admirable *A Gay Synagogue in New York* (1995). Since none of these works cites any of the others, it is particularly significant that despite the diversity of the groups under study all three authors come to similar conclusions. Each of these five congregations (and the anthropologists studying them) bemoaned and puzzled over the dearth of women attendees; the mostly gay men who did take part in these groups came in search of a community with which to worship and a space in which to continue the integration of their sexual and religious identities. Almost all had begun this integration individually, but had eventually become comfortable with the idea of attending a "gay group," and had approached the religious organization most suited to their upbringing and current beliefs. These general trends have been both supported and expanded upon by the sociological studies discussed below.

Within the psychology of religion there has been a smattering of articles on LGBT issues over the past few decades (most recently Mahaffy, 1996; Rodriguez & Ouellette, 2000). Most of these have been concerned with identity negotiation and internalized oppression. Interestingly, religion in general has not been shown to have a simple connection to internalized oppression, and even attendance at LGBT-specific religious organizations does not seem to result automatically in differing levels of self-esteem from those who attend other religious organizations or who do not attend at all. Mahaffy, a sociologist whose predominantly psychological study and analysis are the most complex of the recent works, notes a distinction between lesbian Christians who came out later than they became Christian, and those who became Christian after coming out. While she finds that membership in a conservative Christian organization strongly predicts some level of internal dissonance between lesbian and Christian identities, Mahaffy argues that strategies for resolving that dissonance vary depending on the strength of lesbian identity, the strength of Christian identity, and the level of integration between the two.

The sociology of religion has seen greater development in LGBT studies than has the psychology of religion, but it has been aided in part by the growing rapprochement between fieldwork-oriented sociologists and anthropologists. In fact, a new anthology of ethnographic studies on LGBT religiosity (Thumma & Gray, 2004) includes scholars from anthropology, sociology, and religious studies, whose work and findings differ far more by topic than by discipline.

Sociological approaches to LGBT issues have come from several different angles. Because the so-called "homosexuality debates" in main-line Protestant churches have sometimes been compared to the debates over slavery that split many denominations in the nineteenth century, organizational sociologists have shown a great deal of interest in analyzing denominational responses to these tensions. Most of this work, however, has focused on the coping strategies, adaptive strategies, and debates of heterosexuals and heterosexual denominations; while they provide significant sources for a queer discursive analysis, such interpretive work has not yet been conducted.

As in anthropology, one of the most productive, albeit insufficiently developed, approaches is the sociological study of LGBT people themselves as they express, battle, build, and sustain their religious beliefs, practices, identities, and institutions. Aside from a few early and fairly problematic studies of the Metropolitan Community Church (Bauer, 1976; Enroth & Jamison, 1974), the sociology of religion generally ignored LGBT religiosities until the early 1990s. Three recent studies, however, examine LGBT organizations that are based in fairly standard versions of Christianity–a local support group for lesbian and gay evangelical Christians (Thumma, 1991), and the Metropolitan Community Churches (Warner, 1995; Wilcox, 2003)–and come to conclusions that agree closely with anthropological findings regarding both the functions and the gendered nature of such groups. Another short study, conducted by Gray and Thumma (1997), opens an interesting door to queer analysis with its presentation of "The Gospel Hour," a gospel-music drag show in Atlanta that customers often regarded as an alternative religious service.

Easily the most influential sociologist of LGBT religions is Gary David Comstock, whose 1996 study of lesbians, gay men, and bisexuals in the United Methodist Church and the United Church of Christ was unprecedented and remains unparalleled. In addition to producing a thorough and detailed analysis of the experiences of LGB laypeople and religious leaders within these two denominations, Comstock provides an exhaustive overview of social scientific research on LGBT religious experiences through 1994. Second only to Comstock in productivity is British sociologist Andrew K. T. Yip, who has been publishing prolifically in this area since the mid-1990s (e.g., 1997, 2002). In addition to his earlier work on gay male Christian couples, Yip has recently been studying bisexual Christians and lesbian, gay, and bisexual Muslims in the U.K.

Recently, two studies (Comstock, 2001; Shallenberger, 1998) have followed the lead of both anthropologists and sociologists in reconsidering the position of the researcher. In an attempt to limit their own mediation of their research participants' voices, these two scholars simply published transcripts of their interviews, keeping their own commentary to a minimum. While both authors are to be lauded for thinking critically about their own locations as white, male researchers, they unfortunately fail to take into account the fact that their own questions, projects, presence, and occasional editing (especially in Shallenberger) affect their supposedly "raw" data just as much as overt analysis might do. While both projects have moved the sociology of LGBT religion forward in important ways–Shallenberger's by studying LGBT people outside of religious organizations and Comstock's by focusing on African American religious leaders–their lack of analysis and commentary severely lessens the impact of what could have been extremely important works.

A final approach, that of cultural studies, defies classification within a traditional discipline; I have included it under the social sciences only because it fits within this category better than in any of the others. Two works are especially worth mentioning here. The first, Didi Herman's *The Anti-Gay Agenda* (1997), is an in-depth analysis of the late twentieth-century discourse surrounding "homosexuality" in the *Christian Century*, a slightly-right-of-center news periodical. Tracing a growing focus on the "demonic" through the early 1990s, Herman notes that by the mid-1990s the editors had once again tempered their rhetoric, turning like much of conservative Christianity to gentler (and perhaps more insidious) language of "acceptance" and healing. Jakobsen and Pellegrini pick up on this same language in *Love the Sin* (2003), critiquing both the blatant influence of Christianity in U.S. politics and law, and the rhetoric of tolerance that pervades public discussion of not only sexuality but also of racial and religious "difference" from the white, Christian, heterosexual "norm."

ANALYSIS:
LGBT STUDIES AND RELIGION

In the three decades of its existence, LGBT studies in religion has made impressive progress. There is, however, a great deal more work to be done if this "proto-field" is to become the vibrant enterprise it has the potential to be. Currently, the two most pressing needs are conversation and diversification.

Bibliographies and textual references in many of the works discussed above reveal that the authors are generally aware of, and familiar with, each other's writing. However, it is equally clear that these scholars are not, for the most part, in sustained conversation with each other. That is, they read each other's works and refer to them in their own writings, but each is working, to a certain extent, in isolation. To be sure, there are opportunities for scholars of LGBT religion to meet. A handful of small conferences have been held in recent years; the Center for Lesbian and Gay Studies in Religion and Ministry in Berkeley offers increasing opportunities for conversation; and the American Academy of Religion includes both a Lesbian Feminist Issues in Religion group and a Gay Men's Issues in Religion group, each of which holds several individual sessions and occasionally joint sessions at the AAR's annual meeting. However, the interdisciplinarity of religious studies, and the fact that many scholars work on LGBT issues in passing rather than as a central focus, mean that although such scholars may have met and conversed with each other, they do not meet regularly enough to undertake a sustained conversation about these issues. The result is that while there have been a number of advances in the field, they appear for the most part as isolated fragments with little attempt made to compare findings or develop comparative or theoretical perspectives.

Another symptom of the lack of conversation is the ongoing binary divide of both gender and sexual orientation that appears in conferences and in publishing. This is not to say that male and female scholars do not communicate, collaborate, read each other's work, or attend each other's sessions, because they do all of these things. However, it is worth asking what sort of collaboration (and what sort of understanding of gender and sexuality) is facilitated by the separate existence of groups for gay men's studies and lesbian women's studies in religion? In addition to enforcing a clearly dualistic notion of gender, these two groups nominally exclude bisexuals and transgender people. Again, this is not to say that bisexual and transgender scholars have not presented papers at these sessions, or that studies addressing bisexual and/or transgender issues have not been conducted under these rubrics. But bringing all of these groups into serious and sustained conversation–and creating a location that encourages and facilitates such participation–is critical to the future of LGBT religious studies, not to mention the development of queer approaches to the study of religion.

These multiple forms of exclusion and division echo in past and recent works, as well–though less so among those scholars (mostly the social scientists) who rarely attend AAR meetings. While the work of such social scientists may suffer from the lack of conversation with their religious studies counterparts, the work of religious studies scholars clearly suffers from over a decade of official gender separatism. Rebecca Alpert's masterful work in Jewish theology, for instance, specifically presents itself as centering on Jewish lesbians, offering a few references to Jewish gay men, bisexuals, and transgender people, but basically leaving them to do their own theological work. Likewise, Alpert, Elwell, and Edelson's recently published collection of rabbinical autobiographies is entitled *Lesbian Rabbis* (2001). The exclusion of bisexual women in this volume was apparently inevitable, as the editors note that they attempted to recruit such rabbis but were unable to convince anyone to submit an article. However, the book's editors also note that there are a small handful of openly gay (male) rabbis, yet their volume does not include these men's stories.

I want to emphasize here that I do believe there are good reasons in some cases for studying men and women separately, but I find interesting and somewhat troubling the extent to which this separation currently occurs. Two examples from the opposite side of the gender divide are the recent *Queer Dharma* collections (Leyland, 1998, 2000) and Mark Jordan's superb study, *The Silence of Sodom* (2000), which is unfortunately subtitled *Homosexuality in Modern Catholicism* despite the fact that it explicitly disavows any effort to discuss women's experiences. Leyland's decision to include only gay men, as he explains in the introduction to the first volume of this massive collection (see 1998, p. 9), was based on the fact that his Gay Sunshine Press has historically focused on publishing works about, by, and for gay men. This, I think, is far less defensible than Jordan's reasonable explanation that in a gender-separated religion (he is writing about ordained Catholics) one must expect the experiences of men and women to be radically different. I am troubled, however, by the repeated insistence in such gender-focused (and monosexual, and mono-gendered) works that those who have been left out will eventually come along and write their own works. In an academy that is unremittingly white- and male-dominated and heterosexist, and in a field in which publishing even one LGBT-focused article can threaten one's career, it is naïve at best and grossly irresponsible at worst to blithely assume that "some other scholar" will pick up all the pieces one has disdained to touch. Only one author (Yip, a sociologist) has yet focused on the experiences of bisexuals, and only in the past few years did any work focus on transgender people (Mollenkott, 2001; Sheridan, 2001; Tanis, 2003). Why do gay and lesbian scholars expect that the people we have excluded and ignored will want to join us, and why do we presume they *could*, if they did so choose?

Equally glaring, and irresponsible for many of the same reasons, is the virtually complete exclusion of people of color and of disability issues from these works. Like queer theory and LGBT studies more broadly, LGBT studies in religion is almost completely white-dominated and heavily ethnocentric; published studies also ignore differences in ability and are often forthrightly ableist. Even if a sustained conversation should begin to coalesce around LGBT issues in religion, it will be incomplete and inconclusive without serious consideration of the intersectionality of not only sexuality and gender, but race, class, ability, nationality, postcoloniality, and other factors in our interactions with religion. It will also be glaringly incomplete without the active participation of LGBT people of color, working class people, people with disabilities, and third-world people. Without that kind of participation, gay and lesbian scholars of religion make a mockery of our own demands for inclusion.

Much of the reluctance to study "outside one's own identity" stems, I suspect, from debates over standpoint theory in the early 1990s. Since religious studies tends, on average, to lag about a decade behind the forerunners of academic innovation, it would be logical for the field to be grappling with an issue that feminist and queer studies addressed about ten years ago. Both Jordan (2000) and Comstock (2001), for instance, express great reluctance to analyze or even write about the experience of Others. In Jordan's case it is a gendered Other–Catholic women–and he chooses to focus his work on those whose identities are (apparently) closer to his. Comstock, however, takes heart from Audre Lorde's admonition not to "hide behind the mockeries of separations that have been imposed upon us" (Lorde, 1984, pp. 43-44; see Comstock, 2001, p. 5). Though he does not go so far as to analyze or even comment at any length upon the interviews in his book, Comstock has at least recognized that focusing on those who are "like us" (in itself a highly problematic assumption) only serves to further the ethnocentrism, sexism, ableism, neocolonialism, and other oppressions of the academy. Those of us who benefit from the social power dynamics of academia need to battle such inequities, not by refusing to discuss the experiences of "Others," but by learning from their experiences and from scholars who write about them, by designing our own studies to look beyond sexual orientation, and by discussing sensitively and with great critical caution those experiences with which we are unfamiliar. I offer this critique not as an accomplished practitioner of radical inclusivity, but as someone who struggles with such issues.

Perfection is out of reach for most of us, but I do believe that it is our responsibility to struggle.

QUEER THEORY AND RELIGION

Current Research: Queer Theory in Religion?

At this point, it is probably clear that I see little of the radical promise of queer theory in the current study of LGBT issues in religion. Then again, some contemporary commentators (and even some early ones; c.f. de Lauretis 1994, p. 297) argue that there is little of that promise in contemporary queer theory, either. However, an increasing number of books in LGBT religious studies have claimed the term queer, and a few of them point to the exciting potential of combining queer theory with religion.

To begin with those that claim the term "queer": in many ways, books such as *Queer Dharma* (Leyland, 1998, 2000), *Queer Jews* (Shneer & Aviv, 2002), *Religion is a Queer Thing* (Stuart, Braunston, Edwards, McMahon, & Morrison, 1997), and *Que(e)rying Religion* (Comstock & Henking, 1997) confirm the anxiety of queer theorists that their radical and amorphously complex term will be/is being appropriated by 'the masses' and stripped of its complex (though generally undefined) meanings. *Queer Dharma* and *Queer Jews* are anthologies composed mostly of personal narratives. Despite its apparently broad title, Stuart's volume is a multi-author work of Christian theology, and Comstock and Henking's book is a reader of previously published works in gay, lesbian, and transgender studies in religion. Only Stuart spends any significant time discussing or defining the word "queer"; the other three make no mention of queer theory and either assume or explicitly state that "queer" means simply lesbian, gay, bisexual, transgender, and transsexual. Whether or not this is a useful application of the term is, I think, open to debate. More problematic, however, are Leyland's volumes, which use the word "queer" for books that are solely about gay men.

Interestingly, it is only in Christian theology and in Jewish cultural studies that scholars have seriously taken up the question of interactions between queer theory and the study of religion. For many Christian theologians, it seems that queer theory is a mixed blessing. In her introduction to *Religion is a Queer Thing*, for example, Stuart offers a one-paragraph summary of queer theory and then explains its application to Christian theology:

> Recognition of difference in solidarity is central to queer theology. It acknowledges that black, white, disabled, poor, rich, male, female, and transgendered queers are oppressed in very different ways and that some of us are involved in the oppression of our fellow queers. (Stuart et al., 1997, p. 3)

She hastens to add, however, that "this is not to say that anything goes" (Stuart et al., 1997, p. 4). Kathy Rudy agrees, asserting that "although queer theory is a tool for helping us realize the constructed nature of sexual preference and gender identity as well as for helping us move beyond these identifications, it offers us little insight for ethics" (Rudy, 1997, p. 123). She demonstrates her point by quoting Gayle Rubin (!) at length, and summarizes: "In essence, queers hope to make a place for alternative sexual expression that is completely free of the confining strictures of ethics. . . . The agenda they advocate is–on this point– irreconcilable with the Christian tradition" (Rudy, 1997, p. 124). On the other hand, Goss' *Queering Christ* (2002) and Marcella Althaus-Reid's *The Queer God* (2003) may herald a real queering of Christian theology. Althaus-Reid's work, though dense, is especially notable for its efforts to bring queer, feminist, and Latin American liberation theologies into intimate conversation. Interestingly, though, even as queer Christian theologians begin to push the boundaries and borders of Christian inclusion, religious diversity is rarely part of the discussion.

Yet I hardly wish to argue that religious studies and queer theory are irrelevant to each other. Four works from the past decade demonstrate the immense (if insufficiently realized) potential of this combination. The first, in fact, dates from the early years of queer theory itself. In *God's Phallus and Other Problems for Men and Monotheism* (1994), Howard Eilberg-Schwartz asks a deceptively simple question: why does Judaism forbid divine imagery? Noting that the few sightings of God recorded in the Bible make a point of shielding the divine genitals from human observation, he points to a critical tension created by three aspects of ancient Israelite society. Given the understanding of Israel as the bride of God, and the culture's apparent aversion to male homoeroticism, Israelite priests were in a very awkward position as the male representatives of God's "bride." To lessen the homoerotic implications of their relationship with God, Eilberg-Schwartz argues, they studiously avoided any reflection on the body of God.

Also taking what could be identified as a queer approach to Jewish history is Daniel Boyarin's *Unheroic Conduct* (1997). Exploring, as the subtitle indicates, "heterosexuality and the invention of the Jewish man," Boyarin analyzes Jewish understandings of gender in nineteenth-century Europe. He begins with traditional, Eastern European Jewish culture and the religious texts that influenced it; in the second half of the book his analysis shifts to consider the anxieties around gender and identity that were created by Jewish assimilation into mainstream European cultures. Engaging and innovative, Boyarin's book is one of the few works in the growing field of gender studies in Judaism that treats gender and sexuality as intertwined phenomena. (Incidentally, Boyarin is also one of the editors of a new anthology of explicitly queer analyses of Judaism and anti-Semitism [Boyarin, Iskovitz, & Pellegrini, 2003]. If this anthology is any indication of the direction in which queer theory and religion are traveling together, the future of the field is bright indeed.)

Mark Jordan's *The Silence of Sodom* (2000) offers a similarly nuanced and very queer reading of religious tradition in his exploration of male homosexuality in contemporary Catholicism. In addition to the obvious topics–gay Catholics and Vatican edicts–Jordan considers the cultural aspects of Catholicism, asking why gay men are drawn to the faith, why they stay, and what ramifications the presence of so many closeted gay men might have in a homophobic institution. Two of his proposals are particularly captivating. First, Jordan argues that "clerical culture" (the culture of ordained Catholic men) exhibits stunning similarities to "mainstream" (white, Western, middle-class) gay male culture. Second, in a chapter subtitled "the pleasures of obedience," Jordan suggests that gay men stay within the clerical closet because of the "pleasures" of submission to one's elders as a young priest and domination of one's juniors in the latter years of one's career. "Who can be astonished, then," he asks rhetorically, "that sexually active gay clerics and ex-clerics seem so often to prefer the leather or S&M 'subcultures'? Nor is it shocking," he adds, "that priestly cassocks or monastic robes figure so prominently in some S&M rituals" (Jordan, 2000, p. 218). While Jordan, Boyarin, and Eilberg-Schwartz do not refer extensively to queer theory, perhaps pointing out what has been hidden in plain sight within institutions that lay claim to homophobic moral authority is the queerest way of all to approach religion.

Finally, there is reason to see Jakobsen and Pellegrini's recent work, *Love the Sin* (2003), as an application of queer theory to the study of religion. Though, like the other authors discussed in this section, they rarely reference queer theorists directly, Jakobsen and Pellegrini offer an insightful and important analysis of the roles played by normalizing discourses and discourses of difference in contemporary U.S. politics. Arguing ultimately that "the tolerance of love the sinner, hate the sin is antidemocratic (Jakobsen & Pellegrini, 2003, p. 149), they offer analytical tools for logically dismantling the insidious rhetoric of "tolerance" that reinforces the Othering of queers, ethnic minorities, and other non-dominant groups, closing by advocating instead a radical democracy that values difference and contestation rather than "coercive homogeneity" (p. 149).

These texts offer hope that queer theory can indeed contribute to the study of religion. Does religious studies really need queer theory, though? If queer theory is what its detractors describe—androcentric, ethnocentric, anti-ethical, classist, inaccessible, ignorant of disability theory, Western, and even neocolonial—then religious studies should have nothing to do with it, having its own work to do in those areas. However, as de Lauretis first envisioned it, queer theory has the potential to be far more. With its radical focus on difference and on subverting the "normative," queer theory by definition has the responsibility to question deeply the social power accorded to members of dominant groups—including queer theorists, who have in fact been, to date, predominantly white and middle or upper class, often male, and university-employed (even though that employment has been tenuous for some). If queer theorists have been failing to ask such questions, perhaps instead of giving up on queer theory those left out should be holding such theorists' feet to a queerer flame. In this respect, it is encouraging that some of the authors in Hawley's two volumes (2001a, 2001b) on the intersections of postcolonial and queer theory do in fact claim "queer" for themselves, although it is also understandable that others forcefully reject the term.

What would it mean to "queer" the study of religion, beyond the "add queers and stir" formula that has most frequently been applied to date? It would mean paying close attention to the dynamics of gender and sexuality that religions hide in plain sight, and it would mean examining the roles of religion in both inscribing and challenging heteronormativity and dualistic conceptions of gender. It might also mean queering our concept of what is religious and queering even our methodology—and in this way, queer scholars in religion hold radical potential for change. Both religious studies and queer theory revel (at least theoretically) in their ability to break down methodological and disciplinary boundaries. But do they really do this? Many queer theorists are literary critics; the

American Academy of Religion pigeonholes social science into one session, history into another, literature into a third. But LGBT studies in religion is far too small to fragment in that way; perhaps we can use our methodological diversity to encourage a kind of methodological hybridity. Queering the study of religion thus has the potential to alter religious studies itself.

Future Research: Religion in Queer Theory?

What about the reverse–can the study of religion be of any use to queer theory? Can scholars of religion be queer outlaws too, or only nagging, lesbian and gay in-laws? I suggest that queer theorists would benefit in two ways from greater attention to the study of religion: the first in terms of analytical scope, and the second in terms of methodology.

Upon reflection, it appears quite surprising that queer theory has virtually ignored religion. Indeed, perhaps religious discourse is the secret that queer theory has hidden (in plain sight) from itself. As Jordan has shown (1997), religious discourse played a formative role in the development of the nineteenth-century Western category of the "homosexual." Religion continues to play such roles, and is a powerful force in the creation and perpetuation of hegemonic orders. Thus, even if it were simply an important locus of power and heteronormativity, religion would deserve the attention of queer theorists. However, queer theory must also contend with the important, *positive* roles that religion plays for contemporary LGBT people, and the grassroots sort of queering that religious LGBT people perform on a daily basis. What are the implications, for instance, of a shift from reading Jesus as the son of a divinely-inseminated virgin to reading him as a loving and erotic figure, displayed temptingly in almost full nakedness (and perhaps as a bottom) to the queer, male-attracted (top?) Catholic? Or, as Pattanaik implies in his introduction (2002), we might consider what the ramifications would be of refusing to read gender-crossing and same-sex eroticism in Hindu sacred stories as metaphorical and unrelated to human identities. If queer theory is defined in part by radical inclusivity, then perhaps to include religious queers would be to *queer* queer theory itself.

Furthermore, there is much food for thought in the use of religious symbols in queer cultures. To take but one example: what are we to make of the Sisters of Perpetual Indulgence, groups made up mostly of gay men who appear at benefits, in Pride parades, and in performance art wearing wimples, whiteface, and drag? The Sisters' heretical adoption of Catholic monastic practices goes far beyond the wimple; not only does one take on a formal name upon taking full vows, but an aspiring member must undergo a period of observance, a postulancy, and a novitiate. Surely there is more here than an elaborate mockery of the Catholic church, especially given that, as my own forthcoming research indicates, some Sisters may see their involvement in the organization as a form of spiritual (though probably not Catholic) practice. Unpacking these dynamics in a fully nuanced manner will require the tools of both queer theory and religious studies, and there are other phenomena as well that would benefit from a similar approach.

Also worth noting, especially for those with an interest in literature, narrative, and the cultural inscription of identity, is the curious structural parallel between the standard "coming-out" narrative and the historic and prevalent "conversion narrative" in Christianity. While one analyst has noticed this connection (Cuthbertson, 1996), the topic has yet to be explored in the depth it deserves.

Finally, the field of religious studies has a great deal to offer queer theory in terms of methodology. Perhaps most relevant here is religious studies' understanding of the power of sacred narrative. History of religions scholar Bruce Lincoln (1989) points to a number of ways in which myth, ritual, and classification–all important aspects of religion–can serve to construct, maintain, and deconstruct the social order. Religion, as liberation theologians have known all along, is an important source of both hegemony and counter-hegemony; it is a major conduit of power that offers numerous sites of resistance as well as oppression.

Along these activist lines, it is also interesting to note that the sociology of religion has been interested recently in the construction of religious identities, especially those outside the bounds of the "normative" (c.f. Dufour, 2000). Increasingly, it seems, religious identities are becoming sites of negotiation, fragmentation, and intentional construction. Dufour calls such construction "sifting," explaining that the Jewish feminists in her study maintained their ties to both Judaism and feminism by "sifting out" those aspects of Jewish tradition that were not in accord with their feminist beliefs. Such findings offer an interesting perspective on queer theory's puzzle over the tension between the theoretical force of constructivist theory and the ongoing insistence of the more mainstream activists on essentialism. Non-Christian religious groups are able to agitate for their rights without taking an essentialist perspective on their religious identities; perhaps it would be fruitful for queer theorists to ponder how the acceptance of the constructed nature of religious identities could be applied to new, queer activist strategies.

Indeed, at least two analysts of religion (Hammond, 1998; Jakobsen & Pellegrini, 2003) have already suggested that the relationship between freedom of religion and sexual freedom in the United States may be much closer than is generally thought. Far from being in-laws, then, it just may turn out that LGBT studies, queer theory, and religious studies have the potential to be valuable partners in the land of academic outlaws.

REFERENCES

Al-Haqq Kugle, S. S. (2003). Sexuality, diversity, and ethics in the agenda of progressive Muslims. In O. Safi (Ed.), *Progressive Muslims: On justice, gender, and pluralism* (pp. 190-234). Oxford: Oneworld.

Alpert, R. (1997). *Like bread on the seder plate: Jewish lesbians and the transformation of tradition.* New York: Columbia University Press.

Alpert, R. T., Elwell, S. L., & Edelson, S. (Eds.). (2001). *Lesbian rabbis: The first generation.* New Brunswick: Rutgers University Press.

Althaus-Reid, M. (2003). *The queer God.* New York: Routledge.

Bailey, D. S. (1955). *Homosexuality and the Western Christian tradition.* London: Longmans, Green.

Bauer, P. F. (1976). The homosexual subculture at worship: A participant observation study. *Pastoral Psychology, 25,* 115-127.

Beck, E. T. (Ed.). (1982). *Nice Jewish girls: A lesbian anthology.* Trumansburg, NY: Crossing Press.

Blackwood, E., & Wieringa, S. E. (Eds.). (1999). *Female desires: Same-sex relations and transgender practices across cultures.* New York: Columbia University Press.

Boswell, J. (1980). *Christianity, social tolerance, and homosexuality: Gay people in Western Europe from the beginnings of Christianity to the 14th century.* Chicago: University of Chicago Press.

Boswell, J. (1994). *Same-sex unions in premodern Europe.* New York: Villard.

Boyarin, D. (1997). *Unheroic conduct: The rise of heterosexuality and the invention of the Jewish man.* Berkeley: University of California Press.

Boyarin, D., Iskovitz, D., & Pellegrini, A. (2003). *Queer theory and the Jewish question.* New York: Columbia University Press.

Brooten, B. J. (1996). *Love between women: Early Christian responses to female homoeroticism.* Chicago: University of Chicago Press.

Brown, J. C. (1986). *Immodest acts: The life of a lesbian nun in Renaissance Italy.* New York: Oxford University Press.

Budapest, Z. (1976). *The feminist book of lights and shadows.* Venice, CA: Luna Publications.

Cabezón, J. I. (Ed.). (1992). *Buddhism, sexuality, and gender.* Albany: SUNY Press.

Comstock, G. D. (1996). *Unrepentant, self-affirming, practicing: Lesbian/gay/bisexual people within organized religion.* New York: Continuum.

Comstock, G. D. (2001). *A whosoever church: Welcoming lesbians and gay men into African American congregations.* Louisville: Westminster John Knox Press.

Comstock, G. D., & Henking, S. E. (Eds.). (1997). *Que(e)rying religion: A critical anthology.* New York: Continuum.

Conner, R. P. (1993). *Blossom of bone: Reclaiming the connections between homoeroticism and the sacred.* San Francisco: HarperSanFrancisco.

Corless, R. (2004). Towards a queer dharmology of sex. *Culture and Religion, 5*(2), 229-243.

Countryman, L. W. (1988). *Dirt, greed, and sex: Sexual ethics in the New Testament and their implications for today.* Philadelphia: Fortress.

Cuthbertson, K. L. (1996). Coming out/conversion: An exploration of gay religious experience. *Journal of Men's Studies, 4*(3), 193-207.

Daly, M. (1973). *Beyond God the father: Toward a philosophy of liberation.* Boston: Beacon Press.

Daly, M. (1978). *Gyn/ecology: The metaethics of radical feminism.* Boston: Beacon Press.

Daly, M. (1984). *Pure lust: Elemental feminist philosophy.* Boston: Beacon Press.

de Lauretis, T. (1991). Queer theory: Lesbian and gay sexualities: An introduction. *Differences, 3*(2), iii-xvii.

de Lauretis, T. (1994). *The practice of love: Lesbian sexuality and perverse desire.* Bloomington: Indiana University Press.

Dufour, L. R. (2000). Sifting through tradition: The creation of Jewish feminist identities.*Journal for the Scientific Study of Religion, 39*(1), 90-106.

Eilberg-Schwartz, H. (1994). *God's phallus and other problems for men and monotheism.* Boston: Beacon Press.

Enroth, R. M., & Jamison, G. E. (1974). *The gay church.* Grand Rapids, MI: Eerdmans.

Fosdick, H. E. (1943). *On being a real person.* New York: Harper and Brothers.

Garber, L. (2001). *Identity poetics: Race, class, and the lesbian-feminist roots of queer theory.* New York: Columbia University Press.

Gill, S. (Ed.). (1998). *The lesbian and gay Christian movement: Campaigning for justice, truth, and love.* London: Cassell.

Glaser, C. (1988). *Uncommon calling: A gay man's struggle to serve the church.* Louisville, KY: Westminster John Knox.

Gorman, E. M. (1980). *A new light on Zion: A study of three homosexual religious congregations in urban America.* Ph.D. diss., University of Chicago.

Goss, R. E. (1993). *Jesus acted up: A gay and lesbian manifesto.* San Francisco: HarperSanFrancisco.

Goss, R. E. (2002). *Queering Christ: Beyond Jesus acted up.* Cleveland: Pilgrim Press.

Gramick, J., & Furey, P. (Eds.). (1988). *The Vatican and homosexuality.* New York: Crossroad.

Gray, E. R., & Thumma, S. L. The gospel hour: Liminality, identity, and religion in a gay bar. In P. E. Becker, & N. L. Eiesland (1997) (Eds.), *Contemporary American religion: An ethnographic reader* (pp. 79-98). Walnut Creek, CA: Alta Mira.

Hammond, P. E. (1998). *With liberty for all: Freedom of religion in the United States.* Louisville, KY: Westminster John Knox Press.

Hawley, J. C. (Ed.). (2001a). *Postcolonial and queer theories: Intersections and essays*. Westport, CN: Greenwood Press.

Hawley, J. C. (Ed.). (2001b). *Postcolonial, queer: Theoretical intersections*. Albany: State University of New York Press.

Herman, D. (1997). *The antigay agenda: Orthodox vision and the Christian right*. Chicago: University of Chicago Press.

Heyward, C. (1984). *Our passion for justice: Images of power, sexuality, and liberation*. New York: Pilgrim Press.

Ihara S. (1990). *The great mirror of male love*. (P. G. Schalow, trans.). Stanford, CA: Stanford University Press.

Jackson, P. A. (1998). Male homosexuality and transgenderism in the Thai Buddhist tradition. In W. Leyland (Ed.), *Queer dharma: Voices of gay Buddhists* (Vol. 1) (pp. 55-89). San Francisco: Gay Sunshine Press.

Jacobs, S. E., Thomas, W., & Lang, S. (Eds.). (1997). *Two-Spirit people: Native American gender identity, sexuality, and spirituality*. Chicago: University of Illinois Press.

Jagose, A. (1996). *Queer theory: An introduction*. New York: New York University Press.

Jakobsen, J. R., & Pellegrini, A. (2003). *Love the sin: Sexual regulation and the limits of religious tolerance*. New York: New York University Press.

Jordan, M. D. (1997). *The invention of sodomy in Christian theology*. Chicago: University of Chicago Press.

Jordan, M. D. (2000). *The silence of Sodom: Homosexuality in modern Catholicism*. Chicago: University of Chicago Press.

Jordan, M. D. (2003). *Telling truths in church: Scandal, flesh, and Christian speech*. Boston: Beacon.

Kolodny, D. R. (Ed.). (2000). *Blessed bi spirit: Bisexual people of faith*. New York: Continuum.

Leyland, W. (Ed.). (1998). *Queer dharma: Voices of gay Buddhists* (Vol. 1). San Francisco: Gay Sunshine Press.

Leyland, W. (Ed.). (2000). *Queer dharma: Voices of gay Buddhists* (Vol. 2). San Francisco: Gay Sunshine Press.

Lincoln, B. (1989). *Discourse and the construction of society*. New York: Oxford University Press.

Lorde, A. (1984). *Sister outsider: Essays and speeches*. Freedom, CA: Crossing Press.

Mahaffy, K. A. (1996). Cognitive dissonance and its resolution: A study of lesbian Christians. *Journal for the Scientific Study of Religion, 35*(4), 392-402.

Matter, E. A. (1986). My sister, my spouse: Woman-identified women in medieval Christianity. *Journal of Feminist Studies in Religion, 2*(2), pp. 81-93.

McNeill, J. J. (1976). *The church and the homosexual*. Kansas City: Sheed, Andrews, and McMeel.

Melton, J. G. (1991). *The churches speak on homosexuality*. New York: Gale.

Mollenkott, V. R. (2001). *Omnigender: A trans-religious approach*. Cleveland, OH: Pilgrim.

Mollenkott, V. R., & Scanzoni, L. (1978). *Is the homosexual my neighbor?* San Francisco: Harper and Row.

Murray, S. O., & Roscoe, W. (Eds.). (1997). *Islamic homosexualities: Culture, history, and literature.* New York: New York University Press.

Nugent, R. (Ed.). (1983). *A challenge to love: Gay and lesbian Catholics in the church.* New York: Crossroad.

O'Brien, J. (2004). Wrestling the angel of contradiction: Queer Christian identities. *Culture and Religion, 5*(2), 179-202.

Pattanaik, D. (2002). *The man who was a woman and other queer tales from Hindu lore.* New York: Harrington Park Press.

Perry, T. (1972). *The Lord is my shepherd and he knows I'm gay.* Los Angeles: Nash Publications.

Plaskow, J., & Christ, C. (Eds.). (1979). *Womanspirit rising: A feminist reader in religion.* San Francisco: Harper and Row.

Primiano, L. N. (1993a). *Intrinsically Catholic: Vernacular religion and Philadelphia's "Dignity."* Ph.D. diss., University of Pennsylvania.

Primiano, L. N. (1993b). "I would rather be fixated on the Lord": Women's religion, men's power, and the "Dignity" problem. *New York Folklore, 19*(1-2), 89-99.

Primiano, L. N. (1995). Vernacular religion and the search for method in religious folklife. *Western Folklore, 54*, 37-56.

Rodriguez, E. M., & Ouellette, S. C. (2000). Gay and lesbian Christians: Homosexual and religious identity integration in the members and participants of a gay-positive church. *Journal for the Scientific Study of Religion, 39*, 333-47.

Rudy, K. (1997). *Sex and the church: Gender, homosexuality, and the transformation of Christian ethics.* Boston: Beacon Press.

Shallenberger, D. (1998). *Reclaiming the spirit: Gay men and lesbians come to terms with religion.* New Brunswick: Rutgers University Press.

Sheridan, V. (2001). *Crossing Over: Liberating the Transgendered Christian.* Cleveland, OH: Pilgrim.

Sherkat, D. E. (2002). Sexuality and religious commitment in the United States: An empirical examination. *Journal for the Scientific Study of Religion, 41*(2), 313-323.

Shneer, D., & Aviv, C. (Eds.). (2002). *Queer Jews.* New York: Routledge.

Shokeid, M. (1995). *A gay synagogue in New York.* New York: Columbia University Press.

Stuart, E., Braunston, A., Edwards, M., McMahon, J, & Morrison, T. (1997) *Religion is a queer thing: A guide to the Christian faith for lesbian, gay, bisexual, and transgender people.* London: Cassell.

Swidler, A. (Ed.). (1993). *Homosexuality and world religions.* Valley Forge, PA: Trinity Press International.

Tanis, J. E. (2003). *Trans-gendered: Theology, ministry, and communities of faith.* Cleveland: Pilgrim Press.

Thumma, S. (1991). Negotiating a religious identity: The case of the gay evangelical. *Sociological Analysis, 52*(4), 333-347.

Thumma, S., & Gray, E. (Eds.). (2004). *Gay religion: Innovation and tradition in spiritual practice.* Walnut Creek: Alta Mira.

Tierny, W. G. (1997). *Academic outlaws: Queer theory and cultural studies in the academy.* Thousand Oaks, CA: Sage Publications.

Warner, M. (Ed.). (1993). *Fear of a queer planet: Queer politics and social theory.* Minneapolis: University of Minnesota Press.

Warner, R. S. (1995). The Metropolitan Community Churches and the gay agenda: The power of Pentecostalism and essentialism. In M. J. Neitz, & M. S. Goldman (Eds.), *Sex, lies, and sanctity: Religion and deviance in contemporary North America* (pp. 81-108). Greenwich, CT: JAI.

Wellman, J. K., Jr., (Ed.). (1999). *Religious organizational identity and homosexual ordination: A case study of the Presbyterian Church, U.S.A.* Special issue of *Review of Religious Research, 41*(2), 184-274.

White, D., & White, O. K. (2004). Queer Christian confessions: Spiritual autobiographies of gay Christians. *Culture and Religion, 5*(2), 203-217.

Wilcox, M. M. (2001). Of markets and missions: The early history of the Metropolitan Community Church. *Religion and American Culture, 11*(1), 83-108.

Wilcox, M. M. (2003). *Coming out in Christianity: Religion, identity, and community.* Bloomington: Indiana University Press.

Wilhelm, A. D. (n.d.). Tritiya-prakriti: People of the third sex. Gay and Lesbian Vaishnav Association. Retrieved 28 March 2003 from http://www.geocities.com/galva108.

Wilson, N. (1995). *Our tribe: Queer folks, God, Jesus, and the Bible.* San Francisco: HarperSanFrancisco.

Yip, A. K. T. (1997). *Gay male Christian couples: Life stories.* Westport, CN: Praeger.

Yip, A. K. T. (2002). The persistence of faith among nonheterosexual Christians: Evidence for the neosecularization thesis of religious transformation. *Journal for the Scientific Study of Religion, 41*(2), 199-212.

doi:10.1300/J082v52n01_04

A Queer Anxiety:
Assimilation Politics and Cinematic Hedonics in *Relax . . . It's Just Sex*

Jeff Bennett, PhD

Georgia State University

SUMMARY. This essay explores the commodification of queer identities in independent cinema, offering particular attention to P. J. Castellaneta's 1998 film, *Relax . . . It's Just Sex*. Like many contemporary queer independent productions, *Relax* is ensnared in a representational *cinematic hedonics*, aspiring to sustain a traditional gay and lesbian politics and simultaneously produce pleasure for multiple audiences. While *Relax* attempts to position itself as a queer film that resists normative conceptions of sexuality, the feature inadvertently appropriates more essentialized understandings of identity closely aligned to liberation rhetoric. doi:10.1300/J082v52n01_05 *[Article copies available for a fee from The Haworth Document Delivery Service: 1-800-HAWORTH. E-mail address: <docdelivery@haworthpress.com> Website: <http://www.HaworthPress.com> © 2006 by The Haworth Press, Inc. All rights reserved.]*

The author would like to thank Joan Hawkins and Isaac West for reading earlier versions of this essay and offering instructive and supportive feedback.

Correspondence may be addressed: Department of Communication, 1040 One Park Place, Georgia State University, Atlanta, GA 30302 (E-mail: jefabenn@alumni.indiana.edu).

[Haworth co-indexing entry note]: "A Queer Anxiety: Assimilation Politics and Cinematic Hedonics in *Relax . . . It's Just Sex*." Bennett, Jeff. Co-published simultaneously in *Journal of Homosexuality* (Harrington Park Press, an imprint of The Haworth Press, Inc.) Vol. 52, No. 1/2, 2006, pp. 101-123; and: *LGBT Studies and Queer Theory: New Conflicts, Collaborations, and Contested Terrain* (ed: Karen E. Lovaas, John P. Elia, and Gust A. Yep) Harrington Park Press, an imprint of The Haworth Press, Inc., 2006, pp. 101-123. Single or multiple copies of this article are available for a fee from The Haworth Document Delivery Service [1-800-HAWORTH, 9:00 a.m. - 5:00 p.m. (EST). E-mail address: docdelivery@haworthpress.com].

KEYWORDS. Assimilation, independent film, liberation politics, queer theory

Hollywood has been a consistent source of both liberating messages and constraining archetypes for the queer community. Ellen can come out, but only if she struggles. Will can date, but only if he lives with Grace. John Goodman can be gay, but only if he resides in "Normal" Ohio. Positing such negotiated images has enabled some political progress for quotidian life, but has simultaneously presented new challenges and obstacles. Visibility may be reaching new heights, but so are hate crimes committed against people in the LGBT community.[1] Reflecting on this tenuous conception of progress, *Newsweek* magazine posed a perpetually vexing question for those resisting homophobia and hetero-normativity, asking how queers "live in a culture that loves Rupert Everett but kills Barry Winchell?"[2] (Leland, 2000, p. 49).

The popular implication that gays and lesbians are "just like everyone else" continues to encourage a distorted identification, one in which *only* those individuals who embody the (straight) ideal survive. Recently *Will and Grace* co-creator Max Mutchnick attributed his show's success to its ability to remain apolitical. "It's our *lack* of agenda that's helped make the show a success," he divulges to *Entertainment Weekly.* "We never sit down and say, 'Okay, how can we teach the world about gay marriage?' The minute we start doing that, we fail" (Svetkey, 2000, p. 28). Such editorializing initiated the demise for DeGeneres' sitcom, being canceled by media executives on the grounds that it was too political and issue oriented for typical viewers. Although gay and lesbian programming is generally regarded as marketable, its livelihood frequently depends on its ability to refrain from explicit social commentary. This aggressive apolitical commodification of sexual identity in mainstream media has often forced LGBT populations to explore alternative mediums for addressing conformist ideologies and representational codification.

Independent films have proven to be a rich source of such resistance. Unlike television or mainstream cinema, independent productions have traditionally been less concerned with studio demands and consumer expectations. Films such as *Parting Glances, Go Fish, Poison, The Incredibly True Adventure of Two Girls in Love, Boys Don't Cry, Jeffrey,* and *The Opposite of Sex* have all made attempts (albeit, very different ones) at exploring notions of assimilation, while concurrently attempting to resist it. Independent films have long recognized the need for visible political representations, while simultaneously developing a self-reflexive attitude that acknowledges the effects essentialized images can have. Characterized by its freedom from rigid economic or aesthetic norms, independent film has positioned itself to engage understandings of sexuality in more diverse manners than mainstream cinema or television.

Despite this sovereignty, independent cinema has not remained wholly free of institutional influence. Shifts in the modes of production and distribution throughout the 1990s has made the term "independent" increasingly difficult to define. Some critics suggest that most "independent" films are more easily classified as "appendages" to major studios than autonomous entities. Nonetheless, Emanuel Levy points out in his text *Cinema of Outsiders*, "There never was a single type of independent film–it's the multitude of distinctive voices that makes indie cinema the rich collective phenomena it is . . . in the new American cinema 'independent' is a sufficiently flexible term to embrace a variety of artistic expression" (1999, p. 6). At its base, the term "independent" has simply implied "work different from the dominant or mainstream" (Hillier, 2001, p. ix).

There is a striking parallel between the definitional debates of independent cinema and those concerning sexual politics. In many regards, the concept of "queer" has functioned similarly to the term "independent." Like independent film, gay and lesbian identities continue to be increasingly commodified in popular culture. Similarly, rather than embody an easily delimited idea, the word "queer" connotes a number of meanings and understandings. Just as the word "independent" defies classification, "queer" resists definition, as it is often difficult to judge from the label "exactly what someone is referring to, except that it is something non-straight or non-normatively straight" (Doty, 2000, p. 8).

The increased commodification of both independent cinema and LGBT identities raises important questions about the evolvement of queer politics and the cultural representations being addressed in alternative media. While the "new queer cinema" is often defined as employing irony, pastiche, and fragmented subjectivities to defy traditional identity politics, heightened commodification has the potential to further blur these lines, placing queer filmmakers and their audiences in a precarious hegemonic position (Arroyo, 1997, p. 79). As such, this essay does not attempt to simply read independent film through the competing perspectives of "liberation politics" and "queer theory." Alexander Doty (2000) notes that any text has the potential to be read as queer, depending on the audience viewing it. Rather, this analysis seeks to understand the kinds of identities being constructed by independent films in a culture where the discursive traits of both queer theory and traditional movement theory exist in a common polity, rarely as easily distinguishable paradigms. Michael Warner has argued that these seemingly divergent camps of critique and action are more intertwined than not, explaining that they "belong not to different epochs, or to different populations, but to different contexts" (2002, p. 213).

P. J. Castellaneta's 1998 indie film, *Relax . . . It's Just Sex* (hereafter *Relax*) will be the focal point of this analysis. *Relax* elucidates the tensions inherent in examining contemporary independent films that address queer identities from an aesthetic, ethical, and economic perspective. Like many contemporary independent films, *Relax* is trapped between the necessities of duty and pleasure, ensnared in a representational *cinematic hedonics*. It aspires to sustain traditional gay and lesbian politics and simultaneously wishes to adopt a queer voice that produces pleasure for a multiplicity of audiences. *Relax* recognizes its role as an independent film to transcend the terror that is perpetually in the consciousnesses of queer viewers, as well as produce a product from the "on-going struggle between the extremes of defiance and assimilation, of resistance and complacency" (Griffin, 1992, p. 229).

"NO MORE FILMS ABOUT HOMOSEXUALITY"

At the conclusion of his landmark text, *The Celluloid Closet*, Vito Russo makes an impassioned plea to expand the boundaries of film to present a more eclectic sampling of gay and lesbian identity. He implores his reading audience, "no more films about homosexuality. Instead, more films that explore people who happen to be gay in America and how their lives intersect with the dominant culture" (1987, p. 326). While Russo suggests moving away from the treatment of "homosexuality" as a negative construct, gauging the success of his appeal is elusively difficult. A mainstream film such as *Philadelphia,* for example, purported to represent a "normal" man, who just happened to be gay and HIV positive in a world that isolated people with AIDS. Although the film was well received by popular audiences, queer activists and scholars hardly regarded the production as libratory or progressive. Advocates such as Larry Kramer called it a "heartbreakingly mediocre movie: dishonest, and often legally, medically and politically inaccurate" (1994, p. 1). Critics argued that the film presented distorted views of life with HIV, gay relationships, and the communities where discrimination is perpetuated.

In response, some scholars have suggested that gay rights advocates misstep in their criticism of the film, resorting to the erroneous claim that there is in fact an "authentic" homosexual identity which can be wholly depicted on screen. James Brookey, for instance, encouraged activists to move "beyond" questions of representation and utilize the discursive insights of queer theory to examine "what rules are being made, and what social relations are being enforced" (1996, p. 40). By scrutinizing the discursive forms reiterated in films such as *Philadelphia*, Brookey argued that questions concerning the economic comodification of identity and traditional notions of the family can be more productively engaged. As part of that project, Brookey also emphasized the need for exploring "resistance discourses" produced by gays and lesbians that challenge normative cultural institutions, citing independent films such as *Go Fish* and *No Skin Off My Ass*.

While such potential existed in the new queer cinema of the early 1990s, the last decade has illustrated a movement towards themes that appeal to diverse audience segments and productions which deemphasize political critique. Characters and scripts are created with the intent of appealing to mass consuming audiences, not necessarily engaging forms of cultural resistance. For example, director Tommy O'Haver says of his protagonist in the film *Billy's Hollywood Screen Kiss*, "I wanted people to forget that this is a gay man–it could be anyone" (Levy, 1999, p. 491). Even a film such as *Boys Don't Cry*, which obviously engages in critical cultural critique, appropriates elements of these themes. Director Kimberly Pierce explained on *CNN*, "In the end it's such a universal story–Brandon's celebration of individuality and fluidity of gender, and just being yourself–everybody can relate to that, every teenager, every person" (1999). Of course, appeals to universality can be productive in their own right. Judith Butler, whose theories of performativity speak explicitly against codified understandings of identity, has described their potential writing, "the assertion of universality can be proleptic and performative, conjuring a reality that does not yet exist, and holding out the possibility for a convergence of cultural horizons that have not yet met" (1999, p. xvii).

The move towards universality is closely tied to economic concerns faced by independent filmmakers. Some earlier 1990s productions such as *Go Fish* were exceptionally cost effective to create, so studios could afford to ignore large cross-over appeal, as they would still turn a profit from queer audiences (James, 1994). However, as the decade progressed, the rules for both independent filmmakers and the industry began to shift. In 1996 director Todd Haynes pointed out that increased government cutbacks provided fewer opportunities for grant-funding, forcing indie producers to seek commercial investors (Andrews, 1996). These Hollywood officials were witnessing a blurring of audience segments, as people who would once pay to see a mainstream film were increasingly supporting certain independent productions as well. However, determining whether or not those audiences would appear depended largely on the ability of the studio to market and distribute individual films. Pictures could be edgy and against the norm, but still necessitated justification for theatres to purchase the reels and people to watch them. Because identity politics often failed to appease market considerations, casting and cross-over audience draw became a significant part of developing independent films (Rich, 2001). Economic influence has not only produced "gay films for straight people," but "straight films for gay people" (Darsey, 1997, p. 186; Macnab, 2001, p. 109).

There is little doubt that queer identities and independent films have been increasingly commodified in recent years. But does this commercialization mean that all hope is lost for queer independent cinema? Certainly, such productions have never spoke with one voice, and several continue appealing to a politics understood to be radical by mainstream audiences. Can independent cinema invoke the contours of queer theory to offer insights about normativity and the deployment of sexuality as a continually developing discourse? Or do themes of universality subvert the potential of queer politics to a utopian vision of liberal tolerance? If queer theory and liberation politics exist in different contexts, as implied by Warner, how do we negotiate these tensions in independent texts that attempt to reach diverse audience segments? This analysis will now turn to the film *Relax*, as it deals explicitly with these issues, attempting to navigate a queer politics within a framework that stresses universality.

RELAX . . . IT'S JUST REPRESENTATION

Loosely based on the 1950 production *La Ronde*, the film follows the lives of ten friends living in Los Angeles who struggle with a series of life altering events. Narrated by various cast members throughout the feature, the story unfolds in a quirky manner by using flashbacks, testimonials, a spoofed hygiene film, and witty dialogue. Despite the playful tone of the film, the subject matter is consistently serious as characters recount stories of being tested HIV positive or partner infidelity. The otherwise light-hearted production takes a surprising turn when two of the male characters are assaulted by gay bashers after a party. In the midst of the attack, an assailant is overpowered by the group and then raped by one of the queer men. The remainder of the film chronicles how the friends reconcile their romantic problems and the ethical dilemmas that stem from the sexual assault.

In contrast to the seemingly assimilative tone adopted by many indie films, *Relax* positions itself as an oppositional production. It differs from films such as *Get Real* or *Beautiful Thing* by making a self-conscious effort to critique normativity and include a multiplicity of sexualities, endeavoring to break away from a narrative that revolves around a gay white male protagonist. While it does embrace the stock lonely gay male artist typical in many queer films such as *Billy's Hollywood Screen Kiss*, *The Broken Heart's Club*, and *Trick*, it also attempts to incorporate a number of narratives about less visible members of the LGBT community. The story lines include a lesbian love triangle between a beautiful African-American lesbian, her attractive, but unfaithful bisexual Caucasian partner, and a self-proclaimed butch dyke; A Hispanic man who recently discovers he is HIV positive and his new African-American lover who expresses radical skepticism about the link between HIV and AIDS; A vocal "fag hag" who longs to have a baby and eventually miscarries; and a pair of gay Christian gym-queens who act as stand-ins for the embodiment of "normalized" queers. By integrating a diverse sampling of voices from the LGBT community the film strives to identify the manner in which all relationships are somewhat queer and complicate a "view of coalition politics as the sum of separate identity communities, each locked into its own sexual, gender, class, or racial politics" (Seidman, 1993, p. 105).

Filmmakers such as director Bill Condon (*Gods and Monsters*) have publicly endorsed the development of a cinema that adopts such divergent narratives. He points to films like *The Opposite of Sex* as positive examples, explaining that it had "a gay sensibility but it encompassed all different experiences" (Karger, 1994, p. 36). But how those experiences are performed, the representations of gay and lesbian life they depict, and the political/cultural goals they imagine continue to be hotly contested. Delimiting what is "normalized" and what is "marginalized" is a more pressing question than ever before.

Navigating the area between the Scylla of queer politics and the Charybdis of mass commodification can be a difficult task for independent filmmakers. To alleviate this tension, films such as *Relax* adopt a conceptual cinematic hedonics to meet both ends. While traditionally understood as a form of illicit gratification, hedonics is concerned most with ethics, a philosophy that ponders the relationship between duty and pleasure (Chesebro, 1997, p. 139). Like several contemporary queer independent films, *Relax* continually dances between these two concepts, which are often more connected than isolated. *Relax* is developed in a manner that stresses the aesthetic and political pleasures traditionally associated with independent film and resisting normative behavior. At the same time, it recognizes the hardships accompanying cultural defiance and the obligation to invoke a political message for its queer audience.

A plethora of scenes, characters, and narrative techniques attempt to position *Relax* as an art house exhibition film that produces pleasures traditionally associated with independent cinema. It is important to remember that films are more often than not a source of enjoyment and fantasy for the audiences viewing them. They are instruments of escape and fancy, mediums that are used to help people simultaneously find and lose themselves. Richard Dyer and Derek Cohen remind us that pleasure is often ignored as an integral portion of the industry. They write, "the pleasure of culture gives us a glimpse of where we are going and helps us to enjoy the struggle of getting there" (2002, p. 16). *Relax* isolates this form of cultural pleasure by defining itself as a production with a political message, employing characteristics traditionally associated with art house cinema. It is constructed in a manner that fragments traditional narrative style, is goaded by realism, and is less concerned with action than with audience reaction (Bordwell, 1999). More than any other feature of the film, *Relax* adopts a hostile stance to that which is "normal," invoking a political aesthetic that appeals to queer spectators.

Relax immediately attempts to position itself in opposition to the concept of "normal" identities. It opens with a black and white spoof of a 1950s educational hygiene film. A deep voiced narrator explains, "some of you have never seen homosexuals engaged in any sort of positive physical contact. So we would like to take a moment before we start to acclimate you." The narrator assures viewers that the "lipstick lesbians" and the "gym queens" featured on a revolving platform are nothing to fret. After all, these prototypes strongly resemble the ideals of heterosexual culture. As the two iconic gay men embrace the voice asserts, "Just like two buddies after a ball game."

The nostalgic introduction is designed to resemble a classic text that would be fodder for conventional camp readings. Camp being one of the striking symbols of gay and lesbian film iconography, the movie attempts to establish a "queer" sensibility by mocking that which is usually appropriated as "normal." The segment is intended to be ironic, as its gray, purified *mise en scene* is immediately followed by an explicit sex scene featuring Vincey (Mitchell Anderson), who is put in the precarious position of deciding whether to swallow the semen of a man whom he has just met. As he ponders this decision, he dreams of a lifetime with the attractive man, envisioning everything from crossing the threshold of their new home to selecting china patterns. He justifies ingesting the fluids, only to have the man shatter his reverie, telling him he shouldn't swallow, as it is simply not safe. Unlike traditional notions of camp, there is little need for queer viewers to search for a subtext on the screen. The introduction functions as a parody, establishing the premise that dreams of a "normal" life are more fantasy than reality. While the black and white spoof infers that gay and lesbian relationships are normative, the sexual scene suggests otherwise, pointing to the difficult aspects of building gay relations, including common fears about HIV.

In addition, *Relax* struggles to divorce itself from the normative gay white male protagonist central to contemporary films exploring issues of sexual identity (*Billy's Hollywood Screen Kiss, Get Real, Jeffrey*, and *The Opposite of Sex*). The cast of *Relax* is self-consciously diversified, both racially and sexually, allowing for multiple identifications to transpire. It endeavors to establish, in Arlene Stein's words, that there are "many possible configurations of the relationship between desire, practice, and identity–many more so configurations than there are social categories to describe them" (1991, p. 40). By employing these diverse identities, the producers of *Relax* speak to the concerns of activists who argue that filmmakers must temper themselves when creating oppositional works longing to give underrepresented groups voice (Griffin, 1992). As representations are unavoidably constituted for an unknown public, filmmakers must not assume that they speak on behalf of all members of a group, regardless of how cohesive that collective may seem. While attempting to produce texts that resist the dominant culture, presuming an alternate voice that speaks on behalf of an entire people can unintentionally reinforce stereotypes or be equally totalizing.

To reinforce the importance of personal identity, video footage of individual characters offering testimonials of recent events is employed throughout the film. The audience is given first hand accounts of the problems being grappled with in the narrative. Not only do such scenes help reinforce the aesthetic elements of the traditional art house film by helping break the linear narrative, they also define differences between several of the characters. While film segments speak from an unnamed authority, video shots add an element of authenticity designed to produce a credibility that encourages "us to believe them" (Fiske, 1996, p. 127). The splicing of video footage in the film helps give voice to that which is not easily communicated when dealing with performances that encourage framing a character in a specific manner. The people being video recorded in *Relax* "are trapped in an authenticity that the powerful have the fortune to escape and the misfortune to lose" (Fiske, 1996, p. 127). The testimonials are sad, fearful, and humorous, assigning a level of complexity and humanity to various characters by giving audiences an intimate glimpse into their lives.

Castellaneta used the "experience" of the characters to acknowledge that sexual identities are performed in dissimilar manners, but also utilized "experience" to create a hierarchy of authenticity within the narrative. *Relax* shuns characters who are more traditionally normative in their demeanor while the more developed and prized characters have radical perspectives, are HIV positive, or rape gay bashers. Locating this experience allows the film to explore the needs and interests of people who are seemingly "more queer" than others. In fact, those cast members who are presented as more "heteronormative" are positioned as sites for hostility in the film. Being "normal" is constructed as more dangerous because it reinforces discursive representations that divert attention from the problems "real" gay people confront.

In one segment, for example, the character Javier (Eddie Garcia) tells the group about his experience with a gay couple who scowl at him moments before he discovers he is HIV positive. The pair are described as a "really, really gross Ozzie and Harriet, West Hollywood-type couple that [they] all hate." The "normal" couple and their nasty glances are taken as a "bad omen" for the test results he receives soon after. The men, having recently discovered that they were HIV negative, race past Javier as he describes how cruel the world can be. But as the duo run off to live their "AIDS free life together" they are conveniently hit by a metro bus that is passing by the clinic. In traditional mainstream films it is commonplace for sexually active or promiscuous people to be met by death as the narrative develops (Clover, 1993). In *Relax*, however, there is a queer reversal of this cinematic trope. The "normal" gay people die, not the person marked by the traditionally stigmatized syndrome.

Perhaps the most conspicuous characters to assume assimilative roles in the film are the Christian couple Dwight and Diego (Gibbs Tolsdorf and Chris Cleveland). The men are a beautiful, buffed, Caucasian couple who never argue and continually express concern for others in the film. They wear polo shirts and khakis, go on spiritual retreats together, and their arguments never exceed trivial questions, such as "who should make breakfast today?" Unlike the other characters in the film, their lives are uncomplicated and trouble free. Even their names, "Dwight" and "Diego," mark them as being more alike with each other and different from others in the script. They are never apart, are not featured in the video recorded testimonials, and are not developed as individuals like the other cast members. Dwight and Diego are healthy, happy, and extremely hygienic. They signify what Victor D'Lugin would proclaim the top of the "hierarchy of beauty" in gay male culture. He explains that:

> The image is muscular and very white and very young and very clean . . . That very cleanliness seems to imply there are certain limits with what one would do with that body. The image is so clean and ultimately so safe and nonthreatening that it doesn't allow for us to explore our sexuality, to see what the limits of our fantasies might be." (Mann, 1998, p. 348)

Some critics have labeled this reification of cleanliness "body fascism," arguing that filmmakers should feature a more diverse sampling of the gay community, rather than appealing to cultural ideals that inscribe normativity. Beautiful, buffed gay men in films are almost never HIV positive or African-American. Invoking such images would impede the mystique of cleanliness that is embodied by figures such as Dwight and Diego (Mann, 1998).

Throughout *Relax*, the idealized couple is sympathetic to cultural institutions that are traditionally viewed as central to the oppression of queer populations. In refuting assertions made by T. C. Carson's character about AIDS being a conspiracy theory, they employ scientific proof from medical studies to support their claims. Following the segment in which Vincey rapes an attacker, they are the only characters to suggest going to the police and admit that they told their minister about the assault. There is nothing ideologically secure about these characters under the rubric of traditional queer politics. Not only are they completely "normalized," they support all of the institutions that discursively empower oppression. The church, the law, and medical science are often regarded as "three parts of a mutually reinforcing system of social control" against gays and lesbians and the couple regularly invoke the credibility of these institutions against other characters in film (Darsey, 1997, p. 176).

Dwight and Diego are depicted in sharp contrast to the character of Vincey who is not in a relationship, perpetually insecure, and less attractive. At two points during the narrative, Vincey projects his anxieties about queer life onto the "normalizalized" gay men. For example, in one scene Vincey is repairing his car as he ponders single life with the couple. As he works under the hood, he tells his friends, "the world is a much different place for me than it is for people who look like you . . . things come so easily for you guys, you just have no idea." As he speaks, he inadvertently holds up a pocketknife being used to fix the engine, accidentally pointing it towards the pair. The men cautiously step back as the protagonist pokes fun, saying "would you just relax, I'm just cleaning the crevices. But if you don't quit annoying me . . ." and proceeds to playfully swing the knife at them. Dwight and Diego are made unexplainably uncomfortable by the action, visibly flinching.

In a second shot shown immediately following this discussion, the cast is leaving a nightclub with Vincey dramatically screeching because he failed to meet anyone. He blames the couple for his displeasure, arguing that he was trapped talking with one of their Christian friends. The group laughs, but Vincey insists that the situation is serious because now he is "horny and depressed" and is "going to have to kill somebody and it just might have to be" Dwight or Diego. The scenes with the Christian couple offer a dark foreshadowing to the centerpiece of the film, where Vincey rapes a gay basher at knifepoint after he is attacked.

While mocking notions of normativity, *Relax* maintains a humorous and light tone throughout the first half of the film. The dinner party where Javier announces he is HIV positive, the revealed affair between Megan (Serena Scott Thomas) and her male second-cousin, and the awkwardness of sex are all approached with an eye towards comedy, not tragedy. However, the tenor of the film drastically shifts when the critique of normativity makes a dramatic turn. As the friends leave the nightclub, Vincey and Javier separate from the pack to urinate in an alley and are assailed by a group of men. When Vincey left the club and announced that he was "horny and depressed," he was reiterating the desires that have frustrated him for the duration of the film. While his irritation is directed at queer characters throughout the narrative, they acquire new meaning during this segment. *Relax* shifts from parodying interpolated queers that have been normalized to exemplifying the physical dangers posed by such heteronormativity.

The gay bashers are marked by a number of signs that represent masculinity. They are playing rap music loudly in their car as they approach, reveal baseball bats as weapons, and call the gay men "girls" prior to striking them. One man is dressed in a hockey jersey, and another screams "fore" as he hits Vincey in the stomach with a bat. Most significant, the men threaten to rape Vincey with a dirty beer bottle. As the character beings to struggle, the man in the hockey apparel says, "Baby, you gotta relax or this ain't gonna be pleasant for you."

Hearing their calls, Vincey's and Javier's friends rush back to the alley and immobilize the assailants. During the confusion, most of the aggressors flee, save the man who attempted to sodomize the gay writer with a bottle. Vincey tackles his nemesis, holds him down at knife point, and rapes him with his friends looking on. The scene is symbolically subverted as Vincey whispers the assailant's words back to him, saying, "Relax, relax, or this is not going to be pleasant for you at all." As he continues assaulting his attacker he declares, "Relax, it's just sex . . . gay boys have learned to relax . . . get pleasure from getting fucked over all the time." As the man runs away, Vincey mocks him, asking him for a kiss and asserting that the denigrated man is "just like all the others."

The rape functions, in the words of Judith Butler, as a type of disobedience to discursively interpolating laws. Vincey subverts the disciplining gestures not only to refuse the gay bashers, but to rupture the very laws by which they are operating. Butler explains:

> Where the uniformity of the subject is expected, where the behavioral conformity of the subject is commanded, there might be produced the refusal of the law in the form of parodic inhabiting of conformity that subtly calls into question the legitimacy of the command, a repetition of the law into hyperbole, a rearticulation of the law against the authority of the one who delivers it. (1993, p. 122)

The impending rape is both thwarted and reversed, leaving the masculine figure unable to reproduce the queer subject–Vincey is no longer his to be conquered. By mirroring the attacker's words and quite literally subverting the man's position, *Relax* appeals to a radical discursive politics, one in which those who have been situated as queer can resist cultural domination. Far from being a private act, this attack occurs in the presence of a community whose livelihood is compromised daily by the structures the attacker embodies.

Disrupting masculinity through bodily intrusion is traditionally avoided in films by displacing it from the male body and locating it elsewhere in the *mis en scene* (Neale, 1992, p. 284). *Relax* centralizes this taboo, attempting to strip heterosexuality of the discursive power it derives from stigmatizing homosexual practices. If it is true, that "same sex desire provides the disciplinary terms for normalizing heterosexuality in its compulsory formation," it is important to question how this subversion functions as a mode of queer politics cinematically (Weigman, 1995, p. 99). If heteronormativity recognizes its "phallic potential" in relation to traditionally feminized notions of gay men, does feminizing embodied masculinity aid in the struggle to resist cultural hegemony?

UTOPIA AND ITS DISCONTENTS

Relax operates under a cinematic hedonics that oscillates between the poles of duty and pleasure. It attempts to resist normativity by satirizing seemingly assimilated characters and subsuming discursive structures that act as oppressive agents against gays and lesbians. However, in adopting a radical politics that endeavors to disrupt the discursive authority ascribed to heteronormativity, *Relax* does not resist a hierarchy that oppresses queer bodies as much as it reinforces the very power structures that it is challenging.

In many ways, the rape scene functions as a mode of pondering the limits of queer sexual politics. Questions that address the degree to which violence is justified against an oppressor, the methods of disabling an attacker, and the ways in which those acts might alter power structures are subjects that receive little attention in a movement that stresses tolerance and multiculturalism. *Relax* creates a space in which these matters can be addressed and potentially challenge what audiences might regard as political possibilities. As a cultural text employing a diverse number of voices, *Relax* presents an opportunity for tackling complex issues that are metaphorically encapsulated by the rape.

Despite the discursive potential presented by this surprising twist, the rape is never explicitly engaged in the film. While a mild tension emerges among those characters established as resisting discursive heteronormativity and those who are portrayed as more assimilative, the debate surrounding the assault takes place in a single scene. Rather than converse over the complicated issue, Vincey departs from the group, disappearing for an undetermined amount of time to recollect his thoughts. While there are references alluding to the attack, in the end, the characters simply "agree to disagree" over the incident, and do so in Vincey's absence. Although the assault is the center piece of the film, it is swiftly dismissed.

Discouragingly, the most important function of the rape in the narrative is to empower the film's white male protagonist. By emasculating his attacker, Vincey releases the sexual frustration that has plagued him throughout the storyline. However, in mirroring the basher's words, by literally feminizing the man's body, a disturbing political message unfolds. The assailant is positioned in a fashion similar to that of a person being raped by a man who cannot control his sexual urges. He is crying, being held at knife point, and begging not to be assaulted. But the violence that this man embodies encourages the audience to ponder, "Did he have it coming to him? Did he ask for this?" The public display positions the gay basher's body to be witnessed as both the essential site of difference and the "translation of castration from the metaphorics of the feminine to its literalization" (Weigman, 1995, p. 86). This is not to suggest that the kind of aggression that is inappropriately ascribed to a person who has been sexually assaulted is parallel to the motives of a gay basher. Rather, it is meant to question the degree to which the viewing audience is permitted to justify the means taken to discipline those who inflict violence against queer communities. The rape should provoke ethical discussions that engage the extent to which those who identify as LGBT should "bash back," as well as the repercussions and benefits that might result. Instead it reinforces traditional norms of patriarchy and violence, disempowering one man at the expense of empowering another. In contrast to theories of sexuality that seek to interrupt essentialized understandings of difference, the violation sustains the very discourses it aspires to disrupt. Kate Millet explains that patriarchy "relies on a form of violence particularly sexual in character and realized most completely in the act of rape" (2000, p. 137). It functions by linking feelings of cruelty with images of sexuality, "the latter often equated both with evil and with power" (Millet, 2000, p. 137).

Rather than subvert patriarchal understandings of sexuality, the competing norms of masculinity featured in the rape scene draw attention to a striking element of the story—none of the men in the movie are marked as traditionally effeminate. While the film continually mocks the ideals of normativity, all of the male characters are arguably more masculine than not. Despite *Relax's* efforts to depict itself as a sexually diverse film, the effeminate element of queer identity has been subtly lost. Such a move reinforces Nardi's fears that, "the rhetoric about gender in many gay organizations and communities has often been oppositional in its tone and it questions the role of effeminate men, drag queens, and 'fairies' in the political strategies and media images" (2000, p. 5). Even as the movie attempts to subvert ideals, it reinforces them. The film reproduces anxieties held by contemporary queer activists who fear that unmarketable populations are being erased in media culture.

Vincey's absence and sudden reemergence at the film's conclusion as a gay rights advocate also undermines the production's ability to challenge discursive heteronormativity. After disappearing from the group, Vincey suddenly reappears as a guest on a Los Angeles-based local access television program. The host reveals that Vincey has been printing an on-line series that a lot of "queers" have criticized "as being too political, too preachy." While never disclosing that he is sharing a personal story, Vincey admits that a column he published about a gay basher who is raped by his intended victim is "intense." However, much like the film, he says nothing more about the incident. Instead he asserts, "you really have to wonder why politicians get so upset when all that gay people want are the same rights as everybody else, not special rights."

The empowered protagonist embraces liberal notions of equality, never offering a sense of how the rape changed him, apart from the fact that it enabled him to redefine himself as a tough queer ready to participate in the political system. There is no struggle with the rape in the film, no concern with how it has reshaped his desires or sexual identity. While he suggests that our cultural understandings of sex have been distortedly normalized, at the program's end he asserts little more than "some people are meant to be in relationships" and others are not. The means adopted by the producers of *Relax* are often "queer" in their own right, but their ends continually reproduce a liberal model of tolerance that stresses patriarchal forms.

Relax appears to be a product of both queer politics and more traditional liberation models. Recognizing the flexibility of what is "normal," Castellaneta's film nods to the powers of discursive formations throughout. This is seen most clearly in a scene where Carson's character Buzz, is lecturing the group about the scientific construction of AIDS. Clarifying that AIDS is a "syndrome," not a "disease" he comments, "we carry around dozens of harmless little retroviruses in our system, and HIV is no different, not in its make up . . . the medical community has lumped them all together and they call it AIDS." Rather than simply represent AIDS as "a virus," the production reiterates accounts of the development of AIDS similar to scholars such as Jan Zita Grover, who writes, "In discussions of AIDS, because of distinctions not made–between syndrome and disease, between infections and contagions–there is often a casual slippage from communicable to contagious" (1996, p. 19). However, despite the recognition of individual experience, varying sexual attractions, and resistance to discursive normativity, the manner in which *sexuality* is constructed is problematic throughout the production.

Ironically, sexuality is not depicted as fluid and subject to change in the film. While there are "prototypes" of sexual identity presented, the boundaries of those identities are closely guarded. For example, Lori Petty's butch character Robyn describes herself as a lesbian who makes "Janet Reno look femme." Her non-normative personality is continually positioned against the beautiful, blonde, and successful "lipstick lesbian" Megan, who has abandoned her lover Serena (Cynda Williams) for a man. Attempting to win Serena's affections, Robyn alludes to Megan's distrustful nature asserting "at least with me you know what you get." Here, Megan's bisexuality, or rather her inability to maintain her homosexuality, is directly tied to her deceitful nature. At several points during the narrative Megan is situated as less authentic than other characters because of her straying desires and seemingly normative heterosexual behavior, even if bisexuality is arguably the least normative of the sexualities depicted. Even Megan's parents complain about her new found sexuality, arguing that they had finally come to terms with her identity as a lesbian and have no idea what to tell their friends at PFLAG. The film simultaneously mocks the normative rituals that have been adopted by some heterosexuals to cope with homosexuality and disciplines bisexual identity. Megan is stigmatized because of her fluid sexuality and refusal to maintain essential qualities that sustain the ideals of authenticity. In the end, *Relax* reinforces this secured form of identity by having Megan break off her relationship with a man and attempt reconciliation with Serena. Alas, such compromising is not permitted. In the end, Robyn wins Serena's affections.

In this way, *Relax* adopts a conception of sexual identity that is as stable as those models depicted in mainstream cinema. While the feature evokes an anxiety about the dangers of normativity onto the bodies of Dwight and Diego, it seems unconcerned with the effects of totalizing sexuality. This stabilizing of sexual identity is fast becoming a trope in independent films. Jamie Babbit's independent production, *But I'm a*

Cheerleader tells the story of a teen sent to a reparative therapy camp where gays and lesbians are taught to become straight by performing heterosexuality. Again, however, there is no fluidity of sexual performance at play. All of the characters are staunchly positioned as belonging to one identity group—you are either gay or lesbian, but never crossing the line. Similarly, in the *Opposite of Sex*, a gay man proclaims he is bisexual after sleeping with his partner's sister, but eventually falls in love with a man at the presentation's conclusion.

Indeed, the most "queer" figure in many contemporary films may be the stock heterosexual, or "fag hag." In *Relax*, Jennifer Tilly's character Tara is one of the only heterosexual characters, but is conceived as more stereotypically queer than most of the gays and lesbians. She has strong sexual urges and is constantly seeking the affections of her noncommittal boyfriend. She worries about gay bashing, calls AIDS the biggest tragedy of the 20th century, and invokes Madonna's credibility to prove her point. After longing for a child throughout the film, she becomes pregnant, but decides against sharing the news of her pregnancy with her boyfriend or immediate family, confiding only in her friends. Like Tori Spelling's character in *Trick* or Lisa Kudrow's in *The Opposite of Sex*, Tara is overbearing, loud, annoying, and a source of contention throughout the film.

Despite the appeal of Tara as a "queer" character, however, her role also blurs the line between identity politics and queer performativity. The gloomy narratives surrounding rape and AIDS are eventually replaced by the storyline of Tara's miscarriage. While many interpretations could be made about this sequence, in terms of political struggle, this dramatic conclusion accomplishes numerous goals. First, the death of the baby seeks to subtly reinforce the assimilative tendencies that underlie the film. As opposed to having the stock "homosexual" character depicted as "just like everybody else," Tilly's character embodies the opposite. The death forces a parallel between Tara, one of the only heterosexual characters in the film, and her gay friends that are constantly experiencing pain, suffering, and growth as a result of their sexuality.

This seeming rite of passage into the gay community is problematic for several reasons. At the conclusion of the film Vincey explains that sex leads to many things, both positive and negative, "sometimes life, sometime death." The film produces parallels between heterosexual and homosexual desire, but does so at the expense of trivializing the complex discourses it wishes to critique. The underlying premise of the conclusion is blatantly simple: "we all have sex, see how much we have in common?" While identification is certainly a positive and necessary tool for survival and communication, this construction of sexual normativity undercuts the film's potential as a radical queer text that addresses convoluted issues.

Additionally, the child's death shifts attention away from the tragic gay figures in the picture and allows for a more utopian ending. Traditional films dealing with gay subject matters have long reinforced the notion that gay men and lesbians were self-loathing, suicidal, or destined to die of AIDS. In contemporary queer films, however, we see a new kind of ending. Like productions such as *Longtime Companion* there is an over compensation in many features, a need to have not simply a happy ending, but one that is overtly utopian in its aesthetic and narrative components. Both *Billy's Hollywood Screen Kiss* and *The Broken Hearts Club* end with the entire cast at photo exhibits honoring the protagonist. *The Opposite of Sex* concludes with the characters all jovial and living well. *Relax* also ends on a utopian note, with all of the characters walking along a beach with one another as the sun sets in the background.

In the end, it is difficult to disagree with the film's conclusion. Yes, sex is sometimes good, and sometimes bad. Certainly, community is a wonderful thing. Indeed, gay and straight people can be great friends. Nonetheless, the movie strips all ideological and relational complexities, concluding neatly rather than leaving audiences with any dissonance about sexual hierarchy or power struggles common in independent films. In many regards, normalization had been embraced, not subverted. The film is supposed to be a cross-section of identifications, but "we don't learn much about the characters beyond their sexuality" (Smoron, 1993, p. 33). As such, many issues of striking importance get completely erased. Evidently in Castellaneta's world, interracial relations are without consequence, realizing bisexuality is unproblematic, and religious inclusiveness is easily attained. Jean Baudrillard certainly realized the potential for harm at play here, pointing to the oddities of commodity culture infringing on quotidian life, stressing "an odd paradoxical formula–neither true nor false: but utopian" (1983, p. 50).

The normalizing of racial identities is especially problematic in *Relax*. Despite the film's anxieties concerning ideal representations, it fails to address how being an African-American lesbian or a gay Latino man who is HIV positive varies substantially from being a white, negative, middle-class queer. In many ways, audiences never really escape the gay white man central to this narrative. Following the rape scene, Vincey disappears, but his return remains the focus of the film even as

Tara's child dies, Megan attempts reconciliation with Serena, and Javier comes to terms with the impending threat of AIDS. While the film purports to promote an agenda that deals primarily with people of all kinds and their interpersonal relationships, the film focuses largely on issues that are relatable to white middle-class spectators.

CONCLUSION

Relax asserts itself as a queer film with a defined political agenda, but not in the traditional sense of the word. While it sought to expand the boundaries of queer identity by employing aesthetic and narrative features that subvert heteronormativity, it conceptually and structurally reinforced these concepts in divergent manners. Rather than becoming a nonessentialist text concerned with the performative elements of identity, however, it treats difference on the surface, inevitably feeding feelings of assimilation. This is clearly illustrated in the prose of film critics who proclaim that the movie is " . . . a friendly admonition that the more you look at sexual preference, the less it explains" (Gleiberman, 1999, p. 72). Taking this line of thinking one step further, another writes, "'*Relax . . . It's Just Sex*' is a very down-to-earth picture showing homosexual relationships are the same as relationships between men and women" (Chow, 2000, p. 7).

This is not to say that all independent films are doomed to fall prey to the hegemonic regimes of popular culture. The very nature of independent queer cinema still poses possibilities for developing interesting and provocative depictions of queer life. *Relax* itself is a film that exhibited much potential for engaging issues of identity, normativity, and sexual fluidity, but ultimately stopped short of fully embracing these complicated matters. However, productions such as *Lilies* continue to present intriguing possibilities for performance theory, queer theory, and LGBT studies.[3] Nonetheless, as queer populations and independent films continue to be commodified by mainstream studios, the line between queer sensibilities and liberation politics will continue to blur.

Films that wish to be picked up by major studios will necessarily appeal to mass audiences, making critical analyses of industry politics more pressing than ever before. For example, the copies of *Relax* carried by *Blockbuster Video* carefully edit out two important segments of the film: the explicit sex scene featuring Mitchell Anderson which opens the production and several portions of the violent rape. The very political statements being promoted during both portions of the film have literally been sanitized for consumption by popular audiences who need not deal with gay sex, be it humorous or disturbing. Although critics such as Rich (2001) argue that queer cinema can no longer exist due to contemporary structures of commodity culture, activists would be wise to follow the lead of Stuart Hall who encourages us to remember that identity is not an already accomplished historical fact that the new cinematic discourses represent, it is "a 'production,' which is never complete, always in process, and always constituted within, not outside, representation" (1996, p. 210).

Several year have passed since Russo exclaimed that "homosexuals are powerless by virtue of their unwillingness to be publicly identified" (1987, p. 251). The problem today, however, is not so much a question of becoming more visible, but determining what to do now that we are more visible than ever before. As the line continues to blur between queer theory and LGBT studies, between duty and pleasure, and between normativity and marginalization, queer activists must be more aware than ever of the discourses that subtly and explicitly shape their lives.

NOTES

1. According to FBI statistics posted on the Human Rights Campaign web site as of November 15, 2003. The HRC reports that crimes "committed in 2002 due to bias against the victim's perceived sexual orientation represent 16.7 percent of reported hate crime incidents–the highest level in the 12 years" since the FBI began collecting these statistics.

2. A Pfc. in the military, beaten to death in his bunk at Fort Campbell, Kentucky in July of 1999.

3. While films such as *Lilies* play with conceptions of performance and performativity in interesting ways, I chose not to focus on it extensively because of space constraints and because it was not as widely circulated as *Relax*. Nonetheless, *Lilies* is an interesting feature that deserves detailed analysis. While it shares characteristics of assimilation and resistance as described in this essay, it also does creative work with issues of class, religion, race, and gender.

REFERENCES

Andrews, N. (1996, April 22). Low budget films with a sense of adventure: Nigel Andrews talks to three directors called Todd about the prerogatives and preoccupations of independent American cinema. *Financial Times*, p. 23.

Arroyo, J. (1997). Film studies. In A. Medhurst & S. Munt (Eds.), *Lesbian and gay studies: A critical introduction* (pp. 67-83). London: Cassell.

Baudrillard, J. (1983). *Simulations*. New York: Semiotext[e].

Bordwell, D. (1999). The art house cinema as a mode of film practice. In L. Braudy & M. Cohen (Eds.), *Film theory and criticism: Introductory readings* (pp. 716-724). New York: Oxford University Press.

Brookey, J. (1996). A community like Philadelphia. *Western Journal of Communication, 60*(1), 40-56.

Butler, J. (1993). *Bodies that matter.* New York: Routledge.

Butler, J. (1999). *Gender trouble* (2nd ed.). New York: Routledge.

Chesebro, J. (1997). Ethical communication and sexual orientation. In J. Makau & R. C. Arnett (Eds.), *Communication ethics in an age of diversity* (pp. 126-152). Urbana, IL: University of Illinois Press.

Chow, V. (2000, 28 July). Relax . . . it's just sex. *South China Morning Post.*

Clover, C. (1993). *Men, women, and chain saws: Gender in the modern horror film.* Princeton, NJ: Princeton University Press.

CNN (1999, October 6). Showbiz today.

Darsey, J. (1997). *The prophetic tradition and radical rhetoric in America.* New York: New York University Press.

Doty, A. (2000). *Flaming classics: Queering the canon.* New York: Routledge.

Dyer, R. & Cohen, D. (2002). *The politics of gay culture.* In *The culture of queers* (pp. 15-30). London: Routledge.

Fiske, J. (1996). *Media matters: Race and gender in U.S. politics.* Minneapolis: The University of Minnesota Press.

Glieberman, O. (1999, March 19). 'Relax . . . it's just sex,' 'Dancemaker,' and 'I stand alone' are treats worth seeking out. *Entertainment Weekly,* 72.

Griffin, A. G. (1992). Seizing the moving image: Reflections of a black independent producer. In G. Dent (Ed.), *Black popular culture* (pp. 228-233). Seattle: Bay Press.

Grover, J. Z. (1996). AIDS: Keywords. In D. Crimp (Ed.), AIDS: *Cultural analysis, cultural activism.* Cambridge, MA: MIT Press.

Hall, S. (1996). Cultural identity and cinematic representation. In H. Baker, M. Diawara, & R. H. Lindeborg (Eds.), *Black British cultural studies* (pp. 210-222). Chicago: University of Chicago Press.

Hillier, J. (2001). *American independent cinema: A sight and sound reader.* London: British Film Institute Publishing.

James, C. (1994, January 25). For Sundance, struggle to survive. *The New York Times,* p. 15.

Karger, D. (2000, October 6). Calling their own shots. *Entertainment Weekly,* 34-37.

Kramer, L. (1994, January 9). Lying about the gay 90s. *Washington Post,* p. G1.

Leland, J. (2000, March 20). Shades of gay. *Newsweek,* 46-49.

Levy, E. (1999). *Cinema of outsiders: The rise of American independent film.* New York: New York University Press.

Macnab, G. (2001). The doom generation. In J. Hillier (Ed.), *American independent cinema: A sight and sound reader* (pp. 107-109). London: British Film Institute Publishing.

Mann, W. (1998). Laws of desire: Has our imagery become overidealized? In D. Atkins (Ed.), *Looking queer: Body image and identity in lesbian, bisexual, gay, and transgendered communities* (pp. 345-353). New York: The Haworth Press.

Millet, K. (2000). Theory of sexual politics. In B. A. Crow (Ed.), *Radical feminism: A documentary reader* (pp. 122-153). New York: New York University Press.

Nardi, P. (2000). 'Anything for a sis, Mary': An introduction to gay masculinities. In P. Nardi (Ed.), *Gay masculinities* (pp. 1-11). Thousand Oaks, CA: Sage.

Neale, S. (1992). Masculinity as spectacle. In J. C. & A. Kuhn (Ed.), *The sexual subject: A screen reader* (pp. 277-287). London: Routledge.

Rich, B. R. (2001). Queer and present danger. In J. Hillier (Ed.), *American independent cinema: A sight and sound reader* (pp. 114-118). London: British Film Institute Publishing.

Russo, V. (1987). *The celluloid closet.* New York: Harper and Row.

Seidman, S. (1993). Identity and politics in a 'postmodern' gay culture: Some historical and conceptual notes. In M. Warner (Ed.), *Fear of a queer planet* (pp. 105-142). Minneapolis: The University of Minnesota.

Smoron, P. (1999, July 23). 'Just sex' bores as a gay 'Friends.' *Chicago Sun-Times*, p. 33.

Stein, A. (1991). Sisters and queers: The decentering of lesbian feminism. *Socialist Review*, 20, 33-55.

Svetkey, B. (2000, October 6). Is your tv set gay? *Entertainment Weekly*, 24-28.

Warner, M. (2002). *Publics and counterpublics.* New York: Zone Books.

Weigman, R. (1995). *American anatomies: Theorizing race and gender.* Durham, NC: Duke University Press.

doi:10.1300/J082v52n01_05

INTERSECTIONS

Historicizing (Bi)Sexuality:
A Rejoinder for Gay/Lesbian Studies,
Feminism, and Queer Theory

Steven Angelides, PhD

Monash University

SUMMARY. One of the principal aims of queer theory has been to challenge heteronormative constructions of sexuality and to work the hetero/homosexual structure to the point of critical collapse. Despite an epistemic location *within* this very structure, however, the category of

Correspondence may be addressed: Centre for Women's Studies & Gender, Research/Sociology, School of Political & Social Inquiry, Monash University, VIC 3800, Australia (E-mail: Steven.Angelides@arts.monash.edu.au).

Portions of this article appeared in Steven Angelides, *A History of Bisexuality* (Chicago: University of Chicago Press, 2001) and have been incorporated with the permission of The University of Chicago Press; copyright 2001 by The University of Chicago. All rights reserved.

[Haworth co-indexing entry note]: "Historicizing (Bi)Sexuality: A Rejoinder for Gay/Lesbian Studies, Feminism, and Queer Theory." Angelides, Steven. Co-published simultaneously in *Journal of Homosexuality* (Harrington Park Press, an imprint of The Haworth Press, Inc.) Vol. 52, No. 1/2, 2006, pp. 125-158; and: *LGBT Studies and Queer Theory: New Conflicts, Collaborations, and Contested Terrain* (ed: Karen E. Lovaas, John P. Elia, and Gust A. Yep) Harrington Park Press, an imprint of The Haworth Press, Inc., 2006, pp. 125-158. Single or multiple copies of this article are available for a fee from The Haworth Document Delivery Service [1-800-HAWORTH, 9:00 a.m. - 5:00 p.m. (EST). E-mail address: docdelivery@haworthpress.com].

bisexuality has been largely marginalized and even erased from the deconstructive field of queer theory. This article explores some of the factors behind this treatment of bisexuality and suggests that bisexuality's marginalization and erasure brings into relief the strained relationship between the fields of gay/lesbian history, feminism, and queer theory. In exploring some early influential queer deconstructionist texts, it argues that in overlooking the role the category of bisexuality has played in the formation of the hetero/homosexual structure, the project of queer deconstruction has in important ways fallen short of its goals. The author concludes with a call to rethink conventional deconstructive reading practices. doi:10.1300/J082v52n01_06 *[Article copies available for a fee from The Haworth Document Delivery Service: 1-800-HAWORTH. E-mail address: <docdelivery@haworthpress.com> Website: <http://www.HaworthPress.com> © 2006 by The Haworth Press, Inc. All rights reserved.]*

KEYWORDS. Queer theory, feminism, gay/lesbian studies, bisexuality, social constructionism, deconstruction, history

Any discourse that is based on the questioning of boundary lines must never stop questioning its own.

–Barbara Johnson (1987, p.14)

The field of queer deconstructive theory is heavily indebted to Lacanian psychoanalysis, Foucauldian theory, poststructuralism, and Derridean deconstruction. One of its primary principles is the claim that all identities, sexual or otherwise, are only ever constructed relationally. The central paradigm of analysis has been the axis of sexuality in general and the hetero/homosexual opposition in particular. Queer theorists such as Eve Kosofsky Sedgwick, Diana Fuss, and Lee Edelman, among others, have produced many useful studies that serve to challenge heteronormative constructions of sexuality and work the hetero/homosexual opposition, as Fuss (1991, p.1) puts it, to the "point of critical exhaustion." Despite an epistemic location *within* this very opposition, however, the category of bisexuality has been curiously marginalized and erased from some of the founding texts of queer deconstructive theory. It is an analysis of this phenomenon that concerns me in this article. I am going to suggest that the marginalization and erasure of bisexuality brings into relief the strained relationship between the fields of gay/lesbian history, feminism, and queer theory.

While many bisexual theorists have identified this marginalization and erasure of bisexuality (e.g., Eadie, 1993; Hemmings, 1993; James, 1996; Young, 1997), none has yet provided an adequate explanation of how and why it has occurred. This article attempts to do this by subjecting some of the early foundational works of queer deconstructive theory to historical and deconstructive critique. I will argue that the failure to account for bisexuality is the effect of two interrelated factors. First, contrary to stated aims, one of the tendencies of many queer theorists has been to think the two axes of gender and sexuality vertically or hierarchically rather than relationally and obliquely. Second, interrogations of the axes of gender and sexuality have been subsumed within poorly historicized deconstructive frameworks. What this means, I will contend, is that efforts to deconstruct the hetero/homosexual structure have foundered, on the one hand, because of a failure to address the history of (bi)sexuality and on the other, because of the methodological tensions between gay/lesbian history, feminism, and queer theory.

REREADING THE HISTORY OF (BI)SEXUALITY

In what might appear at first sight to be a statement of the obvious, Jo Eadie (1993, p.139) begins her article on bisexual politics with the claim that "[l]ike all sexualities, 'bisexuality' has a history." Yet as Eadie herself is fully aware, this history has scarcely even begun to be told. Histories of homosexuality, and increasingly of heterosexuality, abound. Yet bisexuality scarcely figures within the historiography of sexuality in general. It is certainly true that the study of bisexuality has received much greater attention in recent years. A history of bisexuality in the ancient world has been written by Eva Cantarella (1992), and a number of articles on aspects of bisexuality in the history of modern sexuality have been produced (e.g., Storr, 1997; Udis-Kessler, 1996). A number of edited collections that contain articles concerned with theorizing bisexuality and bisexual politics have also appeared in recent years (Beemyn & Eliason, 1996; Bristow & Wilson, 1993; Hall & Pramaggiore, 1996; Hemmings, 2002). Merl Storr's edited collection, *Bisexuality: A Critical Reader* (1999), has collated a number of significant historical documents that were pivotal to modern theorizations of bisexuality. In spite of a flurry of publications on the subject of bisexuality in the last decade or so, however, the epistemological category of bisexuality has not been historicized in relation to those of homo- and heterosexuality. Marjorie Garber (1995) has offered the most comprehensive study on bisexuality, demonstrating the centrality of bisexuality to manifestations and meanings of human eroticism. While she traces bisexuality in a wide range of cultural, historical, and literary texts, she is less concerned with historicizing bisexuality as an epistemological category. Garber's book, like most of the texts on bisexuality cited above, is motivated by questions of visibility and representation, and of providing concepts and models for thinking about how we might better understand, theorize, and represent bisexual identities and desires in history and culture.[1] This is a very different enterprise than one concerned with historicizing (and deconstructing) the epistemological conditions of possibility of the very category of bisexuality (and thus of homo- and heterosexuality). Yet it is a diachronic historical analysis of bisexuality in relation to categories of hetero- and homosexuality that is missing in the historiography of sexuality.

It seems to me that there are at least two reasons for the erasure of bisexuality from the historiographical field of sexuality. Dominated by the field of gay and lesbian history, the historiography of sexuality has been marked by a methodological reliance on an identity paradigm. Central to this paradigm has been a distinction between sexual behavior and sexual identity. Constructionist historians, cautious of conflating homosexuality and homosexual identity, have found it useful to examine the history of sexuality through this distinction. This approach has been effective, as Jeffrey Weeks (1990, p. 3) has observed, as a way of distinguishing "between homosexual behaviour, which is universal, and a homosexual identity, which is historically specific." However, this introduces conceptual problems of its own. While homosexual identity is not universalized, a homosexual act is, and this only defers and displaces the problem of identity. The result is that bisexuality is completely erased from the historical record.[2] Chris Cagle (1996, p. 236) describes this approach as "monosexual gay historiography." The "claim that homosexual behavior is universal," he quite rightly points out, "ignores the monosexual presumption of that 'universal.'" Neither an act nor a palpable identity–at least until the late 1960s in the case of the latter–bisexuality merely vanishes into the categories of hetero- or homosexuality.

The second reason for bisexuality's disappearance in the historiography of sexuality is the assumption that bisexuality is merely a by-product or after-effect of the hetero/homosexual opposition. There has been tendency to assume that bisexuality is merely determined by the two poles of this opposition, and that it has no role in the diachronic formation of the opposition and of the identity categories of hetero- and homosexuality. As George Chauncey (1994) declares, "Even the third category of 'bisexuality' depends for its meaning on its intermediate position on the axis *defined by those two poles*" (p.13, emphasis added). In the anthology *Bisexualities* (Haeberle & Gindorf, 1998), Erwin Haeberle argues something similar, stating that the category of bisexuality "did not arise," indeed, "*could not come into existence,*" until after "the simple opposition of homo/heterosexuality had been invented" (p. 14). Embedded in these claims of Chauncey and Haeberle is both a historical question, about the actual invention and formation of the category of bisexuality, and a theoretical, or epistemological, question, about the relationship between the three terms heterosexuality, homosexuality, and bisexuality. I am not convinced that either of the fields of gay/lesbian history or queer theory have fully grasped the extent to which these historical and theoretical questions are mutually informing and, indeed, indissociable. This speaks, I will argue, to the fraught nature of the disciplinary relationship between the two enterprises.

The queer intervention in critical theory and cultural studies has held out enormous promise in its deconstructive critique of identitarian frameworks and of the hetero/homosexual opposition. As Lisa Duggan (1995, p. 197) has suggested, these "critiques, applied to lesbian and gay history texts, might produce a fascinating discussion–but so far, they have not." Outlining the "strained relations" between the fields of queer theory and lesbian and gay history, Duggan goes on to argue that the former have too often failed to acknowledge their debt to the latter; while the latter "have largely ignored the critical implications of queer theory for their scholarly practice." I would like to go some way in initiating a productive exchange between the two fields. While my focus in what follows is the terrain of queer deconstructive theories and not specific lesbian and gay history texts, it is through a queer deconstructive rereading of the historiography of sexuality produced in large part by these texts that has enabled me to mount an historical critique of queer theory itself. My aim in this article is not to ascribe any positive ontological or epistemological meaning to the categories of hetero-, homo-, and bisexuality, but rather to insist on the impossibility of ever finally delimiting their meaning. Hence, my goal is to further the project of deconstruction.[3] I aim, therefore, not to produce yet another theory of sexuality, but rather, to demonstrate the epistemological consequences for anyone attempting such a project. I hope to show how the category of bisexuality, contrary to its marginalization and erasure, is implicated in any attempt to conceptualize hetero- and homosexuality as distinct categories. And this, as I will argue in the conclusion, has profound implications for deconstructive reading practices. However, before I embark on an analysis of some of the early influential works of queer deconstructive theory, and to lay the groundwork for my argument, it is necessary to provide a brief but rather differently oriented examination of some influential moments in the early history of modern categories of sexuality. I shall do this by tracing the important, and largely ignored, role of bisexuality in the epistemological formation of the hetero/homosexual opposition.[4]

The Invention of (Bi)Sexuality

The second half of the nineteenth century was a time of enormous social contestation. Movements for racial and sexual equality, and the proliferation of categories of 'effeminate' men, 'masculine' women and New Women, served to challenge patriarchal boundaries of race, gender and sexuality (Chauncey, 1982-83; Cohen, 1993; Duggan, 1993; Newton, 1990; Smith-Rosenberg, 1990). A new discursive economy for the organization of the sexes and their pleasures was in the making. I call this *the economy of (hetero)sexuality*, the creation of two distinct but interrelated epistemic registers, sex/gender and sexuality. Through a historically strategic alliance, this newly emerging western economy began at the turn of the century to subsume human subjects under a new and more complex ontological order. That is to say that there emerged during this period a significant distinction between sex role (active/passive, masculine/feminine behavior) and sexual object choice (Chauncey, 1982-83). In response to the crisis of gender boundaries and in order contain and codify deviations of sex role behavior, the category of sexuality was individuated and produced as a somewhat distinct but additional component of individual ontology (Davidson, 1987). To qualify as a human being, therefore, an individual was not only bestowed with a distinct sex and gender, but as well, with a sexuality; the latter, if all goes to 'nature's' plan presumed to be the consequence of the former. One was thereby conceptualized as both a man, *and* a heterosexual or homosexual, a woman, *and* a heterosexual or lesbian.

The newly emerging registers of sex/gender and sexuality were inextricably entwined through the hegemonic discourse of evolutionary theory. Determined to reorder dominant social hierarchies, scientists explained deviations of normative being and behavior in terms of a hetero-teleological scale of evolutionary development. Blacks, homosexuals, children, and women were situated at lower points on this scale than white heterosexual men, not able (or not yet able) to reach the highest stage of (hu)man evolution. The category of bisexuality played a central role in this linear model, and thus in the epistemological configuration of the category of sexuality (Angelides, 2001). The human differences of race, age, gender and sexuality were thought to be the effect of a specific temporal and spatial relation to what evolutionists and sexologists referred to as primordial hermaphroditism or embryological bisexuality. Believed to be the earliest form of human ancestry, primordial hermaphroditism, or bisexuality, as Frank Sulloway (1979, p. 179) points out, became the evolutionists "missing bisexual link." This was confirmed by recapitulation theory, which posited that the human embryo repeated "in its own life history the life history of the race, passing through the lower forms of its ancestors on its way to maturity" (Russett, 1989, p. 50). In other words, as Charles Darwin (1927 [1871], p. 525) posited, every individual "bears rudiments of various accessory parts, appertaining to the reproductive system, which properly belong[s] to the opposite sex." This meant that blacks, women, children and homosexuals were thought to be the effect of an unsuccessful evolution, closer to, or retaining many more elements of, the originary (prehistoric) bisexuality of the human race and individual embryo. Put differently, an individual's distance from this state of primordial bisexuality dictated the degree of one's evolutionary advancement. Within this framework, therefore, the axes of race, age, gender and sexuality were defined and aligned by their very *relation* to bisexuality.

However, bisexuality posed a problem for sexological discourse. In the attempt to catalogue human sexual behavior, sexologists were confronted with the dilemma of containing its variant forms within the nascent and rigid oppositional categories of hetero- and homosexuality. After all, even in his 1897 publication, *Sexual Inversion*, Havelock Ellis (1897, p. 133) acknowledged the "person who is organically twisted into a shape that is more fitted for the exercise of the inverted than of the normal sexual impulse, *or else equally fitted for both*" (emphasis added). Similarly, Krafft-Ebing (1965, pp. 373-385) had identified what he called "psychical hermaphroditism." Yet, sexology was unable to account for bisexuality as a form of sexuality. For instance, on the one hand, Ellis (1928 [1901], p. 88) claimed that "[t]here would seem to be a broad and simple grouping of all sexually functioning persons into three comprehensive divisions: the heterosexual, the bisexual, and the homosexual." Yet, on the other hand, he affirmed like Krafft-Ebing, that "[m]ost of the bisexual prefer their own sex . . . [and that this] would seem to indicate that the bisexuals may really be inverts." "In any case," stated Ellis (1928 [1901], p. 278), "bisexuality merges imperceptibly into simple inversion."

The difficulty for sexologists constrained by a linear logic of temporal succession was how to reconcile bisexuality as at one and the same time a biological cause (embryological bisexuality) *and* a psychological effect (bisexual identity). Ultimately, bisexuality as a form of sexuality or identity had to be refused in the present tense.[5] That is to say that bisexuality always had to be somewhere else–in the embryo, the sphere of human prehistory–or something else–either really heterosexual or homosexual. It could never be a stable sexual identity in the here and now otherwise the epistemological integrity of the very categories of man, woman, heterosexual and homosexual would be thrown into doubt (Angelides, 2001). For, on the one hand, it was not possible to define the precise meaning of maleness and femaleness, as all that existed were gradations and combinations of both according the original bisexuality of human beings. Inherent to this notion of universal bisexuality was the physiological fact, accepted by Ellis and other sexologists, that "there is no such thing as a pure male or female."[6] On the other hand, if all individuals are physiologically bisexual to one degree or another then there is no reason why they might not be also potentially bisexual in psychological orientation. Within sexological discourse, therefore, it was less a case of "bisexuality merg[ing] imperceptibly into simple inversion" (homosexuality), as Ellis (1928 [1901], p. 278) had put it, than it was the inverse: *the category of homosexuality, and indeed those of heterosexuality, man and woman, merged imperceptibly into bisexuality*. In this way bisexuality can be seen as an important historical and epistemological regulator of the axes of sex/gender and sexuality.

Freud inherited this problematic relationship to the concept of bisexuality. Despite his attempts to move beyond the biologism of sexology, he retained the theory of primordial bisexuality and made it the bedrock of his psychoanalytic framework. Yet he aimed to erect a psychological theory of gender and sexuality that would complement the biological foundations of psychoanalysis. In this way, psychological bisexuality was seen as a reflection of originary (biological) bisexuality. So according to Freud (1905, p. 141), just as primordial bisexuality manifests physically in every individual by "leaving behind only a few traces of the sex that has become atrophied," so too does it manifest mentally such that each individual is "made up of masculine and feminine traits" and desires (Freud, 1925, p. 255). In a radical move, this meant that for Freud heterosexual and homosexual desires are to be found in each individual. However, this profound challenge to the fixity and mutual exclusivity of hetero- and homosexuality was undermined by his erasure of bisexuality as a viable sexuality. With the dissolution of the Oedipus complex a child's father-identification (masculine) or mother-identification (feminine) is determined by a mutually exclusive structuring of the Freudian axes of identification and object-choice (desire). As the child cannot wish to take the mother as a sexual object and identify with her simultaneously—and vice versa regarding the child and the father—the adult cannot have a feminine identification and take a female sexual object (e.g., Freud, 1923, p.34). As Judith Butler (1990, p. 61) puts it, in Freudian theory "only opposites attract." Bisexuality was thus not an end point but a point of human beginnings. It was that which belonged to the sphere of the precultural, the archaic, the uncivilized, that which had to be repressed for normative and desirable individual and social functioning (e.g., Freud, 1919, p. 261; Freud, 1930).

A number of points require underlining here regarding both sexology and Freudian psychoanalysis. First, the evolutionary concept of biological bisexuality was that which inextricably fused together the axes of gender and sexuality. Second, this teleological model could not accommodate a biological *and* a psychological notion of bisexuality. In other words, bisexuality could not be both origin and effect. Therefore, third, to reinforce the oppositions of *both* man and woman, heterosexual and homosexual, bisexuality as a sexuality or psychological identity had to be refused, or erased in the present tense. As Ellis (1928 [1901], p. 88) himself revealed regarding the trinary taxonomy of heterosexual, homosexual, and bisexual, the latter "is found to introduce uncertainty and doubt." Or as Freud (1940, p. 188) put it more frustratingly in relation to gender (identification) and sexuality (object-choice), this "fact of psychological bisexuality . . . embarrasses all our enquiries into the subject and makes them harder to describe." Bisexuality was not just a conceptual sponge used to absorb the contradictions inherent to the oppositional framing of gender and sexuality. Bisexuality was in fact the repudiated internal *Other* to gender, to sexuality, indeed, to binary logic.

That bisexuality represented a danger to the stability of oppositional notions of gender and sexuality was nowhere more apparent than in the discourse of post-Freudian psychoanalysis. In the three decades following Freud's death the concept of bisexuality was almost unilaterally repudiated as a scientific falsehood within the domains of psychoanalysis and psychiatry. As I have argued in detail elsewhere, the repudiation of bisexuality and the pathologization of homosexuality went hand in hand. The only way for psychoanalysts to circumvent the collapse, into one another, of the boundaries of man, woman, hetero- and homosexuality was to repudiate both the biological and psychological residue of bisexuality. At the level of biology this was initiated by Sandor Rado (1940). At the level of psychology it was initiated by Freud himself and unapologetically completed by Edmund Bergler (e.g., 1962 [1956]) and the dominant American form of post-Freudian, oral-centered psychoanalysis (Angelides, 2001).[7] Refused a referent and rendered a misnomer, bisexuality was elided not only in the present tense but also in any temporal sense at all. This was captured in its most extreme form in the work of Edmund Bergler (1962 [1956]. In his chapter entitled, "Does 'Bisexuality' Exist?" he declared,

> BISEXUALITY–a state that has no existence beyond the word itself–is an out-and-out fraud, involuntarily maintained by some naïve homosexuals, and voluntarily perpetrated by some who are not so naïve. The theory claims that a man can be–alternately or concomitantly–homo and heterosexual. The statement is as rational as one declaring that a man can at the same time have cancer and perfect health. (Bergler, 1962 [1956], p. 80)

The genealogical roots of this mode of thinking can be traced to Freud, for whom the possibility of desiring and identifying with the same (gendered) object is precluded. In various forms this principle has inflected almost all of the influential psychoanalytic theorizations of sexuality in the twentieth century.[8] This was most explicitly captured by Bergler's statement that "[n]obody can dance at two weddings at the same time" (1962 [1956], p. 81). It is also apparent in the pervasive use of the categories of *pseudo*-homo- and heterosexuality, and "spurious" and "overt" homosexuality. Each of these categories was constituted through the law of contradiction. Therefore, as long as no individual could at any given moment occupy two opposing camps, psychological bisexuality was to remain a catachresis. For if all bisexuals are either homosexual or heterosexual, and all homosexuals latent heterosexuals–as post-Freudian psychoanalysis largely maintained–then in order for a state of psychological bisexuality to exist, heterosexuality would no longer be latent at all. Instead, homosexuality, as Freud had argued, would exist somewhere *within* heterosexuality, as one of its structuring elements. And this was too unstable a basis for a discourse attempting to lay claim to a therapeutic cure for homosexuality.

The complete erasure of bisexuality effectively undid Freud's dis-articulation of the sex drive from the reproductive aim and object. It meant that the axes of gender and sexuality could be once again conflated (harking back to nineteenth-century sexology) to represent sexual deviation as a deviation of gender development. In spite of this erasure, however, the category of bisexuality was firmly installed from its inception as the third term in the hetero/homosexual opposition. Yet it always functioned as the repudiated third term, the internal *Other* to sexuality's logic of binary opposition. Moreover, this negation of bisexuality–or what I have called the erasure of bisexuality in the present tense–has structured almost every influential model of sexuality in the twentieth century. The primary reason for this is that our modern, Western epistemology of sexuality has been powered by a binary logic that has as its modus operandi the law of non-contradiction.

Despite its brevity, I hope that the preceding historical précis has gone some way in demonstrating how crucial the category of bisexuality has been to the founding epistemological construction of a mutually exclusive hetero/homosexual opposition and to the maintenance of a discursive alliance of gender and sexuality. As I have demonstrated elsewhere (Angelides, 2001), the hetero/homosexual opposition is less a binary than it is a trinary structure. Of course, from poststructuralism and deconstruction we have learned how the two poles in a binary opposition are mutually constituting. One pole thus requires the other for its meaning. In suggesting that the hetero/homosexual opposition is a trinary structure, I am arguing that instead of two terms, there are in fact three interlocking terms in this epistemological structure. The effect of such an all-pervasive structure means that when a theory or model or text of sexuality posits either one of the terms hetero-, homo-, or bisexuality then the other two terms are unfailingly posited by default. Each of the three terms cannot be posited without the others (even if this means through their negation) precisely because each requires the other two for its self-definition (Angelides, 2001). Therefore, if a theorist is inventing a theory of homosexuality, let's say the gay gene theory, even if the author makes no corresponding claims about heterosexuality or bisexuality, I am arguing that the (binary) logical structure of the hetero/homosexual opposition dictates that s/he will make some kind of corresponding claims whether or not s/he intends to or realizes it. What this means, therefore, is that the hetero/homosexual opposition is epistemologically unthinkable without bisexuality. Each of the three terms has been historically and epistemologically constituted through the logic of binary opposition. This is not to suggest that the meanings of hetero-, homo-, and bisexuality are fixed–far from it; the meanings our theories of sexuality ascribe to these terms are dependent upon the context in which they are invoked. What it does mean, however, is that while there will be multiple meanings of these terms, any shifts of meaning in any one of them will produce shifts of meaning in the others.

It is at this point that I would like to turn to some of the recent attempts within the field of queer theory to *deconstruct* the opposition of hetero/homosexuality and its epistemic fusion with that of gender. Exposing the assumptions made about bisexuality within this work will then enable me to demonstrate my argument about queer theory's deconstructive ahistoricism, and the methodological and political tensions between gay/lesbian history, feminism, and queer theory.

QUEER THEORY AND THE ERASURE OF BISEXUALITY

The impetus for much queer theory has been Eve Sedgwick's claim that any analysis of "modern Western culture" requires a "critical analysis of modern homo/heterosexual definition" (1990, p. 1). That bisexuality has been pivotal to the discursive construction of this opposition, however, has been completely overlooked by Sedgwick. This erasure, I would argue, is in part a structural effect of the central organizing principle of her work: the trope of the closet. For Sedgwick this trope is a useful metaphor for interrogating the "relations of the known and the unknown, the explicit and the inexplicit" (Sedgwick, 1990, p. 3) as they have served to structure modern hetero/homosexual definition. Sexual definition and, indeed, meaning in Western culture itself, she quite rightly argues, have been themselves structured around, among others, the oppositions secrecy/disclosure, knowledge/ignorance, masculine/feminine, natural/artificial, same/different, active/ passive, in/out (Sedgwick, 1990, p. 11). However, what she fails to take into consideration is the fact that in the history of discourses of sexuality it is the force of these very oppositions that has served to elide bisexuality from the present tense.

Bisexuality has been rendered an artifact of our evolutionary prehistory, a state outside or prior to culture or civilization, a myth, a catachresis, and a (utopian) sexual impossibility. This is precisely because bisexuality cannot be represented through these binary formulations, blurring as it does any easy distinction of their terms (by in fact partaking of each of the polar terms). In order to secure its binary structure, one of the primary moves of the epistemology of the closet is to repudiate bisexuality, or else render it consonant with its binary logic. In the former, bisexuality is set up as an interior exclusion; in the latter, it is subsumed either by hetero- or homosexuality. By failing to interrogate the interior exclusions and binary appropriations performed by the epistemology of the closet throughout the history of sexuality, Sedgwick's analysis thus falls short of analyzing its terms.

Sedgwick (1990, p. 11) exposes some of the ways the hetero/homosexual opposition inheres in and structures–through its "ineffaceable marking" of fundamental binarisms–modern Western thought. She also usefully traces the conceptual contradictions responsible for the (continuing) "crisis of modern [homo/hetero]sexual definition" (p. 1) since the turn of the century. By crisis Sedgwick is not celebrating the "self-corrosive efficacy of the contradictions inherent to these definitional binarisms" (p. 11). In other words, discourses concerned with securing sexual definition are not about to disappear as a result of an "incoherence of definition" (p. 11). Rather, what she is attempting to highlight is the way these contradictions drive discourses of sexuality on. In the history of sexuality, therefore, "contests for discursive power" can be seen as "competitions" to "set the terms of, and profit in some way, from the operations of such a an incoherence of definition" (p. 11). An analysis of the centrality of this definitional incoherence thus comprises the primary undertaking of *Epistemology of the Closet*. Yet despite her deconstructive labors, Sedgwick does not inquire into precisely *how* discourses of sexuality vie for "rhetorical leverage" (p. 11), that is, *how* modern homo/heterosexual definition is (in)coherently instantiated. As I have already mentioned, bisexuality is the third term in the hetero/homosexual binary that has absorbed and regulated the contradictions inherent to the (re)production of modern binarized sexual definition. What I would like to suggest, then, is that one important way discourses of sexuality have vied for "rhetorical leverage" and "set the terms" of reference for dominant meanings of sexuality is precisely through the erasure of bisexuality in the present tense. By ignoring bisexuality and, indeed, the metonymical association of bisexuality with binary contradiction, Sedgwick's deconstructive framework does not go far enough in *critically analyzing* modern hetero/homosexual definition. Doing this more effectively would require sustained attention, as I have suggested, to the interior exclusions constitutive of the epistemology of the closet. As it stands, therefore, Sedgwick, perhaps like Foucault, appears content with a description rather than explanation of the production of (hetero/homo) sexual definition. For historians and theorists of (bi)sexuality, however, such a rhetorical analysis only repeats the problematic erasure of bisexuality that is the closet's point of departure.

Diana Fuss's introduction to the edited collection *Inside/Out: Lesbian Theories, Gay Theories* is another of the influential texts of queer deconstructive theory that effects a similar marginalization and erasure of bisexuality. Fuss (1991) follows Sedgwick's lead in analyzing the discursive mechanics of modern hetero/homosexual definition. In a brief theoretical analysis she argues that it is "another related opposition" (p. 1), that of inside/outside, which provides the structural foundations for the opposition of hetero-and homosexuality. Fuss raises a series of questions in order to foreground her analysis:

> How do outsides and insides come about? What philosophical and critical operations or modes produce the specious distinction between a pure and natural heterosexual inside and an impure and unnatural homosexual outside? Where exactly, in this borderline sexual economy, does one identity leave off and the other begin? (p. 2)

Drawing more explicitly from Derridean deconstruction, it would seem that Fuss is asking questions from a position which cannot fail to explore the position of bisexuality in this binary economy. Firstly, she is alluding to the fallacy of a pure inside and a pure outside through which to distinguish hetero- from homosexuality. Secondly, she appears to be setting herself the task of inquiring into precisely *how* these homogeneous fallacies are epistemologically ("philosophical and critical operations") created. And thirdly, she is directly addressing the question of the very threshold between these two sexual identities, that is, the spatial, temporal and discursive points where the boundaries between hetero- and homosexuality are blurred. Bisexuality is unmistakably implicated in every one of these questions. Yet Fuss is confusing on this point, as is evidenced by the problematic parenthetical appearance of bisexuality in the following fourth question. She asks:

> And what gets left out of the inside/outside, heterosexual/homosexual opposition, an opposition which could at least plausibly be said to secure its seemingly inviolable dialectical structure only by assimilating and internalizing other sexualities (bisexuality, transvestism, transsexuality . . .) to its own polar logic? (p. 2)

There are a number of problems with this account. Firstly, as bisexual theorist Michael du Plessis (1996, p. 37) points out, the "identities she lists as somehow in excess of 'homosexuality' and 'heterosexuality' are cordoned off by those parentheses from the body of her own text, taken into consideration only in order to be more insidiously expelled." Secondly, this rendering of bisexuality as excessive or *other* to hetero- and homosexuality implies, rather problematically, the existence of a mode of bisexuality that exists outside the economy of (hetero)sexuality and its binary logic. However, bisexuality *as a sexuality* is historically and epistemologically implicated in this binarized economy, unthinkable outside of its terms. Thirdly, and concomitantly, Fuss is suggesting that the appropriation of bisexuality by the inside/outside, heterosexual/homosexual binaries works *only*, therefore, to *secure* their "seemingly dialectical structure." She appears to ignore the fact that not only is bisexuality internal to the dialectical structure of hetero- and homosexuality, but that bisexuality, in a different yet related definitional guise, preceded and conditioned its historical invention. That is, before its appearance in the economy of (hetero)sexuality–indeed, before the construction of this economy–bisexuality was an evolutionary concept (primordial hermaphroditism) constructed to explain the origins of male and female sex difference. Fuss is not referring to this sense of bisexuality however. Instead, she is referring to bisexuality *as a sexuality*. Had she historicized the dialectical structure of hetero- and homosexuality, therefore, she might have realized that bisexuality has served *both* to secure and, simultaneously, to disrupt its boundaries. For instance, within discourses of sexology, Freudian psychoanalysis and gay liberation, bisexuality has been invoked as an explanatory causal principle in the production of hetero- and homosexuality (Angelides, 2001). Yet within the very same discourses bisexuality has been obscured from the present tense and even repudiated at the very point when it threatens to blur the boundaries between the two.[9]

In fairness to Fuss, however, it is possible that I have misread the thrust of her claim that the hetero/homosexual opposition secures "its seemingly inviolable dialectical structure only be assimilating and internalizing other sexualities (bisexuality, transvestism, transsexualism . . .) to its own rigid polar logic." A more "faithful" reading might be that, with respect to bisexuality at least, it can *only* be accommodated by the hetero/homosexual opposition if it is to conform to the inherent binary logic. On one hand I believe this is the case, and that my first reading interpreted this sentence by ignoring the term "only." On the other hand, however, Fuss appears to diverge from my reading of bisexuality in a way that I think justifies my original critique. To say that bisexuality is *assimilated* and *internalized* by the hetero/homosexual opposition is, as I noted above, to impute a kind of distinctness to bisexuality. This suggests that bisexuality undergoes a kind of 'conversion' by binary logic, and that it can exist as a mode of sexuality outside this oppositional framework. My argument, on the contrary, is that bisexuality is an epistemological part of this framework, *unthinkable outside of binary logic.*

An obvious riposte might well be that Fuss is in fact implicitly referring to a notion of bisexuality that our binary logic refuses to acknowledge, and that this idea is scarcely different to what I refer to as the disavowal of bisexuality in the present tense. Even if this is the case, however, a concept of bisexuality in the present tense is also produced through the workings of binary logic. Any concept of bisexuality can only ever be one of the binary logic's *effects.* By thus situating some version of bisexuality *outside* the hetero/homosexual binary, Fuss is in fact implying precisely what my original interpretation suggests: that all versions of bisexuality *inside* the hetero/homosexual binary *only* reinforce or "secure" its "dialectical structure." Yet in the history of sexuality this is only part of the story. Another part is that bisexuality simultaneously *disrupts*, at every turn, and within the very terms of binary logic, the dialectical structure of hetero/homosexuality (Angelides, 2001).

The problem posed by bisexuality highlights a deeper problem with Fuss's invocation of the inside/outside binary. Inscribed as *other* to the hetero/homosexual opposition, bisexuality is situated *outside* the monogamic and monosexual figuring of the very "couple" inside and outside. It is therefore only possible for Fuss to secure the dialectical structure of this binary *as an explanatory principle* by in turn deploying its self-constituting binary logic. The law of this logic is the law of non-contradiction. Each term in a binary, therefore, is either A or not-A. Any term that is both A and not-A, or, neither A nor not-A is excluded. Fuss relies on this law, however, by failing to consider that which it excludes: the logics of both/and, neither/nor. This effectively repudiates the möbius-like figure that is both inside and outside simultaneously, yet reducible to neither. In reading sexuality through this structure, Fuss aims to turn the categories of hetero- and homosexuality *inside/out.* However, this only demonstrates their logical interdependence. To go one step further in deconstructing the hetero/homosexual structure, Fuss would need to mobilize the repudiated logics and explore that which is undecidable within the terms of this dialectical structure. An analysis of bisexuality as undecidable, as both inside and outside, heterosexual and homosexual (yet at the same time none of these), is one crucial way of doing this. However, bisexuality is bracketed out of the analysis. So rather than expose the workings of binary logic, she merely reinforces its modus operandi.[10]

Yet another startling example of this tendency to render bisexuality parenthetical to queer analysis is Lee Edelman's book *Homographesis*. It exhibits a striking similarity to the case of Fuss. One of the primary objectives of the book is to "explore the determining relation between 'homosexuality' and 'identity' as both have been constructed in modern Euro-American societies" (Edelman, 1994, p. xiv). Following Sedgwick's lead, therefore, he also locates homosexuality as central to any cultural "enterprise of . . . identity-determination" (p. xv). In yet another self-avowedly Derridean mode, this entails and aspires to a deconstruction of the heterosexual logic of identity. Edelman performs this analysis by tracing the rhetorical and contradictory operations of sameness and difference through which (homosexual) identity is instantiated. He suggests that homosexuality is constructed as an *anxious* effect of the very crisis of representation itself. Indeed, and more specifically, "'homosexuality,'" he argues, "is constructed to bear the cultural burden of the rhetoricity inherent in 'sexuality' itself" (p. xiv). Homosexuality thereby stands in for and serves "to contain . . . the unknowability of the sexual" (p. xv).

Interestingly, Edelman affirms his project as a "work of *gay* theory" (p. xvi). Despite this invocation, however, the nomination "gay" is not premised on the stability of a fixed referent. Instead, it is deployed as a "signifier of resistance," a deconstructive tool with which to challenge the logic of identity. In other words, homosexuality becomes the privileged deconstructive site for this project because it is "'gay sexuality' [that] functions in the modern West as the very agency of sexual meaningfulness, the construct without which sexual meaning, and therefore, in a larger sense, meaning itself, becomes virtually unthinkable" (p. xv). Scrutinizing a wide range of cultural productions, *Homographesis* is indicative of the queer deconstructive impulse determined to work the opposition of hetero/homosexuality to the point of epistemological frustration.

What is most startling about Edelman's work is not the almost complete absence of any discussion of bisexuality, although this is in itself rather astonishing (bisexuality does not even make it into the book's index). Rather, it is the fact that bisexuality is called forth in the preface by way of parenthetical reference only to be dismissed as antithetical to the theoretical project of deconstruction. Curiously, however, this reference occurs in the context of locating his work under the rubric of gay theory. Like Fuss's parenthesizing of bisexuality, Edelman's takes place in one rather complex, ambiguous, and perhaps even contradictory sentence:

> By retaining the signifier of a specific sexuality within the hetero/homo binarism (a binarism more effectively reinforced than disrupted by the "third term" of bisexuality) even as it challenges the ideology of that categorical dispensation, this enterprise intends to mark its avowal of the multiple sexualities, the various modes of interaction and relation, that the hierarchizing imperative of the hetero/homo binarism attempts to discredit . . . (p. xvi)

Why does bisexuality dis/appear in this context despite his claim to *avow* that which the "hetero/homo binarism attempts to discredit"? It seems that Edelman is attempting to reassure readers that the theoretical entity of "gay" need not be seen as simply reiterative of the logic of identity and the hetero/homosexual opposition. Is he here attempting to respond to, or reject in advance, the claim that the epistemic category of bisexuality might be equally or better positioned to expose the rhetorical operations of sameness and difference in the construction of sexual identity? If so, it would scarcely be different to an *anxious* gesture of containment. Is homosexuality the only category in the hetero/homosexual binary that provides deconstructive leverage for challenging and exposing the stability and fixity of sexual identity? What kind of reductive and essentializing labor is performed on the category of bisexuality to render it mere reinforcement to this binary?

Edelman purports to be undertaking, perhaps in Foucauldian fashion, an *observation* of "how 'homo' and 'hetero,' 'same' and 'different,' switch places" (pp. xviii-xix) in the rhetorical operations of hegemonic discourse. Yet nowhere does he consider how the category of bisexuality might be implicated in this economy. In fact, such an analysis appears to be wittingly foreclosed in advance by unwittingly performing, to use his words, a "metaphorizing totalization" (p. 11) on bisexuality. Yet in the history of discourses of sexuality bisexuality is both the stabilizing *and* destabilizing element in the epistemic construction of sexual identity: Its erasure in the present tense stabilizes the hetero/homosexual opposition whilst simultaneously and perpetually destabilizing the very terms of the opposition (Angelides, 2001). In fact, bisexuality has been the category through and against which modern sexual identity itself has been discursively constructed. Edelman's claim that bisexuality only reinforces the hetero/homosexual binary thus ignores the historical and epistemological figuring of bisexuality. Like "homosexuality," it cannot be represented as a fixed and stable category.

In addition, Edelman (1994) fails to interrogate the way in which the (absent) presence of bisexuality marks the play of sameness and difference. He quite rightly suggests that "homosexuality marks the otherness, the difference internal to 'sexuality' and sexual discourse itself" (p. xix). What he means is that the logic of identity has installed homosexuality in order to contain the internal crisis of meaning engendered by the *rhetoricity of sexuality*. However, he does not ask what the logic of identity must exclude or disavow in order to perform this operation. That is, how does the discourse of sexual identity ensure the mutual exclusivity of sameness and difference, hetero- and homosexuality? Clearly, bisexuality must be disavowed for these operations. For in relation to hetero- and homosexuality, bisexuality is both same and different. Edelman ignores the fact that it is the repudiation of bisexuality which makes possible, indeed makes coherent, the very switching of places between hetero and homo. His project of "locat[ing] the critical force of homosexuality at the very point of discrimination between sameness and difference" (p. 20) therefore repeats the gesture of bisexual disavowal that sustains the logic of (sexual) identity. So I suggest that it is not only homosexuality which, as Edelman argues, "bears the cultural burden of the rhetoricity inherent in 'sexuality'"; nor is it simply a matter of homosexuality standing in for and serving "to contain . . . the unknowability of the sexual." Historically, bisexuality has also had to bear much of this cultural burden. For in fact it is bisexuality that has had to 'stand out' in order for homosexuality to 'stand in' for the "unknowability of the sexual." That is, it is bisexuality's very *erasure in the present tense* that has accompanied and thus enabled homosexuality to mark the "otherness . . . to 'sexuality.'"

It is clear from the foregoing analysis that, while on the one hand the queer theorists analyzed have sought to challenge the very oppositional terms through which modern sexuality has been historically constructed, on the other hand they have merely reproduced those terms within their own ahistorical deconstructive accounts. To put this another way, queer theorists have in some ways unwittingly reproduced as history the binary framework of sexuality as it has been constructed by (among others) the heteronormative discourses of sexology, Freudian and post-Freudian psychoanalysis/psychiatry. By misrecognizing the epistemological function of bisexuality they have remained blind to one of the logic of (sexual) identity's most telling ruses.

GENDER TROUBLE IN QUEER THEORY

How are we to understand the erasure of bisexuality in some of the fundamental works of queer deconstructive theory? One reason, as I have suggested, is that queer theories have ignored the role of bisexuality in the broader history of sexuality. Whether this is itself the outcome of a reliance on monosexual gay/lesbian historiography is unclear. For as Lisa Duggan (1995) has argued, queer theorists have largely repudiated their intellectual debt to lesbian/gay history. While I would suggest that an uncritical reliance on gay and lesbian historiography is tied up with a form of presentism that is less concerned with rereading history through queer frameworks, even that does not tell us enough regarding bisexuality's erasure.[11] So it is to an interrogation of queer theory's framing of gender that I now turn, for it is here that I suggest we might find some answers.

Within the burgeoning fields of gay/lesbian studies and queer theory the category of sexuality, and its disarticulation from gender, has opened up a promising discursive space for interrogating and deconstructing western discourses constituted through the hetero/homosexual binarism. As the editors to the *Lesbian and Gay Studies Reader* point out, "[l]esbian/gay studies does for *sex* and *sexuality* approximately what women's studies does for gender" (Abelove, Barale, & Halperin, 1993, p. xv).[12] To say that the work of Foucault has been enormously influential in this development is at best an understatement. His genealogical account of the emergence of sexuality as coextensive with modern subjectivity has been absorbed as axiomatic to the field of queer theory (e.g., Sedgwick, 1990). It appears, however, that this productive deployment of Foucault's work has also brought with it a constraining limitation, namely, a problematic relationship to gender.[13]

Increasingly, there is a distinct concern, particularly among feminist theorists, that the category of sexuality has become reified to the point of exclusion in discourses of queer theory. Feminism and the category of gender, so the argument goes, are being cast as redundant explanatory principles as a result of queer theory's attempt to disarticulate gender and sexuality. In this section I will begin by tracing and extending these arguments in order to put forward an argument of my own in relation to bisexuality. I will argue that despite its productive potential, the disarticulation of gender and sexuality, and the Foucauldian-inflected reification of the latter, has proceeded in such a way as to occlude bisexuality from analytic view.

Judith Butler (1994) has problematized the above claim made by the editors of *The Lesbian and Gay Studies Reader*. She argues that it represents an unwitting, yet *aggressive* and *violent* discursive appropriation of sexuality as the "proper object" of gay/lesbian/queer studies over and against a feminism whose proper object is gender (Butler, 1994, pp. 5-6).[14] This appropriation effects, Butler suggests, more than a tendentious methodological distinction between feminism and gay/lesbian/ queer studies. As well, it serves to make feminist inquiry into sexuality obsolete. In interrogating the terms of the analogy between feminism and gay/lesbian/queer, Butler claims that the analogy falls down around the editors' invocation of a Foucauldian-inflected category of "sex":

> the editors lead us through analogy from a feminism in which gender and sex are conflated to a notion of lesbian and gay studies in which 'sex' encompasses and exceeds the purview of feminism: 'sex' in this second instance would include not only questions of identity and attribute (female or male), but discourses of sensation, acts, and sexual practice as well. (p. 2)

Butler argues that the category of 'sex' is common both to feminism and gay/lesbian/queer studies, yet this "commonality must be denied" (p. 2). The "implicit argument," she suggests, "is that lesbian and gay studies does precisely what feminism is said to do, but does it in a more expansive and complex way" (p. 4).

Butler identifies the appropriation of Gayle Rubin's essay "Thinking Sex" as the gesture serving to authorize the methodological founding of lesbian/gay/queer studies. However, she argues that a decontextualized appropriation of Rubin's call for an analytic separation of gender and sexuality effects not only a significant "restriction of the scope of feminism" (p. 8), but breaks the long standing coalition between the two (p. 21). While I remain unconvinced of the mechanics of Butler's argument as it pivots on and is extrapolated from the editors' introduction to *The Lesbian and Gay Studies Reader*–an argument made, I should add, with almost no reference to any texts of queer theory[15]–she has identified an emergent tendency that is perhaps more usefully explored through a grounded analysis of specific queer texts.

Biddy Martin (1994a) takes a first step in this direction in her essay "Sexualities Without Genders and Other Queer Utopias." She provides the basis for a more productive and grounded analysis of some of the issues raised by Butler. Despite welcoming the possibilities opened up by disarticulating gender and sexuality, like Butler, Martin is concerned also that this is taking place at the expense of feminism and important feminist destabilizations of the category of gender. Sexuality, she argues elsewhere, is too often being cast as that which "exceeds, transgresses, or supersedes gender" (Martin 1994b, p. 101). Gender, and indeed feminism, on the other hand, is increasingly being framed as fixed and constraining, hampering the celebration of queerity (Martin, 1994a, pp. 106-7).

Martin argues that Sedgwick's work is indicative of this tendency. In "axiom 2" of *Epistemology of the Closet,* Sedgwick (1990) attempts to keep analytically distinct the two senses of the category of sex: chromosomal sex and sex as sexuality/act/fantasy/pleasure. She goes on to suggest that the latter is "virtually impossible to situate on a map delimited by the feminist-defined sex/gender distinction" (Sedgwick, 1990, p. 29). Instead, Sedgwick stresses that the development of an anti-homophobic discourse more suited to an analysis of sexuality "as an alternative analytic axis" is not just required, but "a particularly urgent project" (p. 32). In collapsing sex and gender "more simply under the rubric 'gender'" (p. 29), she puts forward the claim that sexuality is inflected by a form of conceptual ambiguity in a way unknown to the category of gender. Rendered the more fixed, gender is considered the *proper object* of feminist discourse and less suited to deconstructive analysis. Sexuality, on other hand, is the more apt object of deconstruction, exceeding "the bare choreographies of procreation," perhaps even situated as "the very opposite" to chromosomal sex, to gender (p. 29).

Martin (1994a, p. 107) argues that it is one thing to posit the irreducibility of sexuality and gender, but quite another to react to this, as does Sedgwick, "by making them more distinct, even opposed to one another." She also objects to the way Sedgwick privileges sexuality and defines anti-homophobic analysis not just against but over and above monolithic and fixed notions of both feminism and gender. For example, sexuality, argues Sedgwick (1990, p. 29), "could occupy. . . even more than 'gender' the polar position of the relational, the social/symbolic, the constructed, the variable, the representational." Moreover, sex (an "array of acts, expectations, narratives, pleasures") and sexuality, unlike gender, "tend to represent the full spectrum of positions between the most intimate and the most social, the most predetermined and the most aleatory, the most physically rooted and the most symbolically infused, the most innate and the most learned, the most autonomous and the most relational traits of being" (p. 29). Sedgwick perhaps anticipates the kind of feminist objection raised by Martin with the reassurance that she is not calling for "any epistemological or ontological privileging of an axis of sexuality over an axis of gender" (p. 34). However, in reifying sexuality as the analytically autonomous and "apter deconstructive object" (p. 34), Sedgwick is thus able to install the hetero/homosexual opposition as *the* pivotal organizing principle of western thought over and above that of male/female. Sexuality thereby becomes the *proper object* not of feminist but of anti-homophobic inquiry (as though the two are not overlapping).

The problems encountered with this reified account of sexuality and its disarticulation from gender are made even more palpable when we examine the figure of bisexuality. Recall that it is bisexuality that has in many ways regulated the axes of gender and sexuality as they were constructed in the late 19th and early 20th centuries. And as I discussed earlier, Sedgwick's epistemological mapping of the logic of the closet rests on a repudiation and erasure of bisexuality. Yet despite Sedgwick's acknowledgment that these axes are "inextricable from one another" (Sedgwick 1990, p. 30), her analysis of modern hetero/homosexual definition ignores this very crucial space of overlap between gender and sexuality. Take, for example, her attempt to map the "models" of "gay/straight definition" through which homosexuality has been articulated historically. Sedgwick offers a table with two separate horizontal rows for sexuality and gender. Each row is then vertically divided by two columns, one representing "separatist" models, the other "integrative" or "transitive" ones. On the one hand, homosexuality has been defined *sexually*: as an essentialist minority (separatist); *and* as a universal and cultural potential (integrative). On the other hand, it has been defined in terms of *gender identification*: male and female homosexual desire as a natural effect of male and female gender identification respectively (separatist); *and* as a result of cross-gender identification (integrative) (Sedgwick, 1990, pp. 86-90, esp. p. 88).

While this model captures some of the contradictions and cross-identifications made possible within and between the separatist and integrative axes of homosexual definition, it remains in the end only a model, as she herself calls it, of "gay/straight definition" (p. 88). Bisexuality is incorporated at best only as a universalizing potential, at worst it is implicitly collapsed into hetero- and homosexualities. Sedgwick's reliance on hegemonic constructions of sexual identity thereby repeats the exclusionary gesture necessary to sustain the workings of binary logic. Moreover, her unraveling of gender and sexuality as distinct axes has left her unable to accommodate, as du Plessis (1996, p. 33) points out, "people for whom sexuality and gender may match up differently." This does "damage," argues du Plessis, "to the realities of transgender sexualities and bisexual genders."[16] I would argue also that this kind of exclusionary mapping of sexuality does more than serve to sustain the analytic distance Sedgwick has installed between feminism and gay/lesbian/queer studies. In addition, bisexuality (and indeed transgenderism) is the pawn that is forced out in an act of methodological and disciplinary secessionism.

A similar tendency to privilege and reify sexuality over and against gender is apparent in Fuss's work in *Inside/Out*. Fuss takes the hetero/homosexual binarism as her prioritized point of deconstructive departure. Her primary task is to expose only the interdependence of the hetero on the homo, that is, the homo as always already inside the hetero. However, rather than examine the inextricable enmeshment of the hetero/homo, inside/outside oppositions with that of male/female, Fuss (1991) follows a path similar to Sedgwick's by separating too radically gender and sexuality. This move takes place in her discussion of what is "most urgently" needed in current "gay and lesbian theory": that is, a "theory of sexual borders" which can take into account and promote organizational strategies required to address "the new cultural and sexual arrangements occasioned by the movements and transmutations of pleasure in the social field" (Fuss 1991, p. 5). This new theory, it would seem, is a queer theory of sexuality. In the next sentence she does invoke the opposition of gender but only to dethrone it as the primary paradigm through which to read sexuality:

> Recent and past work on the question of sexual difference has yet to meet this pressing need, largely because, as Stephen Heath accurately targets the problem, our notion of sexual difference all too often subsumes sexual differences, upholding "a defining difference of man/woman at the expense of gay, lesbian, bisexual, and indeed *hetero* heterosexual reality." (Fuss, 1991, p. 5)

This quote of Heath's is also part of an argument that gender and sexuality "can and should be separated from one another" (Heath, 1990, pp. 140-1). However, like Rubin and Sedgwick, Heath is formulating such a claim against Catharine MacKinnon's radical feminist collapsing of sexuality as a mere expression of gender. So by drawing on Heath in order to fault recent and past feminist work on sexual difference, Fuss (1991) is offering somewhat of a reductionist caricature of this diverse body of work. However, she is also suggesting that the vanguard position for this new *theory of sexual borders* is not feminism but gay/lesbian/queer studies. "[G]ay and lesbian readers of culture," she suggests, have a "responsibility ... to reshape and to reorient the field of sexual difference to include sexual differences" (Fuss, 1990, p. 6). Curiously, this responsibility is conferred primarily, or perhaps only, to "gay and lesbian readers." Where are anti-homophobic heterosexual, feminist, bisexual, or transgendered readers of culture situated in relation to this urgent political task?

I suggest that Fuss's failure to incorporate these 'others' within the vanguard of this new sexual theory is the complex product of the problematic reification of sexuality over and above gender. Let us recall the opening statement of her introduction to *Inside/Out*: "The philosophical opposition between 'heterosexual' and 'homosexual' ... has always been constructed on the foundations of ... the couple 'inside' and 'outside'" (Fuss, 1991, p. 1). Here Fuss has immediately elided or at the very least suspended a discussion of gender as an opposition which also fundamentally undergirds the hetero/homosexual opposition. She does invoke gender but only in order to foreground her deconstructive analysis of the hetero/homosexual, inside/outside binaries. Homosexuality, she quite rightly points out, "is produced inside the dominant discourse of sexual difference as its necessary outside, but this is not to say that the homo exerts no pressure on the hetero nor that this outside stands in any simple relation of exteriority to the inside" (p. 5). Fuss indeed seems to be acknowledging the inexplicable interlacing of gender (sexual difference) and sexuality, the latter seen as the expurgated inside of the former. However, she appears to effect a curious analytic slippage whereby gender, or sexual difference, is invoked only to be immediately subsumed or displaced by heterosexuality.[17] Homosexuality is then called forth as the internally erected border that works "to define and defend" the heterosexual inside. It is identified as the subversive element "occupying the frontier position of inside out" in the "discourse of sexual difference," "neither completely outside" it "nor wholly inside it either" (pp. 5-6).

In representing (homo)sexuality as transgressive or excessive of sexual difference, Fuss is attempting to gesture towards a theory of sexuality not beholden to an analysis of gender. The axis of sexuality appears to be superimposed on top of the axis of gender, subsuming gender as a subsidiary component. Lee Edelman (1994) appears to perform a similar move. He suggests that

> "[w]here heterosexuality ... seeks to assure the sameness or purity internal to the categorical 'opposites' of anatomical 'sex' ... homosexuality would multiply the differences that desire can appre-

hend in ways that menace the internal coherence of the sexed identities that the order of heterosexuality demands." (p. 10)

Again, it is homosexuality that is identified as subversive agent. I would argue, following Butler (1994), however, that this maneuver performed by Fuss and Edelman reads as an allegory of the relationship being unwittingly instantiated between feminism and gay/lesbian/queer studies. Feminism is metonymically associated with gender, gay/lesbian/queer studies with (homo)sexuality, the latter in a relationship of subversive excess to the former. In other words, queer theory is that through which Fuss's new theory of sexual borders and Edelman's project of *Homographesis* can be advanced over a redundant feminism.

Fuss's new theory of sexual borders, I would add, appears to be the exclusive domain not of anti-homophobic feminists, bisexuals, and transgenderists, but of 'gays and lesbians.' For it is they who are seen to occupy the subversive "frontier position" of homosexuality. In this way such a move evacuates the very self-reflexive mode–the critical queer reflex–that is, I would argue, the most significant and important force of this new (queer) theory of sexual borders.

Despite acknowledging the fact that homosexuality is constituted inside the discourse of gender or sexual difference, Fuss and Edelman tend to construct sexuality as synonymous with the hetero/homosexual opposition, distinct from and superimposed over the top of this discourse. Partially displacing gender, sexuality, or the hetero/homosexual opposition, is then identified as the privileged upper layer of deconstructive analysis. In other words, there is a sense in both Fuss's and Edelman's–and indeed in Sedgwick's–work that sexuality must first be deconstructed in order to prize it away from, and thus render it autonomous of gender. However, this reification of a sexuality disarticulated from and epistemologically privileged over gender obfuscates an analysis of their mutual interrelation. As a result, an analysis of bisexuality as the figure shoring up binary sexual identity is occluded. For it is bisexuality which has not just traversed but historically and epistemologically regulated the axes of sexuality and gender in the production of modern hetero- and homosexual identities.

CONCLUSION

Like Foucault (1980), and perhaps partly as a result of his enduring legacy, some of the prominent queer theorists have rendered gender "historically subordinate to sexuality" (Foucault 1980, p. 157).[18] As I have argued, however, sexuality was constituted as an effect of a difference internal to phallocentric gender. That is to say, that sexuality was produced around crises or deviations of normative gender. So the axis of sexuality was never entirely, nor even nearly, separate from that of gender in the modern economy of (hetero)sexuality. The former was produced in and through the latter.

Queer theorists are certainly cognizant of this historical fact. Indeed, it is upon this knowledge that the call to separate sexuality from gender is predicated. In other words, it is because of this historical reduction of sexuality to gender dynamics that such a future-oriented project to disarticulate the two is undertaken. However, this future-oriented project of the present appears to have distorted the terms of a deconstructive project oriented to dismantling figurations of sexuality inherited from the past. That is, it is perhaps a presentist tendency in queer theory that has undermined more properly historicized deconstructive analyses. In subordinating gender to sexuality and insisting on a degree of analytic autonomy for the latter, many queer theorists have thought the two axes vertically or hierarchically rather than relationally and obliquely. As a result, bisexuality, an important historical regulator of the axes of gender and sexuality, has been elided in the present tense and, indeed, in almost any sense at all.

Here it is perhaps pertinent to offer as a reminder Fredric Jameson's infamous slogan: "Always historicize!" (1981, p. 9). Clearly, deconstructive critique of all kinds presupposes the historicity of identity categories. However, in the case of the queer deconstructive theory I have examined, a reliance on this presumption–a reliance on an unexamined historiography–has meant the evacuation of a significant part of the very history at the heart of sexuality's historicity. The historiography of modern sexuality has been remarkably inattentive to the discursive and epistemological function of bisexuality. Gay/lesbian constructionist history has been concerned primarily with tracing the emergence of homosexual identities, and rarely with tracing the epistemological processes informing their formation. One result of this is that bisexuality has made only a fleeting appearance in the historiography of sexuality. The emphasis on identity, and the fact that bisexuality has been barely (if at all) visible as a cultural identity until recent decades, have meant that in constructionist histories bisexuality's mention is limited for the most part to the ways it has cropped up in the particular theories of sexuality. It has also meant that the identity paradigm, and thus the hetero/homosexual opposition, has been unwittingly reproduced in a queer deconstructive theory derivative of such historical accounts. So despite the assault on essentializing notions of identity, both queer theory and gay/lesbian history have failed to address important aspects of the relationality of identity within the very history and theory of (bi)sexuality.

It seems to me not unreasonable to suggest that *any* deconstruction of historically overdetermined identity concepts and categories must engage the history on whose behalf it speaks. Alternatively, it is equally as important for constructionist scholars to engage a deconstructive critique of the very terms through which their historical accounts are formulated. I propose, then, that historicization and deconstruction must always be seen as two sides of the same conceptual process. In suggesting this, it follows that social constructionist gay/lesbian studies and deconstructive queer theories ought not be framed as adversaries or wholly distinct methodologies; even less ought they disavow their epistemological intersection with feminism. Instead, we might facilitate the production of a deconstructive historicism more attentive to the workings of difference if we remember always to acknowledge the mutually implicating and mutually constituting nature of these seemingly distinct analytic models.

I have argued that one way of furthering the project of a deconstructive historicism is to rethink conventional binary-based representations of sexuality. While gay/lesbian constructionism and queer deconstructionism have correctly identified the hetero/homosexual structure as the epistemological linchpin of modern western concepts and representations of sexuality, what I have suggested is that they have misunderstood the workings of this seemingly binary structure. Instead of functioning as a binary of two mutually constituting poles, the hetero/homosexual structure has, both historically and epistemologically, functioned strictly speaking as a trinary. It is important to reiterate, however, that to argue that each of these terms are meaningful only in relation to the other two–that is, that each requires the other two for its self-definition–is not to argue that these terms are somehow truthful reflections of individual sexualities. It is simply to argue that, however ill-conceived or inadequate for the representation of the wide range of cultural forms of sexuality, this trinary structure has nonetheless been the primary organizing principle of modern western thought on sexuality. This has significant ramifications not just for queer theory and gay and lesbian history, but, indeed, for any research into modern western sexualitiess. Not only do our deconstructive analyses of the hetero/homosexual structure need recasting in order to unravel more accurately the workings of this structure in the myriad cultural texts and discourses in which it appears. In addition to this, any researcher who lays claim to any of these three terms is beholden to specify the trinary interrelationships contained therein. This is because any effort to invoke any one of the categories of hetero-, homo-, and bisexuality inevitably results in default claims about the other two terms—whether or not a researcher intends to make such claims. For queer theorists critical of any attempt to impose rigid and homogeneous definitions of sexuality and distinctions between hetero- and homosexuality, this trinary-based deconstructive reading practice promises to make researchers far more accountable in their use of such unstable terms as hetero-, homo-, and bisexuality. It might also help to undermine the continued production of spurious essentialist theories of sexuality.

Dean Hamer's (Hamer and Copeland, 1994) infamous 'gay gene' research provides a useful example to illustrate this last point. Hamer, like the vast bulk of scientists searching for the origins of (homo)sexuality, deliberately overlooked bisexuality, "because our first goal was to determine whether genes had any influence on sexual orientation, which meant it was important to study only those individuals whose orientation was unambiguous" (1994, p. 146). The problem with Hamer's methodology is that he fails to appreciate how the very term 'homosexuality' can only gain meaning by way of distinctions between both hetero- and bisexuality. His claim to be dealing only with homosexuality is therefore patently false, for in order to define homosexuality at all he must draw boundaries around each of the three terms—although this boundary marking is most often unintentionally rather than intentionally achieved. The point I wish to underscore is that the trinary-based deconstructive method I am advocating is far more effective in exposing the flaws in Hamer's methodology than the usual poststructuralist binary-based method that merely repeats the erasure of bisexuality and unwittingly reinforces a dualistic reading of the hetero/homosexual structure.

I share the deconstructive view that any attempt to provide definitive meanings and to draw strict boundaries around the categories of hetero-, homo-, and bisexuality is doomed to failure. I am also of the view that the hetero/homosexual structure ought not to be presumed as an uncritical point of departure for thinking about sexualities. I just hope that in delineating the trinary-based deconstructive in this article, I have gone some small way towards furthering the interminable project of deconstructive criticism.

NOTES

1. What I am arguing is that the bulk of the work on bisexuality has been driven largely, or even implicitly, by the desire to somehow represent that which goes by the name of bisexual identities and bisexualities. For instance, in suggesting that bisexuality is "neither the 'inside' nor the 'outside' but rather that which creates both [homosexuality and heterosexuality]" (1995, p. 526), Garber is attempting to provide a theory *of* bisexuality. Similarly, the editorial objective of Storr's (1999) collection is an interrogation of the question of "what bisexuality is" (p. 3); and BiAcademic Intervention's collection, as revealed by the title, *The Bisexual Imaginary: Representation, Identity, and Desire* (1997) is concerned with representing bisexuals and bisexualities.

2. In his recent collection of essays, *How to do the History of Homosexuality*, while David Halperin (2002) attempts to avoid instating a simplistic distinction between representation and reality, and thus discourse and desire, he nonetheless fails to consider how bisexuality, as both an epistemological category and an identificatory axis of desire, informs the historical production the hetero/homosexual opposition.

3. This argument is detailed in the concluding section.

4. It might be useful at this stage to point out that when I refer to the historicization of categories of sexuality and the epistemological formation of the hetero/homosexual opposition, I am not referring to the ways in which these categories and the opposition are negotiated by individuals or communities. The focus of my discussion is on the epistemological conditions of possibility for the articulation of the categories hetero-, homo-, and bisexuality in dominant theories of sexuality. In short, I am referring to the way in which each of these three terms can only be defined with reference to the other two; that is, that each term derives its meaning through distinctions with the other two. This argument will be elaborated throughout the article.

5. In relation to bisexuality, the phrase "present tense" was first used by Amanda Udis-Kessler (1991). While my usage of this phrase in some ways overlaps with Udis-Kessler's–and I am therefore indebted to her for applying it to bisexuality–it is also significantly different. Udis-Kessler is using it in a contemporary context to refer to the crisis of meaning she thinks bisexuals and bisexuality pose to essentialist understandings of sexuality. She argues that bisexuals and bisexuality bring home the constructionist understanding of sexuality as fluid and amenable to choice, thereby challenging the fixity of both hetero- and homosexualities. I am using the phrase as a way of interrogating and describing the specific historical and epistemological processes by which bisexuality has been erased as a legitimate identity in discourses of sexuality in the modern west. In this way, my analysis may complement Udis-Kessler's, and indeed provides an historical and theoretical framework upon which to ground some of her claims

6. This is a quote by a physiologist whom Ellis endorses (1928 [1901], 313).

7. At most, bisexuality was deployed in a statistical or behavioral sense in terms of an individual taking part in both homosexual and heterosexual practices throughout a lifetime. So despite the fact that most theorists and analysts of this period describe some of their subjects as bisexuals, in terms of the structures of individual identity they seem to be either homosexual or heterosexual. There was no such thing as a bisexual at the level of ego structure.

8. I should point out that I am referring to influential psychoanalytic models that have constituted a kind of dominant, global discursive field of (homo)sexuality. The reason I placed the "homo" in parentheses is that all too frequently normative "sexual-

ity" has been the default by-product of a discourse concerned with mapping homosexual "deviance". It is also worth noting that psychoanalytic models such as Lacanian theory had virtually no influence on this hegemonic field of (homo)sexuality.

9. Of course, in post-Freudian psychoanalysis this threat was contained by the outright repudiation bisexuality's existence.

10. Ironically, Fuss (1991) points out that: "The problem, of course, with the inside/outside rhetoric, if it remains deconstructed, is that such polemics disguise the fact that most of us are both inside and outside at the same time" (p. 5).

11. See Henry Abelove's (1995) discussion of presentism in queer theory.

12. I should point out that the editors to this reader may refuse a distinction between lesbian/gay studies and queer theory. They consider queer a structuring part of lesbian and gay studies. "[O]ur choice of 'lesbian/gay,'" they point out, "indicates no wish on our part to make lesbian/gay studies look less assertive, less unsettling, and less queer than it already does"(p. xvii).

13. The list of feminist critiques of this kind is endless. For good examples see Diamond and Quinby (1988); Hartsock (1990); Dean (1994).

14. Butler (1994) suggests that it was an unintentional move, "given that all three have made strong contributions to feminist scholarship" (p. 5).

15. Butler (1994) refers to Sedgwick, but only in a footnote (pp. 23-4, note 8).

16. Butler (1994, p. 24, note 8) argues along similar lines to du Plessis.

17. While Lacanian influenced theorists such as Fuss might distinguish sexual difference from a more sociological category of gender, I am using gender along lines similar to Judith Butler (1994), whereby she has attempted to construct a theory of gender which retains some of the insights of Lacanian sexual difference whilst also incorporating a transformative notion of gender (pp. 18, 24-5, note 13). In this way, following Butler I see the notion of sexual difference as already constituted through a matrix of gender. When I discuss the separation of gender and sexuality in the work of theorists such as Fuss, therefore, I use gender interchangeably with sexual difference.

18. Foucault (1980) actually uses the term "sex," however this term encompasses not just sexual practice, pleasure, etc., but also gender.

REFERENCES

Abelove, H., Barale, M.A., & Halperin, D. M.. (Eds.). (1993). *The lesbian and gay studies reader*. New York: Routledge.

Abelove, H. (1995). Critically queer: Interview with Henry Abelove. *critical inQueeries*, *1*(1), 7-14.

Angelides, S. (2001). *A history of bisexuality*. Chicago: University of Chicago Press.

Beemyn, B., & Eliason, M. (Eds.). (1996). *Queer studies: A lesbian, gay, bisexual, and transgender anthology*. New York: New York University Press.

Bergler, E. (1962 [1956]). *Homosexuality: Disease or way of life?* New York: Collier Books.

Bristow, J., & Wilson, A. R. (Eds.). (1993). *Activating theory: lesbian, gay, bisexual politics*. London: Lawrence & Wishart.

Butler, J. (1990). *Gender trouble: Feminism and the subversion of identity*. New York: Routledge.

Butler, J. (1994). Against proper objects. *differences: A Journal of Feminist Cultural Studies*, 6(2-3), 1-26.

Cagle, C. (1996). Rough trade: Sexual taxonomy in postwar America. In D. E. Hall & M. Pramaggiore (Eds.), *RePresenting bisexualities: Subjects and cultures of fluid desire* (pp. 234-252). New York: New York University Press.

Cantarella, E. (1992). *Bisexuality in the ancient world*. Translated by Cormac Ó'Cuilleanáin. New Haven: Yale University Press.

Chauncey, G. (1982-83). From sexual inversion to homosexuality: Medicine and the changing conceptualization of female deviance. *Salmagundi, 58-59*, 114-146.

Chauncey, G. (1994). *Gay New York: Gender, urban culture, and the making of the gay male world, 1890-1940*. New York: Basic Books.

Cohen, E. (1993). *Talk on the Wilde side: Toward a genealogy of a discourse on male sexualities*. New York: Routledge.

Darwin, C. (1927 [1871]). *The descent of man, and selection in relation to Sex*. New York: The Modern Library.

Davidson, A. I. (1994). Sex and the emergence of sexuality. *Critical Inquiry, 14*, 16-48.

Dean, C. J. (1994). The productive hypothesis: Foucault, gender, and the history of sexuality. *History and Theory, 33*, 271-96.

Diamond, I., & Quinby, L. (Eds.). (1988). *Feminism and Foucault: Reflections on resistance*. Boston: Northeastern University Press.

Doty, A. (1993). *Making things perfectly queer: Interpreting mass culture*. Minneapolis: University of Minnesota Press.

Duberman, M., Vicinus, M., & Chauncey, G. (Eds.). (1990). *Hidden from history: Reclaiming the gay and lesbian past*. New York: Meridian.

Duggan, L. (1993). The trials of Alice Mitchell: Sensationalism, sexology, and the lesbian subject in turn-of-the-century America. *Signs, 18*(4), 791-814.

Duggan, L. (1995). The discipline problem: Queer theory meets lesbian and gay history. In L. Duggan & N. Hunter, *Sex wars: Sexual dissent and political culture* (pp. 194-206). New York: Routledge.

du Plessis, M. (1996). Blatantly bisexual; or, unthinking queer theory. In D. E. Hall & M. Pramaggiore (Eds.), *RePresenting bisexualities: Subjects and cultures of fluid desire* (pp. 19-54). New York: New York University Press.

Eadie, J. (1993). Activating bisexuality: Towards a bi/sexual politics. In J. Bristow & A. R. Wilson (Eds.), *Activating theory: lesbian, gay, bisexual politics* (pp. 139-170). London: Lawrence & Wishart..

Edelman, L. (1994). *Homographesis: Essays in gay literary and cultural theory*. New York: Routledge.

Ellis, H., & Symonds, J. A. (1897). *Sexual inversion*. London: Wilson & Macmillan.

Ellis, H. (1928 [1901]). *Studies in the psychology of sex, Volume II, Sexual inversion*. Philadelphia: F.A. Davis Company.

Freud, S. (1905). *Three essays on the theory of sexuality. The standard edition of the complete psychological works of Sigmund Freud*. Vol. 7. Translated. and edited by. James Strachey. London: Hogarth, 24 vols. 1953-74, 123-243.

Freud, S. (1919). Preface to Reik's *Ritual: Psycho-analytic studies. Standard edition*, 17, 257-63.

Freud, S. (1923). *The ego and the id. Standard edition*, 19, 3-66.

Freud, S. (1925). Some psychological consequences of the anatomical distinction between the sexes. *Standard edition*, 19, 241-60.

Freud, S. (1930). *Civilization and its discontents*. Edited by James Strachey. London: Hogarth Press, 1975.

Freud, S. (1940). *An outline of psycho-analysis. Standard edition*, 23, 141-207.

Foucault, M. (1980). *The history of sexuality, Volume One: An introduction*. Translated by Robert Hurley. New York: Vintage Books.

Fuss, D. (1991). Inside/out. In D. Fuss (Ed.), *Inside/out: Lesbian theories, gay theories* (pp. 1-10. New York: Routledge.

Garber, M. (1995). *Vice versa: Bisexuality and the eroticism of everyday life*. New York: Simon & Schuster.

Goldman, R. (1996). Who is that *queer* queer?: Exploring norms around sexuality, race, and class in queer theory. In B. Beemyn & M. Eliason (Eds.), *Queer studies: A lesbian, gay, bisexual, and transgender anthology* (pp. 169-182). New York: New York University Press.

Haeberle, E. J. (1998). Bisexuality: History and dimensions of a modern scientific problem. In E. J. Haeberle & R. Gindorf (Eds.), *Bisexualities: The ideology and practice of sexual contact with both men and women* (pp. 14-51). New York: Continuum.

Haeberle, E. J., & Gindorf, R. (Eds.). (1998). *Bisexualities: The ideology and practice of sexual contact with both men and women*. New York: Continuum.

Hall, D. E., & Pramaggiore, M. (Eds.). (1996). *RePresenting bisexualities: Subjects and cultures of fluid desire*. New York: New York University Press.

Halperin, D. M. (2002). *How to do the history of homosexuality*. Chicago: University of Chicago Press.

Hamer, D., & Copeland, P. (1994). *The science of desire: The search for the gay gene and the biology of human behavior*. New York: Simon & Schuster.

Hartsock, N. (1990). Foucault on power: A theory for women? In L. Nicholson (Ed.), *Feminism/Postmodernism* (pp. 157-175). New York: Routledge.

Heath, S. (1990). The ethics of sexual difference. *Discourse, 12*(2), 128-153.

Hemmings, C. (1993). Resituating the bisexual body. In J. Bristow & A. R. Wilson (Eds.), *Activating theory: lesbian, gay, bisexual politics* (pp. 118-138). London: Lawrence & Wishart..

Hemmings, C. (2002). *Bisexual spaces: A geography of sexuality and gender*. New York: Routledge.

James, C. (1996). Denying complexity: Dismissal and appropriation of bisexuality in queer, lesbian, and gay theory. In B. Beemyn & M. Eliason (Eds.), *Queer studies: A lesbian, gay, bisexual, and transgender anthology* (pp. 217-249). New York: New York University Press.

Jameson, F. (1981). *The political unconscious: Narrative as a socially symbolic act*. Ithaca: Cornell University Press.

Johnson, B. (1987). *A world of difference*. Baltimore: Johns Hopkins University Press.

Krafft-Ebing, R. (1965). *Psychopathia sexualis: A medico-forensic study*. Trans. Harry E. Wedeck. New York: G.P. Putnam's Sons.

Martin, B. (1994a). Sexualities without genders and other queer utopias. *Diacritics, 24*(2-3), 104-121.

Martin, B. (1994b). Extraordinary homosexuals and the fear of being ordinary. *differences*, *6*(2-3), 100-125.

Newton, E. (1990). The mythic mannish lesbian: Radclyffe Hall and the new woman. In M. Duberman, M. Vicinus, & G. Chauncey (Eds.), *Hidden from history: Reclaiming the gay and lesbian past* (pp. 281-293). New York: Meridian.

Rado, S. (1940). A critical examination of the concept of bisexuality. *Psychosomatic Medicine*, *2*, 459-467.

Russett, C. E. (1989). *Sexual science: The Victorian construction of womanhood.* Cambridge: Harvard University Press.

Sedgwick, E. K. (1990). *Epistemology of the Closet.* Berkeley: University of California Press.

Smith-Rosenberg, C. (1990). Discourses of sexuality and subjectivity: The new woman, 1870-1936. In M. Duberman, M. Vicinus, & G. Chauncey (Eds.), *Hidden from history: Reclaiming the gay and lesbian past* (pp. 264-280). New York: Meridian.

Storr, M. (Ed.). (1999). *Bisexuality: A critical reader.* New York: Routledge.

Sulloway, F. (1979). *Freud, biologist of the mind.* London: Burnett Books.

Udis-Kessler, A. (1991). Present tense: Biphobia as a crisis of meaning. In L. Hutchins & L. Kaahumanu (Eds.), *Bi any other name: Bisexual people speak out* (pp. 350-358). Boston: Alyson Publications, Inc.

Udis-Kessler, A. (1996). Identity/politics: Historical sources of the bisexual movement. In B. Beemyn & M. Eliason (Eds.), *Queer studies: A lesbian, gay, bisexual, and transgender anthology* (pp. 52-63). New York: New York University Press.

Weeks, J. (1990). *Coming out: Homosexual politics in Britain from the Nineteenth Century to the present.* London: Quartet Books.

Young, S. (1997). Dichotomies and displacement: Bisexuality in queer theory and politics. In S. Phelan (Ed.), *Playing with fire: Queer politics, queer theories* (pp. 51-74). New York: Routledge.

doi:10.1300/J082v52n01_06

Troubling the Canon:
Bisexuality and Queer Theory

Mark A. Gammon, ABD

University of Massachusetts-Amherst

Kirsten L. Isgro, PhD

University of Massachusetts-Amherst

SUMMARY. This essay explores the notion that bisexuality and contemporary bisexual political movements both align and trouble canons of queer theories of sexuality and gender. This project provides an historical review and assessment of recent bisexual theorizing to highlight key themes in its evolution as well as a discussion of how these themes have shaped the relationship of bisexuality and queer theory. Drawing on this assessment and a wider discussion of GLBT scholarship, we invite critical inquiry regarding the implications of bisexual theorizing on

The authors would like to thank Karen Mock, Heather Richard, and Kristy Thomas for their comments and editorial suggestions. They would also like to acknowledge and thank two very important mentors, Lisa Henderson and Janice Irvine, for their suggestions on this project and for helping them to continually refine their intellectual arguments about sexuality and culture.

Correspondence may be addressed: Mark A. Gammon, Department of Sociology, University of Massachusetts-Amherst, Thompson Hall, Amherst, MA 01003 (E-mail: gammon@soc.umass.edu).

[Haworth co-indexing entry note]: "Troubling the Canon: Bisexuality and Queer Theory." Gammon, Mark A., and Kirsten L. Isgro. Co-published simultaneously in *Journal of Homosexuality* (Harrington Park Press, an imprint of The Haworth Press, Inc.) Vol. 52, No. 1/2, 2006, pp. 159-184; and: *LGBT Studies and Queer Theory: New Conflicts, Collaborations, and Contested Terrain* (ed: Karen E. Lovaas, John P. Elia, and Gust A. Yep) Harrington Park Press, an imprint of The Haworth Press, Inc., 2006, pp. 159-184. Single or multiple copies of this article are available for a fee from The Haworth Document Delivery Service [1-800-HAWORTH, 9:00 a.m. - 5:00 p.m. (EST). E-mail address: docdelivery@haworthpress.com].

queer theory and vice versa. We address questions of bisexual epistemologies, its discursive roles within queer theory, and its impact on queer politics and organizing. Noting bisexuality's absence in much of this research and scholarship, we suggest these projects have been limited in their ability to fully and effectively address sexual subjectivity both in theory and in its everyday lived experience. doi:10.1300/J082v52n01_07 *[Article copies available for a fee from The Haworth Document Delivery Service: 1-800- HAWORTH. E-mail address: <docdelivery@haworthpress.com> Website: <http://www.HaworthPress.com> © 2006 by The Haworth Press, Inc. All rights reserved.]*

KEYWORDS. Bisexual activism, bisexual epistemology, bisexuality, queer theory, sexuality

Bisexuality has always been sexual identity's most fearful ghost.

(Angelides, 2001, p. 203)

The modern historical emergence of sexual categorization has been plotted and theorized by a range of historians and social scientists.[1] Within this context the category of bisexuality has been variously noted as absent, under-recognized, under-theorized, and more recently, as central to conceptualizing sexual identities.[2] Wishing to speak more directly to recent bisexual theorizing, particularly its location within GLBT studies and queer scholarship, we begin with a brief critical historical review divided into three major sections: bisexual activist narratives, psychological research and perspectives, and social science/ humanities accounts. We focus our attention on these three particular areas because we believe that they embody and engage most intimately our concerns and arguments regarding bisexual theorizing. They also provide a set of key contemporary characteristics from which we develop our arguments regarding how these themes have shaped the relationship of bisexuality, LGBT studies, and queer theory. In addition, these three areas of activism and scholarship highlight important chronological and epistemological shifts from early gay and lesbian studies to current queer theory discussions. Following this historical assessment and discussion we investigate the interrelationship of bisexuality and queer theory by addressing questions of knowledge production, bisexuality's discursive and political roles within GLBT and queer theorizing, and its impact on sexual politics and organizing. We conclude our essay by arguing that bisexuality, as a lived experience and an epistemological perspective, can be an integral part of the canon of queer theory.

HISTORICAL REVIEW OF BISEXUAL THEORIZING

Within the context of sexual minority activism and scholarship, attending to the topic of bisexuality is uneven at best and more often simply absent. Those scholars and activists who do address bisexuality as a political and sexual identity often underscore the multiple ways bisexuality is marginalized. In their 1977 social psychology article on bisexuality, Phillip Blumstein and Pepper Schwartz argue that, "such behavior has been seen as a curiosity, and no attempt has been made to integrate the occasional data on bisexuality into any coherent scientific view of sexuality" (p. 31). Writing in 2000, sociologist Paula Rust notes that,

> in the midst of the explosion of research on sexuality in the 1970s and early 1980s, few people noticed the absence of research on bisexuality. For the most part researchers had adopted the popular conception of sexuality as dichotomous, that is, as composed of two opposite and opposing forms of sexuality known as homosexuality and heterosexuality. (p. xiv)

The dearth of research and scholarly input regarding bisexuality as a concept itself continued until the mid 1980s when several factors, including HIV/AIDS, nascent bisexual political activity, and theoretical/epistemological shifts across academic disciplines, converged and led to the development of a more sustained and coherent discussion of bisexuality.

The following sections provide a brief review of this recent bisexual history, focusing primarily on scholarship and activism within a U.S. context.[3] While seeking to avoid hard and fast disciplinary distinctions, we have loosely grouped our discussion under the headings of bisexual activist narratives, psychological research, and other social sciences/humanities accounts of bisexuality. Each of these categories points to the various ways in which bisexuality has been conceptualized and argued for by activists and scholars.[4] The historical review we provide sets the stage for better understanding how bisexuality is integral to current queer theory, as an academic area of study as well as an epistemological position. Drawing from film scholar Maria Pramaggiore's (1996) description, we understand bisexual epistemologies as "ways of apprehending, organizing and intervening in the world that refuse one-to-one correspondences between sex acts and identity, between erotic objects and sexualities, between identification and desire" (p. 3).[5]

Bisexual Activist Narratives

Bisexuality became visible through its exposure and emergence in popular media and culture at three specific moments in the latter half of the twentieth century. The first of these appearances occurred in the early-mid 1970s with the publication of prominent articles on the topic in both *Time* and *Newsweek* in 1974.[6] These happened simultaneously with the embodiment of bisexuality chic in such popular media figures as David Bowie and Elton John. Bisexual behavior was highlighted in the 1980s with the onset of the HIV/AIDS epidemic, often targeting men who engaged in sex with other men as the main carriers of the virus into the heterosexual community.[7] Bisexuality's third entrée into mainstream media came in mid-1990s on the heels of increased political organizing with the publication of a *Newsweek* cover story in 1995.[8] The 1990s also witnessed not only an increase in media exposure for bisexuality, but also the first sustained and critical investigation of bisexual representations among activists and academics (c.f. Bryant, 1997; Garber, 1995). Yet nearly a decade into the United States' HIV/AIDS epidemic, bisexual behavior continued to be either ignored or socially stigmatized. The HIV/AIDS epidemic brought discussions of private sexual practices out into the public, often challenging people's assumptions and perceptions about sex. Social responses to HIV/AIDS also contributed to polarities between heterosexuals and gays, white people and people of color, monogamous and non-monogamous relationships, and those who do not use drugs and those who do, especially since the disease has specifically affected these latter groups (Hutchins, 1991).[9] Critical cultural theorist Jo Eadie (1993) discusses the many ways that bisexual people have been perceived as "polluters" of gay and lesbian culture. Eadie (1993) calls attention to the myths surrounding bisexuality that are shared by both gay and straight people: "if you get involved with them they convert you; they always leave you for a partner of the other sex; they drain the vital energies of gay politics; they are an HIV risk; they are psychologically unstable" (p. 131). Reacting to these stereotypes and ambivalences about bisexuality, particularly within gay and lesbian communities, some bisexual identified individuals began organizing, both politically and socially, in the early 1980s. Coinciding with the larger emergence of a queer politics, this bisexual movement was part of a response to the 1970s Gay and Lesbian Liberation Movement and conventional civil rights politics.

While bisexuals were involved in the earlier Gay Liberation Movement, bisexual activism bloomed in the early 1980s, beginning with the West Coast BiPol (founded in 1983)–a bisexual, lesbian, and gay political action group–and the Bay Area Bisexual Network (Weise, 1992). Also in 1983 the Boston Bisexual Women's Network began meeting and publishing their bi-monthly newsletter, *Bi Women*. These early regional political organizations were quickly followed by the birth of the North American Multicultural Bisexual Network, which later became BiNet USA in 1991. Formed out of the first nationwide gathering of bisexuals at the 1987 March on Washington for Gay and Lesbian Rights, BiNet USA became the first and largest national bisexual organization in the country whose mission is "to collect and distribute information regarding bisexuality, and to facilitate the development of bisexual community and to work for the equal rights and liberation of all oppressed people" (Bisexual Network, 1993; see also Hutchins & Ka'ahumanu, 1991). Similar to second wave feminist efforts to correct and include women's contributions to social history, some bisexual activists sought to include bisexuality as a valid part of sexual minority communities. As activists Loraine Hutchins and Lani Ka'ahumanu (1991) state, "Bisexual people–by any other name, by every other name–have lived and loved since the beginning of time. Yet we're told we don't exist, that we're really heterosexual or really gay, that nothing exists except these two extremes" (p. xx). As a result of the perpetuation of this "unhealthy, unrealistic, hierarchical dichotomy," political efforts were geared towards inclusion of bisexuals and bisexuality–as part of the diverse range of human sexuality–in the history of gay and lesbian activism (Hutchins & Ka'ahumanu, 1991, p. xxii). These early activist narratives were complex and often contradictory with some arguing for bisexuality as an identity (somehow more authentic, transgressive, and transcendent than others), while other queer/bi activists questioned and challenged the assumed stability of identity in relation to anatomical sex, gender, and sexual desire (Hemmings, 2002; Young, 1997).

In addition to expanding national and international bisexual political organizing, this period also witnessed a surge of books and other publications about bisexuality.[10] In the introduction to their groundbreaking *Bi Any Other Name*, editors Hutchins and Ka'ahumanu state, "In this book bisexual people tell the stories of our lives, name our experiences, and take pride in ourselves. *Bi Any Other Name* is a primer for the bisexual community and movement, and for everyone who seeks to understand" (1991, p. xx). A year later, Elizabeth Reba Weise edited another anthology, *Closer to Home: Bisexuality and Feminism*. In these anthologies, authors of diverse backgrounds address the psychological, spiritual, cultural, and political aspects of bisexual pleasures, identities and epistemologies. These authors assert that bisexuality calls

> into question many of the fundamental assumptions of our culture: the duality of gender; the necessity of bipolar relationships; the nature of desire; the demand for either/or sexualities; and the seventies' gay and lesbian model of bisexuality as a stage in working through false consciousness before finally arriving at one's 'true' sexual orientation. (Weise, 1992, p. ix)

Both anthologies take up questions of community, principles, and practices of bisexuality; although Weise's anthology begins to inquire more theoretically into bisexuality as an identity and political position, engaging explicitly with U.S. feminist theories. Paula Rust (1993) summarizes these questions:

> If we follow the lead of the black, women's, gay and lesbian movements in adopting a liberationist ideology, the bisexual movement might succeed in adding one more group of people to a growing list of oppressed minorities. If we break with recent political tradition, however, the bisexual movement has the potential to radically alter the way we think about gender and sexuality. Is such a change possible in the current political climate, or would it doom the bisexual movement to failure? (p. 281)

These questions of identity and political strategy permeate much contemporary theorizing about sexuality (and the potential for political mobilization which we take up below). Speaking to these questions, Judith Butler (1993) acknowledges the necessity of identity categories for political struggle, however, she argues that it is also impossible to sustain "mastery over the trajectory of those categories within discourse" (p. 227). These bisexual narratives do not operate in isolation from larger theoretical and political concerns about sexual minorities. In fact, bisexuality as a concept and subject position foregrounds many of the debates that surround GLBT studies and queer theory, especially essentialist and social constructionist arguments of sexual identity formation.[11] For example, several scholars (Angelides, 2001; Ault, 1996; Hemmings, 2002) argue that bisexuality as an identificatory and analytical category functions as the sexual *Other* through which homosexual and heterosexual identities are constituted as different.

Psychological Research

Along with activist narratives, a range of research and scholarship on bisexuality has been generated by, and located in, psychological and counseling paradigms as well as psychosexual perspectives on human behavior.[12] These works clearly view sexuality and sexual identity as orientations, a term which Bailey (1995) describes as broadly referring to an individual's pattern of sexual attraction to men and/or women.

Within early sexology, bisexuality had been operationalized in a variety of ways. For example, the term bisexuality is present, though certainly not central, in the works of late nineteenth and early twentieth century sexologists such as Richard von Krafft-Ebing and Havelock Ellis as a way of addressing the presence of maleness and femaleness within a single individual (hemaphroditism). However, historian Steven Angelides (2001) argues that within their work, an ontological category of bisexuality never fully developed because any stain of homosexuality was enough to subsume bisexuality into homosexuality. Bisexuality is also present, though never effectively conceptualized, in Freud's turn-of-the-century theorizing on human sexuality. Alfred Kinsey's 1940s and 1950s research on human sexual behaviors revealed tendencies within his respondents to engage in sexual activities/fantasies with both men and women; however, he avoided employing the term "bisexuality" due to its historical association with hemaphroditism (Angelides, 2001).[13]

Within the body of later psychological research, sexual orientation has often been broken down into the three major categories of heterosexual, homosexual, and bisexual. Such thinking about sexual orientation and identity has typically been based on the assumption of "monosexuality," represented by exclusivity of homosexual or heterosexual "object choice" (Blumstein & Schwartz, 1977; Fox, 1995). When viewed in this context, bisexuality or multiple object choices has resulted in erasure. For example, in his review of psycho-sexual literature, A. P. MacDonald (1983) found that bisexuals were usually excluded or subsumed by lesbian and gay categories in research on sexual orientation.

In order to understand and validate bisexual identity and behaviors, a number of psychologists have employed many different routes, typologies, models, and conceptualizations. For example, Gary Zinik (1985) proposes three forms of bisexuality: *simultaneous bisexuality*, which includes having sex with at least one partner of the same and different sex in the same time period; *concurrent bisexuality*, which includes having sex separately with females and males during the same time period; and *serial bisexuality*, which is defined as alternating between male and female sexual partners over time. Similarly, Klein (1993) distinguished four major types of bisexuality: *transitional, historical, sequential*, and *concurrent*. Still other authors have proposed similar typologies such as *defense bisexuality, married bisexuality, equal bisexuality, experimental bisexuality, secondary bisexuality*, and *technical bisexuality* (Fox, 1995; Fox, 1996). As these typologies show, a significant effort has been made to label and categorize bisexual behaviors. However, by displacing gender as *the* primary means for understanding sexual pleasure, desire, and identity, some scholars suggest that, "by definition, bisexuals defy categorization" (Schuster, 1987, p. 57).

Psycho-social examinations (c.f. Klein, 1993; MacDonald, 1981; Paul, 1984) of bisexuality often reveal as a common theme the ability and/or desire to connect with women and men in terms of attraction, love, affection, and desire. Others argue that it is more appropriate to view individuals who have sexual/affectional partners of both sexes as people who challenge the relevance of gender to sexual experiences. In what has been labeled as the "third paradigm shift' in modern understandings of sexuality, some contemporary theorists question the central role that biological sex and gender play in the definition of sexual orientation" (Rust, 2000, p. 38). This transformation is exemplified by John De Cecco and Michael Shively (1983/1984), who suggest that research about sexuality should shift the unit of analysis from the individual to the sexual relationship. Efforts such as De Cecco and Shively's demonstrate the varying possibilities for research and represent new possibilities for understanding sexual orientation as more than simply a sex/gender-centric concept. This psychological research on bisexuality then is a contribution significant to the theoretical and research literature on identity formation, particularly its effort to affirm rather than pathologize these sexual orientations. Additionally, the development of multidimensional approaches to sexual orientation allow for more accurate representations of people's sexual behavior and identity (Firestein, 1996; Fox, 1996). Despite these promising shifts within psychological research, this literature generally treats sexuality as an individualized psychological impulse instead of a social construct with particular histories, practices, taboos, social rules and mores (De Cecco, 1985; Firestein, 1996).

Social Sciences/Humanities Accounts

In addition to psychological accounts of bisexuality, several social science and humanities scholars have addressed the concept of bisexuality. Distinctive from psychological perspectives this literature explores the ways that sexuality, much like race and gender, is meaning-laden, and tied to larger historical, economic, political, and social structures and conditions (Valocchi, 2003). Three main themes are predominant within this literature: bisexuality is everywhere, bisexuality as a challenge to monosexuality, and bisexuality as a postmodern sexuality. In her book *Vice Versa: Bisexuality and the Eroticism of Everyday Life*, cultural theorist Marjorie Garber (1995) argues against traditional two-dimensional models favored by some bisexuals, which through their reliance on gender, often reestablish a heterosexual/homosexual binary. In their place, Garber offers a 'möbius strip' model that "has only one side, not two, and, if split down the middle, remains in one piece" (Garber, 1995, p. 30). Garber uses this model to introduce the notion of one space that incorporates "concepts of 'two,' 'one,' and 'three'" (p. 30). Drawing on literary history, popular culture, mythology, science, sexology, psychoanalysis, and anecdotes, Garber argues that bisexuality is one of the key destabilizing forces of postmodern culture (Cresap, 1996). By resisting two-dimensional models, Garber challenges a long history of simplistic understandings of bisexuality as the "middle ground" between homosexuality and heterosexuality. Instead, Garber offers a conception of bisexuality as omnipresent, a pervasive organizing logic for sexual subjectivity which epitomizes any deviation from a fixed object choice.

While useful, Garber's capacity for finding bisexuality literally everywhere also raises serious theoretical concerns. The sheer scope of Garber's historical and cultural assessments ultimately leads her to question, both analytically and theoretically, the very separability of bisexuality from sexuality itself. However, this line of thinking reintroduces a problematic assertion of bisexuality as *more* authentic than lesbian, gay, or straight sexualities. Garber broadly suggests that bisexuality is in fact "not just another sexual orientation but rather a sexuality that undoes sexual orientation as a category, a sexuality that threatens and challenges the easy binaries of straight and gay and queer and 'het,' and even, through its biological and physiological meanings, the gender categories of male and female" (Garber, 1995, p. 65). Feminist theorist Clare Hemmings (2002) argues that Garber's work is representative of bisexual theorizing which seeks to locate bisexuality "everywhere and nowhere," an approach that she argues can serve to "reconfigure bisexuality simply as a carrier of difference for lesbian and gay men" (p. 47). Literary theorist Michael Du Plessis (1996) is also skeptical of such overgeneralizations and suggests that Garber's work promotes a limited and ahistorical accounting in which bisexuality becomes the equivalent of eroticism and narrative. This is to say, while such claims of a vast existence can feel both exciting and liberating, it can also obfuscate the complexities of sexual identity and often has profound repercussions for politics and organizing. Political theorist Stacey Young (1997) also cautions against this line of thinking about bisexuality and suggests that an effective interrogation of the conventional hetero/homo binarism will entail moving beyond claims that bisexuality somehow surpasses this opposition.

The suggestion that bisexuality effectively transcends dualistic oppositions highlights a second current theme in approaches to bisexuality. Rust (2000) suggests that,

> bisexuality is a qualitatively different form of sexuality. The distinction between gender-specific and non-gender specific sexuality is embodied in, and essentialized by, the concept of the 'monosexual' who, unlike the 'bisexual,' restricts her or his sexuality to partners of only one sex or the other. (p. 40)

As Hemmings (2002) observes,

> bisexuality is thus posited as a consistent and self-evident challenge to lesbian, gay and straight oppositions, the fluidity and transgressive nature of the former contrasted with the static and conservative nature of the latter. (p. 5)

This deployment of the term "monosexuality" can serve a strategic function by establishing a position through which bisexuals are able to develop a sense of community as determined by their difference from "monosexuals" (Ault, 1996; Highleyman, 1995).

In spite of these useful aspects, however, this conception is often criticized for positioning bisexuality as a stand in for multiplicity and complexity. All too often bisexuality is "then banished together with all of that multiplicity in order to restore the appearance of a stable, binary world" (Young, 1997, p. 61). In addition, Hemmings (2002) argues that in terming all non-bisexuals "monosexuals" the differences between gay men/lesbians and heterosexuals are erased, thereby "equating the power dynamics that exist between bisexuals and lesbians/gay men with those between homosexuals and heterosexuals" (p. 29). Further, such efforts continue to value bisexuality and bisexual critique in its difference from both homosexuality and heterosexuality. The inquiry focuses on the uniqueness of bisexuality itself rather than a critical evaluation of bisexual emergence(Young, 1997). Both Hemmings and Young base their critiques on the perception that to position bisexuality as outside, or in opposition to, a hetero/homo dyad serves only to reinscribe binary logic and fails to locate bisexual epistemologies as central to the analysis.

This leads us to a third main theme in social science and humanities research, the linkage of bisexuality to postmodernity and/or postmodernism. A common perception is that the fluid, ambiguous, and inconsistent "character" of bisexuality naturally intersects with various analogous threads in postmodernist discourse such as indeterminacy, multiplicity, and the blurring of "identity." Literary critic, Donald E. Hall (1996) for example, examines the proposition, "BISEXUALITY = POSTMODERNISM EMBODIED" (p. 9, capitalization in original). Although he does ultimately reject this proposition, it continues to allure Hall and others. Sociologist Merl Storr (1999) observes about Hall's proposition, "it is clear . . . from his characterization of bisexuality as destabilizing, polyvalent and disruptive, that he still finds the temptation a seductive one" (p. 310). This association of bisexuality and postmodernity has been used by Storr (1999) as an explanatory model to understand the contemporary emergence of bisexual narratives. Storr offers an understanding of postmodern*ism* as a cultural and aesthetic movement, and postmodern*ity* as a particular set of material conditions. In her assessment, bisexuality's alignment with these movements is more properly situated in postmodernity rather than postmodernism, that is, it lies in the realm of material conditions. Thus, she suggests

> narratives of bisexuality in the US and UK have been newly audible in recent years because–in part, at least–they are part of a more generalized (and, of course, still very incomplete) shift from the modern to the postmodern which began to pick up speed around the time of Stonewall. (Storr, 1999, pp. 315-316)

Storr marks recent debates about non-linear identity as a potentially substantial turning-point in the history of sexual identity and politics, and "one which is making the articulation of bisexual identity increasingly possible" (p. 316). While the relationship of bisexuality and postmodernity certainly remains open to debate, Storr agues for the grounding of bisexuality in a set of historical material conditions and encourages a more critical reflection of its location *within* those conditions.

As these three bodies of literature show, bisexuality can be understood both as an identity/subject position and an epistemological perspective. Bisexual narratives, psychology literature, and social science/humanities theorizing all reveal the potential of bisexuality as a lived experience as well as a particular way of knowing the world. Early 1990s bisexual activist narratives emphasized that one's personal and collective identities were "real" for many individuals. As a result, these personal testimonies aimed to make visible not only people's personal experiences, but also the potential of a vibrant multicultural bisexual political movement, suggesting a new way to conceptualize sexuality as the lived embodiment of non-stationary sexuality. At the same time, psychologists and social scientists during the 1980s and 1990s were trying to research, classify, and understand the individual and social impact of bisexual activities. Such activism and theorizing allows us to explore the relationship between bisexuality and queer theory.

BISEXUALITY AND QUEER THEORY

Using this brief historical sketch as a backdrop and drawing on our assessments of narratives and scholarship on bisexuality, we now turn our attention to a discussion of the developing relationship between bisexuality and queer theory. First, we trace the trajectory of gay and lesbian studies of the 1970s and 1980s to the more recent queer theory scholarship of the 1990s and beyond. Second, we briefly review the many ways that "queer" circulates, assessing where bisexuality and queer theory diverge and unite. We note that within these various canons of sexuality research, bisexuality, as both an epistemology and subject position, has often been deemed absent. We conclude with a brief exploration of the political ramifications of queer activism and scholarship.

GLBT/Queer Scholarship

The contemporary study of sexual minorities can be organized into three different paradigms: essentialist, social constructionist, and deconstructionist. Concerned with asserting and creating a gay identity and a sense of pride in self-definition, post-Stonewall gay liberation mobilized around newly coherent and political sexual identities (Altman, 1971; Altman, 1982; Seidman, 1997). While never a universal project, early 1970s gay liberation tended to focus its attention on examining the structures of lesbian and gay oppression and the methods by which such oppression might be eliminated.[14] In this process gay liberation claimed that homosexuality as an identity location holds the potential to liberate various forms of sexuality and sex/gender constraints. As a result, gay liberation was structured by, and primarily organized around, gay identity and gay pride. However, Annamarie Jagose (1996) argues that gay liberation "had political affinities with other sexually marginal identities like bisexuals, drag queens, transvestites and transsexuals" and that "the principles of gay liberation benefitted a range of other identificatory categories" (p. 40). Despite such optimistic assertions however, the growth of this generation of gay activists was intimately tied to essentialist notions of homosexuality and the increasing institutionalization of gay identity (Epstein, 1987; Weeks, 1977). Gay rights, then, relied on an ethnic/essentialist model in which a minority sexual identity, much like racial identity for example, is a static category. And, arguably, such collective and unified identity categories are necessary for successful political resistances and gains (Gamson, 1996). The parallel establishment of gay and lesbian studies as an academic area included an analytical focus directed towards *sex* and *sexuality*; "it is informed by the social struggle for the sexual liberation, the personal freedom, dignity, equality, and human rights of lesbians, bisexuals, and gay men; it is also informed by resistance to homophobia and heterosexism" (Abelove, Barale, & Halperin, 1993, p. xvi). However, within this context of gay liberation and expanding lesbian and gay scholarship, theorizing about bisexuality and bisexual identity remained relatively limited (Rust, 2000).

Sociologist Steven Seidman (1997) notes that challenges to the dominance of this "ethnic model" and unitary gay identity began in the mid-late 1970s and continued throughout the 1980s, and was led by "those whose lives were not reflected in the dominant representations" (p. 120). The notion of a universal sexual identity category was under attack, reflecting struggles over difference–particularly as exposed through racial and ethnic minorities, marginalized socio-economic classes, and non-normative sexualities such as bisexuality. Together with these assertions of difference, the development of constructionist approaches to sexuality also placed into doubt the reign of a universal, transnational, and transhistorical sexual subject (Epstein, 1987; Seidman, 1997). Constructionist scholars (c.f. Gagnon and Simon, 1973; McIntosh, 1968; and Weeks, 1977, among others) proposed an epistemological shift in the understanding of sexuality, moving away from natural, biological, and essentialist assumptions toward perspectives that accounted for sexuality as a socially, historically, and inter-subjectively constructed experience.

Working in tandem, constructionist scholarship and declarations of difference significantly altered the political, social, and intellectual terrain of sexuality. Although bisexuality was often invisible or marginalized in many constructionist accounts, this scholarship exposed new cracks, fissures, and possibilities for sexuality and sexual subjectivity. It is within this landscape that bisexuality as a social and political identity as well as an epistemological perspective began to take shape. Indeed, explorations of how bisexual knowledges are produced in the margins of dominant sexual discourses becomes a focus of attention in the next wave of bisexual scholarship. Arguing that one's sexual identity, experience and/or behavior may be in contradiction with one's way of understanding/knowing the world, many of these scholars (c.f. Angelides, 2001; Ault, 1996; Däumer, 1992; Hemmings, 2000/2002) challenge the premises of earlier bisexual research and theorizing.

A third wave of scholarship–queer theory–embarks on a larger deconstructive project, and questions the very terms on which "gay" and "lesbian" are based. Expanding on the underpinnings of constructionist studies and integrating poststructuralist critiques of the 1980s, queer theory further shifts the emphasis away from homosexuality as a minority group toward assessing how sexuality (in broad terms) creates and structures knowledge, culture, and social life as a whole (Sedgwick, 1990; Seidman, 1993; Valocchi, 2003).

Terminology and the Politics of "Queer"

Although many meanings attach themselves and are subsumed under this sign, "queer" remains a fluid and ambiguous term. However, several scholars (c.f. Angelides, 2001; Jagose, 1996) elaborate "queer" as circulating in (at least) three distinct ways. First, in many arenas "queer" is mobilized as a stand-in for the partnering of lesbian and gay. Which is to say, "queer" is often simply "invoked as style and symbol for homosexuality" (Angelides, 2001, p. 165). Originally proposed by feminist theorist Teresa de Lauretis in 1991 as a disruptive term intended to generate a critical distance from lesbian and gay, de Lauretis herself later renounced queer theory as "a conceptually vacuous creature of the publishing industry" (1994, p. 297).[15] This first deployment of the term "queer" then offers a relatively narrow conception of sexual identity and has not typically provided bisexuals and other marginalized individuals, activities, or arrangements with a new or increased location within the realm of sexual politics. Queer Nation is one possible example of this use of "queer."[16]

In contrast however, a second formulation of "queer" speaks directly to this challenge and denotes "queer" as a collective term for a wide range of marginalized sexual desires, formations, and subjects (Angelides, 2001; Duggan, 1995b; Valocchi, 2003). In this articulation "queer" obviates the troublesome and inconvenient "laundry list" (i.e., GLBTQ[2]) approach to creating and communicating inclusive social and political practices. Therefore, while reflecting its deployment as a cover for lesbian and gay, "queer" also finds instrumental resonance in its potential to rhetorically reduce without necessarily becoming philosophically or theoretically reductive. In this regard "queer" offers a linguistic shortcut that, through its ambiguity and instability, suggests both inclusiveness and a "big-tent" philosophy which suits many of its proponents. Ault (1996) notes that the queer label "glosses distinctions among sexual identity categories and differences between men and women" and, consequently, constructs a safe and often anonymous space for stigmatized sexual categories like bisexual and transgender (p. 457).

The third articulation of "queer" highlights its theoretical and analytic opposition to both the heterosexual and homosexual mainstream (Seidman, 1997; Warner, 1999). Further, queer theory and its politics seek to disrupt normative conceptions of identity as is typically practiced in both heterosexual and homosexual arrangements, to resist "regimes of the normal" (Warner, 1993, p. xxvi). As Seidman (1997) argues, "queer theory put into permanent crisis the identity-based theory and discourses that have served as the unquestioned foundation of lesbian and gay life" (p. 141). Advocating instead an infinite range and configuration of sexual identities, practices, and discourses, "queer" extends beyond simple pluralism to arrive at the negotiation and dismantling of the very concept of identity itself.

In this sense "queer" is, in part, a response to, and a break with, the perceived limitations of the liberationist philosophy and identity conscious politics of the lesbian and gay movement (Angelides, 2001; Gamson, 1996; Jagose, 1996). Historian Lisa Duggan (1995a) argues that queer theorists, informed by critical theory and cultural studies, are engaged in three areas of critique: (1) humanist/liberationist narratives, (2) empiricist methods that rely on "experience" as if objective evidence, and (3) identity categories as authentic, unitary, and unwavering. Thus, while the long dominant logic of lesbian and gay politics has been battling heterosexism and homophobia in an effort to legitimate homosexuality, queer theory and its proponents have sought to expose the limits of this project and instead focus their attention on heternormativity. As sociologist Steve Valocchi (2003) notes, "heteronormativity refers to the set of norms that make heterosexuality seem natural or right" operating often in unconscious and unmarked ways "that make it particularly difficult to expose and dislodge" (p. 8). Queer theory attempts to make visible the hetero/homo dichotomy and to illustrate its prominence as *the* defining logic of Western cultural and social practice(Sedgwick, 1990). Therefore, "queer theory is less a matter of explaining the repression or expression of a homosexual minority than an analysis of the hetero/homosexual figure as a power/knowledge regime that shapes the ordering of desires, behaviors, social institutions, and social relations–in a word, the constitution of the self and society" (Seidman, 1997, p. 150).

Bisexual Epistemology and Queer Theory

We now turn our focus to an examination of the unexpected and ongoing absence of bisexuality in much of queer theory.[17] While highlighting limits, shortcomings, and/or disconnections, our discussion primarily seeks to advocate a conversation between these projects and a reassessment of the many ways in which a more active and explicit investigation of bisexuality as both a subject position and theoretical framework might present new and innovative avenues of inquiry and political mobilization. To this end, a number of scholars have evoked the notion of *bisexual epistemologies* (see Angelides, 2001; Ault, 1996; Däumer, 1992; Hemming, 2002; Pramaggiore, 1996; Young, 1997). While the scope of this epistemological approach warrants a much larger discussion than is possible here, we briefly address the topic below (see Angelides, 2001 and Hemmings, 2000/2002 for an elaboration of this approach).

While bisexuality in and of itself may not necessarily transcend binary oppositions, it does offer a lens through which to observe and explore such dichotomies within queer theory. Literary theorist Elisabeth Däumer (1992) proposes understanding bisexuality as an epistemological and ethical vantage point "from which we can examine and deconstruct the bipolar framework of gender and sexuality" (p. 98). Drawing on feminist poststructuralism and queer epistemology, many scholars explore how meanings about bisexuality are generated in particular ways within the axes of sexuality and gender. They argue a more explicit engagement between bisexuality and queer theory is a worthwhile endeavor because of the interdependence of het/homo/bi categorizations. Engaging with difficult questions about how knowledge is produced based on sexual difference, for example, sociologist Amber Ault (1996) asks: "what becomes of subjects asserting discursively produced identities not clearly, wholly, or only located in either of the categories in the binary oppositions of sex and gender structures?" (p. 451).

Angelides (2001) suggests locating bisexuality *"precisely where the definition of heterosexuality leaves off and homosexuality begins*–that is, *at which point heterosexuality becomes homosexuality*, and vice versa (p. 205, italics in original). In further developing his proposition that "bisexuality is *both* the stabilizing *and* destabilizing element in the epistemic construction of sexual identity," Angelides argues that it has served to both secure and, simultaneously, to disrupt the homo/hetero dichotomy. As an example of bisexuality's contradictory presence, he argues that bisexuality can both *"foreground* gender in analyses of identity, sexuality, desire, and pleasure–and thereby highlight the interconnections of gender and sexuality" and "it can also *displace* gender as the primary means for understanding certain forms of identity, sexuality, desire, and pleasure" (Angelides, 2001, p. 189). Hemmings (2000) echoes this formulation when she notes "the consistent partiality of bisexual experience, and thus the consistent presence of bisexuality in the formation of 'other' sexual and gendered subjectivities" (p. 4). In arguing that *all* subjectivities are partial, these authors debunk the notion that there is a single bisexual/homosexual/heterosexual identity and experience. Thus, queer theory's valuable commitment to exposing dichotomous epistemological configurations clearly has something to gain from a more attentive and nuanced recognition of bisexuality and its epistemic, discursive, and structural arrangements.

Identity Politics, Bisexuality, and Queer Political Organizing

Despite a common perception that bisexuality disrupts sexual identity categories, a tension still exists, because these categories, including bisexual, appear to be both indispensable to, and restricting of, political projects (Young, 1997). Arguing for a socially and politically grounded project, Seidman (1997) suggests that a refusal to "anchor experience in identifications ends up, ironically, denying differences by either submerging them in an undifferentiated oppositional mass or by blocking the development of individual and social differences through the disciplining compulsory imperative to remain undifferentiated" (p. 135). Thus, the queer deconstructive project seeks to do away with the very subjects through which social and political changes are currently produced. Joshua Gamson (1996) refers to this as the *queer dilemma*: "At the heart of the dilemma is the simultaneity of cultural sources of oppression (which make loosening categories a smart strategy) and institutional sources of oppression (which make tightening categories a smart strategy)" (p. 413). While it seems clear that neither bisexuality nor a bisexual subject position inherently transcends or solves these dilemmas of the politics of identification, bisexuality does offer a valuable location for interrogating epistemological underpinnings of sexual subject formation. Thus, following Angelides' (2001) proposition, we suggest that attention be given not only to the social, historical, and political emergence of homosexual identities, but also to the epistemological assumptions that informed and configured them. This undertaking might then expose new possibilities for engaging with previously overlooked contributions of bisexual epistemologies.

As previously noted, a more sustained interrogation of bisexuality, its scholarship, sexual practices, and identities, might reveal certain inert configurations and absences within contemporary sexual theory while also contributing to a larger reconsideration of sexuality. Such efforts are suggested by Young (1997) who argues that theoretical work about sexuality in general would be greatly enhanced by examining not only what bisexuality means for bisexuals, but also how it is constructed and deployed in larger discourses of sexuality. She asks,

> When does it get invoked, and how? When and why does it disappear, and with what effects? What other issues seem to attach to it, what questions does it perennially raise? What complications that appear when we theorize bisexuality actually exist for, but are obscured in theories about, lesbianism, male homosexuality, and male and female heterosexuality? (Young, 1997, p. 71)

In these ways, a bisexual epistemological position might buttress queer theory's ongoing interrogation of the hetero/homosexual figure as a structuring power/knowledge regime. However, in contrast to queer theory's potentially anti-identity vantage point,[18] bisexual epistemologies might allow for an analysis of binary configurations while fostering the pragmatic political and social realities of identity politics (see also Däumer, 1992; Hemmings, 2002). In this way, bisexual epistemologies could mitigate the critique that, while producing a coalition of non-normative sexual identities, queer reduces the efficacy of lesbian and gay politics.

CONCLUSION

Our intent in this essay has been to highlight the ways that bisexuality and bisexuals have been an intrinsic, although not always explicit, part of both gay and lesbian studies/activism and queer theory/activism. As highlighted throughout our essay, we believe that bisexuality, both as an identity and as an epistemology, has often been obscured within gay/lesbian studies, psychological research, constructivist scholarship, and much of queer theory's canon. As a result, all of these projects have been limited in their ability to fully and effectively address sexual subjectivity both in theory and in its everyday lived experience.

Whereas gay and lesbian scholarship has often focused on homosexuality as an individual and collective identity, queer theory has challenged meta-narratives based on a unified sexual identity and the dominance of the hetero/homo binary. Where gay and lesbian studies highlighted the similarities between sexual minorities, queer theory has focused on fragmentation and differences across sexualities. Additionally, the tension between lesbian and gay studies and queer studies has been variously posited as both a generational issue (e.g., Stonewall era and post-Stonewall era academics, see Duggan, 1995a; Gamson, 1996), and as political versus academic (see Duggan, 1995a; Seidman, 1997). In highlighting these features, we echo Angelides' (2001) observation that the failure to acknowledge debts to gay/lesbian history has left some queer theorists "uncritically reliant upon a historiography of sexuality built squarely around the identity paradigm" (p. 187). Therefore, while both recognizing and supporting queer theory's deconstructive tendencies, we share with other sexuality theorists and activists the concern that such efforts effectively make invisible that which is already a decentered and marginalized subject position, bisexuality.

According to Seidman (1997), "the notion of a unitary gay identity has been fundamental to the evolving gay communities of the 1980s."

> *Even more basic to the framing of the gay community as an ethnic group has been the assumption that gender preference defines sexual orientation.*" (p. 123, italics in original)

This fundamental reliance on a unitary identity and gender preference has kept bisexuality marginal or absent in much of the political and academic activity of post-Stonewall lesbian and gay movements. Further, the continued invisibility of bisexuality in much queer theory begs a larger question: if academia has become the chief site for queer discourses, and if gay and lesbian-identified academics are the ones who have controlled the production of lesbian and gay knowledge, who gets excluded or marginalized in the process? (Seidman, 1997). Thus, by stretching the boundaries of identity categories, and disregarding the distinctions between various forms of marginalized sexual identification, "queer has provoked exuberance in some quarters, but anxiety and outrage in others" (Jagose, 1996, p. 101).

Yet there is much potential for a union between queer theory and bisexuality. As mentioned earlier, gay and lesbian studies focuses more on *homophobia* and *heterosexism*, whereas queer theory tends more to address *heteronormativity*. Binary sexual structures, whether heterosexual or homosexual, actively construct hierarchical boundaries and systems through which particular acts, desires, activities, identities, and formations are divided and framed as deviant, to be excluded and marginalized. By contrast, instead of reifying identity categories, queer theory takes as its purpose exposing the "operations of heteronormativity in order to work the hetero/homosexual opposition to the point of critical collapse" (Angelides, 2001, p. 168). Similarly, bisexuality, as both a lived experience and an epistemological position, has the potential to refuse one-to-one correspondences between sexual desire and identity, and between identification and activity. In this regard, bisexuality can be seen as a vital partner to queer theory and queer political projects aimed at the exposure and dismantling of binary structures and the workings of heteronormativity.

Many scholars assert that there is a distinction between the macro/structural levels that privilege heterosexuality and the micro/meso levels of people's individual sexualized lives (Eadie, 1993; Valocchi, 2003; Warner, 1999). In this regard, then, heteronormativity and heterosexuality cannot be reduced to each other, although they certainly may overlap and co-exist. As Eadie (1999) warns, "the conflating of all heterosexual desire with the destructive mechanisms of heterosexist and heteronormative oppression does nothing to enable people to accept their own sexual diversity" (p. 135). This seems particularly relevant for those individuals who may not neatly fit into the dichotomous categories of heterosexual or homosexual. Sexual relations between straight people may be organized such that they are not heteronormative, just as sexual relations between gay men and between lesbians may be organized such that they are (Valocchi, 2003). The term "queer" then can include, not only gays and lesbians and bisexuals, but all people "who find themselves at odds with straight culture" (Warner, 1999, p. 38). These non-normative relationships and sexual expressions are targets of what Warner (1999) terms sexual "moralism"–wherein some idealized sexual tastes or practices are mandated for everyone. Thus, the exposure and dislodging of heteronormativity is not queer's burden exclusively nor is it a taken-for-granted by the very existence of queer, rather, this project is an active and ongoing process that demands the participation of a wide variety of contributors and collaborators.

A number of activists and scholars have called for a more intersectional approach that looks at the multiple factors and identities (including not only sexuality and gender, but also race, class, nationality, religion, and age) that contribute to various social positions (DuPlessis, 1996; Firestein, 1996; Fox, 1996; Hutchins and Ka'ahumanu, 1991; Seidman, 1997; Valocchi, 2003). Our efforts here are concerned with historical and intellectual trends in sexuality studies, current polemics, and pragmatic concerns stemming from the recognition of multiplicity. However, we want to underscore the importance of looking at both cultural and structural features (such as fundamentalism, nationalism, colonialism, racism, and globalization) in the shaping of our understandings of sexuality. Recognizing that both structural and cultural arenas must be explicated for a more complete understanding of how identity formation and queer politics occur, we suggest it is this interface between the structural and cultural realms where sexuality moves and lives.

NOTES

1. Despite our focus on more contemporary scholarship, we want to note the importance of wider historical and cultural perspectives. See for example: Chauncey, G. (1994). *Gay New York: Gender, urban culture, and the making of the gay male world, 1890-1940*. New York: Basic Books; Halperin, D. (1993). Is there a history of sexual-

ity. In H. Abelove, M. A. Barale, & D. M. Halperin (Eds.), *The lesbian and gay studies reader* (416-431). New York: Routledge; Katz, J. (1995). *The invention of heterosexuality*. New York: Dutton; Minton, H. L. (2002). *Departing from deviance: A history of homosexual rights and emancipatory science in America*. Chicago and London: The University of Chicago Press; Plummer, K. (1992). Speaking its name: Inventing a lesbian and gay studies. In K. Plummer (Ed.), *Modern homosexualities: Fragments of lesbian and gay experience* (pp. 3-28). London and New York: Routledge; Weeks, J. (1985). *Sexuality and its discontents: Meanings, myths, and modern sexualities*. London; Boston: Routledge & K. Paul; Weeks, J. (1996). The construction of homosexuality. In S. Seidman (Ed.), *Queer theory/sociology*. Cambridge, MA: Blackwell Publishers.

2. See the 1985 special issue on bisexuality in the *Journal of Homosexuality* for examples of research which addresses some of these dilemmas. For a history of early accountings of bisexuality and an argument for its centrality to sexual categorization see S. Angelides (2001).

3. Hemmings (2002) notes that while bisexual theorizing from the U.S. draws heavily on empirical sociological and psychological approaches, British bisexual theorizing has drawn more on critical/cultural approaches. In this regard, although our paper engages with both bodies of literature, our primary focus is the former.

4. In discussing bisexuality as a theoretical concept, sexual behavior, identity, and epistemological position, we want to note the complexities and limitations of linguistic terms to fully convey and capture the range of perspectives regarding bisexuality. As Merl Storr notes, there is an ongoing question about "what bisexuality actually consists in"–maleness/femaleness, masculinity/femininity, and/or heterosexuality/homosexuality (p. 3). And further that the "binarism implied by the 'bi' in bisexuality has itself been cause for concern for some authors, especially those whose epistemological perspectives are broadly opposed to the prevalence of binary division in conceptual thought" (p. 11, n.1) (Storr, M. (1999). Editor's introduction. *Bisexuality: A critical reader*. (pp. 1-12). New York: Routledge).

5. The use of "bisexual epistemologies" in the plural echoes various scholars of bisexuality and conveys our acknowledgement of the partiality and contingent nature of knowledge production and subjectivity.

6. See, The new bisexuals. (1974, May 13). *Time*, 79-80; Bisexual chic: Anyone goes. (1974, May 27). *Newsweek*, 90.

7. See Gelman, D. (1987, July 13). A perilous double love life (Bisexuals and AIDS), *Newsweek*, 44-46; Nordheimer, J. (1987, April 3). AIDS spector for women: The bisexual man, *New York Times*, pp. A1, D18; Randolph, L. B. (1988, January). The hidden fear: Black women, bisexuals and the AIDS risk. *Ebony*, 120, 122-123, 126.

8. See Leland, J. (1995) "Bisexuality: Not gay. Not straight. A new sexual identity emerges," *Newsweek*, July 17, 44-50. Unlike the 1974 articles that were far from front page news, the 1995 *Newsweek* article was the cover story.

9. As Hutchins notes in her essay, Love that kink with the onset of AIDS, "I began thinking a lot more about sex; what was safe, what was not, what was kinky, what was straight. Lo and behold, old distinctions didn't hold. What was straight could be unsafe, what was kinky could be safe. Extremes met in the middle" (p. 338).

10. In 1991, the Bay Area Bisexual Network begins publishing the first and only national bisexual quarterly magazine, *Anything that moves: The bisexual magazine*. Examples of additional publications that came out during this period include: Klein, F. & Wolf, T. J. (Eds.). (1985). *Bisexualities: Theory and research*. The Haworth Press;

Geller, T. (Ed.). (1990). *Bisexuality: A reader and sourcebook.* Times Change Press; Klein, F. (1993). *The bisexual option* (2nd edition). The Haworth Press; Sharon, L. (Ed.). (1994). *The very inside: An anthology of writing by Asian and Pacific Islander lesbian and bisexual women.* Sister Vision Press, Toronto; Rust, P. (1995). *Bisexuality and the challenge to lesbian politics: sex, loyalty, and revolution.* New York University Press.

11. For a more detailed discussion of these essentialist and constructionist debates see: Epstein, S. (1987). Gay politics, ethnic identity: The limits of social constructionism. *Socialist Review, 93/94,* 9-56; Seidman, S. (1997). *Difference troubles: Queering social theory and sexual politics.* Cambridge; New York: Cambridge University.

12. The *Journal of Homosexuality* has published a number of such studies and essays. See for example: Berkey, B. R. T. Perelman-Hall, & L. Kurdeck. (1990). The multidimensonal scale of sexuality. *Journal of Homosexuality, 19*(4), 67-87; Coleman, E. (1987). Assessment of sexual orientation. *Journal of Homosexuality, 14*(1/2), 9-24; De Cecco, J.P., & Shively, M. (1983-84). From sexual identity to sexual relationships: A contextual shift. *Journal of Homosexuality, 9*(2/3), 1-26; Klein, F. Sepekoff, B., & T. Wolf. (1985). Sexual orientation: A multi-variable dynamic process. *Journal of Homosexuality, 11*(1-2), 35-49; J. Paul. (1985). Bisexuality: Reassessing our paradigms of sexuality. *Journal of Homosexuality, 11*(1-2), 21-34; Shively, M. & De Cecco, J.P. (1977). Components of sexual identity. *Journal of Homosexuality, 3*(1), 41-48. Two special issues of *The Journal of Homosexuality* addressed critical theoretical and clinical issues of bisexual and homosexual identities (see winter 1983/spring 1984, Volume 9 (2/3) and summer 1984, Volume 9 (4) respectively). See also, *Journal of Homosexuality.* 1984, *10* (3/4).

13. While Kinsey's sexuality scale has been criticized by some scholars for presenting homosexuality and heterosexuality as mutually exclusive and failing to clarify what was measured in the middle of his continuum (see Klein, F. (1993). *The bisexual option* (2nd ed.). New York: Haworth Press and Udis-Kessler, A. (1993). Appendix: Notes on the Kinsey scale and other measures of sexuality. In E. R. Weise (Ed.), *Closer to home: Bisexuality & feminism* (pp. 311-318). Seattle, WA: Seal Press), others argue that his methods and research were more nuanced (see Irvine, J.M. (1990). *Disorders of desire: Sex and gender in modern American sexology.* Philadelphia: Temple University Press).

14. Gay liberation was not a males-only endeavor. Many lesbians were involved in its creation; it is important to note the concurrent emergence of lesbian-feminism as a vital aspect of the story of a post-Stonewall homosexual politic.

15. See, de Lauretis, T. (1991). Queer theory: Lesbian and gay Sexualities. *Differences: A Journal of Feminist Cultural Studies, 3*(2), iii-xviii. And, de Lauretis, T. (1994). Habit changes. *Differences: A Journal of Feminist Cultural Studies, 6*(2-3), 296-313, respectively.

16. Angelides (2001) argues that Queer Nation's use of the term "queer" was a "revalorized and reanimated substitute for gay and lesbian" (p. 164). See also, Berlant, L. & Freeman, E. (1993). *Queer nationality.* In M. Warner (Ed.), *Fear of a queer planet: Queer politics and social theory* (pp. 193-229). Minneapolis: University of Minnesota Press.However Rosemary Hennessy disagrees and purports that, "Queer Nation shared many of the presuppositions of queer theory:

deconstructing the homo-hetero binary in favor of a more indeterminate sexual identity; targeting a pervasive heteronormativity by miming it with a campy inflection; employing a performative politics that associated identity less with interiority than with the public spectacle of consumer culture." (Hennessy, R. (2000) *Profit and pleasure: Sexual identities in late capitalism.* New York: Routledge. p. 127)

17. In his history of bisexuality, Angelides (2001) argues, "In the canonical deconstructive texts of queer theory a palpable marginalization at best, and erasure at worst, surrounds the theoretical question of bisexuality" (p. 172).

18. Steven Seidman (1997) argues that some poststructuralist gay theory goes "beyond a critique of identity politics to a politics against identity" (p. 135).

REFERENCES

Abelove, H., Barale, M., & Halperin, D. (1993). Introduction. In H. Abelove, M. Barale, & D. Halperin (Eds.), *The lesbian and gay studies reader* (pp. xv-xxii). New York and London: Routledge.

Altman, D. (1971). *Homosexual oppression and liberation.* New York: Avon.

Altman, D. (1982). *The homosexualization of America.* Boston: Beacon Press.

Angelides, S. (2001). *A history of bisexuality.* Chicago and London: University of Chicago.

Ault, A. (1996). Ambiguous identity in an unambiguous sex/gender structure: The case of bisexual women. *The Sociological Quarterly, 37*(3), 449-463.

Bailey, J. M. (1995). Biological perspectives on sexual orientation. In A. R. D'Augelli & C. J. Patterson (Eds.), *Lesbian, gay, and bisexual identities over the lifespan* (pp. 102-135). New York: Oxford University.

Bisexual Network of the United States (BiNet USA). "The mission of BiNet USA." *Bylaws of the Bisexual Network of the United States (BiNet USA).* Adopted February 14, 1993. p. 3.

Blumstein, P., & Schwartz, P. (1977). Bisexuality: Some social psychological issues. *Journal of Social Issues, 33*(2), 30-45.

Bryant, W. (1997). *Bisexual characters in film.* New York and London: The Haworth Press.

Butler, J. (1993). *Bodies that matter: On the discursive limits of "sex."* New York, Routledge.

Cresap, K. (1996). *Bisexuals, cyborgs, and chaos. Postmodern Culture, 6*(3). Retrieved October 14, 2002, from http://muse.jhu.edu/journals/postmodern_culture/v006/6.3r_cresap.html

Däumer, E. (1992). Queer ethics: Or, the challenge of bisexuality to lesbian ethics. *Hypatia, 7*(4), 90-105.

De Cecco, J. (1985). Preface. *Journal of Homosexuality, 11*(1/2), xi-xiii.

De Cecco, J. P., & Shively, M. G. (1983/1984). From sexual identity to sexual relationships: A contextual shift. *Journal of Homosexuality, 9*(2/3), 1-26.

Duggan, L. (1995a). The discipline problem: Queer theory meets lesbian and gay history. In L. Duggan & N. Hunter (Eds.), *Sex wars: Sexual dissent and political culture* (pp. 179-191). New York and London: Routlege.

Duggan, L. (1995b). Making it perfectly queer. In L. Duggan & N. Hunter (Eds.), *Sex wars: Sexual dissent and political culture* (pp. 155-172). New York and London: Routledge.

Du Plessis, M. (1996). Blatantly bisexual: Or, unthinking queer theory. In D. E. Hall & M. Pramaggiore (Eds.), *RePresenting bisexualities: subjects and cultures of fluid desire* (pp. 19-54). New York: New York University Press.

Eadie, J. (1999). Extracts from Activiting sexuality: Towards a bi/sexual politics. In M. Storr (Ed.), *Bisexuality: A critical reader* (pp. 119-137). London and New York: Routledge.

Ellis, H. (1928). *Studies in the psychology of sex*. Philadelphia: F.A. Davis Co.

Epstein, S. (1987). Gay politics, ethnic identity: The limits of social constructionism. *Socialist Review, 93/94*, 9-56.

Firestein, B. (1996). Bisexuality as paradigm shift: Transforming our disciplines. In B. Firestein (Ed.), *Bisexuality: The psychology and politics of an invisible minority* (pp. 263-291). Thousand Oaks, CA: Sage.

Fox, R. C. (1995). Bisexual identities. In A. R. D'Augelli & C. J. Patterson (Eds.), *Lesbian, gay, and bisexual identities over the lifespan* (pp. 48-86). New York: Oxford University.

Fox, R. C. (1996). Bisexuality in perspective: A review of theory and research. in B. Firestein (Ed.), *Bisexuality: The psychology and politics of an invisible minority* (pp. 3-50). Thousand Oaks, CA: Sage.

Gagnon, J., & Simon, W. G., (1973). *Sexual conduct: The social sources of human sexuality*. Chicago, Aldine.

Gamson, J. (1996). Must identity movements self-destruct? In S. Seidman (Ed.), *Queer theory/sociology* (pp. 395-420). Cambridge, MA: Blackwell.

Garber, M. B. (1995). *Vice versa: Bisexuality and the eroticism of everyday life*. New York: Simon & Schuster.

Hall, D. E. (1996). BI-ntroduction II: Epistemologies of the fence. In D. E. Hall & M. Pramaggiore (Eds.), *RePresenting bisexualities: Subjects and cultures of fluid desire* (pp. 8-16). New York: New York University Press.

Hall, D. E., & Pramaggiore, M. (Eds.). (1996). *RePresenting bisexualities: Subjects and cultures of fluid desire*. New York: New York University Press.

Hemmings, C. (2000). *A feminist methodology of the personal: Bisexual experience and feminist post-structuralist epistemology*. Retrieved October 14, 2003 from http://www.women.it/ cyberarchive/files/hemmings.htm

Hemmings, C. (2002). *Bisexual spaces: A geography of sexuality and gender*. New York: Routledge.

Highleyman. L. (1995). Identity and ideas. In N. Tucker (Ed.), *Bisexual politics: Theories, queries, and visions* (pp. 73-92). New York: The Haworth Press.

Hutchins, L. (1991). Love that kink. In L. Huchins & L. Ka'ahamanu (Eds.), *Bi any other name: Bisexual people speak out* (pp. 335-343). Boston: Alyson Publications.

Hutchins, L., & Ka'ahumanu, L. (Eds.). (1991). *Bi any other name: Bisexual people speak out* (1st ed.). Boston: Alyson Publications.

Jagose, A. (1996). *Queer theory: An introduction*. New York: New York University Press.

Klein, F. (1993). *The bisexual option* (2nd ed.). New York: Haworth Press.

Klein, F., Sepekoff, B., & Wolf, T. J. (1985). Sexual orientation: A multivariable dynamic process. *Journal of Homosexuality, 11*, 35-49.

Krafft-Ebing, R. V. (1931). *Psychopathia sexualis.* New York.

MacDonald, A. P. (1981). Bisexuality: Some comments on research and theory. *Journal of Homosexuality, 6*(3), 21-35.

MacDonald, A. P. (1983). A little bit of lavender goes a long way: A critique of research on sexual orientation. *Journal of Sex Research, 19*(1), 94-100.

McIntosh, M. (1968). The homosexual role. *Social Problems, 16,* 182-193.

Paul, J. P. (1984). The bisexual identity: An identity without social recognition. *Journal of Homosexuality, 2/3,* 45-63.

Pramaggiore, M. (1996). BI-ntroduction I: Epistemologies of the fence. In D. E. Hall & M. Pramaggiore (Eds.), *RePresenting bisexualities: Subjects and cultures of fluid desire* (pp. 1-7). New York: New York University Press.

Rust, P. C. (1993). Who are we and where do we go from here? Conceptualizing bisexuality. In E. R. Weise (Ed.), *Closer to home: Bisexuality & feminism* (pp. 281-310). Seattle: Seal.

Rust, P. C. (2000). *Bisexuality in the United States: A social science reader.* New York: Columbia University Press.

Schuster, R. (1987). Sexuality as a continuum: The bisexual identity. In B. L. P. Collective (Ed.), *Lesbian psychologies: Explorations and challenges* (pp. 56-71). Urbana, IL: University of Illinois Press.

Sedgwick, E. K. (1990). *Epistemology of the closet.* Berkeley and Los Angeles: University of California Press.

Seidman, S. (1993). Identity and politics in a postmodern gay culture. In M. Warner & Social Text Collective. (Eds.), *Fear of a queer planet: Queer politics and social theory* (pp. 105-142). Minneapolis: University of Minnesota Press.

Seidman, S. (1997). *Difference troubles: Queering social theory and sexual politics.* Cambridge; New York: Cambridge University Press.

Storr, M. (1999). Postmodern bisexuality. *Sexualities, 2*(3), 309-325.

Valocchi, S. (2003). *Can sociology be queered: The limits and possibilities of queer theory for sociology.* The 73rd Annual Meeting of the Eastern Sociological Society, Philadelphia, PA.

Warner, M. (1993). Introduction. In M. Warner & Social Text Collective (Ed.), *Fear of a queer planet: Queer politics and social theory* (pp. vii-xxxi). Minneapolis: University of Minnesota Press.

Warner, M. (1999). *The trouble with normal: Sex, politics and the ethics of queer life.* New York: Free Press.

Weeks, J. (1977). *Coming out: Homosexual politics in Britain, from the nineteenth century to the present.* London: Quartet.

Weise, E. R. (1992). *Closer to home: Bisexuality & feminism.* Seattle, WA: Seal Press.

Young, S. (1997). Dichotomies and displacement: Bisexuality in queer theory and politics. In S. Phelan (Ed.), *Playing with fire: queer politics, queer theories* (pp. 51-74). New York: Routledge.

Zinik, G. (1985). Identity conflict or adaptive flexibility: Bisexuality reconsidered. *Journal of Homosexuality, 11,* 7-19.

doi:10.1300/J082v52n01_07

Cape Queer?
A Case Study
of Provincetown, Massachusetts

Karen Christel Krahulik, PhD

Brown University

SUMMARY. Cape Queer is a case study that details how sexuality intersects with race, gender, and class in the development of the gay and lesbian resort community, Provincetown, Massachusetts. It asks scholars to pay closer attention to the ways in which methodologies and practices utilizing LGBT studies and queer theory can combine rather than separate to interrogate LGBT and queer histories, politics and communities. In the process, it assesses how the global mechanics of capitalism led to the local queering and eventually un-queering of a gentrified, white, gay and lesbian enclave. doi:10.1300/J082v52n01_08 *[Article copies available for a fee from The Haworth Document Delivery Service: 1-800-HAWORTH. E-mail address: <docdelivery@haworthpress.com> Website: <http://www.HaworthPress.com> © 2006 by The Haworth Press, Inc. All rights reserved.]*

Correspondence may be addressed: Associate Dean of the College, Brown University, Box 1939, UH 201, Providence, RI 02912 (E-mail: Karen_Krahulik@brown.edu).

[Haworth co-indexing entry note]: "Cape Queer? A Case Study of Provincetown, Massachusetts." Krahulik, Karen Christel. Co-published simultaneously in *Journal of Homosexuality* (Harrington Park Press, an imprint of The Haworth Press, Inc.) Vol. 52, No. 1/2, 2006, pp. 185-212; and: *LGBT Studies and Queer Theory: New Conflicts, Collaborations, and Contested Terrain* (ed: Karen E. Lovaas, John P. Elia, and Gust A. Yep) Harrington Park Press, an imprint of The Haworth Press, Inc., 2006, pp. 185-212. Single or multiple copies of this article are available for a fee from The Haworth Document Delivery Service [1-800-HAWORTH, 9:00 a.m. - 5:00 p.m. (EST). E-mail address: docdelivery@haworthpress.com].

KEYWORDS. Capitalism, heteronormativity, Provincetown, queer theory

Nestled neatly into Cape Cod's outer fist of shifting land and seascapes, curls Provincetown, Massachusetts, a narrow strip of sand shifting constantly under the weight of its own historic and contemporary claims to fame. From the late 1800s to today, Provincetown has capitalized on its currency as the landing place of the *Mayflower* pilgrims, birthplace of Yankee whaling captains, home of Portuguese fishermen, base for the United States Navy, theater for the Provincetown Players, canvas to Charles Hawthorne, and playground for gay tourists. Throughout the twentieth century, individual and national imaginaries invested in "American" promises of freedom, whiteness and economic success enticed any number of visitors to visit this distant but attainable "Land's End" destination. My larger project examines the making and marketing of Provincetown in detail (Krahulik, 2000, 2003). Here I track some of those who answered Provincetown's call to the persecuted and their complicated relationship to post-WWII circuits of resistance and power. Before doing so, I provide a brief overview of my methodological approach.

Purposefully, I utilize both gay and lesbian studies and queer theory. My most memorable introduction to the "contested terrain" between the two took place at the 2001 American Historical Association's annual meeting in Boston. There I delivered a paper on what the *Provincetown Advocate* in 1951 called, "The 'Queer' Question"–the postwar moral panic facing residents in Provincetown and elsewhere. When I finished, a self-identified gay man, lay historian, and frequent Provincetown visitor launched the first comments and question. After praising the two men on the panel for presenting refreshingly thoughtful and well-written papers, he accused me of using the term "queer" offensively and irresponsibly. In his mind, queer was used in the past and present in one, and only one, way: as a derogatory term heterosexuals invoked to mark and hurt effeminate, gay men. He had no knowledge of the field of queer theory, no experience in queer activism, and he ignored my historical contextualization of the term. He ended his rant by asking me, since I used the term queer, how I would like it if he called me a "cunt." While I would have preferred a collegial rather than an embittered and sexist exchange, the encounter prompted me to ponder the following: how misogyny functions within gay and lesbian communities, how the terrain of sexuality gets linked to discipline and punishment, how relieved I am in the knowledge that my worst conference experience has happened already and how salient are past and present investments in the term queer.

My more formal introduction to queer politics and practices began in graduate seminars at New York University during the mid 1990s. As a student, I studied the historiography of gay and lesbian history and took brief forays into what a queer history might look like. The space of the classroom allowed me safely to debate and challenge a queer analysis that questioned the logics of social history projects dedicated to "usable pasts" (Stein, 2001). Among other interrogations, I recall four methodological and theoretical modes of inquiry: social history, cultural history, lesbian and gay history, and queer theory/history. Informed by the "bottom up" politics of the civil rights and women's movements, social history set out in the 1970s and 80s to recuperate people and events previously neglected. Social historians sought to legitimize the following as worthy of historical inquiry: everyday life and ordinary or disempowered people. They aimed to give voice to the voiceless, to render the invisible visible, and to do so through empiricist and quantitative research methods (Stein, 2001).

Cultural historians departed from this approach in the 1980s and early 90s by critiquing the essentialist assumptions and empiricist methods used in the hunt for those "hidden from history." Informed by the growing field of cultural studies, cultural historians attended to the various meanings and *processes* embedded in understandings of culture. They studied culture as "high," "low," and popular; as processes rather than fixed entities; and as systems of meaning deciphered from rituals and representations. Instead of recuperating social movements per se, they analyzed subcultural formations as modes of resistance (Escoffier, Kunzel, and McGarry, 1995; Stein, 2001).

Following the work of early sexologists and homophile writers, the "modern" field of gay and lesbian history sprang from both social and cultural history projects (Rubin, 2003). Beginning in the 1970s, the first set of texts paralleled other social history endeavors by recuperating homosexuals, both extraordinary and ordinary, from history (Berube, 1990; D'Emilio, 1983; Duberman, Vicinus, and Chauncey, 1989; Faderman, 1981; Katz, 1976;). Appearing in the early 1990s, the second set approached variations in identity, desire and representation more decidedly by focusing, in the spirit of cultural studies, on the historically and culturally specific meanings embedded in same-sex erotic practices, relationships and performances (Chauncey, 1994; Kennedy and Davis, 1993; Newton, 1993). Although the move from social to cultural history was chronological, it was not neatly linear. Gay and lesbian history texts like George Chauncey's *Gay New York* (1994) and Esther Newton's (anthropological) *Cherry Grove* (1993) utilized both social and cultural history approaches as they rendered the invisible visible while attending to the ways in which gay men and lesbians mobilized subcultural practices of resistance in historically specific moments and geographies.

Historians in general were slow, and often refused, to engage the burgeoning literary fields of poststructuralism and queer theory that took off in the late 80s and early 1990s, finding themselves sandbagged in what Lisa Duggan (1998) has referred to as the "theory wars." Queer theorists led by Eve Sedgwick and carried forth by Judith Butler and others made central the project of destabilizing rather than recuperating identities of the past, present and future; focused on the performative, repetitive, and representational aspects of identity that debunked claims of authenticity; and attended to discourses and power relations that mapped, maintained and intervened in constructions of normalcy and deviance (Butler, 1990; Escoffier et al., 1995; Duggan, 1998; Sedgwick, 1990, 1993; Stein, 2001; Warner, 1993, 1999).

From this alchemy of methods and politics, *at least* two kinds of queer history projects have emerged. One takes the literary-based "queer turn," as Marc Stein (2001) has called it, and seldom looks back. Lisa Duggan's *Sapphic Slashers* (2000) best exemplifies this approach as she shifts, in her words, "from researching the social history of lesbians to investigating the narrative representation of 'the lesbian' and its imbrication with social and material life" (2000, pp. 17-18). Rather than focusing on bodies engaged in homoerotic acts to locate and reclaim a lesbian past, Duggan (2000) examines how "a broad clash of stories and categories of sexual and gender difference produced a highly influential if contested cultural narrative" that disseminated a "tale about sexually deviant 'types'" and "produced the figure of the 'lesbian'" (p. 16).

Another kind of queer history differs in emphasis. Rather than making the "queer turn," it hesitates at the corner, shuffles and inhales, but keeps close lgbtq bodies and communities in need of recuperation. This kind of queer history still uses social and cultural history methods to locate voices and movements previously unheard or undocumented. It privileges everyday acts of resistance and their accompanying power relations, reading both as cultural narratives. It analyzes history through a queer lens, meaning, it asks how gays, lesbians and other deviant "types" disrupted or reinforced heteronormativity. Martha Umphrey's

(1995) essay, "The Trouble with Harry Thaw," works well with the emphasis of this second model. In tracing Thaw's queer, meaning eccentric and sexually non-normative, past, Umphrey calls for a *queered* history–"a process of doing history, an antihomophobic mode of inquiry"– that takes "instability and scandal as its subjects" (pp. 20-21).

My work on Provincetown falls within the expansive realm of the latter queer project. Like Umphrey, I understand the term queer as an adjective–what looks disruptive, odd, non-normative–and a verb–the action of disrupting heternormativity. Instead of attempting to claim certain people in Provincetown's past as queer, I focus on the queering process. I am less interested, as Umphrey (1995) puts it, in the "self-consciousness of the historical subject" and more interested in tracing "the history of sexual outlawry as a way to critique homophobia and compulsory heterosexuality" (p. 20).

My project also differs from Umphrey's as I look historically at how that which looked queer and disruptive in one place and moment–gay and lesbian space-taking in Provincetown during the 1950s–evolved decades later into a kind of queer-less conservatism that reinforced rather than disrupted dominant notions and systems of gender, race and class. In other words, rather than taking an anachronistic approach and requiring the term queer to understand disruptions across historical circumstances and locations as similar, I ask it to measure that which was disruptive and risky in Provincetown for certain people at certain moments. Thus, the term queer surfaces in this paper in three temporal and relational ways: first, as a derogatory descriptor used in the mid twentieth century to mark effeminate men; second, as an inclusive analytic tool that reads certain post-WWII economic and/or demographic processes as disruptive to heteronormativity; and, finally, as a mode of analysis that is critical of gay and lesbian politics that reinscribe rather than challenge class and race exploitation. In this latter sense I use queer to indicate that which aspires to disrupt heternormative spaces, discourses and practices *without* erasing or conflating the intersections of sexuality with class, race, national and ethnic differences (Hennessey, 1995). In this way, I deploy and redeploy a queer analysis in the same project to map desire and deviance, and to assess the politics of space-taking projects that require critique and not just celebration.

Based on a three-year ethnographic community study–during which time I lived in Provincetown, conducted seventy oral history interviews, and perused reams of archival papers–my work at Provincetown speaks to many of the postindustrial capitalist projects that affected and continue to influence the making of ethnic resort towns and identity-based urban enclaves globally and locally. Tourist attractions, like Niagara Falls, New York; Steamboat Springs, Colorado; Monterrey, California; and Santa Fe, New Mexico bore witness to similar processes as their working-class, ethnic enclaves became resort destinations (Coleman, 1997; Dubinsky, 2000; Horton, 2000; Norkunas, 1993). Countless urban and rural locations such as Manhattan's Lower East Side and Virginia's Loudoun County have struggled under similar strains of gentrification (Mele, 2001; Spain 1993). The seasonal importation of foreign-born workers of color, specifically Jamaican laborers sponsored by hotels and restaurants and holding H2B visas, that Provincetown turned to in the mid 1990s, takes place now in resort towns from Wilmington, North Carolina, to Boothbay Harbor, Maine. And the gay enclave-making that shaped Provincetown resembled that in urban and suburban places like Park Slope in Brooklyn, the Castro in San Francisco, Greenwich Village and Chelsea in Manhattan, and New Orleans in Louisiana; and in resort areas such as Cherry Grove on Fire Island, Miami Beach in Florida; and Rehoboth Beach in Delaware (Boyd, 2003; Chauncey, 1994; Knopp, 1990; Krahulik, 2003; Newton, 1993; Rothenberg, 1997).

In the end I offer both a narrative of gay and lesbian resistance, territoriality, and pleasure as well as a critique of the queering process–a closer look at the local and transnational socioeconomic relations that shaped gay life in Provincetown and made "Queersville, U.S.A." (Cunningham, 1995, p. 83) possible and desirable. Even more important than evaluating Provincetown for its measure of queer-ness, I question the politics mobilizing lgbt quests for safe space. To do so I consider how gay enclaves like Provincetown–which I contend has re-articulated many of the race-ethnic and class exclusions one might find in any postindustrial tourist town–can begin but then eclipse a queering process.

The layout of this paper mirrors its theoretical underpinnings. The next section, "Queering Land's End," charts forms of resistance and dissent as Provincetown turned unevenly into a gay and lesbian resort mecca. This part heeds Lila Abu Lughod's (1990) call to illuminate "diagnostics of power" (p. 42) rather than romantic readings of freedom and agency by "respect[ing] everyday resistance not just by arguing for the dignity or heroism of the resistors but by letting their practices teach us about the complex interworkings of historically changing structures of power" (p. 53). Like George Chauncey, Jr.'s (1994) interpretation of New York City's early twentieth-century gay worlds, I read Portuguese and gay narratives of resistance as politically conscious and/or socially collective acts that had a cumulative effect on local power relations, in this case on what constituted acceptable or unacceptable behavior in Provincetown. I also locate responses of those in power to these moments of resistance, the responses indicative in and of themselves of resistance, to make central the tension between those thwarting and those courting a gay presence in Provincetown. The final part, "Displacements," hones in on the exclusionary outcomes of this evolution, on the ways, as Abu-Lughod (1990) notes, that "resisting at one level may catch people up at other levels" (p. 53). In this section I argue that the socioeconomic effects of making spaces gay are as important as the process, and that without such a critique we–scholars interested in questions of social change and transformation–risk reproducing the very systems of oppression we aim to expose (Hennessey, 1995).

QUEERING LAND'S END

Building on yet also diverging from other narratives of lesbian and gay history, this story begins not in the semi-public spaces of bars, parks, theaters, or homophile meetings, nor in the semi-private spaces of house or neighborhood parties, but in the households of heterosexual-acting or identified Portuguese women who took in gay boarders (Beemyn, 1997; Boyd, 2003; Chauncey, 1994; D'Emilio 1983; Garber, 1989; Kennedy and Davis, 1993; Newton, 1993; Rothenberg, 1994; Stein 2000; Thorpe, 1996). This is not to say that restaurants and nightclubs did not play a significant role in the making of gay identities and communities at Land's End; they clearly did. But rather that a critical mass of socioeconomic relationships between gay tourists and Portuguese natives were forged in these boarding homes before, during and after the postwar era (1946 through the 1950s). Feminist historians and theorists, particularly those attending to race, have documented the ways in which families functioning as private training grounds feeding systemic action have been central to the creation of oppositional cultures (Hunter, 1990; Jones, 1985; Kelley, 1993). Portuguese households in Provincetown functioned in a slightly different, yet no less significant, way as matriarchal, income-pooling breeding pens for economically driven, cross-cultural alliances.

Immigrating en masse from the late 1800s to 1924, Portuguese men and women were instrumental to Provincetown's transition from a Yankee whaling seaport to a fishing village, art colony and resort town. As "picturesque" (Edwards, 1918, p. 151), racialized foreigners, Portuguese immigrants were sought after by pens, paintbrushes and cameras that strove to capture their "black to creamy olive" (Edwards, 1918, p. 151) complexions and their "joyousness and vivacity" (Nutting, 1923, pp. 17-18). While becoming Portuguese-Americans, Portuguese residents moved closer to the category of whiteness–literally, by articulating that they were white and not black, and, symbolically, by producing and starring in blackface minstrel shows from the 1930s through the 1950s (Krahulik, 2000, 2003). While becoming white and American, Portuguese immigrants enjoyed economic success and were valued by native-born residents and journalists as "law-abiding, industrious and thrifty" laborers (Tarbell, 1932, p. 233).

In the mid 1800s, Yankee whaling captains and their families ruled over all of Provincetown and prospered. By the early twentieth century, however, as Agnes Edwards (1918) described, a noticeable shift had occurred: "Portuguese-Portuguese-Portuguese everywhere," she exclaimed (p. 151). "They are the fishermen, the storekeepers . . . their daughters are waitresses in the hotels and teachers in the schools" (p. 151). While Portuguese husbands, brothers and fathers were out fishing, or, increasingly, taking tourists out to see fish, Portuguese women engaged in a number of income generating enterprises. Some left their homes to bait hooks, work in the cold storage freezers, or wait on tourists in restaurants and shops. Others turned their spare rooms, kitchens and parlors into boarding homes (Krahulik, 2000, 2003). It was in the spaces of these boarding homes that Portuguese women and their families not only came into direct contact with white, homosexual acting, appearing and identifying men and women, but also built symbiotic and trusting relationships with them. The household of Clement Arthur Silva was typical. In the 1930s and 40s, while his father was out fishing, Clem's mother took in boarders at their home at 557 Commercial Street. Silva (1997) reminisced recently:

> we used to have at any time two or three gay guys that my mother rented to who were very nice . . . in my home on the water. And we had gay girls . . . my mother used to feed them, rent the room and everything else for three dollars a night.

If the accommodations suited them, the "gay guys" and "girls" (also known at the time as "confirmed bachelors" and "maiden ladies"), who hailed mostly from the Northeast but also from Canada and Europe, often returned annually to the same boarding home for both short–a weekend or week–and long–a month or season–visits, further ensconcing themselves within Portuguese households and families. These long-term economic relationships often became caring, social ones as well. Amelia Carlos, born in Provincetown in 1910, rented small cottages in her backyard to gay men for decades. "Especially in the summer the young people move in and they're wonderful and I look forward to seeing them every spring and they're so nice," Carlos (1998) explained not long ago. "I have a boy that came in across the street this winter and at Christmas time he brought me a tin full of homemade cookies that he had made. And he said this is for you and have a happy Christmas." Carlos was delighted to receive the gift and made sure to reciprocate in kind: "I always give [sic] him banana bread. I pound on the window and tell him to come get banana bread when I make it." Representing the perspective of white gay men, Peter Hand (1990), a Canadian who first visited Provincetown in 1932, noted simply and nostalgically, "we became one of the family. They cried when we came and they cried when we left. And we did too."

During a time when homosexuality was suspect and criminalized, Portuguese women and their families welcomed sex and gender "deviants" into their homes for any number of reasons. They did so because they needed the income, especially but not only during the Great Depression; because their neighbors did the same, thus normalizing associations and kindnesses toward effeminate men, masculine women and gender-normative gays and lesbians; because housing homosexual rather than heterosexual men allowed Portuguese women to rent rooms in their homes without risking questions of sexual impropriety (gay men revel in telling tales of these harmonious matches wherein Portuguese women appreciated having a "man" about the house to "protect" them and to exchange recipes and such with them); because, having lived in an art colony, they had grown accustomed to and developed a fondness for eclectic artists, many of whom behaved or identified as homosexual; and because after decades of *becoming* white Portuguese Americans, Portuguese constructions of "desirable" guests hinged on race and class more so than sexual or gender orientation (Krahulik, 2000, 2003; Sanchez, 1993). In other words, as long as sex- and gender-bending men and women were white and arrived with income to spare, Portuguese homeowners were pleased, more often than not, to take them in. This is not to suggest that all Portuguese homeowners were racist or elitist or that all tourists were white, but rather that collectively and symbolically Portuguese and other residents participated in shaping Provincetown as a welcoming destination for a racialized (as white) leisure class of gay and lesbian vacationers and consumers.

Along with a handful of Yankee-owned accommodations, like the Pilgrim House and Delft Haven Cottages, Portuguese households made room in Provincetown for countless "confirmed bachelors" and "maiden ladies." Arriving alone and coupled in the 1910s and 20s, visiting artists such as Charles Demuth, Marsden Hartley, Maude Squires, Ethel Mars, Fred Marvin and his "all man Friday," Cesco, and "wash-ashores" (local term for visitors who become residents) like Eleanor Bloomfield, Ivy Ivans, and Peter Hunt introduced non-normative erotic sensibilities and relationships to Land's End (Krahulik, 2000, 2003).

By the dawn of WWII, according to Tennessee Williams, another set of "belles" descended upon Provincetown. In his 1940 sojourn to Land's End, Williams fell in quickly with a group "dominated by a platinum blonde Hollywood belle named Doug and a bull-dike named Wanda who [was] a well-known writer under a male pen-name" (Windham, 1976, pp. 5-6). The "crowd" was, he bragged to friends elsewhere, "the most raffish and fantastic crew that I have ever met and even I–excessively broadminded as I am–feel somewhat shocked by the goings-on" (Windham, pp. 5-6). Offering a glimpse of Provincetown's 1940 summer options, Williams noted that he was enamored with a ballet dancer; courted by a musician, a dancing instructor, and a language professor; and duped by "a piece of trade, a Yale freshman . . . [who] got away" (Windham, pp. 5-6). In 1944, again from Williams's point of view, gay visitors became even more flamboyant. As opposed to his 1940 visit when the "belles [were] jingling gaily all over town" (Windham, 1976, pp. 10-11), in 1944 he found Provincetown "screaming with creatures not all of whom are seagulls," and "full of really *surrealist* belles," who make for a "social atmosphere [that] has been utterly vile" (Windham, 1976, pp. 141, 144-145). Regardless of Williams's preferences, his letters support the premise that by the mid 1940s Provincetown was fast on its way to becoming a gay resort mecca–a reputation coexisting with its other incarnations as an "exotic" Portuguese seaport, eclectic art colony, and quaint "colonial" village.

In the 1940s and 50s, Provincetown housed at least four subsets of gay men and lesbians. Williams described the party atmosphere of the first set when he noted that it entailed, "camping with a bunch of . . . queens" (Windham, 1976, p. 139). Joining or alongside this festive group of gay men was the second subset: Williams and his elite circle of artists who resided for months, seasons and years at Land's End in order to write, paint, dance or act. The third was comprised of gay and lesbian wash-ashores, like Pat Shultz, Lenore Ross, and Beverly Spencer, who spent summers working and accumulating capital in the bars and restaurants that the gay tourists and elite artists patronized (Krahulik, 2000, 2003). Finally, having been born at Land's End, were Portuguese, Yankee and mixed-race gays and lesbians, known locally as, "our queers" (Krahulik, 2000, 2003).

I distinguish between these groups not to naturalize differences, but to highlight the way gender, race and class shaped different kinds of same-sex or homoerotic experiences in Provincetown. The first two subsets, the vacationing gay men and visiting artists, were, for the most part, white, financially well-off men. They came to Provincetown to "camp," relax, or succeed in the arts. The next two sets, the wash-ashores and native gay men and lesbians, made up Provincetown's laboring rather than leisure or artistic classes. These residents were also more diverse than the visiting groups in terms of ethnicity, gender and income. To be sure, intermingling and identity blurring amongst the artists, natives, "queens," "bull-dikes," and laboring wash-ashores were common. Wash-ashores like Peter Hunt sometimes slipped into the category of "our queers"; native gay men and lesbians went "camping with [the] . . . queens," or took paints to easel; and more than one artist found it necessary to labor alongside others in the service industry. In their distinctions and fluidities, they contributed collectively to the project of queering Land's End.

In addition to households, local businesses were critical to the production of a queer culture in Provincetown. Like most resort areas at the time, Provincetown enticed tourists with a fleet of entertainment venues in the form of restaurants and clubs. In contrast to establishments in more demure vacation destinations like Martha's Vineyard or Hyannisport, but like some of New York City's more risqué cabaret clubs, Provincetown's nightclubs featured gender transgressive entertainment and catered to tourists of varying ethnic, gender, and sexual backgrounds. The clubs spearheading this postwar entertainment culture included: the Weathering Heights Club, the Atlantic House, the Pilgrim House, the Moors Restaurant, and the Townhouse. By the 1950s Provincetown's visiting and native gay men and lesbians had invented an elaborate social ritual organized in and around these establishments.

The seasonal and daily–weather permitting–ritual grounded Provincetown's non-normative tourist community in the postwar era and continues more than a half century later to shape gay leisure time at Land's End. New Beach, presently called Herring Cove, kicked off the festivities at high noon. After a few hours of sun, surf, and, for some, sex, the largely white crowd of "belles," plus a smattering of straights, "bull-dikes," lesbians, and gays of color, paraded at approximately four o'clock from the beach down the road to the Moors Bar and Restaurant. A local Portuguese couple, Maline and Naomi Costa (the latter of whom was reputed to have bisexual affairs), owned the Moors; offered "authentic" Portuguese linquica, lobster rolls, and chowder; employed visiting and native gay men and lesbians; and hosted an elaborate cocktail hour featuring the festive pianist, Roger Kent. Kent entertained by orchestrating at least one hour of audience participation comedy skits and Broadway sing-alongs, favorite past-times of a certain collection of white gay men who found the fantasy aspects and the homosexual undertones of the theater empowering (Krahulik, 2000, 2003). At least twice a week, gay wash-ashore Jack Richtman (1997) and others remembered recently, fellow members of the staff or patrons hoisted Kent to the top of his piano where he donned a wide-brimmed straw hat, held a long cigarette holder, and sang "torch songs in soprano."

At five o'clock the revelers made their way down a sandy path (now Shank Painter Road) to the Weathering Heights Club. The infamously "robust" Phil Baione, a Boston-based "teamster" who was, according to one native, "as queer as a three dollar bill" (Napi Van Derek, personal communication, December 12, 1997), owned the Weathering Heights and was also its headline feature. A number of cross-dressing men and women waited on tables and performed as Baoine's "Weathering Knights," while Alice King, whom some have described as a short, stout, Italian "butch," managed the club and at times acted as the emcee. Baoine delivered female impressions, told jokes after descending into the crowd from the ceiling on something akin to a trapeze or a large swing, and invited audience members on stage to participate in his skits. Richtman's (1997) memories position Provincetown and Weathering Heights as liminal places: "We all crawled up there [to Weathering Heights] . . . it was a place away from everything in a place that was away from everything. So that made it more cozy and wonderful." And Phil Baoine's act, he recalled nostalgically, smacked of "the girl in the velvet swing all covered with tulle again."

A leisurely change of clothes then dinner typically followed happy hour festivities. Some guests chose Lenore Ross and Pat Shultz's Plain And Fancy Restaurant, which steered gays and lesbians downstairs while herding straight couples and families upstairs. Others patronized the Bonnie Doone Restaurant, located where Muscle Beach is today, or the lively Flagship Bar and Restaurant in the East End (now Jackson's). The night for many gay and lesbian vacationers, however, was still young. Night-time entertainment in the form of black, white and mix-raced comedians, singers, and female impressionists could be found at the Town House Restaurant and Lounge (now Steve's Alibi); the Madeira Room in the basement of the Pilgrim House (now Vixens); the Carriage Room upstairs at the Atlantic House (now the Macho Room); or at the Crown and Anchor Hotel complex. A number of smaller bars including the Pilgrim Club, near the Old Colony Tap, and the Ace of Spades, which attracted a lesbian crowd and eventually became the Pied Piper, also catered in the postwar era to a mixed crowd of gays and straights (Krahulik, 2000, 2003).

For many gay men, though certainly not all, the daily ritual also included opportunities for anonymous or semi-anonymous public sex. Besides capitalizing on Provincetown's acres of sand dunes during the day, after midnight many men looked for sex near the Pilgrim Monument or at a constantly changing but designated area of the bay beach, known now as the "dick dock." Others chose to meet friends at one of Provincetown's after-hours cafés like the Hump Inn or Mary Spaghetti's place. The routine even subsumed the late morning hours as gay men and lesbians enjoyed breakfast often at the Cottage restaurant, which a local family, the Feltons, ran before their gay son "Dickie" assumed control (Krahulik, 2000, 2003). Just before noon vacationers headed back to New Beach to witness, among other things, the Weathering Knights, who carried Baoine over the dunes on a litter before ceremoniously tossing him into the surf: "He'd be covered in tulle all flowing and everything," Richtman (1997) remembered, "like something out of 'Priscilla, Queen of the Desert' . . . and of course everyone would scream." In this way the clubs and their inhabitants functioned as moving theaters of celebration and resistance, creating and performing layer upon layer of rituals within rituals–the ritual of the secular pilgrimage to Provincetown, the ritual of club-hopping, the ritual of Baoine tossed into the surf or Kent conducting sing-alongs, to name just a few.

In Provincetown's cabaret clubs, cross-dressed bodies and performances that were denigrated elsewhere moved closer to and at times occupied the center. Because of this, gays and lesbians had the opportunity to experience, at least for a limited amount of time in a contained space, what it meant to become "symbolically central," to use Peter Stallybrass and Allon White's (1986) term. In these cabaret clubs, in other words, gay and straight onlookers celebrated rather than demonized an environment in which queer sensibilities thrived. Certainly some queer sensibilities, like female impressionists, thrived more so than others, notably male impersonators; thus begging the question of which gender disruptions were most celebrated and at whose or what expense. Imbalances of this sort call forth analyses made by cultural critics and historians such as Robin D. G. Kelley (1993), who has reminded scholars to note how "the creation of an alternative culture can simultaneously challenge and reinforce existing power relations" (p. 88). In this case, the creation of a gay male subculture simultaneously challenged and reinforced power relations between men and women.

Still, symbolically, these semi-public clubs assured Provincetown's less queer natives and visitors that gender disruptive performances would not spill out onto the streets of the landing place of the *Mayflower* Pilgrims. It was exactly, however, this spillage, this crossing of a critical threshold, that mobilized the rhetoric and disciplinary measures of Provincetown's postwar moral panic–a panic that mirrored all too well the "signification spiral" outlined in Stuart Hall, Chas Critcher, Tony Jefferson, John Clarke, and Brian Robert's (1978) *Policing the Crisis*. In their analysis, a signification spiral entails six levels of demise: (1) identification of a specific problem; (2) identification of a subversive group; (3) "convergence" or the association of this problem with other concerns; (4) a "threshold," which, if crossed, will necessarily lead to further destruction; (5) the prophecy of more trouble to come unless specific measures are taken; (6) the call for strict regulations (p. 223). As long as queer bodies and celebratory performances were contained within the semi-public cabaret clubs, thus available to select rather than random or unsuspecting onlookers, Provincetown's social order remained intact. Let them loose on the streets, however, and the following would swiftly and progressively occur. First, increasing numbers of queers would play out their brazen acts on Provincetown's streets. These interventions would surely drive middle-class tourists out of town. Economic ruin would soon follow, and, unless strict regulations were implemented, complete moral degradation.

Paul C. Ryan ("Of Ill Report," 1949) of the *Worcester Telegram* was among the first to make public Provincetown's queer ritual and emerging politics of containment. Ryan's piece, "Provincetown 'Boys' A Problem," illuminated for western Massachusetts and surrounding areas the gender sensibilities, ineffectual policing tactics, and welcoming attitudes one might find at Land's End. Ryan first congratulated eastern Massachusetts for a successful recreation business year, then stated that Provincetown claims to offer "quaintness, old dwellings, the sand dunes and sea," which attract "legitimate artist[s] and art student[s]." Yet it is also, he exposed, "with this backdrop that P-Towners have found an increasing number of 'tourists' who flock into the town in early Summer and attempt to give the place a little 'atmosphere.' These 'boys' as the townies call them, are somewhat of a problem." The boarding homes, which make up a significant portion of the business community, cannot agree on whether or not to house gay men and "local enforcement officials cannot cope with the situation until some of the 'boys' get into trouble. Then they are heaved out of town. But for every two that go, two more appear." Ryan concluded by lampooning parts of the well-worn queer routine, "It is only after dark that the freak parade starts. The 'boys' flutter along Commercial Street to their various evening entertainment spots or snake along in their brightly colored convertibles to beach parties. Zebra-striped seat covers were vogue this year for the open cars." After this brief description, he added, "Labor Day weekend was the season's climax. Out at New Beach the 'boys' held their annual 'convention' or mass beach party and more than 300 showed up for the affair. Everyone entertained" ("Of Ill Report," 1949). Far from rendering Provincetown's gay vacationers as self-loathing inverts, like many writers, sexologists, and psychiatrists were prone to do at the time, Ryan's column instead revealed the resilient, fun-loving and festive nature of Provincetown's postwar gay community.

The "'Boys' Problem" soon escalated into a battle between Portuguese and Yankee elected officials, police officers, conservative residents, and clergymen intending to rid Provincetown of its "boys," and Portuguese and Yankee residents and business owners (some of whom were gay or gay-acting) hoping to profit from Provincetown's popularity with a largely solvent subculture. Some business owners despised most gay men and lesbians, and some elected officials were sympathetic to them, but, for the most part, relationships of authority and dissent fell along these lines.

To bridge this rift and regain some semblance of social control, Police Chief William N. Rogers criticized Chamber of Commerce business owners who employed "boys" and who "provide[d] them with quarters and [were] not loath to provide them with congregating places" ("Chamber to Ponder," 1950). Rogers asked the Chamber to support a stricter set of town by-laws so that law enforcement officials could more effectively prosecute the "exhibitionists" who, he argued, behaved in Provincetown as they would not dare in their own hometowns. Chamber President and Portuguese native Joseph E. Macara echoed Rogers's plea and made more explicit how cagey the terms of local morality and normality had become:

"each season . . . the number of 'The Boys' continues to increase . . . and the abnormal actions of many become more public and brazen with the result that more and more normal people turn away from the town in disgust. . . . The problem will be difficult to handle," he insisted, "but it must be met and solved before the summer trade of the town is seriously damaged and before some climax in abnormality occurs." ("Chamber to Ponder," 1950)

The *Provincetown Advocate* responded to the Chamber's concerns by rousing Cape Tip's hibernating residents in the winter of 1951 and likening their hometown to a guardian beast battling nothing short of gender immorality. In an article entitled, "The 'Queer' Question," it warned: "Sometime, and the sooner the better, Provincetown will have to take between its paws a somewhat baffling and knotty problem. The problem isn't pretty, pleasant or wholesome. But it is definitely with us." The "'queer' question" elaborated on "the problem" by deferring to an (in retrospect highly suspicious) anonymous letter from "a patron of long standing who [was] a physician in Deep River, Connecticut." Apparently, the Connecticut physician had informed Ralph C. Carpenter, a Yankee native, owner of Delft Haven Cottages, and member of Provincetown's highest elected board, the board of selectmen, that he and his wife, "with regret," must cancel their trip to Land's End. The town and Carpenters' West End resort complex were "perfect vacation spot(s)," the physician conceded. However, "the swarming numbers of 'queer boys' . . . [who] flood all over our favorite eating spots . . . cavort around Long Nook Beach, [and] almost fill the walks in Provincetown" ("'queer' question," 1951), convinced them to vacation elsewhere.

One year later, the board of selectmen decreed a set of regulations meant to rid Land's End not of gay men or lesbians altogether, but of the more flamboyant and visible gender transgressors. "Selectmen Clamp Down on Gay Spots with New Regulations to Curb Evils," the *Provincetown Advocate* declared in 1952. "Determined to raise the standards of Cape End places . . . [and] eliminate objectionable features which have been on the increase in recent years," the selectmen hand delivered the regulations to each licensed liquor establishment. The new by-laws insisted that, "No licensee shall employ or allow to perform on the licensed premises any so-called female impersonators, nor employ, cater to, or encourage the licensed premises to become the habitual gathering place for homo-sexuals of either sex" ("Selectmen Clamp," 1952). Other rules attempted to ferret out obscene or suggestive language and dancing in ill-lit spaces; some prohibited the presence of intoxicated persons and female bartenders.

Despite these regulations, business owners refused to police gender and sexual morality within their establishments. One Portuguese lesbian remembered recently that her immediate relatives, who owned and operated a popular local bar, were aghast at the selectmen's audacity even to propose what locals mocked as the "ten commandments." The general attitude, she recalled, amongst most natives was that the regulations were "ridiculous" and "crazy" (Anonymous, personal communication, January, 1997). One imagines this was especially true for local entrepreneurs who fit into one of the following categories: those who behaved or identified as gender or sex deviants; those who had close friends or relatives that were gender or sex deviants; and those whose clientele was made up primarily of tourists and natives that were gender or sex deviants.

In the face of this refusal, local officials changed tactics slightly–from decreeing to cajoling–as they called next on God-fearing "decent" residents. In a formal letter entitled, "An Appeal to All Decent People In The Town of Provincetown," selectmen Frank Barnett, William White, and Ralph Carpenter launched an impassioned, Christian-based, anti-homosexual plea: "We can no longer say 'it can't happen here.' It has and we are at this moment overrun with a throng of men described by Archbishop Cushing as 'the lowest form of animal life.' Unbelievable as it may seem, they have their friends, defenders, and supporters among our own people" ("An Appeal," 1952). Portuguese women house them, "night club operators cater to them." We need everyone's help, they pleaded, to eliminate the "nests where the homosexuals congregate" and to succeed in "this crusade."

To be sure, a good number of residents, local clergymen in particular, stood behind and probably helped to draft the selectmen's "appeal," but a critical mass of natives, wash-ashores, and entrepreneurs disregarded this plea and instead, as we shall soon see, put forth their own ideas about decency and democracy. Before business owners articulated these ideas, the selectmen made one last attempt to exert power by using their capacity as the local licensing board to shut down at least one of the "nests where homosexuals congregate." They strategically targeted Phil Baoine and his Weathering Heights Club first. Although Weathering Heights was one of the most popular clubs patronized by straight, gay, and bisexual natives and tourists, Baoine was an easy target for these reasons: first, unlike other clubs owners, Baoine was not a native or resident of Land's End and could not, therefore, claim exemption in the category of "our queers"; second, instead of using local suppliers, Baoine conducted business with associates in Boston, thus further distancing himself from community support; finally, Baoine and his Weathering Knights were some of the only "professional" gender transgressors whose performances moved from their liminal nightclub venues into Provincetown's streets and beaches. Backed by local clergymen and conservative townsfolk, the selectmen succeeded in denying Baoine a liquor license in July, 1960, and in permanently closing the Weathering Heights Club despite protests from countless residents and visitors (Krahulik, 2000, 2003).

One week following the closing of the Weathering Heights Club, a group of summer business owners petitioned the board of selectmen to cease its "arbitrary and discriminating nature of the delay and denial of business licenses," because they pretend to know "what is good for Provincetown" ("Shopkeeper's Plea," 1960). In their formal petition, which the *Provincetown Advocate* reprinted on July 28, 1960, they made clear that their concern lay not necessarily with standards of morality, but rather with the "effect that possible closings and future denials will have on the prospects of Provincetown as a resort town." "Provincetown," the letter continued, "is no longer a comfortable place to vacation and is quickly becoming also uninteresting and even annoying . . . as it becomes less comfortable and less interesting and less entertaining, our 'summer people' also become less." If the summer people, meaning gays and lesbians, depart, they explained, the only guests who will remain are the frugal "transient tourists." The business owners agreed, "to deliver justice to an individual who is persistently offensive is democratic; select a business or attack a group and cause economic suicide are other questions." If the board persists on its path of arbitrary policing, they ensured, businesses will suffer irreparable damage, townsfolk will lose jobs, vacationers will go elsewhere, and "a great deal of color and quality that brings the summer source of income into this town," will be lost. Only "Coney-Island seekers and beatnik viewers" will make time for Provincetown, they assured ("Shopkeeper's Plea," 1960).

In one sense, the attack on the Weathering Heights Club and by extension Provincetown's ceremonial gay community was short lived. Even though Baoine never again entertained from his sturdy swing, gay men and lesbians continued making annual pilgrimages to Land's End and by 1997 had laid claim to Provincetown as, "*our* town" (Provincetown Business Guild, Annual Guide, 1997). In another, it represents a perennial negotiation between residents and local officials attempting to regulate normality and morality at Land's End. In other words, the post-WWII moral panic was not the first nor would it be the last time Provincetown questioned the "kind"–meaning class, race and sexual/gender orientation–of guests populating Land's End, or the acts these guests engaged in once at Land's End.

Indeed, like most other resort towns and many small communities, Provincetown has concerned itself consistently with the status and behavior of its visitors. While mapping these dynamics in detail is beyond the scope of this paper, a brief overview of local policing moments will suggest the breadth of those beyond Provincetown's "charmed circle," to use Gayle Rubin's (1993) term. In the late 1930s, for instance, residents and local officials targeted Boston-based day tourists of the "boat people" crowd, especially those donning "short shorts" and "halter tops" as particularly "undesirable" (Krahulik, 2000, 2003). These working-class "transient tourists," or "Coney-Island seekers and beatnik viewers," as the above caption notes, were also not welcome during or after the postwar queer crusade simmered down (Krahulik, 2000, 2003). Following the postwar era, hippies, lesbians, ACT UP activists, and, eventually, heterosexual as well as gay and lesbian people with children ("breeders") all faced official and unofficial resistance to their claims on Land's End. Concurrently, throughout the twentieth century, some residents and business owners symbolically and literally discouraged black tourists from visiting by refusing to admit them into restaurants or boarding homes, by advocating for the continuation of minstrel shows, and by perpetuating blackface performances into the late 1990s (Krahulik, 2000; 2005). The economist Thorstein Veblen's theory seems to work well regarding Provincetown's negotiations over bodies and consumption: "The basis on which good repute in any highly organized industrial community ultimately rests is pecuniary strength. And the means of showing pecuniary strength, and so of gaining or retaining a good name are leisure and a conspicuous consumption of goods" (Veblen, 1934, in Badgett, p. 470).

DISPLACEMENTS

White gay men and a lesser number of lesbians supported by Portuguese and Yankee residents and natives, queered Land's End in the postwar era by challenging heteronormative sexual practices and gender representations during a time when explicit challenges as such were prosecutable offenses. In this way they took risks and put job and housing security aside in order to respond collectively to the moral panics and politics of containment saturating Land's End and most of postwar America. The socioeconomic outcome of this kind of queering process, however, disrupts celebratory readings of gay, space-taking projects. Indeed, the panoply of effects and reassignment of community authority resulting from Provincetown's evolution into a gay resort were and continue to be widespread and complicated. I address these effects at length elsewhere. Here I consider briefly some of the material and structural changes related to gender, labor and the social reproduction of goods and people in late twentieth century Provincetown (Krahulik, 2000, 2003).

Provincetown's turn into a gay resort mecca moved the local economy's gender balance in an unexpected direction. Even as residents' anxieties were on the rise–due to the perceived emasculating effects of the decline in fishing and concurrent rise in gender transgressions– male economic authority lived on and thrived at Land's End in the postwar era as men displaced women as much, if not more, than any other category of business owners. The accommodation sector of the service industry illustrates this trend well: In 1966 men owned 107 accommodation establishments (classified by size and amenities as "camps and cabins," "inns," and "lodges") while women owned 110. By 1997 men owned 83 while women owned 27 (License Records, 1966, 1997). This shift reflects three kinds of movements: first, that of gay men into Provincetown; second, that of native and resident men who were either forced or chose to leave fishing and instead joined the service industry; and, third, that of Portuguese women, who, in some but not all cases, lost authority as boarding house entrepreneurs when husbands, fathers, and brothers remained shore bound.

Similarly, although gay men did not necessarily displace lesbians, they certainly carved out more of Provincetown as their own. White gay men arrived in Provincetown with greater financial resources than gay women, they gained access to Provincetown's capitalist service economy more rapidly, and they made up the majority of Provincetown's leisure class of vacationers. Besides cornering the market on nightclubs and bars, with few exceptions, men owned most gay-owned businesses, including, but not limited to, bed and breakfast establishments, retail shops, and hotels. The lodging facet of the new service industry again best illustrates this shift. In 1966 gay men owned approximately six accommodation businesses and gay women owned one. This discrepancy continued as time went on. By 1973 gay men owned fifteen and gay women four, and in 1990 gay men owned forty-four while gay women owned eight. Gay men also had considerably larger stakes in Provincetown's budding real estate market (License Records, 1966, 1973; Provincetown Business Guild, 1990). They facilitated Provincetown's turn into a gay mecca by withdrawing from the Chamber of Commerce because it did not intentionally advertise Provincetown as a gay place to gay tourists, and in 1978 founded one of this country's first gay business guilds, the Provincetown Business Guild (PBG). At the suggestion of PBG officers and members, who wanted more gay control over local licensing decisions, gay men gained access to Provincetown's local government well before gay women. In 1979 PBG members helped Marvin Coble, an openly gay man, win a seat on the board of selectmen (Krahulik, 2000, 2003).

Although dominated by white gay men, the gentrification process that escalated in the 1980s and 90s and eventually consumed Land's End included white lesbians as well a lesser number of lesbians of color. Lesbians washed ashore incrementally rather than descending upon Provincetown en masse as the gay "boys" had done. Lesbians participated in Provincetown's gay ritual in the prewar era by attending the sing-alongs, participating in the Weathering Heights shows, and infiltrating the routine at nearly every twist and turn, partaking in public sex being the possible exception. They also staked out a number of gender-specific spaces for themselves, first a lesbian bar called the Ace of Spades, and, later, in the 1980s the short-lived Ms. Room (in the Crown & Anchor). And they split the south side of Herring Cove Beach–the "gay" side–into two. Upon approaching the beach from the parking lot, lesbians claimed the middle and right side, now called "the lesbian section," and relegated gay men to the far left (a more remote section that allowed for greater privacy and opportunity for public nudity and sex).

Women established themselves economically, politically, and culturally in part by gaining control of a portion of the local service economy. By the 1980s lesbians had set up women-oriented nightclubs, retail shops, and, most important, a series of women-only guest homes. The guest house sector, a traditionally feminine enterprise of the larger service industry, seemed to make room relatively easily for a small number of lesbians. Gay women did not own the majority of guest houses or even a majority of gay guest houses in Provincetown. They did, however, command a highly visible guest house presence by joining together as a group, the Women Innkeepers of Provincetown (WIP), and by carving out women-only space and time in Provincetown, known now as Women's Week. Lesbians also advanced in the arts with painters like T.J. Walton, in the entertainment sector with comedians like

Kate Clinton, and in local politics with selectmen such as Cheryl Andrews. Their ascendancy was fraught with tension, as townsfolk and gay men voiced resentment over and attempted to explain away the apparent lesbian "takeover," yet soon a women's movement emerged within what had become a predominantly white gay male space (Krahulik, 2000, 2003).

Despite the "takeover" rumor, gay women were far from correcting the gender imbalance following the gay male influx. Indeed, the ways in which gay men and lesbians built community did not then and does not now automatically translate into a disruption of white male privilege and its relation to capitalism. Lesbians still, however, systematically challenged Provincetown's new male-centered order, and, in so doing, changed the way women lived and vacationed in Provincetown. Gay women created women-only spaces in Provincetown, they encouraged lesbians to take pride in their identities, and they drew distinctions between themselves and Provincetown's gay male world. Gay women were the first to deliberately tap into a gay retail market by peddling lesbian-specific goods and music in the late 1970s in a store called Womenscrafts. Indeed, they used the mechanics of capitalism to shape and build a gay consumer culture at Land's End decades before other entrepreneurs and corporations followed suit elsewhere. In this way a gay consumerist identity emerged at Land's End by the 1980s as lesbians sought economic independence on the heels of the feminist movement and in the face of gay men's shifting economic options due to the onset of AIDS (Krahulik, 2000, 2003).

Provincetown's demographic shift and new international reputation as a white gay and lesbian mecca complicated the locations of Portuguese residents and cultures. Unlike some ethnic villages that are now resort towns, like Aspen, Colorado, or Niagara Falls, New York, the sets of material and spatial winners and losers in Provincetown did not fall out neatly according to ethnicity or residential status (newcomers v. natives). Some Portuguese natives, like Debbie Silva and her gay brother Clement Arthur Silva, who own Clem and Ursies Seafood Restaurant (named after their parents), have prospered alongside more solvent wash-ashores. Most other Portuguese natives, however, sold their homes and businesses or gave up expensive rentals and moved up-Cape or off-Cape. For some emigration was a choice, for others a matter of economic necessity. Similarly, Portuguese cultural events, such as the Blessing of the Fleet, once integral to Provincetown as an annual Portuguese religious ritual, have become showcase tourist events meant to celebrate Provincetown's alluring ethnic past in the face of its diminishing present (Krahulik, 2000, 2003). These patterns have led to two distinct demographic shifts: first, working-class residents of all sexual and ethnic backgrounds have emigrated, thus leaving a laboring void filled in now by foreign-born, seasonal workers; and, second, of those (im)migrating as full or part-time residents, most have identified, appeared and/or behaved as lesbian, gay, bisexual or transgendered, and as white.

New family and reproductive structures are now taking shape in Provincetown as gay tourists and part-time residents, most of whom do not have children, continue to displace year-round residents and traditional nuclear families. It remains to be seen whether longstanding civic institutions–churches, schools, firehouses–will disintegrate since the most frequented sites in town have become the bars, shops, museums and beaches (Krahulik, 2000, 2003). Displacing Provincetown's traditional nuclear families, the individual has assumed the primary role as a unit of consumption. This trend follows John D'Emilio's (1993) important argument about the way capitalism and gay identity produced alternative family mechanisms that differed in fundamental ways from nuclear family patterns and expectations.

The terrain of material reproduction and consumption has also changed. Retail stores in Provincetown, exemplifying a new "boutique capitalism," now cater to a gay and lesbian tourist market. In Provincetown residents can find ample rainbow-colored candles, stationary, and tee-shirts, but few if any affordably-priced household items. What was once a ten-minute walk downtown to replenish linens or household staples is now a thirty or sixty mile drive up-Cape to larger towns. Provincetown's location at the end of a sixty-mile peninsula in this respect becomes especially significant for residents without the time or means for such lengthy excursions (Katz, 2001).

Its isolation from other towns has also, in part, led to its most recent demographic shift: the importation of a racialized laboring class that enables gay, lesbian and Portuguese economic success. In the final years of the twentieth century, real estate and rental costs skyrocketed as Provincetown's gentrification process surged ahead despite the widespread displacement of native-born workers. Although several employers, concerned residents and local officials advocated for and created an "affordable housing" program, it proved largely ineffective in terms of retaining a critical mass of low-income residents. Increasingly, employers paid less attention to the project of local worker retention and more to the option of foreign-born worker recruitment. By 2002 close to one hundred business owners imported foreign-born workers of color from Jamaica under the H2B-visa seasonal job program (Patricia Fitzpatrick, personal communication, August 7, 2002). Just as Provincetown's white Yankees imported "dark-skinned" Portuguese seamen in the mid to late nineteenth century because American sailors found greater opportunities onshore, white gay entrepreneurs and Portuguese natives are importing black and to a lesser degree white, Eastern European student laborers because native-born workers will not or cannot afford to reside permanently at Land's End. Unlike some communities participating in similar transnational exchanges of bodies and labor, Provincetown has a Human Rights Resolution Working Group that counsels foreign-born workers and attempts to oversee their labor and housing conditions. Even so, this group is not likely to solve the larger challenge of labor exploitation if class displacement continues (Krahulik, 2000, 2003).

The larger issue of creating a racialized laboring class, of patching class displacement with foreign-born workers of color instead of interrogating the social processes leading to location-specific exclusions, is not unique to Provincetown. This widespread phenomenon will continue to place native- as well as foreign-born workers in the most menial and least promising labor arrangements as transient and expendable community members. Indeed, this study raises questions for all towns facing the twin challenges of gentrification and displacement. What kind of communities take shape in the leveling of class, race and sex diversity? What investments are gay communities making in whiteness, normality, and assimilation, and at whose expense? Marc Stein (2000) asked similar questions of homophile activists in postwar Philadelphia and concluded that, "while lesbians and gay men have challenged many dominant values, they have participated in and contributed to a conservative consensus about the nature of differences between women and men. Rather than representing a 'queer' alternative, lesbians and gay men, by and large, have reproduced the dominant system of relations between the sexes" (p. 386).

Unlike Philadelphia, Provincetown is one of the only places on the East Coast where certain gay people feel at "home," or free to be "out" on streets, in bars, in public spaces and in private. Yet access to Provincetown is limited and it is not at all clear that tourists, who return annually, understand how their pilgrimages have contributed to the following: the effacement of local residents and cultures, the creation of a gay enclave grounded in male-centered privilege and identity-based consumer capitalism, and the building of a racialized laboring class that serves and sustains the interests of those who are primarily white and wealthy. What are the implications of creating identity-based enclaves that become exclusive and exclusionary? Can places like Provincetown, despite its status as a resort destination, keep close the ideals of community as a site of political mobility?

Provincetown's history offers new ways of understanding identity-based, space-taking projects. It also speaks to widespread processes of class, gender and race-ethnic displacement and importation as it exposes the price of gay participation in transnational capitalist exchanges of goods and people. To call again on the "contested terrain" with which we began, assessing the project of gay liberation in Provincetown has demonstrated, ultimately, how gays and lesbians who once took risks have moved away from a politics that one might call queer and toward a rearticulation of race, class and gender norms and inequalities that play out elsewhere, indeed, anywhere. In other words, the desires for community and public space in Provincetown that have been born out of historic exclusions complicate the fantasy of what gay evolutions and enclaves have and continue to promise. If, as Rosemary Hennessy (1995) writes, "politically, the aim of queer visibility is not to include queers in the cultural dominant but to continually pressure and disclose the heteronormative" (p. 35), how can white gay men and lesbians residing or vacationing in Provincetown, who hail from or worked their way into places of privilege, begin to derail rather than reinscribe a capitalist consumer ethic based on identity celebration and class-race exploitation?

REFERENCES

Abu-Lughod, L. (1990). The romance of resistance: Tracing transformations in power through Bedouin women. *American Ethnologist, 17,* 41-55.

An appeal to all decent people in the town of Provincetown. (1952, August 7). *The Provincetown Advocate.*

Badgett, M.V. (1997). Thinking homo/economically. In M. Duberman (Ed.), *A queer world: The Center for Lesbian and Gay Studies reader* (pp. 467-476). New York: New York University Press.

Beemyn, B. (Ed.). (1997). *Creating a place for ourselves: Lesbian, gay, and bisexual community histories.* New York: New York University Press.

Berube, A. (1990). *Coming out under fire: The history of gay men and women in World War Two.* New York: Free Press.

Boyd, N.A. (2003). *Wide open town: A history of San Francisco, to 1965.* Berkeley: University of California Press.

Butler, J. (1990). *Gender trouble: Feminism and the subversion of identity.* New York: Routledge.

Carlos, A. (Speaker). (1998). *Oral history interview for Provincetown Oral History Project* (Cassette Recording). Provincetown, MA: Provincetown Public Library.

Chauncey, G., Jr. (1994). *Gay New York: Gender, urban culture and the makings of the gay male world, 1890-1940.* New York: Basic.

Coleman, A.G. (1997, January). *Call of the mild: The Rocky Mountain skiing industry.* Paper presented at the American Historical Association Annual Meeting, New York, NY.

Cunningham, M. (1995). Social Studies: Out Town. *Out, June.*

D'Emilio, J. (1993). Capitalism and gay identity. In H. Abelove, M. Barale, & D. Halperin (Eds.), *The gay and lesbian studies reader* (pp. 469-475). New York: Routledge.

D'Emilio, J. (1983). *Sexual politics, sexual communities: The making of a homosexual minority in the United States, 1940-1970.* Chicago: University of Chicago Press.

Duberman, M., Vicinus, M., & Chauncey, G., Jr. (Eds.). (1989). *Hidden from history: Reclaiming the gay and lesbian past.* New York: New American Library.

Dubinsky, K. (1999). *The second greatest disappointment: Honeymooning and tourism at Niagara, Falls.* Rutgers: Rutgers University Press.

Duggan, L. (1998). The theory wars, or, who's afraid of Judith Butler? *Journal of Women's History, 10,* 9-19.

Duggan, L. (2000). *Sapphic slashers: Sex, violence and American modernity.* Durham, NC: Duke University Press.

Escoffier, J., Kunzel, R., & McGarry, M. (1995). Editor's introduction. *Radical History Review, 62,* 1-5.

Edwards, A. (1918). *Cape Cod: New and old.* Boston: Houghton Mifflin.

Faderman, L. (1981). *Surpassing the love of men: Romantic friendship and love between women from the Renaissance to the present.* New York: Morrow.

Garber, E. (1989). A spectacle in color: The lesbian and gay subculture of jazz age Harlem. In M. Duberman, M. Vicinus, & G. Chauncey (Eds.), *Hidden from history: Reclaiming the gay and lesbian past* (pp. 318-331). New York: New American Library.

Hall, S., Critcher, C., Jefferson, T., Clarke, J., & Robert, B. (1978). *Policing the crisis: Mugging, the state, and law and order.* London: Macmillan.

Hand, P. (Speaker). (1990). *Oral history interview* (Videocassette Recording). Provincetown, MA: Provincetown Public Library.

Hennessy, R. (1995). Queer visibility and commodity culture. *Cultural critique, 29,* 31-76.

Horton, S. (2000). Maintaining Hispano identity through the Santa Fe Fiesta: Reappropriating key symbols and resisting Anglo dominance. *Kiva, 66* (2), 249-265.

Hunter, T. W. (1990). *Household workers in the making: Afro-American women in Atlanta and the New South.* (doctoral dissertation, Yale University, Unpublished. New Haven, CT.

Jones, J. (1985). *Labor of love, labor of sorrow: Black women, work, and the family from slavery to the present.* New York: Basic.

Katz, C. (2001). On the grounds of globalization: A topography for feminist political engagement. *Signs, 26,* 1213-1237.

Katz, J. N. (1976). *Gay American history: Lesbians and gay men in the U.S.A.* New York: Crowell.

Kelley, R. D. G. (1993). "We are not what we seem": Rethinking black working-class opposition in the Jim Crow South. *Journal of American History, 80,* 75-112.

Kennedy, E. L., & Davis, M. (1993). *Boots of leather, slippers of gold: The history of a lesbian community.* New York: Routledge.

Knopp, L. (1990). Some theoretical implications of gay involvement in an urban land market. *Political Geography Quarterly, 9,* 337-352.

Krahulik, K. C. (2000). Cape queer: The politics of sex, class and race in Provincetown, Massachusetts, 1859-1999. (DAI and UMI No. 9970901)

Krahulik, K. C. (2003). *Provincetown: New England village and gay resort.* New York: New York University Press.

Krahulik, K. C. (2005). *Provincetown: From pilgrim landing to gay resort.* New York: New York University Press.

License records, Innholders. (1966, 1973, 1997). Provincetown Town Hall Archives.

Mele, C. (1996). Globalization, culture and neighborhood change: Reinventing the Lower East Side. *Urban Affairs Review, 32,* 3-22.

Newton, E. (1993). *Cherry Grove, Fire Island: Sixty years in America's first gay and lesbian town.* New York: Beacon Press.

Norkunas, M. K. (1993). *The politics of public memory: Tourism, history and ethnicity in Monterey, California.* Albany, NY: University of Albany Press.

Nutting, W. (1923). *Massachusetts beautiful.* New York: Bonanza Books.

Of ill report. (1949, September 22). *The Provincetown Advocate.*

Provincetown Business Guild. (1990). *Provincetown Business Guild 1990 brochure & directory* [Brochure]. Provincetown, MA.

Provincetown Business Guild. (1997). *Provincetown Business Guild 1997 brochure & directory* [Brochure]. Provincetown, MA.

The 'queer' question. (1951, February 2). *The Provincetown Advocate.*

Rubin, G. (1998). Thinking sex. In H. Abelove, M. Barale, & D. Halperin (Eds.), *The gay and lesbian studies reader* (pp. 3-44). New York: Routledge.

Rubin, G. (2003, December). *Geologies of queer studies: It's déjà vu all over again.* Paper delivered as part of the City University of New York, Center for Lesbian Gay Studies, David R. Kessler Lecture Series, New York, NY.

Richtman, J. (Speaker). (1997). *Oral history interview for Provincetown Oral History Project* (Cassette Recording). Provincetown, MA: Provincetown Public Library.

Rothenberg, T. (1994). "And she told two friends": Lesbians creating urban social space. In D. Bell & G. Valentine (Eds.), *Mapping desire: Geographies of sexualities* (pp. 165-181). New York: Routledge.

Sanchez, G. (1995). *Becoming Mexican American: Ethnicity, culture, and identity in Chicano, Los Angeles, 1900-1945.* New York: Oxford University Press.

Sedgwick, E. K. (1990). *Epistemology of the closet.* Berkeley, CA: California University Press.

Sedgwick, E. K. (1993). *Tendencies.* Durham, NC: Duke University Press.

Selectmen clamp down on gay spots with new regulations to curb evils. (1952. June 5). *The Provincetown Advocate.*

The shopkeeper's plea puzzles selectmen. (1960. July 28). *The Provincetown Advocate.*

Silva, C. A. (Speaker). (1997). *Oral history interview for Provincetown Oral History Project* (Cassette Recording). Provincetown, MA: Provincetown Public Library.

Spain, D. (1993). Been-heres versus come-heres: Negotiating conflicting community identities. *Journal of the American Planning Association, 59,* 156-171.

Stallybrass, P., & White, A. (1986). *The politics and poetics of transgression.* Ithaca, NY: Cornell University Press.

Stein, M. (2000). *City of sisterly and brotherly loves: Lesbian and gay Philadelphia 1945-1972.* Chicago: University of Chicago Press.

Stein, M. (2001, March). *The queering of Philadelphia lesbian and gay history.* Paper presented at Swarthmore College, Swarthmore, PA.

Tarbell, A. (1932). *Cape Cod ahoy! A travel book for the summer visitor.* Boston: A.T. Ramsay & Co.

Thorpe, R. (1996). "A house where queers go": African-American lesbian nightlife in Detroit, 1940-1975. In E. Lewin (Ed.), *Inventing lesbian cultures in America* (pp. 40-61). Boston: Beacon.

Umphrey, M. (1995). The trouble with Harry Thaw. *Radical History Review, 62,* 8-23.

Warner, M. (1993). *Fear of a queer planet: Queer politics and social theory.* Minneapolis, MN: University of Minnesota Press.

Warner, M. (1999). *The trouble with normal: Sex, politics and the ethics of queer life.* New York: Free Press.

Windham, D. (Ed.). (1976). *Tennessee Williams's letters to Donald Windham, 1940-1965.* New York: Holt, Rinehart, and Winston.

doi:10.1300/J082v52n01_08

Jewish Disappearing Acts and the Construction of Gender

Ruth D. Johnston, PhD

Pace University, NYC

SUMMARY. In this essay I propose to investigate the interarticulation of race/ethnicity and gender at two fin de siècle moments: the conceptualization of the Oedipus complex at the turn of the twentieth century and the conceptualization of gender as performative in contemporary queer theory. Though these gender constructions contrast strikingly with one another–queer theory opposes and calls into question the heteronormativity of the Oedipal itinerary–both theories are produced through the displacement of racial/ethnic difference onto sexual and gender difference.

One line of investigation in this essay is to relate their difference to the distinct situations of ethnic in-betweenness in which they were produced. Freud's situation as a Jew undergoing assimilation to Western European customs has been compared to that of the post-colonial subject. Judith Butler's and Eve Kosofsky Sedgwick's theories of queer performativity have been located in a post-assimilationist situation in the U.S. of the 1990s. At both moments a doubling takes place but with a radical shift in perspective. Whereas the post-colonial subject undergoes

---

Correspondence may be addressed: Pace University, Department of English, Pace Plaza, New York, NY 10013 (E-mail: rjohnston@pace.edu).

[Haworth co-indexing entry note]: "Jewish Disappearing Acts and the Construction of Gender." Johnston, Ruth D. Co-published simultaneously in *Journal of Homosexuality* (Harrington Park Press, an imprint of The Haworth Press, Inc.) Vol. 52, No. 1/2, 2006, pp. 213-235; and: *LGBT Studies and Queer Theory: New Conflicts, Collaborations, and Contested Terrain* (ed: Karen E. Lovaas, John P. Elia, and Gust A. Yep) Harrington Park Press, an imprint of The Haworth Press, Inc., 2006, pp. 213-235. Single or multiple copies of this article are available for a fee from The Haworth Document Delivery Service [1-800-HAWORTH, 9:00 a.m. - 5:00 p.m. (EST). E-mail address: docdelivery@haworthpress.com].

a psychic splitting in which the point of view of the colonizer predominates and promotes assimilation via mimicry, the post-assimilation subject performatively constructs difference, often by a reverse mimicry that involves identification with a subaltern group.

Finally, in both situations the notion of "queer incoherence" is deployed not to negate gay and lesbian specificity, but rather to articulate such specificity as historically emergent, on the verge of definition. *doi:10.1300/J082v52n01_09 [Article copies available for a fee from The Haworth Document Delivery Service: 1-800-HAWORTH. E-mail address: <docdelivery@ haworthpress.com> Website: <http://www.HaworthPress.com> © 2006 by The Haworth Press, Inc. All rights reserved.]*

KEYWORDS. Anti-semitism, gay and lesbian, queer performativity, homosexuality, invention of heterosexuality, multiculturalism, post-colonial subjectivity, race/ethnicity

INTRODUCTION

In this essay I propose to investigate the interarticulation of race/ethnicity and gender at two fin de siècle moments: the conceptualization of the Oedipus complex, which Daniel Boyarin (1995) terms "the invention of heterosexuality" (p. 131), at the turn of the twentieth century and the conceptualization of gender as performative in contemporary queer theory. Though these gender constructions contrast strikingly with one another–queer theory opposes and calls into question the heteronormativity of the Oedipal itinerary–both theories are produced through the displacement of racial/ethnic difference onto sexual and gender difference. Judith Butler (1993) uses the term interarticulation to describe identity categories as "vectors of power" that "require and display one another for the purpose of their own articulation" (p. 18). The interarticulation of identity categories not only recognizes their interstructuration but also makes possible the location of theories of sexuality and gender in a specific socio-historical context and thereby responds to the frequent criticism of psychoanalysis for its neglect of such considerations. Hence my use of the term "queer" rather than "gay" or "homosexual." For as Eric Savoy (1999) argues, the notion of "queer incoherence" is most usefully deployed not to negate gay and lesbian specificity, but rather to articulate such specificity as "on the threshold of tentative definition" (p. 154). Savoy's project and mine are similarly

framed by a concern to explore the "uncanny resonances between tumultuous historical moments that mark the 'pre' and the 'post' of clarified gay and lesbian identities" (Savoy, 1999, p. 154). In this connection
my use of the construction "racial/ethnic" above is also historically motivated. That is, it registers a contradiction as well as a historical shift in
the representations of Jewish identity in this century that is implicated in
the construction of sexual categories. Since both sexual and ethnic definitions are riven by contradictions, the notion "queer incoherence" is
especially suited for describing the historical possibilities that emerge
from their interstructuration or mutual perversion.[1]

It is also possible to relate these two constructions of gender as
"masked repetitions" of each other insofar as both are produced by the
same displacement process, albeit with very disparate effects. The term
"masked repetition" derives from Jeffrey Mehlman's reading of three
Freudian texts which reveal the operation of the same displacement process, but "masked" insofar as its function changes radically with each
text. Thus the genesis of jokes in *Jokes and Their Relation to the Unconscious* is a masked repetition on the one hand of anaclisis, the process by
which sexuality is generated in *Three Essays on the Theory of Sexuality*
and on the other hand of deferred action, the process by which sexuality
is repressed in "Project for a Scientific Psychology." Mehlman's work
demonstrates the vast diversity of effects that the process of displacement can generate. In the present context the displacement process enacted by Freud's Oedipus theory functions to disavow the construction
of the Jewish male as sexually deviant in fin de siècle Vienna. That is,
the theory suppresses the racial particularity of this gendering by displacing the Jewish male/Christian male opposition with the more universal opposition of female/male. Interestingly, queer theory, which
defines gender as performative, has also been read as being structured
by suppressing ethnic (Jewish) particularity–in this case exclusion from
the multiculture in fin de siècle USA–and translating this (lack of)
ethnic identity into terms of gender incoherence.

Even though both theoretical operations involve displacement, they
are masked repetitions because their radically diverse contexts produce
starkly contrasting effects. Thus while in both cases the representation
of race/ethnicity is displaced onto gender and in the process generalized, the two constructions of gender reverse one another: queer theory
defines gender as performative and therefore potentially resistant to the
heteronormative constructions of gender formulated in the wake of
Freud. One line of investigation in this essay will be to relate their difference to the different situations of ethnic in-betweenness in which

they were produced. In this connection Boyarin, building on the work of Sander Gilman, has compared Freud's situation as a Jew undergoing assimilation to Western European customs to that of the post-colonial subject, drawing on Franz Fanon's and Homi Bhaba's analyses of this cultural situation. Jon Stratton, Naomi Seidman, and others locate Judith Butler's and Eve Kosofsky Sedgwick's theories of queer performativity in a "post-assimilationist" situation in the United States of the 1990s. At both moments a doubling takes place but with a radical shift in perspective. Whereas the post-colonial subject undergoes a psychic splitting in which the point of view of the colonizer predominates and promotes assimilation via mimicry, the post-assimilation subject performatively constructs (and legitimates) difference, often by a reverse mimicry that involves identification with a subaltern group.

THE INTERARTICULATION OF RACE AND GENDER IN "THE INVENTION OF HETEROSEXUALITY"

The work of Sander Gilman and others demonstrates that Freud's theories about the construction of gender involve a displacement of racial onto sexual and gender difference. But this interarticulation was already at work in the conceptualization of the Jew. For the definition of the Jew in racial terms occurs in the nineteenth century: "The Jews are black, according to nineteenth-century racial science, because they are not a pure race, because they are a race that has come from Africa" (Gilman, 1991, p. 99). Their status as a "mixed race" or "mulattos" is opposed to the status of the Germans (Aryans) as a "pure" race. Moreover, Gilman demonstrates that there is simultaneously a strong linkage between Jewish males and women in European culture dating back to the middle ages, largely because of their practice of circumcision. Gilman explains that this equation is based on the analogy of the circumcised penis and the clitoris: each was seen as a "truncated penis": "The clitoris was known in the Viennese slang of the time simply as the 'Jew' (*Jud*). The phrase for female masturbation was 'playing with the Jew'" (Gilman, 1993a, pp. 38-39). Consequently, the Jew in Europe was seen as a feminized male, that is, as sexually deviant, and circumcision functioned as both a racial and sexual sign. As Ann Pelligrini (1997) points out, in this reading "Jewishness becomes as much a category of gender as of race" (p. 17).

Gilman's thesis (1993a) is that "what Freud constructed in his image of the woman was the absolute counter image of the Jew" (p. 47), translating the description of the Jew's racial difference strictly into a definition of femininity as a defense against the representation of Jewish males as feminized. And the use of the "Dark Continent" metaphor to describe female sexuality was determined by the fact that Jews were considered blacks by anti-Semites (Gilman, 1993a, p. 38).[2] As Mary Ann Doane (1991) explains, the phrase, taken from Victorian colonialist texts which used it to designate Africa, merges "two unknowabilities, racial difference and sexual difference," which are "usually articulated as a problem of the limits of knowledge and hence of visibility, recognition, differentiation" (pp. 211-12). Insofar as the trope serves to dissociate the Jewish male from such "darkness," it exposes Freud's complicity with both the misogyny and colonialist racism of this historical period, even as it expresses Freud's own conflicted condition as a colonized subject. Thus a difference internal to masculinity (i.e., between Aryan and Jewish males) is projected onto the heterosexual model of difference, or as Boyarin (1998) puts it, "the binary opposition phallus/castration functions to conceal the third term: the circumcised penis" (p. 229).

The historical moment is important to take into account here, not only vis-a-vis race but also sexuality, for as Michel Foucault's work establishes, prior to the nineteenth century, that is prior to the "invention" of the homosexual (Edelman, 1994, p. 11), men who engaged in sexual relations with other men were not thought of as partaking of sexual behavior that ruled out sexual relations with women. Thus the effeminacy associated with sodomy from the twelfth through the eighteenth centuries was thought of as sporadic behavior. However, the discursive shift noted by Foucault transformed the occasional sodomite into the fixed and exclusive identity of the homosexual, who desired relations only with other men. This transformation in turn constituted a radical discontinuity between homosexual and heterosexual identities.

However, it is crucial at this juncture to qualify Foucault's conception of this discursive shift as a linear development in which one model of same-sex relations supersedes another. For as Sedgwick (1990) argues, the most powerful effects of homo/heterosexual definition are generated rather by the co-existence and contradiction among minoritizing/universalizing and gender transitive/intransitive models of sexual identity. Accordingly, to re-conceive of the discursive shift noted by Foucault as giving rise to logical incoherence rather than as eliminating previous notions of same-sex relations helps to explain why male sexuality was so vulnerable to misinterpretation at this historical moment. Lee Edelman (1994) argues that the susceptibility of mis-reading male sexuality in relation to the homosexual/heterosexual discontinuity installed by the conception of the homosexual as a distinct identity produces the imperative to "posit the marker of 'homosexual difference' in terms of visual representation" (p. 11). For the absence of such a visible marker threatens the reliability of anatomical sameness to guarantee sexual identity. Moreover, the residual force of the earlier model of same-sex relations is evident in that the visible marker was drawn from the cultural linking of sodomy and effeminacy, now transformed into an inveterate sign of sexual difference that was projected onto a binary conception of gender difference (Edelman, 1994).[3]

Interestingly, this imperative coincides with the growing controversy in the nineteenth century over the significance of circumcision as a visible sign of racial difference just at the moment of the disappearance of other visible markers of Jewish distinction. For as Gilman points out, though the linkage of male Jew and woman has a long history in Europe, the growing social significance of this marker of Jewish difference in the mid-nineteenth century may be associated with the need for some visible sign of difference in a social context in which other marks of difference were becoming illegible: Western European Jews were becoming indistinguishable from other Western Europeans in matters of language, dress, occupation, location of home, cut of hair (Gilman, 1993b). Consequently, as we shall see, the constructions of the Jew and the homosexual share striking similarities.

For this reason as well it is possible to describe the situation of Western European Jews at this time, including Freud, as that of the post-colonial subject, in other words the hybrid subject whose cultural world is doubled (Boyarin, 1998). For the representation of the male Jew as female was not only externally imposed by anti-Semites, but was also internalized by Jews as defining a distinct Jewish cultural difference. Boyarin (1995) explains that "within traditional rabbinic Jewish culture, the feminization of the male . . . was experienced as a . . . positive sense of self-identification and differentiation from the Romans. . . ." But for the "emancipated Jew this representation would have been transvalued into something negative and shameful," especially at the moment when the discourses of misogyny and homophobia were intensifying (pp. 131-32). The configuration of Jewish difference "not only as feminine but also as queer," just at the moment when queer was being "solidified into an identity toward the end of the century," illuminates Freud's invention of the Oedipus complex as a "family romance of escape from Jewish queerdom into gentile, phallic heterosexuality" (Boyarin, 1995, pp. 133, 134).

In contrast to Gilman, who maintains that Freud's response to anti-Semitism was to universalize Jewish difference by displacing it with a male/female opposition, Boyarin (1998) argues that "Freud's racial difference [also] helped him understand sexual differentiation and its general intersection with race" (p. 217). Boyarin (1998) draws on the work of Franz Fanon and Homi Bhaba to relate the production of misogyny and homophobia in Freud's theories to a shift in position from the perspective of the colonized to a kind of psychic splitting or double consciousness in which the subject adopts the point of view of the oppressor, abjects what is deemed "contemptible," i.e., what has been represented as "feminine," and projects it onto women and gays. In other words, the assimilating process for the Jew entails an identification with the colonizer that results in a different masculine gendering, which functions to repudiate the feminine position ascribed to the Jewish male. As evidence, Boyarin (1998) cites *Analysis of a Phobia in a Five-Year-Old Boy*, known as the case of "Little Hans" (1909), the first time that the term "castration complex" appears in Freud's texts, which Freud describes as having a double etiology: the fantasies that women are castrated and that the circumcised Jew's penis is damaged (castrated). Little Hans's castration anxiety emerges through the process of deferred action ("Nachträglichkeit"). More specifically, his mother threatened him with castration to stop him from masturbating, but the threat itself did not produce castration anxiety at the time. Only when his father explained the difference between men's and women's sex organs more than a year later did Hans recall his mother's threat, which assumed a new significance thanks to his acquisition in the meantime of the knowledge of sexual difference:

> the piece of enlightenment which Hans had been given a short time before to the effect that women really do not possess a widdler was bound to have a shattering effect on his self-confidence and to have aroused his castration complex . . . they could take his own widdler away, and . . . make him into a woman! (Freud, 1909, p. 36)

In a footnote to this statement Freud supplies the second reason for Little Hans's castration anxiety, this time linked to anti-Semitism, which itself is tied to sexual difference:

The castration complex is the deepest unconscious root of anti-Semitism, for even in the nursery little boys hear that a Jew has something cut off his penis–a piece of his penis, they think–and this gives them the right to despise Jews. And there is no stronger unconscious root for the sense of superiority over women.

In the same footnote Freud offers the example of Otto Weininger, who committed suicide after completing his book *Sex and Character* (1903), in which he "treated Jews and women with equal hostilit. . . . Being a neurotic, Weininger was completely under the sway of his infantile complexes, and from that standpoint what is common to Jews and women is their relation to the castration complex" (p. 36, n. 1). Boyarin (1998) points out that the conspicuous omission in this account is the fact that Weininger was Jewish, which underscores the importance of another parallel omission, that "Little Hans" was Jewish too, and hints at a third parallel with Freud himself. For Boyarin argues that "in presenting 'Little Hans' and [Otto] Weininger as if they were gentiles gazing at . . . the Jewish penis and filling with fear and loathing, Freud . . . represents himself (or at least an aspect of himself) gazing at his own circumcised penis. . . . Like Fanon, Freud is 'forever in combat with his own image'" (p. 215). Boyarin (1998) therefore argues that the case of "Little Hans" offers "an anatomy not only of misogyny and anti-Semitism . . . but of Jewish and (post)colonial self-contempt" even in cases where the sign of circumcision might not figure racial difference, as in the colonized subjectivity analyzed by Fanon (p. 217).[4]

However compelling Boyarin's argument, it still requires qualification because anti-Semitism and racism are not exact equivalents. The structure of doubling or mimicry is not the same in each case precisely because the sign which figures racial difference is not the same, a difference one may be tempted to overlook because both Fanon and Bhabha deploy psychoanalytic categories and concepts relating to sex in the colonial context. More specifically, Homi Bhabha models the process of colonial othering on fetishism, which in psychoanalysis describes a structure that operates to deny sexual difference by endowing the woman with a substitute penis (the fetish). Fetishism involves a doubling of consciousness, a split between belief and knowledge: the fetishist both believes the woman has a penis and knows that she does not. In the colonial situation, disavowal of difference produces in the Other "a misfit-grotesque mimicry or doubling" (Bhabha, 1994, p. 73). Such mimicry is encouraged through education and a "civilizing" process that stops short of full assimilation, so the colonized subject is "almost the same, but not quite" (Bhabha, 1994, p. 86).

However, though Bhabha argues that not having the penis is equivalent in the colonial context to skin/race/culture, such marks of exclusion do not uniformly limit the possibility of national identification. That is, for the colonial subject described by both Bhabha and Fanon "almost the same, but not quite" translates into "almost the same, but not white" (Bhabha, 1994, p. 86). Here, the category "white" appears to designate an *essential* difference. In contrast, as Jon Stratton (2000) points out, whiteness is ambiguously defined in relation to Jews because, on the one hand, the opposition Aryan/Jewish constructed Jews as other, but on the other hand, Jews were also considered "white." It is this ambiguity, this confusion of the category of whiteness itself, that proves more profound and threatening and marks the difference between racism and anti-Semitism (Stratton, 2000).[5] Paradoxically, the Jews' ambivalent whitenesss not only made them more threatening, but, as we shall see, also enabled them, in a different context, the United States, to be more fully incorporated (assimilated) into whiteness (Stratton, 2000).

To conclude this section with yet another paradox, Freud's invention of the Oedipus complex not only reveals his racism, misogyny, homophobia, and self-contempt, but also constitutes a tremendous theoretical advance insofar as it de-essentializes both sexual and racial difference by presenting them as constructions produced by deferred action rather than traits existing intact at birth. Freud's concept of "Nachträglichkeit" (translated as "deferred action") refers to a complex temporal logic that subverts the linear conception of time and its corollary, the erosion of the notion of origin, by representing memory as serial inscription or repetition. We have noted its operation in the case of "Little Hans," which does not dwell on all of the concept's radical implications. These are more fully elaborated in the 1895 "Project for a Scientific Psychology" as part of Freud's seduction theory in the case history of a hysteric named Emma.

Freud resorted to a theory of seduction as *proton pseudos* ("primal deceit") because he could not establish seduction as an event. The theory does not invoke deliberate simulation on the part of hysterics. Rather, *proton pseudos* refers to a fundamental duplicity inscribed in the conjunction of circumstances in the case history. Freud's analysis reveals that Emma's phobia of entering shops alone results from the conjunction of two scenes because the event as such escapes consciousness, and only the memory excites the affect. When Emma was eight, she was twice assaulted by a shopkeeper who grabbed at her genitals through her clothes. However, at this time she was too young to understand the sexual significance of his actions. At the age of twelve, she entered a shop alone and saw two shop assistants laughing, perhaps at her clothes. This banal, non-sexual detail of resemblance activated the memory of the grinning shopkeeper's assault, which she now understood for the first time because of the onset of puberty in the interval between the scenes. Freud (1895) writes, "the recollection aroused [through the displacement of affect] (what the event when it occurred could certainly not have done), a sexual release, which turned into anxiety," which instituted a repression of the earlier scene and symptom formation (p. 411). The notion of deferred action thus undermines the very idea of original or grounding "event" as it suspends trauma in the structural relation between two events as well as two registers of meaning, perception and consciousness (i.e., the unconscious). Freud here assumes a psychical apparatus structured through the repeated revision of a memory, which renders any linear notions of causality untenable because it reveals the non-coincidence of chronology and causality. For despite its chronological placement, "cause" is the after-effect or inference of an interpretive process. The absence of a determinate origin or cause also means that the subject is not predetermined.

If we tend to underestimate Freud's radicality at times it is perhaps because in subsequent texts in which Freud detaches the function of trauma from the hysteria scenario and generalizes its application, his misogynous statements detract attention from the process he describes. For instance, in his 1925 description of the castration scenario, deferred action structures only the little boy's interpretation of sexual difference: "he begins by showing irresolution and lack of interest" in the perception of the girl's anatomical difference; "he sees nothing or disavows what he has seen." Later, after "some threat of castration has obtained a hold upon him," the memory "arouses a terrible storm of emotion in him," and he retroactively interprets the girl's difference as *her* castration (p. 252). In the process the earlier scene–the initial uncertainty of his perception–is repressed. In this scenario, the little girl serves two functions. First of all, she confirms the boy's displacement of castration onto her, even though this interpretation means that she inexplicably disregards her own difference and adopts a masculine perspective. She thereby confirms the boy's wholeness and integrity. Secondly, the fact that her corroboration takes the form of an immediate perception ("she makes her judgment and her decision in a flash. She has seen it and knows that she is without it and wants to have it") simultaneously excludes her from the knowledge process that constructs the boy's understanding and reinforces the repression of the uncertainty of perception. Even more curiously, Freud, like the boy and the girl, also locates castration in the girl's anatomy, thereby repeating their failure to acknowledge castration as a trauma, suspended in the gap between experience (the initial "irresolution" of perception) and understanding (the misinterpretation of sexual difference). Like the little boy, he disavows the implication of castration for himself, much as he does in the case of Little Hans. It is significant that at the time of writing the "Project" Freud had not yet identified seduction scenes with the feminine Oedipus complex. Precisely because his theory of female sexuality was *not* at stake, he was able to elaborate the knowledge process that constitutes the feminine subject. In short, the transfer from the hysteria to the castration scenario registers the shift from a tentative or queer to a consolidated sexuality by means of a textual practice that foregrounds meaning or interpretation and mutes the process itself, i.e., the text's performativity. This emphasis is precisely what will be reversed in the next fin de siècle.

"PARENTHETICAL JEWS" AND THE PERFORMATIVITY OF DIFFERENCE

Part II shifts the focus to another fin de siècle, the 1990s in the USA, which entails as well a shift from a post-colonial to a post-assimilationist situation. In this connection, Jon Stratton traces the changes in post World War II definitions of ethnicity decade by decade which produced such a shift. Even though his account demands modification because it conforms to a linear narrative that does not sufficiently acknowledge the co-existence of competing definitions, it is useful nonetheless in that it provides a taxonomy of different ideologies of ethnicity. Prior to this time, specifically in the 1930s, Jews were invisible, "cloaked under other types of bodies" (Stratton, 2001, p. 143) in accordance with the prevailing ideology of assimilation and the melting pot. It is worth pointing out that in film and vaudeville this cloaking often involved the use of blackface, as in *The Jazz Singer*, which, Michael Rogin argues, furnished a way for Jews to integrate into a society in which African Americans were positioned as the Other, a point to which I will return (Seidman, 1998). In the 1950s, Jews of the USA began to be represented in terms of their religious rather than their racial difference (Stratton, 2001). Though other groups–Italians, Greeks, Irish– were also "whitened" during this period, Jews were accepted as more white, more Anglo-American because they were conceived as "prefiguratively white," meaning that initially their difference was presented in terms of religion and their integration facilitated "through the rhetoric of a Judeo-Christian tradition" rather than culture (e.g., in contrast to Italians) (Stratton, 2001, p. 155). In short, the peculiarity of the Jews is that they were assimilated on two levels–both ideologically and culturally. It should be noted as well that during this time ethnic specificity is interarticulated with class. Thus Karen Brodkin argues that "job degradation and racial darkening were linked" and that "economic prosperity also played a very powerful role in the whitening process" (Stratton, 2000, p. 288).

But in the 1960s, after the whitening of the Jews was achieved, they came to be defined more in terms of their cultural rather than their religious or racial difference. At the same time, many of these cultural features were applied to other contexts, available to generalization: the Jewish American Princess; the Jewish Mother; (you don't have to be Jewish to love) rye bread, bagels (Stratton, 2001). This definition marked a shift from the ideology of the melting pot, which in its most conservative construction meant Anglo-conformism, to the ideology of cultural pluralism, which allowed for cultural diversity within a system of shared values and norms. This negotiation of difference and similarity was achieved by means of a private/public distinction, relegating specific cultural practices to the former realm.[6] By the 1960s, cultural pluralism had become a "household word" (Stratton, 2001, p. 155). Cultural pluralism led to a re-definition of whiteness, one that extended to the entire "European" community within the United States but that excluded African Americans and other racialized groups:

> It is, in fact, 'race,' and specifically the 'black' race, which has been the excluded excess in the pluralist ideology in which Jews were deracialized as a people in their own right and re-racialized as an ethnic group within the 'white' race. (Stratton, 2000, p. 276)[7]

Stratton remarks on the waning of the desire for assimilation during the 1970s and 1980s as the politics of multiculturalism gradually supplanted those of cultural pluralism and argues that this shift once again placed Jews in a peculiar, i.e., post-assimilationist, situation. More specifically, multiculturalism in the United States may be conceived as registering a disillusionment and resistance to the philosophy of pluralism (Stratton, 2000). It not only promotes the public display of diversity, thereby collapsing the private/public distinction on which pluralism depends, but it also legitimates identification and solidarity with origins outside the United States (thereby posing a possible menace to the conception of a unified nation-state) (Stratton, 2000).

In this context, "what was at issue, representationally speaking, was how to produce and present difference for a group which had, for three decades, been presented as white, and as subscribing to the key value system of Anglo-America . . ." (Stratton, 2001, p. 155). From the point of view of subaltern groups espousing multiculturalism, Jews are seen as part of the "white" elite, which explains why anti-Semitism is more likely to be expressed by such groups than by "white" society at this time (Stratton, 2000). Naomi Seidman (1998) describes even more forcefully the exclusion of Jews from the multiculture:

> If the founding moment of American multiculturalism is in the shift from the liberalism of the civil rights movement to the identity politics of Black Power in the mid-to late 1960s, then multiculturalism, from the beginning, signalled the expulsion of Jews from a comfortable home on the left. (p. 260)

At the same time, the production of post-assimilationist Jewish-American difference indicates a reversal in the role of performance. Whereas in earlier decades ethnic difference was understood to be based on tradition and descent, while being American (assimilated) was based on choice and was therefore performative, in the 1980s and 1990s, performance came to be associated instead with the establishment of (ethnic) difference (Stratton, 2001) because ethnicity itself was re-conceived as consent-based, as something that must be "constantly invented, consented to, and negotiated . . . " (Sobchack, 1991, p. 348). Drawing on Homi Bhaba's concepts of doubling and mimicry, but to very different ends than Boyarin writing about Freud, Stratton (2001) argues that whereas the production of the double by the colonizer functions to prevent the full assimilation of the post-colonial subject (usually because of some racial marker of difference), United States films in the 1980s represent the production of the double by the subordinate group in order to express difference or dis-assimilation.

Moving from a consideration of 1980s films to the context of gender theory, Stratton (2001) argues that Judith Butler's work in queer theory is a displacement of writing about herself as being Jewish, which suggests certain parallels to Freud's theoretical moves. However, the explanation of how Butler's work involves the production of a double and a displacement of ethnic onto sexual difference is more clearly demonstrated by Naomi Seidman. Seidman (1998) locates Butler in a

longstanding "subterranean tradition of Zeligs and Zebraheads, parenthetical Jews and identifiers with an 'other' identity" (p. 256).[8] More
particularly, Seidman cites Butler's response to bell hooks's criticism of
Jennie Livingston, the documentary film director of *Paris is Burning*,
for representing "blackness" from a perspective complicit with "hegemonic whiteness" without in any way interrogating whiteness.[9] Butler
(1993) challenges hooks's description of Livingston as white:
"Livingston is a white lesbian (in other contexts 'a Jewish lesbian from
Yale,' an interpellation which also implicates this author [Butler] in its
sweep)" (p. 133). According to Seidman (1998), while for Butler the
identification of Livingston as lesbian establishes a bond between the
director and the gay men who are the subjects of her film, putting her
Jewishness in parentheses (and by implication Butler's as well) de-
politicizes that ethnic difference. Here we have an example of a double
doubling: on the one hand Livingston and Butler, on the other and more
importantly, the doubling of lesbianism and Jewishness. The assertion
of lesbianism produces a difference that Jewishness by itself cannot.

However, this reference to Jewishness is anomalous in Butler's
work. But then so is her self-description as a lesbian. In "Imitation and
Gender Insubordination" (1991), for example, Butler explains her discomfort with "identity categories [because they] tend to be instruments
of regulatory regimes" (p. 13). And her conception of identity as
performative, i.e., the site of a compulsory repetition that produces only
the semblance of identity, underscores the instability of such categories:

> does or can the 'I' ever repeat itself, cite itself, faithfully, or is there
> always a displacement from its former moment that establishes the
> permanently non-self-identical status of that 'I' or its 'being les-
> bian'? . . . the repetition, and the failure to repeat, produce a string
> of performances that constitute and contest the coherence of that
> 'I'. (p. 18)

A few points of clarification are in order at this point.

(1) Juxtaposing Seidman's reading of Butler with the latter's definition of performativity indicates that displacement occurs not only from
ethnicity onto sexuality/gender, but also within (between acts of) sexu-
ality/gender. The displacement of ethnicity onto sexuality/gender, because it moves from one identity category to another, is only more
obviously identity-fracturing than a displacement from one "I" to another "I" which does not cross definitional lines. Yet the destabilizing
effects of displacement occur in both.

(2) Consequently, Stratton's terminology requires qualification, for he uses the terms performative and performance interchangeably and conceives of both as volitional, as Sobchack's notion of "consent-based" ethnicity implies as well. As a result, Stratton (2001) downplays the disruptive effects of performativity. In contrast, Butler (1991) distinguishes between performance and performativity and insists on the compulsory, unconscious aspect of the latter:

> the psyche calls to be rethought precisely as a compulsive repetition . . . if every performance repeats itself to institute the effect of identity, then every repetition requires an interval between the acts . . . in which risk and excess threaten to disrupt the identity being constituted. The unconscious is this excess that enables and contests every performance, and which never fully appears within the performance itself. (p. 28)

(3) Because Stratton (2001) emphasizes the naturalization of identity through performativity, he argues that Butler's writings legitimate performative difference, including ethnic difference, and suggest a way to "produce a distinctive Jewishness in the USA," thereby enabling Jews to participate in the multiculture: Just as gender is naturalized through repeated performance, "Jewishness, like other ethnicities, can . . . be thought of as a set of attributes which are repeated and naturalized as identifiably Jewish" (p. 160). However, this account ignores the compulsory aspect of performativity and the incoherence that repetition produces, factors that suggest rather a theoretical legitimation of a *resistance* to the identity politics associated with multiculturalism.

Ultimately, despite the reference to Butler, Stratton's emphasis on the naturalization of Jewish identity suggests what Seidman (1998) describes as "a straight road of Jewish self-identification in the multiculture" (p. 267). This "road" co-exists with another which de-naturalizes identity per se. Thus Seidman (1998) more persuasively argues that the peculiar post-assimilationist position of the Jews, produced by a long "tradition of Jewish universalist secularism," means that the Jew can secure a place in the multiculture only through "a different kind of blackface, lifting a marginality wholesale from elsewhere" (p. 260), what I am calling a reverse mimicry. And instead of the performative production of a Jewish identity, "adopting the particularist position of another group paradoxically becomes a distinctively Jewish act" (p. 261).

Nowhere is this act better displayed than in Eve Kosofsky Sedgwick's *Epistemology of the Closet* (1990). Her first chapter not only describes, but enacts doubling through a sustained performance. More specifically, Sedgwick compares gay self-disclosure and the drama of Jewish self-identification in the biblical story of Esther. Although she recognizes the convergence of racial/ethnic and gender categories in Esther's identity, Sedgwick reads both components in a reductive way in order to sharpen the contrast to gay self-disclosure. Thus she argues that in its "clear ancestral linearity and answerability, in the roots of cultural identification through each individual's originary culture of . . . the family," the story of Esther offers a "simplified" model of coming out, different from the gay version, whose distinctiveness derives from the "plurality and cumulative incoherence of modern ways of conceptualizing same-sex desire and gay identity" (pp. 75, 85). According to Sedgwick, other differences derive from this key distinction. For instance, Esther's communal ties make it possible for her to control others' knowledge of her as well as to set limits on the effects of her self-disclosure. Such epistemological control contrasts markedly with the unsettling and unpredictable effects of gay self-disclosure, which has the potential of destabilizing all identities, both of the one coming out and of the one receiving the disclosure.

At the same time, Sedgwick's own coming out as (Jewish) in this very chapter de-essentializes Jewish identity by placing it in parentheses. Commenting on Esther's subordination of gender issues to the interests of minority rights, she writes:

> (Even today, Jewish little girls are educated in gender roles–fondness for being looked at, fearlessness in defense of 'their people,' a non-solidarity with their sex–through masquerading as Queen Esther at Purim; I have a snapshot of myself at about five, barefoot in the pretty 'Queen Esther' dress my grandmother made [white satin, gold spangles], making a careful eyes down pointed-toe curtsey at [presumably] my father, who is manifest in the picture only as a flashgun that hurls my shadow, pillaring up tall and black, over the dwarfed sofa on the wall behind me). (p. 82)

I have argued elsewhere that the biblical story of Esther is more complex than Sedgwick's account suggests because it presents Esther as an instance of womanliness as masquerade par excellence. That is, Esther's female submissiveness indicates not so much "a firm Jewish choice of minority politics based on a conservative reinscription of gender roles" (Sedgwick, 1990, pp. 81-82), but rather serves as a mask to conceal a non-identity, for the story ends not with the consolidation but with the disintegration of Jewish identity as non-Jewish subjects of the kingdom profess themselves to be Jewish in order to protect themselves from persecution by the Jews, who come to power when Mordecai, Esther's uncle, replaces Haman as the King's adviser (Johnston, 2003).

In a parallel argument, Seidman (1998) questions the solidity of Jewish identity in so far as she argues that Sedgwick's "coming out as a (Jew) neatly reverses Esther's" by theatricalizing the self-disclosure, thereby transforming it into an instance of ethnic drag (p. 263). Recall that in Butler's definition (1991) "drag is not an imitation or a copy of some prior and true gender; . . . drag enacts the very structure of impersonation by which any gender is assumed" (p. 21). Butler's conception of drag thus permits Seidman (1998) to conclude that "both Eve-Esther and Queen Esther are simulacra, (Jewish) drag queens" and that both self-disclosures are "carefully crafted performance[s]" (p. 263).

For my purposes, I wish to emphasize the idea of coming out as performative–insofar as it involves both repetition and a failure to repeat exactly–so as to contest Stratton's claim that

> the image of the closet is a utopian, liberal idea bound up with both essentialism and privacy. . . . [and associated with a] sense of an obligatory and obliging confinement [that has] been replaced by a liberatory politics of public self-expression, something intimately bound up with the rise of the ideology of multiculturalism . . . (2000, p. 14)

First of all, this quotation clearly reveals Stratton's adherence to a linear model of history in which one ideology "replaces" another. Sedgwick (1990) explicitly rejects this model as she seeks to draw our attention instead to a performative space of contradiction produced by co-existing understandings of same-sex relations: "This project does not involve the construction of historical narratives. . . . Rather, it requires a reassignment of attention . . . on a performative space of contradiction that they both delineate and . . . pass over in silence" (pp. 47-8). Secondly, Stratton's understanding of performativity is no less reductive than his model of history. As I have indicated above in my discussion of Butler, Stratton conflates it with performance. In fact, the quotation from Sedgwick suggests that the two are related in that both such a historical model and notion of performativity suppress contradiction. Consequently, Stratton reads Sedgwick's conception of the closet and her comparison of coming out stories reductively as well.

Elsewhere, Sedgwick (1995) herself suggests an alternative to the kind of reading that Stratton presents. That is, she demonstrates precisely how we may translate Butler's theory of quotidian gender performativity into specifically textual terms insofar as she draws on Paul de Man's "demonstration of 'a radical estrangement between the meaning and the performance of any text.'" Sedgwick explains that such textual performativity designates "not so much the nonreference of the performative, but rather . . . its necessarily 'aberrant' relation to its own reference–the torsion, the mutual perversion of reference and performativity" (p. 3).

In the two coming out stories discussed above, the aberrant relation of performativity to reference is evident in the tension between Sedgwick's statement on the one hand that Queen Esther represents a solid Jewish and gender identity and her own drag performance as Esther on the other hand, which exposes the imitativeness and contingency that belie that description. For the doubling of Sedgwick and Esther means that Sedgwick's ethnic drag is simultaneously a gender performance. Furthermore, as Seidman (1998) points out, the name–Eve Kosofsky Sedgwick–raises questions not only about the author's ethnicity, but also about her sexuality: "there is a double tension in this coming-out scene: Sedgwick simultaneously does and does not come out as Jewish and, less explicitly, she almost but doesn't quite come out as not-heterosexual" (p. 264). Yet for all her sensitivity to the performative dimension of Sedgwick's coming out as a (Jew), Seidman (1998) reads Sedgwick's vicarious identification more reductively as "the position of the fag-hag, the heterosexual woman who loves gay men" (p. 265), whose unintelligible identity politics "throws the multicultural vision into anxious question" (p. 266).

Sedgwick's own description of the "openly vicariating cathexis from the outside that motivates [her] study" is rather more complex, having to do with her "experience as a woman; as a fat woman; as a nonprocreative adult; as someone who is, under several discursive regimes, a sexual pervert, under some, a Jew" (Sedgwick, 1990, pp. 62, 63). Moreover, Sedgwick goes on to suggest that vicariousness in particular is what draws her to study "the closet" and pre-Stonewall gay self-definition (rather than "out" liberatory gay politics):

> "the vicarious becomes particularly charged in association with the homo/heterosexual definition" as a result of the discursive

shift that instituted a radical discontinuity between homosexual and heterosexual identities, making identification with/as especially problematic. At the same time, just as Butler extends the notion of drag to include the assumption of any gender, so Sedgwick maintains that *all* identification is vicarious, for "not only identifications *across* definitional lines . . . require . . . explanation . . . the same is equally true of any person's identification with her or his 'own' gender, race, sexuality, nation" (pp. 60-61).

I would therefore qualify Seidman's reading and argue that it is Sedgwick's insistence on the vicariousness of all identification, rather than her position as a "fag-hag," that "throws the multicultural vision into anxious question" (Seidman, 1998, p. 266).

In resisting a "straight" road to identification Butler and Sedgwick thus embrace the queerness that Freud sought to escape through his construction of the heterosexual male. Yet this reversal is an instance of masked repetition in that the disparate effects produced by these theories conceal the operation of a common process. Its discovery requires that we read Freud performatively as well. That is, if Sedgwick's performance as Queen Esther exhibits the aberrant relation of performativity to reference, is this "torsion" not also evident in Freud's case of "Little Hans," in which the anatomy of Jewish anti-Semitism is relegated to a footnote and the circumcisions of Hans, Weininger, and Freud himself never mentioned, or in the 1925 castration scenario in which Freud's conclusions contradict his earlier insights (1895) into the operation of deferred action in trauma?

In fact, deferred action, whose operation is muted in Freud's two later texts is, I maintain, a theory of queer performativity. This theory may be reconstructed by invoking the Heisenberg uncertainty principle, which describes the scientist's implication in an experiment. The principle states that it is impossible to ascertain the location of a particle and to measure its velocity simultaneously. Accordingly, in reading Freud, to focus on a particular effect or meaning blinds us to the lost cause of its production. For to focus on effect or substance commits us to repetition governed by the logic of identity. This is what happens in the castration scenario. The repetition of a specific content represses the prior discovery of repetition as a structure. Thus the little girl and Freud repeat the little boy's misconstruction of castration. In this scenario, deferred action makes no difference, for all–the girl, the boy, and Freud/narrator– see the same *thing*. By the same token, to focus on the hysteric erects hysteria into the universal meaning of the earlier scenario, an origin that determines all future readings of the scene. In each case the fixation on a single meaning conceals its contingency on a specific, time-bound interpretive context, which is open to re-vision.

Attending to the operating mode or text's performativity, on the other hand, brings into relief the structuring function of deferred action in disparate scenarios and its production of different effects. Thus focusing on repetition as a structure reveals the significance of discontinuities and failures of representation which allow differences to emerge and come into play, thereby opening a space for queer incoherence. For the absence of a determinate origin or cause means that the subject is not predetermined in some originary moment once and for all, hence not reducible to any particular cultural construction—be it hysteria, castration, femininity, or any other interpretation of sexuality for that matter. To say that the subject remains in question, or subject to repeated re-vision, is rather to insist on its arbitrariness (sexuality does not refer to an "identity" that exists outside its construction in a specific representation).

Attention to the process operative in Freud's texts permits a different reading of their crucial discoveries, one at odds with the sexual bias of certain recuperative tactics in their conclusions. It is to regard castration as a crisis in vision rather than as an anatomical distinction and the past as the effect of narration rather than its cause or origin. It is therefore not surprising to discover from such a reading that Freud's notion of deferred action comes close to approximating the temporality of performativity as described by Judith Butler (1993), which also conceives of time in terms of repetition and the retroactive production of cause: "Performativity must be understood not as a singular or deliberate 'act,' but, rather, as the reiterative and citational practice by which discourse produces the effects that it names" (p. 10). And just as Freud undermines the notion of singular event and describes memory as serial inscription, Butler insists that an "act" is not discrete but itself a repetition that cannot be separated from the process that produces it (p. 244, n. 7) and that "moments" are also not distinct and uniform (p. 245, n. 8). Hence her use of the term "sedimentation" to designate this temporality.

My argument that shifting attention from meaning to process brings to light the queerness of Freud's theory of deferred action invites a return to and a re-vision of Eric Savoy's argument (1999) cited at the beginning of this essay. Savoy maintains that contemporary queer theory is especially suited to provide a reading of an incipient gay and lesbian specificity of queerness in 1950s cinema, which at the time existed only in silences and connotative excess. We can now identify such a reading as an instance of retroactive interpretation or re-vision according to the operation of deferred action. For his analysis does not seek to supply the meaning of such silences and excesses but rather to note their function as resistance to solidified meaning. Similarly, my reading of queerness in Freud's texts, which foregrounds its silences and its failures to make sense in order to make present the functioning of the process, is also a deployment of the same interpretive practice.

Finally, to foreground the performativity of Freud's texts helps us to understand the uncanny resonances between the historical moments that mark the "pre" and "post" of all clarified (sexual) identities, not only those relating to gay and lesbian specificity, as in Savoy's reading. That is, these "moments" do not suggest a "before" and "after" located along a historical continuum but the displacement of such a historical model by the repetitive emergence and undoing of identity discovered by attending to the process. For just as in Freud's writings queerness co-alesces into a firm identity (the heterosexual male) as a result of a textual practice that privileges a particular inference and blinds us to its construction, so may queerness in the context of homosexuality also involve a shift of focus from the contradictory and tentative process of definition to an achieved gay or lesbian identity. In both cases the Heisenberg uncertainty theory applies and transforms a choice between two identities or binary opposites (i.e., queer vs. heterosexual or queer vs. lesbian/gay) into a displacement of attention to their construction. From this perspective, consolidated gay and lesbian specificity refers to *what* one comes out as. But queer describes coming out as performative—a compulsory iterative process that subjects such specificity to change.

NOTES

1. More specifically, Savoy argues that the queer paradigm more accurately demonstrates the incipient specificity of homosexual identification in 1950s cinema because in that period the explicit representation of homosexuality was proscribed, resulting in an oblique representation that relied heavily on connotation and circumlocution. Though the "pre" moment with which I am concerned is turn of the century Vienna, it shares with 1950s American cinema the tentativeness of definition of the homosexual which is the focus of Savoy's analysis and is therefore also best described in terms of the queer paradigm, not only because homophobia generates a wealth of representation around lesbian and gay potentiality in both 1950s cinema and in Freud's Vienna, but also because in the latter context homophobia is intertwined with racism. Actually, Daniel Boyarin (1995) identifies *three* intertwined cultural events in the discursive configuration imposed on Freud: "the racialization/gendering of anti-Semitism, the fin-de-siècle production of

sexualities, including the 'homosexual,' and the sharp increase in contemporary Christian homophobic discourse (the 'Christian Values' movement)," all of which produced a "perfect match between homophobia and anti-semitism" (p. 129).

2. The "Dark Continent" trope appears in Freud's "The Question of Lay Analysis" (1926), where it is used to explain the psychoanalyst's limited understanding of female sexuality (p. 212). However, as Mary Ann Doane (1991) explains, "the adjective 'dark' in dark continent signifies not only unknowability but blackness in its racial connotations" (p. 211).

3. Boyarin (1995) argues that "homophobia is at this time almost subsumed under misogyny, to which anti-Semitism bears a strong family resemblance" (p. 142, n. 33).

4. Boyarin's argument (1998) builds on many parallels between Freud and Fanon: For both, the more educated the colonial subject, the greater his discomfort upon returning to his native land. Language is another mark of the split subject, the adoption of French/"high" German in place of Creole/Yiddish. Like the Jew, the black is also "feminized" by the dominating European culture. Finally, Fanon's misogyny and homophobia parallel Freud's and are evident in his claim to know "nothing" of the woman of color, which echoes Freud's description of female sexuality as a "dark continent," and in Fanon's denial that homosexuality exists in Martinique (pp. 222-225).

5. The ambivalence is registered as well in the descriptions of Gilman and Boyarin. Gilman (1991) describes Jews both as "blacks" and as "mulattos" (p. 99); Boyarin (1998) describes them as "off-white," "ecru" (p. 219).

6. Stratton (2000) traces the roots of cultural pluralism to the 1920s and 1930s and describes it as a reaction to the Anglo-conformist movement, advanced by Jewish thinkers such as Horace Kallen. Cultural pluralism represents an attempt to preserve a minority group's religious and cultural practices and a reaction against total assimilation (pp. 265-266).

7. One might even consider this as an instance of blackface, as it functions in Rogin's argument, for the presence of African Americans in the United States "distracted concern from the Jews," facilitating their acceptance (Stratton, 2000, p. 276). In this connection, Naomi Seidman (1998) argues that both the use of blackface and Jewish participation in the civil rights movement indirectly provided a way for Jews to be integrated as white.

8. *Zebrahead* (1992) is a film about a Jewish teenager who assumes the role of an African American; Woody Allen's *Zelig* (1983) is a film about a Jewish man's chameleonism, which enables him to assume the accent, profession, and ethnicity of those he comes into contact with.

9. bell hooks's criticism of Livingston is only one instance in which she defends black culture from being appropriated and commodified by "white supremacist culture." For instance, hooks (1992) calls Madonna a modern day Shirley Temple, whose video *Like a Prayer* recalls "those Shirley Temple films where Bojangles was trotted out to dance with Miss Shirley and spice up her act" (p. 162). And she compares Sandra Bernhard to Madonna: "Like her entertainment cohort Madonna, Bernhard leaves her encounters with Others richer than she was at the outset. We have no idea how the Other leaves her" (p. 39). Underlying hooks's defense of black culture against encroachment from whites is a separatist assumption that black culture can somehow "belong" exclusively to blacks. Certainly she is bound to find Butler's conception of identity as imitative and contingent inimical to her own project, which can be accommodated in the multiculture as Butler's cannot.

REFERENCES

Bhabha, H. (1994). *The location of culture.* New York: Routledge.

Boyarin, D. (1995). Freud's baby, Fliess's maybe: Homophobia, anti-Semitism, and the invention of the Oedipus. *GLQ: A Journal of Lesbian and Gay Studies, 2*(1-2), 115-47.

Boyarin, D. (1998). What does a Jew want?; or, The political meaning of the phallus. In C. Lane (Ed.), *The psychoanalysis of race* (pp. 211-40). New York: Columbia University Press.

Butler, J. (1991). Imitation and gender subordination. In D. Fuss (Ed.), *Inside/outside: Lesbian theories, gay theories* (pp. 13-31). New York: Routledge.

Butler, J. (1993). *Bodies that matter: On the discursive limits of "sex."* New York: Routledge.

Doane, M. A. (1991). *Femme fatales: Feminism, film theory, psychoanalysis.* New York: Routledge.

Edelman, L. (1994). *Homographesis: Essays in gay literary and cultural theory.* New York, Routledge.

Foucault, M. (1980). *The history of sexuality.* (Vol. 1: *An introduction*). (R. Hurley, Trans.) New York: Vintage Books.

Freud, S. (1895). Project for a scientific psychology. In M. Bonaparte, A. Freud, & E.Kris (Eds.), *The origins of psycho-analysis: Letters to Wilhelm Fliess, drafts and notes: 1887-1902* (pp. 355-445). (E. Mosbacher & J. Strachey, Trans.) New York: Basic Books.

Freud, S. (1953-74). *The standard edition of the complete psychological works of Sigmund Freud.* (J. Strachey, Ed.). (Vols. 1-24). London: Hogarth Press.

_____ [1909]. Analysis of a phobia in a five-year-old boy (Vol. 10, 5-140).

_____ [1925]. Some psychical consequences of the anatomical distinction between the sexes (Vol. 19, 248-58).

_____ [1926]. The question of lay analysis: Conversations with an impartial person (Vol. 20, 183-258).

Gilman, S. L. (1991). *The Jew's body.* New York: Routledge.

Gilman, S. L. (1993a). *Freud, race, and gender.* New York: Routledge.

Gilman, S. L. (1993b, Spring). Male sexuality and contemporary Jewish literature in German: The damaged body as the image of the damaged soul. *Genders, 16,* 113-40.

hooks, b. (1992). *Black looks: Race and representation.* Boston: South End Press.

Johnston, R. D. (2003). The Jewish closet in *Europa, Europa. Camera Obscura, 52,* 1-33.

Mehlman, J. (1975). How to read Freud on jokes: The critic as *Schadchen. New Literary History, 6*(2), 439-61.

Pelligrini, A. (1997). *Performance anxieties: Staging psychoanalysis, staging race.* New York: Routledge.

Savoy, E. (1999). "That ain't all she ain't": Doris Day and queer performativity. In E. Hanson (Ed.), *Outtakes: Essays on queer theory and film* (pp. 151-82). Durham: Duke University Press.

Sedgwick, E. K. (1990). *Epistemology of the closet*. Berkeley: University of California Press.

Sedgwick, E. K., & Parker, A. (Eds). (1995). *Performativity and performance: Essays from the English institute*. New York: Routledge.

Seidman, N. (1998). Fag-hags and bu-Jews: Towards a (Jewish) politics of vicarious identity. In D. Biale, M. Galchinsky, & S. Heschel (Eds.), *Insider/outsider: American Jews and the multiculture* (pp. 254-68). Berkeley: University of California Press.

Sobchack, V. (1991). Postmodern modes of ethnicity. In L. D. Friedman (Ed.), *Unspeakable images: Ethnicity and the American cinema* (pp. 329-52). Urbana: University of Illinois Press.

Stratton, J. (2000). *Coming out Jewish: Constructing ambivalent identities*. New York: Routledge.

Stratton, J. (2001). Not really white-again: Performing Jewish difference in Hollywood films since the 1980s. *Screen 42*(2), 142-66.

doi:10.1300/J082v52n01_09

Desiring Mates

Dean Durber, PhD

Independent Scholar

SUMMARY. The discourse of gay liberation reads silence surrounding personal participation in same-sex sexualized pleasures as a sign of repression, oppression and a positioning in the closet. In contrast, coming out is an important step towards accepting one's true homosexual self. The demand for the emancipation of the homosexual type further suggests that all same-sex sexualized contact signifies the homosexuality of the subjects involved, regardless of whether they recognize this or not.

This compulsory homosexualization of men who have sexualized contact with men does not apply to relationships between male friends ("mates"). A "mateship" union grants a level of privacy otherwise eradicated by a gay liberation movement insistent on the public confession of a homosexual orientation. To remain silent about corporeal pleasures poses a threat to the modernist preference for control of bodies and to the established gay identity. Silence offers a space for the construction of new modes of same-sex intimate relationships within a queer framework. doi:10.1300/J082v52n01_10 *[Article copies available for a fee from The Haworth Document Delivery Service: 1-800-HAWORTH. E-mail address:*

This research has been assisted by funding provided through a Curtin University Postgraduate Scholarship.

Correspondence may be addressed: P.O. Box 233, Hamilton Hill, WA 6963, Australia (E-mail: deandurber@optusnet.com.au).

[Haworth co-indexing entry note]: "Desiring Mates." Durber, Dean. Co-published simultaneously in *Journal of Homosexuality* (Harrington Park Press, an imprint of The Haworth Press, Inc.) Vol. 52, No. 1/2, 2006, pp. 237-255; and: *LGBT Studies and Queer Theory: New Conflicts, Collaborations, and Contested Terrain* (ed: Karen E. Lovaas, John P. Elia, and Gust A. Yep) Harrington Park Press, an imprint of The Haworth Press, Inc., 2006, pp. 237-255. Single or multiple copies of this article are available for a fee from The Haworth Document Delivery Service [1-800-HAWORTH, 9:00 a.m. - 5:00 p.m. (EST). E-mail address: docdelivery@haworthpress.com].

KEYWORDS. Articulation, closet, desire, homosexual, mateship, queer, silence

CLASH OF THE QUEER

When queer theory is interpreted as having a responsibility to expose the enforced silencing of other non-heteronormative sexual minorities, to bring these "censored subjugated knowledges and social voices" out of "shame, fear, and despair" (Seidman, 1997, p. 105), it too acts within the naturalized discourse of sexuality from which the homosexual and the heterosexual have emerged as truthful articulations of being. A queer theory that speaks of multiple sexualities, insisting that visibility can help prevent foreclosure on possible future mutations (Butler, 1991), participates in the ongoing attempt to locate all forms of sexualized corporeal contact within the limitations of a progressive narrative of sexuality. This multiplication–what is naively assumed to offer a more mature politics than the singular ethnic model of sexual identity (Fuss, 1989)–serves no better purpose than the enlargement of the regulatory field of normalization (Dean, 2000). When "the queer project" is (mis)interpreted as that which must seek to support "forms of personal living that are public in the sense of accessible, available to memory, and sustained through collective activity" (Warner, 2002, p. 203), the queer critique is contained and restrained by the continuing demand for confession of our pleasures.

This article addresses the regulating effect caused by the articulation of same-sex sexualized contact within the naturalized category of homosexuality. In contrast to the demand imposed on queer theory to bring sex out of the "closet," I suggest that silence offers a space in which a man who has sexualized contact with his male friend ("mate") can resist an enforced interpellation into a system of classification that requires all of his desires–past, present, and future-to be related to this one momentary physical act. In order to recognize the doing of same-sex sexualized pleasures outside of the metanarrative of being a homosexual, the possibilities of rearticulation of desire must include the act of non-articulation: a queering of silence.

DEFINING MATES

Within the Australian culture, the term "mateship" is commonplace but widely disputed. For some, it is "part of the Australian heritage. The male heritage, born in the bush in colonial days, nurtured in the male-dominated isolation of sheep stations and gold fields, glorified by the Anzacs" (Arndt, 1986, p. 36). Despite Australia's historical and continuing allegiance to and dependence on other Western nations—England and America, in particular-the concept of mateship is upheld as proof of the uniqueness of this nation. "Mateship" signifies a truly Australian relationship between men who best personify the Australian character. For others, however, the ideology of mateship offers an evasion of any in-depth critique of this country's class system (Buchbinder, 1994) and continuing marginalization of women and indigenous cultures (Edgar, 1997). This it does through a promotion of the superiority of friendships between working-class white men as the foundation of the Australian nation.

Although Edgar (1997) makes an attempt to critique a part of this evasion through reclassifying mateship as central to the family, thereby hoping to remove it from the exclusively male domain of "beer-swilling, pants-dropping foolery" (p. xii), nevertheless, his approach reinforces another important and often taken-for-granted aspect of the mateship ideology. "Being a 'real man,'" Edgar contends, "is not to be measured by his ability to control or dominate others, rather by his capacity to create a compassionate, sharing marriage and father children in an intimate and loving way" (p. xvi). "Mateship" is a signifier of the heterosexuality of the men involved in this union. For a man to refer to another man as a "mate" is to describe a bond absolutely devoid of mutual sexualized desire. Any action that begins the process of intimate sexualized physical contact between the men is outside of the normative position of heterosexuality in which these mateship relationships are ideally located. Such contact is the marker of the segregation between homosocial mateship and homosexuality. One only has to be certain about an absence or presence of "sex" to be able to know the "truth" of a relationship between men.

Sedgwick (1990) has posed the question: "What does it mean—what difference does it make—when a social or political relationship is sexualised?" (p. 5). In his recent investigations into the troubles of gender "down under," David Coad (2002) attempts such a sexualization by exposing how the Australian myth of heterosexual men surrounded by their heterosexual mates is dependent on the elision from history of the homoerotic and the homosexual within these unions. This he does through linking traditional stories of iconic figures in Australian culture–Ned Kelly, Henry Lawson, Crocodile Dundee–to the emergence of a queer landscape that demands and justifies the rewriting he has done. Similarly, in his analysis of the film *Gallipoli*, David Buchbinder (1994) has noted how the concept of a heterosexualized mateship can offer "subversion of patriarchal authority and of certain patriarchal norms [. . .] by simulating or approaching forbidden homosexuality through the exposure of homosocial desire" (p. 130). Such attempts to rewrite the history of normative masculinity in Australia–and the masculinization of normative Australian history–successfully note the eternal presence of homosexual desire even in the narratives that silence it.

However, an exposure of the intimacy experienced between men, the articulation of it within the discursive confines of the normalized homo-hetero positions, works to displace any real possibilities of trouble and difference. To claim there is evidence of sexualized desires and/or contact in a relationship between two men is to bring it into the regulatory system of a language of sexuality and to allow it to be tamed as "homosexual" accordingly. To argue that a particular relationship contains no "sex" is to allow it to be known and therefore controlled as "heterosexual." We may never be certain of the outcomes of this compulsory sexualization. We may never know for sure if the men are truly gay or truly straight. However, our obsessive will to know sexual types can be comforted at least by the knowledge that all men and their relationships with other men are "normal" because they comply with already established modes of being and being with others. They are always understandable within the homo-hetero binary. In order to disrupt this normative process of attaining knowledge about and containing bodies, the question that needs to be asked is: What does it mean–what difference does it make–when a relationship that involves sexualized contact is removed from the social and the political?

Certainly, the truth of a union of mates as homosocial and of the men involved as heterosexual is never guaranteed, never stable. Any insistence on the innate heteronormativity of the relationship produces suspicion of a homosexuality buried deep beneath the skin. Gay theory–and, at times, queer theory–readily goes in search of this hidden desire. Similarly, any attempt to define the relationship as homosexual and the men as homosexuals is hard to prove with absolute certainty given the culture's preference for heterosexuality. The general constructionist recognition of a distinction between act and identity also means that even the observation of a man engaging in an act of sexualized contact with another man cannot secure his position as a homosexual. Despite his participation in such an act, a man may choose to define his sexual identity otherwise, as is evidenced in the rise in popularity of such self-labeling terms as "men who have sex with men (MSM)" and "bi-curious." The "truth" of the heterosexuality or homosexuality of the union and the men is, therefore, always both culturally specific and historically contingent.

"Mate" is a signifier that both elides and contains same-sex physical intimacies. It is incapable of totally eradicating the possibility of same-sex sexualized contact or desire between men, while simultaneously incapable of affirming the presence of such things with absolute certainty. It therefore helps to deconstruct the normative binary of homo-hetero in which all bodies and their pleasures are sexualized. Its applicability is not restricted to Australia. The desire for heterosexual exclusivity extends well beyond the borders of this one part of the English-speaking world, as does the reality and suspicion of homosexuality. The importance the entirety of Western culture places on sexualized contact as a signifier of a whole(some) sexual identity works discursively to render impossible any sexualized contact between men who purport to be just friends ("mates"). Such an intense focus on what bodies do with other bodies also helps to reaffirm the existence of the homosexual other in a naturalized and universalized homo-hetero binary (Sedgwick, 1990). "Mate" therefore offers an alternative to the homo-hetero narrative wherever this narrative exists. As used elsewhere, "mate" also carries connotations of breeding and marriage, thus rendering the term even more confusing to the stability of the homo-hetero binary, even queerer.

ENSNARED INTO A DEVIANCY

Although there is certainly wide—and rightfully queer-dispute over the exact timing and context of the emergence of a homosexual consciousness (Fuss, 1989; Jagose, 19963; Norton, 1997), the introduction of the signifier "homosexual" into the culture in the late nineteenth-century (Adam, 1995; Halperin, 1990; Katz, 1997) reveals a formal attempt to isolate sexualized contact with a person of the same-sex from other forms of sexual "perversion" and to thus identify and institutionalize the act as an independent character trait. It is a popular understanding of the human experience because it relies on the simple process of observing who is having sex with whom (Halperin, 1989). As Foucault (1978) argued, it took specific corporeal acts already defined as "sex," held them up as proof of the individual's fixed sexual orientation and thereby produced a permanent species. "Homosexuality" sought to assign to the act of sexualized contact between men an interior and innate desire, and "homosexual" therefore became-and continues to become-any man who engages in such an act.

This establishment of a homosexual category is congruent, therefore, with the general shift of the "Enlightened" era of modernity towards the disciplining of the individual body. It allows for the "whole" person–and not the singular act–to become the focus of study and the object of accessible knowledge (Cohen, 1991; Foucault, 1977; Seidman, 1997). Although same-sex sexualized contact existed and continues to exist across histories and cultures, "homosexual" offers a convenient means of identifying men who participate in same-sex sexualized pleasures by framing and ensuring their essentialized (homo)sexed materiality (Butler, 1993). With the identification of the homosexual species, the sexualized body more readily becomes an acceptable site of surveillance (Danaher, Shirato & Webb, 2000). As McWhorter (1999) critically notes:

> Our classification system–both its requirements that people be their sexualities and the division of sexualities into hetero and homo–is a social control used to manipulate and manage people and to distribute or withhold goods; it is a political tool, and its employment is never disinterested. (p. 81)

This attempt to categorize bodies according to the kinds of corporeal pleasures they experience presupposes a unified understanding of the meaning attached to any particular activity carried out by the body. To claim that all forms of sexualized contact between two men signify homosexuality, for example, is to accept as axiomatic the notion that these corporeal interactions are focused on and constructed through a recognition of biologically ascribed sex. To say that any man who has sexualized contact with another man is a "homosexual" is to normalize the taxonomy of sexuality that seeks to encage such contact within an accessible system of classification. "Homosexuality" thus connotes an essentialist interpretation of sexualized pleasures because it claims that the desire for sex emerges from "a determinate source from which all sexual expression proceeds" (Halperin, 1990, p. 24). Acceptance of this arbitrary system of classification fails to recognize that "bodies, sensations, pleasures, acts, and interactions are made into 'sex' or accrue sexual meanings by individuals, groups, discourses, and institutional practices" (Seidman, 1997, p. 81).

THE LIBRATORY INCITEMENT

Within the context of a wider, late 1960s countercultural claim that the personal is political–that "everyone's political views should be read as expressing his or her particular, subjective interests" (Warner, 2002, p. 34)–the gay liberation movement declared that the ability to make public one's homosexuality was a major step towards removing discrimination against the homosexual subject. Rejecting the earlier twentieth century homophile notion of the private as sacred, the post-Stonewall gay liberation movement instead demanded that private lives become public (Bronski, 1998). Within the discourse of gay liberation, coming out of the closet is a "valuable catalyst for personal growth" (Chekola, 1994, p. 71) and a necessary step towards achieving full citizenship. It is expected that every gay-identifying man will have a coming out story to tell. Based on a belief that control of a label can grant the speaking subject power (Cruikshank, 1992), the coming-out process seeks to establish legitimate gay subjects as "active participants" in the writing of their history in order to permit them "more control over its interpretation" (Hall Carpenter Archives, 1989, p. xi).

Undoubtedly, this movement has assisted in removing much of the negativity attached to same-sex sexualized unions. As a result, increasingly, the labeling of a person as "homosexual," "gay," or "faggot"–to name but a few of the less provocative terms regularly used to describe those who appear to express same-sex desire–often fails to have the intended result of inflicting "injury" (Butler, 1997b) on the named subject. On the contrary, these terms are accepted by those who publicly admit to having same-sex desires and are used widely as positive descriptions of self. Within the discourse of gay liberation, it is suggested that when a man can define himself with reference to such terms, this reveals a comfortable acceptance of self. The articulation of "I am gay" incurs no injury on the speaking subject, but has "an immensely exhilarating and self-healing effect" (Adam, 1995, p. 90). In contrast, the closet–a space of non-articulation of a homosexual identity for the self–is viewed as "a manifestation of heteronormative and homophobic powers" and a space whose "materiality mediates a power/knowledge of oppression" (Brown, 2000, p. 3).

Foucault's *History of Sexuality* speaks of an "Incitement to Discourse," an imperative and compulsion to speak. In contrast to the belief in the past as en era of censorship of sex, Foucault (1978) claims there has been a "steady proliferation of discourses" concerned with naming it; "an institutional incitement to speak about it [. . .], a determination on the part of agencies of power to hear it spoken about, and to cause *it* to speak through explicit articulation and endlessly accumulated detail (p. 8). He warns against becoming docile to a system that accepts the ability of sex to "tell us our truth, or rather, the deeply buried truth about ourselves which we think we possess in our immediate consciousness" (p. 69), for this kind of discourse is a tool of power and control. A sexual identity can be seen as both creative and constraining (Creet, 1995). However, the former understanding is promoted to the exclusion of the latter within the discourse of gay liberation.

Still, sexual identities are touted as "necessary fictions" (Weeks, 1999, p. 18). Still, the political is made personal through an insistence that our corporeal pleasures need legitimating and therefore articulation. Despite warnings to the contrary (Foucault, 1978), despite the concern that legitimacy is what we are expected to think we need (Humphreys, 1972), a culture of confession of our sexualized habits continues. The belief is upheld that the truth of who we are rests in our ability to offer better communication, in telling all (Plummer, 1995). Freedom is said to emerge through the articulation of our pleasures within the context of the construction of a determinable sexual identity for the self. The irony is that although coming out stories may differ in specifics, the overall structure of these narratives remains the same. What the discourse of gay liberation defines as a joyful coming out, Foucault therefore suggests is a form of enforced confession deeply entrenched in the construction of a bourgeois subject with a will and a capacity to know and be known.

THE INJURY OF COMING OUT

Early gay theorists saw problems in adopting a homosexual identity that sought to exclude heterosexual desires. Instead, they insisted "gay" signified a freedom from identification with sexual roles and sexual identities (Reynolds, 2002). Dennis Altman (1971) once wrote of a liberation that would enable people to use their bodies for "sensual enjoyment as an end in itself, free from procreation or status-enhancement" (p. 99). He later noted the failure to sustain this approach, turning instead to applaud the shift from behaviour to identity as the "greatest single victory of the gay movement" (Altman, 1982, p. 9). Today, for most people, "gay" does not suggest fluidity of sexual expression. The insistence that "gay" should no longer signify only those who have a conscious recognition of the importance of same-sex desires to their being, but also incorporate all who display such desires (Boswell, 1989), reveals the extent and strength of this signifier's borders. "Gay" has become a naturalized category that enables the containment of the body by insisting, whether we like it or not, that anyone who engages in same-sex sexualized activities must move now into the identity of a being to which these activities have been pre-allocated.

The proclamation of a homosexual identity–"I am gay"–therefore produces a paradox elided in the suggestion of "coming out" as an act of liberation. The insistence on the existence of a repressing closet and on the corresponding need to dismantle this space through articulation of one's desire as "homosexual" promises release from oppression. However, it does not acknowledge sexual categories themselves as the products of systems of regulation. Speech does not name what already exists. It only helps construct what later is assumed natural within the discourses that come to define it (Bhabha, 1994; Butler, 1997b). It is not the act of sex, but rather the act of articulation of the sex that reveals the man who has sexualized contact with another man to be a homosexual. To label oneself as "gay" is an injurious act, therefore, because it reveals the successful normalization of a process of self-discipline. As Grosz (1995) notes:

> To submit one's pleasures and desires to enumeration and definitive articulation is to submit processes and becomings to entities, locations, and boundaries, to become welded to an organizing nucleus of fantasy whose goal is not simply pleasure and expansion but control, the production of endless repetition, endless variations of the same [. . .]. (p. 226)

"I am gay" accepts the injury of corporeal classification and ignores how the establishment of the homosexual as a distinct and separate category goes hand in hand with the murder of our desires (Hocquenghem, 1972; Stavrakakis, 1999).

Despite this, the discourse of gay liberation continues to (mis)read "homosexuality" as the truthful signifier of all same-sex desires. It accepts as axiomatic that sexualized contact between men signifies homosexuality regardless of whether this is recognized or not by the subjects involved. It stresses that for a man to have sex with a man *is* to be a homosexual, whereas any failure to recognize this identity stems from a repression both external and internal to the sexualized subject: either this repression is the result of compulsory heterosexuality or internalized homophobia (Cruikshank, 1992; Halley, 1994). The gay movement's obsession with attaining legitimacy for the homosexual subject upholds compulsory homosexualization of all men who have sexualized contact with men, while ignoring the historical and cultural containment of bodies and pleasures evident within this naming. So intense is the demand to speak of the sexualized self as a homosexual that any refusal to comply can be met with the claim that the silent subject is "not experiencing real human existence" (Mark, 1994, p. 257). The "failed gays " (Davies, 1992, p. 77), the "psychological cripples" (Reynolds, 2002, p. 94), can live only false and unhappy lives (Seidman, Meeks & Traschen, 1999). Those who do not come out as a homosexual, those who do not articulate self according to the demands of the discourse of gay liberation, are denied humanity.

THE QUEER INTERRUPTION

Gay liberation therefore offers no epistemological shift away from the cultural disciplining of the body. Instead, it merely reinforces such discipline through promoting the control of corporeal pleasures. Such a system of control is assisted now by a self-policing, liberating mode of regulation: the "coming out" that internalizes "the state's desire that we have our identity papers in order, and take up the work of policing our own conceptions of what constitutes a legitimate sexual minority" (Lehring, 1997, p. 192). The pathologizing of corporeal acts into sexual types, into a "life form and a morphology" (Foucault, 1978, p. 43), is not a closed chapter in history, but an ongoing process reinforced by gay liberationist demands for the establishment of equal rights for the essentialized homosexual species. These demands work to normalize the binary between the already socially legitimate heterosexual and the desiring-to-be socially legitimate homosexual. Thus, they occlude space for consideration of other forms of sexualized unions (Butler, 2002; Halperin, 1990). The suggestion that these sexual categories are "omnipresent" not only closes our eyes to the "historical varieties of gender, affection and eroticism past" (Katz, 1997, p. 180), but also to the multiplicity of intimate unions of the present (Altman, 1999) and possible ones of the future.

The rise of the gay liberation movement may have permitted the invention of "a way of being, a sense of identity, and a way of speaking about ourselves that has made it possible to claim 'rights'" (Plummer, 1992, p. 22), but this is not sufficient to ignore the processes of marginalization-consciously political or unconsciously discursive–this movement participates in. Gay liberation is a utopian ideal that strives for unity through the dismissal of any conflict to this unity as abject, as abnormal (Seidman, 1998). It promotes homonormativity. The political and social benefits gained by constructing a homosexual community through the promotion of self-articulation as "gay" are not enough to ignore the continuation of the regulation of bodies within arbitrary systems of sexual classification, especially if these classifications result in the marginalization of alternative ways of experiencing pleasures of the flesh.

It is an important part of the queer project to offer criticism of the processes that permit the construction of a naturalized being (Bower, 1997). Queer theory must maintain a continuous and disturbing challenge to the institutionalization of pleasures (Edelman, 1995). The missing sexual revolution, then, is one in which there is a need to challenge the assumption that sexualized pleasures can be organized into a binary of homosexuality and heterosexuality (Stein & Plummer, 1996). A queer theory that simply lies back and thinks of already naturalized conceptions of sexuality fails to critique how "homosexuality" does not reveal the truth of all male-male sexualized contact, but merely exposes our willingness to offer articulation of corporeal pleasures within the boundaries of a discourse of sexuality that has produced this very system of categorization.

In order to establish possibilities of intimate unions independent of normative sexual categorizations, queer theory must move beyond a claimed intent to establish substantive, positive, alternative identities (Halperin, 1995), and instead strive to assert an acknowledged mutability (Butler, 1997a) that can avoid any appeal for a unified "family" (Edelman, 1995, p. 344). The missing sexual revolution is one in which there is a need to challenge the assumption that sexualized pleasures need to be organized at all. For queer to remain queer, it is necessary to question/queer the reliance upon articulation as the truthful means of defining our sexualized experiences; for what is dismissed in the demand for speech is the possibility that a non-articulation of desire (silence) can offer the construction of alternative male-male intimate unions that stand outside of the normalized understanding of such corporeal contact.

BRINGING BACK THE CLOSET

Creet (1995) defines the speech act of coming out as a process of "naming or categorizing feelings that had previously existed" (p. 182). This interpretation mirrors the understanding most people have when they articulate a homosexual orientation. The discourse of gay liberation reads any suggestion of the non-existence of the homosexual as enforcing a repressive silence on what is natural and real. According to this discourse, silence is a force of disempowerment, consciously applied to limit access to choices of history and lifestyles. In addition, the deployment of silence as a means of evading articulation of a homosexual identity by those who participate in same-sex sexualized activity helps to maintain an inequitable heterosexualized status quo (Gross, 1993). Those who manage to "pass" as heterosexuals merely reap "the benefits of expanded psychological and social breathing space [for homosexuals] created through others' efforts" (p. 128). Their refusal to acknowledge their naturalization into a "queer nation" offers no input into the demanded attack on a compulsory heterosexuality deemed the cause of the closet in the first place (Smith, Kippax & Chapple, 1998, p. 61).

Although it may bring into question what we hold to be some of our most intense human emotions (Simon, 1996), I share Reynolds's (2002) concern that the construction of the binary of an "in" and an "out" assists in obscuring the fiction of the homosexual state in which the speaking subject now assumes itself to exist (p. 55). A closet that contains a repressed and/or oppressed homosexual is one that already assumes the existence of a natural homosexual being. Indeed, the notion of a closet is complicit with the construction of a homosexual type, for this is the space in which the homosexual is born and naturalized (Fuss, 1991). It maintains its position as the "fundamental feature of [our] social life" (Sedgwick, 1990, p. 68) because we have docilely accepted a system that understands our same-sex sexualized contact as indicative of our being homosexuals. We–those who experience the pleasures of same-sex sexualized contact–must know what it means to exist in an oppressive closet because we now already know ourselves to be homosexuals. The continuing failure of the discourse of gay liberation has been a refusal to consider that its notion of an oppressive closet, and its corresponding belief that it can help to eradicate this space through speaking of all men involved in same-sex affairs as "homosexual," is an act of colonization complicit with the demands of a culture obsessed with seeing all bodies, knowing all bodies. A restricting of the possibilities of intimate unions occurs when it is suggested that silence signifies a closet of unquestionable repression and therefore something irrefutably undesired. As Diana Fisher (2003) has expressed, for some bodies silence can be useful. It can help to construct the kind of closet in which bodies are able to "escape from the dominant ideology organizing and monitoring" their lives (p. 174).

Norton contends that "[q]ueer people and subcultures are actively hidden from view so as not to jeopardize the definition of normal people and cultures" (Norton, 1997, p. 84). This is not necessarily the case. In some instances, the silence may reflect the inadequacy of the normative discourse of sexuality to define the subject and his/her acts of same-sex sexualized contact. It is not that marginalized voices are inaudible because "we have taken their speech away from them, deprived them of the means of enunciation" (Hall, 1996, p. 140), but because the discursive formations that dominate interpretations of our corporeal pleasures do not permit us to hear them. Although it may be true that "homosexual sodomy itself involves a discourse of genders, requiring for its commission the articulation of two bodies *as the same*" (Halley, 1994, p. 190), the fact that two bodies "of the same" are involved in sexualized contact does not signify a desire that can be read as essentially homosexual, as essentially a desire for this already discursively "same-d" body.

Western culture assumes the homo-hetero binary to be knowledgeable–and therefore in control–of all relationships between men in its ability to demand or eradicate sexualized contact between male-d bodies respectively. The assumed stability of the in/out binary is undermined, however, by the suggestion that one can never fully be one or the other. The poststructuralist notion of identity as "a constellation of multiple and unstable positions" (Jagose, 1996, p. 3) emphasizes the importance of the exterior to the construction of the interior. Diana Fuss (1991) has argued, for example, that any sexual identity necessarily contains the opposite of what it seeks to claim for self. While she contends that "heterosexuality secures its self-identity and shores up its ontological boundaries by protecting itself from what it sees as the continual predatory encroachment of its contaminated other" (p. 2), she similarly concedes that "any sexual identity, based on the complicated dynamics of object choice, works through a similar defensive procedure" (p. 2). Homosexuality is included, therefore, in such an active process of defense.

Signifiers of a sexual orientation not only seek to know a person's innate desires based on an arbitrary interpretation of acts committed by the body, but also aim to preclude any further realization of desire outside of the boundaries established in the labeling process. Heterosexuality strengthens homosexuality through its repudiation of it (Butler, 1995), while similarly "an articulation of non-heterosexuality bolsters the centrality of heterosexuality itself" (Namaste, 1996, p. 201). "Coming out" into homosexuality is, therefore, an attempt to maintain an identity for self through a continuous rejection of abject sexual desires (Creet, 1995). It is, as Fuss (1991) adds "less a matter of final discovery than perpetual reinvention" (p. 7). For the homosexual, the "coming out" and an existence in the "closet" can never end.

Silence offers an active form of resistance to the constraints imposed on the body by this ceaseless process of sexual identity categorization. The closet, rather than a space of essentialized oppression and repression, of compulsory and enforced silence, can be "a strategy of accommodation and resistance which both reproduces and contests aspects of a society organized around normative heterosexuality" (Seidman et al., 1999, p. 10) and, indeed, normative homosexuality. It can be a space in which bodies are able to play around with and disrupt the cultural demand to speak of who we are with the belief that such speech can offer us liberation (Fisher, 2003). In this more postmodern concept of the closet (Reynolds, 1999), corporeal experiences can be held within a productive space of silence that can refute the normative interpretation of these experiences within the naturalized homo-hetero binary. This silence enables the subjects involved to organize their same-sex intimacies otherwise, if any such organization is required at all.

There are immense and intense pleasures to be found in the act of non-articulation. Such pleasures cannot be contained by a language always out of touch with bodies (Dean, 2000), always unable to capture reality (Stavrakakis, 1999). It is within the unrepresentable "Third Space" (Bhabha, 1994, p. 37) where the signs of "sex" formerly understood to be reflexive of an unquestionable existence can be read anew. Although the signifiers "homosexual" and "heterosexual" may grant the possibility of future contestations and rearticulations through the elisions they enforce (Butler, 1997b), it is when "boundaries collapse, in that minute intermission before we draw new ones" (Stavrakakis, 1999, p. 86), at the moment when a man has same-sex sexualized contact (real or fantastical) without bringing this experience into articulation, that he *does* queer–a queer that reminds us

> that we are inhabited always by states of desire that exceed our capacity to name them. Every name only gives those desires–conflictual, contradictory, inconsistent, undefined–a fictive border, a definition that falsifies. (Edelman, 1995, p. 345)

The ability to engage in same-sex sexualized contact without interpreting this as a desire for an object of the same sex requires a shift away from normative heterosexuality and away from the promoted alternative of normative homosexuality. Where the former denies the possibility of a sexualized union, the latter insists upon it in order to maintain their definitions in language and in culture. Thus, there occurs the eradication of possible understandings of the contact beyond those already available within this binary. The suggestion by the discourse of sexuality that all forms of sexualized experience can be located within a homo-hetero binary imposes limitations on constructing intimate same-sex unions outside of the structures already in place to control them. Indeed, these structures work to make any non-homosexual and non-heterosexual union unsustainable. Queer culture, however, can and must be "independent of the dominant culture, self-determined rather than socially controlled" (Norton, 1997, p. 241).

DESIRING MATES

The discourse of sexuality has a desire to know sexual types through its insistence on bringing all corporeal doings between men into the bedroom of the homosexual being. To refer to a man as a "mate" helps to bring confusion to this will to knowledge. What has formerly been labeled as indicative of a natural "homosexuality" and implanted into the interior of the sexed and sexualized body to construct the homosexual being can be rearticulated within the space of silence provided by "mate" to suggest a kind of corporeal intimacy unconcerned with imagined notions of identity, legitimacy and being. In the non-articulation of sexualized acts into knowable terms, mates are able to perform moments of mutual pleasure without having to carry the memory of these pleasures into the normative construction of a homosexual identity. The silencing of any sexualized experience permits a man to avoid interpellation into a system of classification that requires all of his desires to be related to the sexed body and regulated accordingly. It permits the *doing* of a queer relationship no longer merely confined to *being*. In this "hybrid region," the will to knowledge demanded by the discourse of sexuality is displaced by a savoring of "unthinkability" (Butler, 2002, pp. 16-17). The unspoken becomes the unknowable, which in turn removes the man from the enforced position of a controllable (homo)sexualized subject.

Mateship relationships suggest a bond between men that is extremely close. A mate is someone to whom a man is connected emotionally already. What need is there to explain further the content of such a union with specific reference to the sexualized pleasures that may or may not be a part of it? In the non-articulation of sexualized acts in known and knowable terms, mates are able to be just mates. They can focus on the intensity of the multiple pleasures that make them mates. Such pleasures may include the act of sexualized contact, but these acts do not have to be understood as resulting from a natural (homo)sexualized desire on the part of the individual bodies involved. Instead, these acts can be viewed as one example of the kind of pleasures that produce and sustain the closeness of the bodies in the mateship.

This reclaiming of silence instigates a challenge to the naturalized homosexualization of the male-male sexualized union that has not been offered at any time in the aftermath of the nineteenth century pathologization of sexualized acts. Here, bodies and pleasures act as the counterattack against the deployment of sexuality to regulate and restrain (Foucault, 1978). The corporeal form negates its demanded role as a signifier of an essentialized sexual orientation, entering a space of silence in which it can avoid being identified as existing either at the center or at the periphery (Fisher, 2003). It is neither heterosexual nor homosexual. It is something other. It surpasses the normative discursive definitions of its own actions, and thereby denies the claimed right of the discourse of sexuality to name the sexualized positionalities of the subjects involved. The silence makes it impossible to establish whether the subject has had sexualized contact with his "mate" in the past, will have in the future or is having right now as we all continue to speak incessantly about sex and about a self involved in sex.

Such a position is likely to arouse fierce emotions of resistance out of a frustration that stems from an inability to decipher the subject within normalized constructions of sexual identity, but such a reaction is the dream of a queer. The threat to the normative taxonomy of sexuality is not that abhorrent and/or minority sexual behaviors might be exposed, but that these behaviors might be removed from the constraints of the orientations to which they have been historically and culturally ascribed. The threat to the discourse of gay liberation is not that men might have sexualized contact with other men while in denial of their sexuality, but that men might form physically pleasurable relationships with each other based on desires not focused on sexed bodies; that they might find ways of doing corporeal pleasures outside of the expectancy that such pleasures reveal a responsibility to identify with its cause. The threat to the normative taxonomy of homosexual is that men might fuck with other like-minded men in ways that the signifier "homosexual" cannot control.

REFERENCES

Adam, B. (1995). *The rise of a gay and lesbian movement.* New York: Twayne Publishers.

Altman, D. (1971). *Homosexual oppression and liberation.* Ringwood, Australia: Penguin Books.

Altman, D. (1982). *The homosexualization of America, the Americanization of the homosexual.* New York: St Martin's Press.

Altman, D. (1999). The internationalization of gay and lesbian identities. In D. Epstein & J. T. Sears (Eds.), *A dangerous knowing: Sexuality, pedagogy and popular culture* (pp. 135-149). London; New York: Cassell.

Arndt, B. (1986, January 21). The myth of mateship: Why men have no real friends. *The Bulletin,* 36-41.

Bhabha, H. (1994). *The location of culture.* London: Routledge.

Boswell, J. (1989). Revolutions, universals, and sexual categories. In M. Duberman, M. Vicinus, & J. G. Chauncey (Eds.), *Hidden from history: Reclaiming the gay and lesbian past* (pp. 17-36). New York: Penguin.

Bower, L. (1997). Queer problems/straight solutions. In S. Phelan (Ed.), *Playing with fire: Queer politics, queer theories* (pp. 282-291). New York: Routledge.

Bronski, M. (1998). *The pleasure principle: Sex, backlash, and the struggle for gay freedom.* New York: St. Martin's Press.

Brown, M. (2000). *Closet space: Geographies of metaphor from the body to the globe.* London, Routledge.

Buchbinder, D. (1994). Mateship, *Gallipoli* and the eternal masculine. In P. Fuery (Ed.), *Representation, discourse and desire: Contemporary Australian culture and critical theory* (pp. 115-137). Melbourne: Longman Cheshire.

Butler, J. (1991). Imitation and gender insubordination. In D. Fuss (Ed.), *Inside/out* (pp. 13-31). New York: Routledge.

Butler, J. (1993). *Bodies that matter.* New York: Routledge.

Butler, J. (1995). Melancholy gender/refused identification. In M. Berger, B. Wallis, & S. Watson (Eds.), *Constructing masculinity* (pp. 21-36). New York: Routledge.

Butler, J. (1997a). Critically queer. In S. Phelan (Ed.), *Playing with fire: Queer politics, queer theories* (pp. 11-30). New York: Routledge.

Butler, J. (1997b). *Excitable speech: A politics of performative.* New York: Routledge.

Butler, J. (2002). Is kinship always already heterosexual? *Differences, 13*(1), 14-31.

Chekola, M. (1994). Outing, truth-telling, and the shame of the closet. In T. F. Murphy (Ed.), Gay ethics: *Controversies in outing, civil rights, and sexual science* (pp. 67-90). New York: The Haworth Press.

Coad, D. (2002). *Gender trouble down under: Australian masculinities.* Valenciennes: Presses Universitaires de Valenciennes.

Cohen, E. (1991). Who are "we"? Gay "identity" as political (e)motion (a theoretical rumination). In D. Fuss (Ed.), *Inside/out* (pp. 71-92). New York: Routledge.

Creet, J. (1995). Anxieties of identity: Coming out and coming undone. In M. Dorenkamp & R. Henke (Eds.), *Negotiating lesbian and gay subjects* (pp. 179-199). New York: Routledge.

Cruikshank, M. (1992). *The gay and lesbian liberation movement.* New York: Routledge.

Danaher, G., Schirato, T., & Webb, J. (2000). *Understanding Foucault.* St. Leonards, Australia: Allen & Unwin.

Davies, P. (1992). The role of disclosure in coming out among gay men. In K. Plummer (Ed.), *Modern homosexualities* (pp. 75-83). London: Routledge.

Dean, T. (2000). *Beyond sexuality.* Chicago: University of Chicago Press.

Edelman, L. (1995). Queer theory: Unstating desire. *GLQ, 2*(4), 343-346.

Edgar, D. (1997). *Men, mateship, marriage.* Sydney: HarperCollins.

Fisher, D. (2003). Immigrant closets: Tactical-micro-practices-in-the-hyphen. In G. A. Yep, K. E. Lovaas, & J. P. Elia (Eds.), *Queer theory and communication: From disciplining queers to queering the discipline(s)* (pp. 171-192). New York: Haworth Press.

Foucault, M. (1977). *Discipline and punish: The birth of the prison.* New York: Vintage Books.

Foucault, M. (1978). *The history of sexuality, volume 1: The will to knowledge.* London: Penguin Books.

Fuss, D. (1989). *Essentially speaking: Feminism, nature & difference.* New York: Routledge.

Fuss, D. (1991). Inside/out. In D. Fuss (Ed.), *Inside/out* (pp. 1-10). New York: Routledge.

Gross, L. (1993). *Contested closets: The politics and ethics of outing.* Minneapolis: University of Minneapolis Press.

Grosz, E. (1995). Bodies and pleasures in queer theory. In J. Roof & R. Wiegman (Eds.), *Who can speak? Authority and critical identity* (pp. 221-230). Chicago: University of Illinois Press.

Hall Carpenter Archives. (1989). *Walking after midnight: Gay men's life stories.* London: Routledge.

Hall, S. (1996). On postmodernism and articulation. In D. Morley & K. H. Chen (Eds.), *Stuart Hall: Critical dialogues in cultural studies* (pp. 131-150). London: Routledge.

Halley, J. E. (1994). The politics of the closet: Towards equal protection for gay, lesbian and bisexual identity. In J. Goldberg (Ed.), *Reclaiming Sodom* (pp. 145-204). New York: Routledge.

Halperin, D. M. (1989). Sex before sexuality: Pederasty, politics, and power in classical Athens. In M. Duberman, M. Vicinus, & J. G. Chauncey (Eds.), *Hidden from history: Reclaiming the gay and lesbian past* (pp. 37-53). New York: Penguin.

Halperin, D. (1990). *One hundred years of homosexuality.* London: Routledge.

Halperin, D. (1995). *Saint Foucault: Towards a gay hagiography.* Oxford: Oxford University Press.

Hocquenghem, G. (1972). *Homosexual desire.* Durham: Duke University Press.

Humphreys, L. (1972). *Out of the closets: The sociology of homosexual liberation.* Englewood Cliffs, NJ: Prentice-Hall.

Jagose, A. (1996). *Queer theory.* Melbourne: Melbourne University Press.

Katz, J. N. (1997). "Homosexual" and "heterosexual": Questioning the terms. In M. Duberman. (Ed.), *A queer world* (pp. 177-180). New York: New York University Press.

Lehring, G. (1997). Essentialism and the political articulation of identity. In S. Phelan (Ed.), *Playing with fire: Queer politics, queer theories* (pp. 173-198). New York: Routledge.

Mark, R. (1994). Teaching from the open closet. In E. Hedges & S. F. Fishkin (Eds.), *Listening to silences: New essays in feminist criticism* (pp. 245-259). New York, Oxford University Press.

McWhorter, L. (1999). *Bodies and pleasures: Foucault and the politics of sexual normalization.* Bloomington, IN: Indiana University Press.

Namaste, K. (1996). The politics of inside/out: Queer theory, poststructuralism, and a sociological approach to sexuality. In S. Seidman (Ed.), *Queer theory/sociology* (pp. 194-212). Cambridge, MA: Blackwell Publishers.

Norton, R. (1997). *The myth of the modern homosexual: Queer history and the search for cultural unity.* London; Washington: Cassell.

Plummer, K. (1992). Speaking its name: Inventing lesbian and gay studies. In K. Plummer (Ed.), *Modern homosexualities* (pp. 3-28). London: Routledge.

Plummer, K. (1995). *Telling sexual stories: Power, change and social worlds.* London: Routledge.

Reynolds, R. (1999). Postmodernizing the closet. *Sexualities, 2*(3), 346-349.

Reynolds, R. (2002). *From camp to queer: Remaking the Australian homosexual.* Melbourne: Melbourne University Press.

Sedgwick, E. K. (1990). *Epistemology of the closet.* New York: Harvester Wheatsheaf.

Seidman, S. (1997). *Difference troubles: Queering social theory and sexual politics.* Cambridge: Cambridge University Press.

Seidman, S. (1998). *Contested knowledge.* Malden, MA: Blackwell Publishers.

Seidman, S., Meeks C., & Traschen F. (1999). Beyond the closet? The changing social meaning of homosexuality in the United States. *Sexualities, 2*(1), 9-34.

Simon, W. (1996). *Postmodern sexualities.* London: Routledge.

Smith, G. S., Kippax, S., & Chapple, M. (1998). Secrecy, disclosure, and closet dynamics. *Journal of Homosexuality, 35*(1), 53-73.

Stavrakakis, Y. (1999). *Lacan and the political.* London: Routledge.

Stein, A., & Plummer, K. (1996). I can't even think straight. In S. Seidman (Ed.), *Queer theory/sociology* (pp. 129-144). Cambridge, MA: Blackwell Publishers.

Warner, M. (2002). *Publics and counterpublics.* New York: Zone Books.

Weeks, J. (1999). Myths and fictions in modern sexualities. In D. Epstein & J. T. Sears (Eds.), *A dangerous knowing: Sexuality, pedagogy and popular culture* (pp. 11-24). London; New York: Cassell.

doi:10.1300/J082v52n01_10

CONTEXTS

Teaching Queer Theory at a *Normal* School

Jen Bacon, PhD

West Chester University

SUMMARY. This article presents a case study of the ongoing struggle to queer West Chester University at the level of the institution, the curriculum, and the classroom. Part of that struggle includes an effort to establish a policy for free speech that accommodates the values of the institution toward diversity. Another part involves attempts to introduce LGBT Studies into the curriculum, and the resulting debates over whether the curriculum should be "gayer" or "queerer." I discuss the personal struggle to destabilize ready-made categories and encourage non-binary

Author note: Many thanks to Karen Fitts, Vicki Tischio and the students in my Tutoring Writing class for their feedback on this essay. Also, special thanks to Rodney Mader, whose commitment to a just world at my institution has inspired me to keep traversing this contested terrain, even when my feet are blistered. Thank you for showing me that the right shoes matter.

Correspondence may be addressed: Women's Studies, 211 Main Hall, West Chester University, West Chester, PA 19383 (E-mail: jbacon@wcupa.edu).

[Haworth co-indexing entry note]: "Teaching Queer Theory at a *Normal* School." Bacon, Jen. Co-published simultaneously in *Journal of Homosexuality* (Harrington Park Press, an imprint of The Haworth Press, Inc.) Vol. 52, No. 1/2, 2006, pp. 257-283; and: *LGBT Studies and Queer Theory: New Conflicts, Collaborations, and Contested Terrain* (ed: Karen E. Lovaas, John P. Elia, and Gust A. Yep) Harrington Park Press, an imprint of The Haworth Press, Inc., 2006, pp. 257-283. Single or multiple copies of this article are available for a fee from The Haworth Document Delivery Service [1-800-HAWORTH, 9:00 a.m. - 5:00 p.m. (EST). E-mail address: docdelivery@haworthpress.com].

thinking, while honoring the identities we live, and perform, in the class-room. In the last four years, WCU has hired half a dozen out gay or lesbian faculty members, some of whom identify as "queer." In many ways, those faculty members have entered a climate open to new ideas for adding LGBT content to the curriculum and to queering the structure and curriculum of the university. But as faculty, staff, and students engage this cause–along with the broader cause of social justice at the University–we have found that our enemies are often closer than we might have guessed. Detailing the tensions that have characterized the landscape at WCU during my three years and half years there, this essay elaborates on the epistemological and pedagogical issues that arise when queer Theory meets LGBT Studies in the process of institutional, curricular, and pedagogical reform. I argue that questions about content and method, inclusion and exclusion, and identity and performance can be answered only with a concerted effort and continued attention to the cultural tendency to re-assert binaries while simultaneously learning from them. What is true of West Chester, I argue, is true of the larger social system where the contested terrain of the queer has implications for the choices we make as both stakeholders and deviants in the systems we chronicle and critique. doi:10.1300/J082v52n01_11 *[Article copies available for a fee from The Haworth Document Delivery Service: 1-800-HAWORTH. E-mail address: <docdelivery@haworthpress.com> Website: <http://www.HaworthPress.com> © 2006 by The Haworth Press, Inc. All rights reserved.]*

KEYWORDS. Queer theory, lesbian and gay studies, curriculum, institutional reform, pedagogy

Judith Butler (1991) has, in essence, gotten her wish that when she appears under the sign of "lesbian" she would like to "have it permanently unclear what precisely that sign signifies" (p. 308). Identities have destabilized, particularly in the last five years, and some lesbians and gays aren't too thrilled about it. While the destabilizing force could be the on-the-ground impact of queer theory, which began as a mode of literary criticism and developed into a norm-questioning lifestyle, it seems likely that the destabilized bodies and lifestyles that queer theory describes were already living on a contested terrain, and on college campuses across the U.S., before academic theorists even considered calling them queer.[1] It's hip to be queer, and down right pathetic to be normal.

At my mid-sized, regional, state school in eastern Pennsylvania, the terrain of the queer is contested in subtle, but persuasive ways: A cross-gendered student pair runs for Homecoming king and queen; a preacher spews homophobic venom in the middle of the quad, and the LGBT student group sells lemonade and candy bars at the spectacle; a female student sports a pin to class that reads "Proud Daddy." In short, the "queer" interacts with the "normal" here every day, despite the Normal School history of the institution, and despite the suburban, middle-class, white, Republican "bodies" that largely populate the campus.[2]

The above cited incidents are "queering"–but in the process they are also indicative of a mounting tension between LGBT Studies and queer theory. By "queering," I refer to practices, linked to post-structuralism in the form of queer theory, whereby cultural norms are tested, played with, and even turned upside down in the interest of challenging the very idea of normal. If LGBT Studies is a progressive campaign to "de-other" lesbians and gays by creating safe spaces in the institution, the curriculum, and the classroom for lesbian and gay bodies, queer theory is a progressive campaign to "re-other" everything in the culture that has occupied a position of privilege, power, or normalcy, starting with heterosexuality. Both have the potential to make lesbian and gay subjectivities less contested, but these two campaigns bump into one another at precisely those places where LGBT Studies is most successful, because in those places, lesbian and gay bodies have begun to look "normal"–and lesbian and gay subject positions risk assimilation in a culture that may decide to extend the boundaries of inclusion to lesbians and gays–but only at the expense of some new "other" who will be excluded.[3] By examining the politics of the local, and the manner in which the terrain is contested at the institutional, curricular, and classroom levels, this essay will provide one traveler's guide to approaching, resolving, or tolerating this tension. The context for this particular moment of inquiry is 2003, a special issue of the *Journal of Homosexuality*, and the slippery terrain where LGBT Studies meets queer theory and engages in an academic contest with very non-academic ramifications.

In particular, in looking at West Chester University at three levels, the institution, the curriculum, and the classroom, this essay will explore three sites of contestation that happen to have played out in those levels during my four years on the faculty here. At the institutional level, I will discuss the contested terrain of free speech. At the curricular level, I take up the process of curricular reform, and in the classroom, the politics of identity. In every case, these "contests" raise similar

questions for those of us at the front lines of both campaigns: What are
the costs of inclusion and exclusion? How can we advance an agenda
that self-consciously resists the double-binds that relentlessly appear,
and why would we want to? And what do we want our institutions, curricula, and classrooms to provide for students who are struggling with
these binds?

FREEDOM OF SPEECH/THE FREEING OF SPEECH: QUEER RESPONSES TO INSTITUTIONAL HOMOPHOBIA

Two incidents will provide my point of entry to the contested terrain
of LGBT Studies and Queer Theory at the institutional level. In both
cases, that "contest" ended up being about free speech issues. This is not
all that surprising, given the national debate over hate crimes and hate
speech, which has had LGBT political organizations, including the Human Rights Campaign, lobbying for legislation that would place certain
limits on Free Speech. At public universities, like WCU, the "place,
time, and manner" restrictions on free speech function as the only
imposable limit that can prevent speakers from disrupting "classes or
other essential operations."[4] And yet those restrictions, if applied uniformly and in keeping with the stated values of the University, can provide for responses from the university community that communicate
tolerance, civility, and equity. Unfortunately, those opportunities are
not "normally" exercised.

First, let me provide a little institutional history. As of 1999, West
Chester University has included sexual orientation in its non-discrimi-
nation policy, but has yet to adopt a policy providing same-sex spousal
equivalency benefits. The University has a long-standing and stable
Women's Studies program, one that offers courses called "Women and
Sexuality" and "Lesbian Studies"–and the English Department has included "Queer Theory" in its list of desirable secondary specializations
for job candidates for the last three years. A literature seminar in "Queer
Theory" has been offered for three consecutive years, and course titles
like "Manhood and Masculinity," from outside the English Department,
would seem to indicate that the University is entering the queer
zone–albeit slowly.

In the Fall of 2001, a preacher from a local evangelist organization
screamed anti-gay epithets and taunts on the University quad for several
hours while public safety officials protected his rights to free speech.
With minions wearing T-Shirts that spelled G-A-Y down one side but

read "Got AIDS Yet?" the preacher singled-out students with a pointed finger and yelled, "Fags burn in hell," "only sluts wear mini-skirts," and "homosexuality is an abomination." A large crowd of students gathered to witness this spectacle, and though most found it offensive or ridiculous, the tone of the campus was altered that day.

As an out queer faculty member, I found myself feeling oddly vulnerable in front of my classroom that day, wondering if the students before me had been listening to the rant on the quad only moments before they sat looking at me in the classroom. I remember wondering if it was possible for them to disassociate everything that had filtered through them from the body who sits, now, in the 12:00 position of the circle. The same logic that protects my right to be queer, and to share ideas with students about what Queer Theory offers to the pursuit of knowledge, protects the rights of that speaker. But this queer body has been employed by an institution that promises to provide equal opportunity to individuals regardless of sexual orientation–an institution that pledges to value diversity, but remains chillingly silent when opportunities for representing those values present themselves.[5]

So when the LGBT Concerns Committee met later that week to discuss the situation, we were torn by our alliances. Ultimately, we decided, as a group, that we wanted to weigh in on the side of free speech, but we wanted to protect our students at the same time. We devised, with public safety and university legal counsel, a new policy regarding public speakers that requires such speakers to register two hours in advance, giving the Office of Public Safety enough time to send out emails to the LGBT public safety liaisons, who would then enact a project-lemonade-style counter protest, whereby members of the LGBT student group sell lemonade, candy, and queer buttons and stickers on the sidelines of the spectacle.[6] In the first implementation of the new policy, the student organization made $100.00, and the speaker abandoned campus after only two hours. During the 2002-2003 school year, there were no registered speakers preaching hate on West Chester University's campus.

But you put out one fire, and you send sparks to another patch of dry grass, I suppose. During fall 2002, a homophobic article was posted, by a member of the history faculty, on a bulletin board in the history department. Pennsylvania's recent, and "unfortunate," ruling to allow second-parent adoptions was apparently "Of Historical Interest"–as the bulletin board was titled. Another faculty member, from the English Department, stumbled upon the article, and added another bulletin, anonymous and handwritten, alongside it, which read, "This is homophobic crap. Whose "BULLetin board is this?" The faculty union gets wind of the situation (aided by irate members of the history department who claim "freedom of speech" protects their right to put anything they want on their bulletin board) and threatens to grieve the individual who posted the handwritten note for "uncivil" behavior, except that they don't know who did it. The issue is ultimately resolved peacefully, but not before the public debate over free speech gets scattered over the red-hot coals of the queer, and queers find themselves, once again, questioning whether homophobic texts are as protected as any other texts. But we also begin to articulate a connection between free speech and ethics, arguing that ethics requires more agency of those texts on an institutional bulletin board–where it is agreed that all postings should be "authored" if not authorized.

Ultimately, what these battles over free speech teach us is that institutional "stake" in free speech is capable of being redirected so that the core values of the institution can continue to matter. Diversity, as a core value at my particular institution, is trumpeted in matters of hiring, in the general education goals of the University, and in the civility code for campus climate. But as a public institution, the guidelines regarding free speech are clear cut. The KKK can indeed come and demonstrate on the student quad, so long as they stay 50 feet away from the classroom buildings, don't block the entry or exit of students, and don't amplify their speech. West Chester, like most institutions, is inherently normal. It will resist challenges to the base plan of "do nothing," because to do "something" requires an agency that the institution would rather avoid. Where the institution has remained consistently silent, that silence has been interpreted by the LGB Concerns Committee as a ringing endorsement of the status quo. Calling that silence into question, however, has proven to be extremely effective. The loud clamor of queer faculty members, and the suggestion that the institution has contributed to a hostile work climate with its silence, got us a meeting with the acting President, an offer to work with public safety officers on a training program that would make them better allies, and a continued audience at our meetings by the provost. In short, creating a space that is safe for queer inquiry, on our campus, has required that LGBT bodies step forward, with real stories about real identities, to speak about the personal consequences of teaching in an environment that does not send out consistent messages about the inclusion of lesbian and gay subjects.

And that is the continuing challenge. Can we use lesbian and gay bodies, codifying their stability in the process, in the service of institutional changes that will ultimately question that very stability? Can *this* lesbian body champion the process, and the language, that will get "domestic partner benefits" for WCU employees, while she simultaneously questions the values that would allow monogamous gay couples to receive benefits that other families might not be entitled to? Knowing that the terrain is contested, is it ever okay to stake a claim to a piece of it anyway? The answer to these questions, at a practical level, has been "yes." But the circle of bodies, the "allies" in this contest, has proven to be a queer one. By arguing for free speech, and simultaneously using it to our own advantage, by challenging institutional silence, and simultaneously using it to our own advantage, the contested terrain can change in ways that accommodate lesbian and gay bodies, while making it perpetually impossible to determine where the queer might be said to begin.

A Recklessly Simple Strategy: Queering Curriculum Reform

Many events will enter into my analysis of the contested terrain where LGBT Studies meets Queer Theory in the process of curricular reform at West Chester University. But all of the events are related, at least tangentially, to the attempts by a small cadre of faculty members to launch a Lesbian and Gay studies minor–or a Queer studies minor–or a sexuality studies minor (well, you'll see, by the time we got rolling, one of the most contested sites turned out to be the name, and content, of the minor itself).

In the Introduction to *The Lesbian and Gay Studies Reader* (1993), editors Henry Abelove, Michele Aina Barale, and David Halperin write that "[t]he history of the field to which these essays all contribute, lesbian/gay studies, has yet to be written. When such a history comes to be written, it is likely to be contested" (xv). The editors go on to analogize lesbian/gay studies to Women's Studies, writing that "[l]esbian/gay studies does for sex and sexuality approximately what Women's Studies does for gender" (xv). The "work" of lesbian/gay studies, using this analogy, is to establish the centrality of sex and sexuality as a fundamental category of analysis and understanding within many different fields of inquiry.

If that sounds queer to you, as it does to me, then it will make sense to both of us that the anthology includes works often "marked" as the cornerstones of Queer Theory–Eve Sedgwick's introduction to *Epistemology of the Closet*, Judith Butler's "Imitation and Gender Insubordination," Teresa de Lauretis's "Sexual Indifference and Lesbian Representation." And yet even in this relatively early compilation of "the field," there are hints of a brewing tension. The editors write of their difficulty titling the anthology, "reluctantly" shunning queer in favor of lesbian and gay, but arguing, as if there was already a need to convince, that lesbian and gay studies includes inquiry into "many kinds of sexual non-conformity" and that the terms lesbian and gay are "more widely preferred than is the name 'queer'" and "are not assimilationist" (xvii). If we use this decade old statement as a harbinger of the tensions to come, then a fairly accurate picture emerges of where the tensions may be said to reside: origins, naming, inclusivity, assimilation.

Eve Sedgwick's 1990 text, *Epistemology of the Closet*, (excerpted in *The Lesbian and Gay Studies Reader*) was an early spectator in this "contest"–offering up the terms "universalizing" and "minoritizing" as a lens for rethinking the question of essentialism and social construction that seemed to be the quagmire of discussions up to that point. LGBT Studies, according to this view, is the study of LGBT individuals, a study that depends on such individuals actually existing in order to become objects of study. Early LGBT Studies programs, many of which continue today, offered courses in Gay History, Gay Studies, Psychology of Gays and Lesbians, Lesbian Writers, The Rise of a Gay and Lesbian Movement, Gay/Lesbian Literature, among others, in an attempt to rescue from erasure the lives of gay men and lesbians who had hitherto been invisible in the curriculum (Younger, 2003). Offering the sort of corrective that Women's Studies brought to issues of sex and gender, LGBT Studies sought to ask, and answer, questions about what sociology, or anthropology, or literature had missed by ignoring queers. This is extremely important work.

At the same time, courses that did not necessarily link themselves to an LGBT curriculum existed in universities across the country, with titles that have since come to indicate a potential "queer" thread. Courses like Human Sexuality, Intro to Sexuality Studies, Deviant Sexualities, Variant Sexualities, or Sociology of Sex Roles likely included homosexuality as one thread, or unit, in the conversation–but certainly not the focal point. At the same time, many of these courses were on the books long before LGBT Studies was even conceived of as a legitimate discipline for academic research. The "queers" who showed up in such courses, might well be the deviant or variant "other" who normalizes heterosexuality just by showing up.

According to John Younger's "University LGBT/Queer Programs" list, 150 universities in the U.S. and Canada currently offer degree programs, courses, or web-based information relating to LGBT issues, and many of the courses listed mirror those above–in both categories

(2003). So where is the contested terrain? Why not have courses that include homosexuality among other sexualities co-exist with courses that are specific to LGBT concerns? And where they do co-exist, are there not theoretical and pedagogical ties that might make such offerings a coherent curriculum?

Sedgwick (1990) wrote, in Axiom 2 of *Epistemology of the Closet* that: "The study of sexuality is not coextensive with the study of gender; correspondingly, anti-homophobic inquiry is not coextensive with feminist inquiry. But we can't know in advance how they will be different" (p. 27). Part of my project here is to elaborate on the ways that they are different at West Chester University and to discuss what we might learn from the ways that such differences play out that will allow for better traversing of the contested terrain. One of the major tensions between LGBT Studies and Queer Theory mirrors a tension in feminist inquiry—namely—the tension between identity politics and post-structural critiques of essential identities.

I did not always know that the terrain was contested. Now I have a much more acute understanding of institutional politics, and a much keener sense of the position held by Women's Studies. The director of Women's Studies, at our yearly retreat last year, discussed her concern about the potential erasure of women as a historical category by post-structural theories, by queer theories. Can we promote definitional incoherence, indeterminacy, and the prominence of the fluid identity while still supporting women? Or is one of the tensions between LGBT Studies and Queer Theory the incompatibility of Queer Theory with feminism? At West Chester University, the analogy that Women's Studies is to Gender Studies as LGBT Studies is to Queer Theory is particularly apt, and important, given that the curricular reform movement for the LGBT Studies minor began, in many ways, in Women's Studies. But let me go back for a minute and provide some context.

According to the brochures which describe the Women's Studies program at West Chester University, Women's Studies is:

- a way of looking at the world that questions historical and current gender arrangements
- an interdisciplinary field of study that examines how the social constructions of gender, race, and class affect our lives
- an exploration of women's thoughts, feelings, and experiences
- an analysis of interactive patterns among women and men

- a program whose faculty show their commitment to the development of students through interactions inside and outside the classroom
- a safe place where students come to recognize the obstacles that may hinder their educational goals, clarify their academic interests, and explore career opportunities
- a body of knowledge that ultimately serves as a basis for social change

What, then, is gender studies? Why are faculty who teach in the Women's Studies Program are afraid to utter the words "gender studies" at steering committee meetings where we discuss the future of the major and strategies for recruiting more students? For newer faculty, faculty who more clearly align themselves with a third or fourth wave agenda, the "gender" flag is a flag worth waving–not only for student recruitment, or for "steering" the major in a direction that is in keeping with current theoretical debates, but for personal reasons that play out in our classrooms. Putting the spotlight on one gender, rather than gender itself, reinforces the idea that gender is binary, that we understand gender best by looking at one *in contrast to* the other. But putting the spotlight on gender as a construct, has its limitations as well, given the gendered bodies in the classroom who are struggling to maintain that binary, or beginning to come to terms with sexism by understanding the women's plights.

Women's Studies at West Chester, as at many institutions, has a history. Battles waged in the 1970s and 1980s were hard-fought–curricular battles to protect programs or institute courses, as well as battles to reform the University's sexual harassment procedures, to promote equity in hiring, to educate health care workers and counselors, and to provide campus programming for women students on eating disorders, acquaintance rape, and self-esteem. We continue to benefit from those struggles over what it means to be a feminist both in and out of the classroom. And along comes Queer Theory–inserting itself into a curriculum that has only begun to include LGBT Studies.

During the 2001-2002 school year, a group of faculty on the LGBT Concerns Committee began the process of building a Queer Studies minor at West Chester. We first formed a sub-committee, and then members of that sub-committee attended a regional workshop run by John Younger about his work building the Sexuality Studies program at Duke. We came back energized and enthusiastic for what we saw as the first important steps. We began thinking about curriculum–what core courses and what electives would best serve students?–surveying the courses already available that might fit within the minor and creating syllabi for courses that we felt we should add to the curriculum. We began thinking about institutional structure–where would the courses for the minor "live?"–surveying the programs and departments on campus whose work seemed most clearly aligned. We began thinking about resources–who would administer and teach?–surveying the potential for borrowing faculty from other departments, for getting the necessary approvals from the administration, and for marketing the program to students.

In all of these efforts, we encountered, again and again, tension. We were happy to find many existing courses in the curriculum at West Chester that seemed appropriate for our minor. We found "Gay America" and "Manhood and Masculinity" in the History Department, "Women and Sexuality" in Women's Studies, "Human Sexuality" in the Health Sciences Department, and "Sexuality in Society" in the Sociology Department, among others. We began the paperwork of putting courses, like my Lesbian Studies course, through with their own names and numbers, rather than the "special topics" designations that had allowed us to offer them in the past. And we began to create core courses–including a course titled "Q-101"–that would provide an introduction to the minor.

Imagining that an obvious home for this sort of work was Women's Studies, we put together a brief description of the plan and brought it to the Women's Studies Steering Committee. By this time, I knew enough to fear the result. If faculty members were afraid to mention the possibility of moving toward a gender studies model in Women's Studies at the steering committee, then the potential seemed great that the steering committee would raise serious, substantial objections to offering a course in the Women's Studies department called "Manhood and Masculinity." Not so. The Women's Studies steering committee voted unanimously to house the new Queer Studies minor in Women's Studies, providing that the curriculum was compatible with the bylaws already in place for the Women's Studies Program.

Naïvely, we imagined this to be an easy win. Looking over the above-mentioned bylaws, we saw very few stumbling blocks. One of the "requirements" specified that course content in Women's Studies should be "by, for, and about women," but even here, we imagined that there was room to work, assuming that the Women's Studies faculty would likely amend the requirement to say something more like "women and other marginalized populations." But that conversation never happened, because we ran into so many other stumbling blocks.

First, one of the faculty members who teaches courses that will potentially be part of the minor challenged the notion that courses must utilize "feminist" pedagogy. Instead, he insisted, teachers must present the material in an objective manner and let students determine how to judge them. "Manhood and Masculinity," he went on, "is not a feminist course." The room started spinning then, and I imagined myself in a scene from the film *Go Fish*, the talking heads in the room a blur of self-parody. I vaguely remember hearing myself say, "the concept of masculinity itself cannot be presented outside of the feminist scholarship that has allowed us to see masculinity as a manifestation of a binary gender system," and I remember realizing, at that moment, that I might have been walking with blinders on again–and that Manhood and Masculinity, for all I knew, was a course on "how to be a man," and that maybe I should take it to get fashion tips.

The name of the minor itself–from LGBT Studies, to Queer Studies, to Sexuality Studies, to "Special Populations"–became the next contested territory in the ongoing battle over post-identity politics at a University that is still struggling, vehemently, to be "normal." We decided, as a sub-committee, to call the minor "Sexuality Studies" rather than "Queer Studies" or "Lesbian and Gay Studies," as had previously been proposed. Our thinking here was that Lesbian and Gay Studies would be too exclusionary, implying that the minor was a study in the special interests of a minority population, and entrenching the curriculum in one corner of the contested terrain this essay addresses. Queer Studies, though potentially accommodating the above concern, had problems of its own, in that we imagined the minor to include both "queer" and "non-queer" sexualities, potentially including adapted versions of courses like "Sociology of the Family" or "Love and Marriage" in the curriculum. Make no mistake; we imagined a queer curriculum in that the minor would be an interrogation of customs, laws, politics, and ideas surrounding sexuality, but we saw the curriculum as MORE queer for including the potential for interrogating the "norms" around sexuality alongside the variance.

The students were the first to react to this news, proffering their concern that we were "diluting" the curriculum, or "cleaning it up" for the bureaucrats in Harrisburg who wouldn't like the word "queer" showing up in the Undergraduate Catalogue. And as we worked, as faculty, to quell these suspicions among students, we realized via our interactions with administrators that the fears were legitimate. At a meeting with the

Associate Provost and the Vice President for Advancement, we were given packets of material about the procedures necessary for implementing a new minor, but told in no uncertain terms that no new minors would be approved that were not directly related to health or technology, areas the University has identified for job growth potential in eastern Pennsylvania. Instead, they proposed a plan of "quiet incrementalism," suggesting we work toward getting courses in place that might, in a better political climate and better fiscal situation, be part of such a minor. Meanwhile, a well-intentioned faculty member in Health Sciences suggests that we propose a minor on "special populations in our society" including "a course(s) that deals with LGBT–and that the course can be entitled what best represents the course content (i.e., Queer Studies)" (Personal Communication, December 9, 2002). While all this is going on, members of the Women's Studies steering committee are offering me behind-the-scenes "bribes" to keep the minor out of Women's Studies, suggesting that Sociology or Anthropology might provide a better home.[7]

In subtle ways, all of these gestures and machinations are indices of the tension between LGBT Studies and Queer Theory. The study of "special populations" in and of itself is contested territory at a school as "normal" as West Chester. Just last year, as the University made a move to include a "diversity" requirement in the general education curriculum, the inclusion of a requirement that courses designated as "diversity" courses include an "analysis of structural inequality" sent some members of the curricular planning body into a tailspin. And while the more leftist reaches of the University, including Women's Studies, are completely comfortable with an LGBT Studies model, as demonstrated by the Lesbian Studies course that I teach, they may not be entirely comfortable with a Queer Studies model that has students working to unravel categories like "woman" and "lesbian" that are the basis for much of the political action done by Women's Studies in the last three decades. And perhaps that is a good thing.

Sitting in the Director of Women's Studies office, one-on-one, the end result of phase one in this process was recklessly simple. We talked. We talked Queer Studies and LGBT studies–we talked Sexuality Studies, and we talked about the history of the institution. Ultimately, we decided that "Sexual Identity and Culture" would address the concerns we both had about the place of an intro course in the curriculum of Women's Studies, where it would get its curricular "prefix," and in the curriculum of a yet-to-be-hatched minor that traverses the contested territory of both LGBT Studies and Queer Theory. The binary we had imagined, it turns out, was already crumbling. By focusing on the sites that were likely to be contested, we were distracted from noticing all of the places that common enemies could enter the contest. Bureaucracy, sexism, and fear nearly got in the way of a curriculum that was well-positioned to do important work for both programs–work that would honor identity, while specifying its historicity. The pace of change is recklessly fast. And yet the strategy I am suggesting here is recklessly simple–when you find an opportunity, build on it in as queer a way as you can, using both "sides" of the binary as a while continuing to historicize that queering.

L/G/B/T/S/Q–The Contested Territory of Sexual Identity in the Normal Classroom

The last arena of the contested terrain, although likely the first we encounter in our day-to-day lives as faculty members, is the classroom. Here, the consequences for the "contest" are played out in every interaction, every assignment, and every seized, or missed, opportunity for pointing out to students that the categories we rely on are both empowering and necessary, and also disabling and exclusionary.[8] The struggle became clear to me when I accepted an appointment to the English Department of West Chester University, hired as the result of a search that included Queer Theory as a desirable secondary area of expertise, my primary area being composition and rhetoric. While Queer Theory–in its application to the theory and pedagogy of writing instruction–was certainly of interest to my colleagues in composition and rhetoric, the only course in Queer Theory offered by the department was taught as a Literature Seminar, a seminar that composition/rhetoric specialists were not then invited to teach.

Nevertheless, I was asked to teach Lesbian Studies during my first year at West Chester by the Women's Studies Department. The course had been offered once or twice before as a special topics course in Women's Studies, but not in several years. The faculty member who taught the course, however, was taking a medical leave of absence, and as the most recent and most "out" faculty member with expertise in the subject area, I was asked to fill in and teach the course in her place. I was thrilled, but also naive.

I had one conversation with the faculty member who previously taught the course–a very pleasant one–where she told me a bit about how she had conceived of the course, but also about her intention to change it if she ever taught it again. She made no inquiries about my intentions for the course, and expressed no concerns about what I might do there. I left the meeting thinking that my course would probably be quite different than hers, but also that she would be perfectly happy with what I planned to do. She used Faderman's (1999) *To Believe in Women: What Lesbians Have Done for America–a History* as her primary text, where I compiled an interdisciplinary packet of readings including Butler, Wittig, Rich and, yes, Faderman (though I chose one chapter from her *Odd Girls and Twilight Lovers* (1991) book, the one that discusses the problem of looking backward in history to find "lesbians," given that the term, and concept, is historically specific).

My idea of what a Lesbian Studies course would be was informed by my recent immersion in graduate study, when Queer Theory had emerged, and flourished, during the period of time in which I was a student. I had no idea what the Women's Studies department had come to expect from the course as it was taught previously. Queer, Lesbian–what's the difference, right? But these are institutional politics, and I was clueless about them, so I constructed a syllabus, made a readings packet, and proceeded under the ready assumption that I was certainly equipped to make judgments about appropriate curriculum and pedagogy on a topic on for which I claim expertise. It seems incredibly naïve now, but I assumed a Lesbian Studies course would be an interrogation of the category "lesbian." To study lesbians, I imagined, meant beginning the course with a question "What is lesbian studies?" And the map of the course I planned was a mirror of my own journey through lesbian subjectivity as a graduate student. My dissertation was an analysis of "queer" tropes in women's identity narratives, using data I collected by traveling around the country for three months, interviewing women about their coming out experiences. In short, I had been doing "Lesbian Studies" of my own for the past two years, and those studies relied heavily on queer applications of rhetorical theory and cultural analysis. I know now, having taught the course twice, that students who registered for it were expecting something different than what they received.

Day One: Course introduction. I want to begin to get to know my students, and to begin the slow process of connecting identities to texts, labels, and institutional structures. I realize now that this process was partly about my understanding of what a "lesbian studies" course should be, and partly about my own agenda as a lesbian who was trying to figure out the costs and benefits of that label in an increasingly queer academy. Here I was, teaching this course because I had been an "out" lesbian in the job market. And here I was, teaching this course because I had academic expertise in a subject area called "Queer Theory." I say this to showcase that the "contested terrain" is a terrain that real bodies inhabit. When I appear under the sign of lesbian at WCU, I might like it to be "permanently unclear precisely what that sign signifies" (Butler, 1993, p. 308), but it is more likely that the sign will signify something fairly clear, and that I will be the one who is "unclear" about that signification.

I began the course by telling a coming out story–mine–which is different than saying that I told "my" coming out story, because there are many. I gave them the "standard" model: grew up in the south, always felt "different," had crushes on female teachers and coaches but didn't think of them as crushes, hit adolescence and found that my interest in boys was more feigned than real, so I made feeble attempts at performing my femininity, but gave the performance up quickly when I found myself kissing a girl at a slumber party during my first year of high school. So I fell in love, came out to my parents, and became increasingly involved in the gay community, eventually leading my college LGBT student organization, speaking and writing and marching for the cause, and ultimately studying queer subjects as part of my graduate education. I included a few funny anecdotes along the way, because coming out stories are supposed to be a little funny. I told about some harsh reactions and heartaches, because coming out stories are supposed to be poignant. I ended with a libratory theme–stable identity realized, white picket fence and subscription to California Cryobank's artificial insemination clinic surely right around the corner.

According to Biddy Martin (1993), the coming out narrative represents at some level the struggle for self-determination among lesbians. There is a pleasure in self-expression, particularly for individuals who feel that their identities are poorly represented by the dominant culture). To tell such stories is to speak one's way into existence in an almost tangible way, because without self-narrative, individuals with queer self-understandings risk the possibility that lesbians will be defined by those very forces who would deny their existence (Martin, 1993). With such self-representation comes power, or at least the lure of power. But the lure of self-definition that individuals find so pleasing in the coming out story, may also be a trap confining the individual in a specific definition of self based in sexual identity.

They liked my story; I could see that immediately. For the lesbian-identified students in the room, I probably managed in the first ten minutes of class to become a new role model. For some of the straight-identified students, I was the first "real" lesbian they had ever known, and they could see, already, that they'd made an excellent choice in taking this class, because they were going to "understand what it's like" to be a lesbian by hearing about the lives, loves, and trials of women like me. I was friendly and smart and funny, and I allowed my students to read those things on to my lesbian identity–as if all lesbians might be as friendly and smart and witty as this one sitting compactly in the 12:00 position of the circle.[9]

I asked them to "brainstorm" their own coming out stories–to take a few minutes and jot down ideas about what they would include if they had to tell such a story. Ten of the twenty-eight students begin furiously writing. Another three or four were tentative. The rest sat dumbfounded. A minute elapsed. A hand shot up. "I don't have a coming out story," sighed a student in the back, and several other students nodded in agreement. "Do you want us to write about how we would come out if we were lesbians?"

Eleven minutes. That's how long it took for someone to claim a heterosexual identity in my lesbian studies class. And if I hadn't sucked up the first 10 minutes telling my own story, I bet it would have happened sooner. So we paused the coming out story brainstorming activity (and here I must admit that I never intended the activity to work; I knew they didn't have the necessary information to complete the assignment) and began a discussion of what it means to "come out" or to tell a "coming out story." I asked them to reflect on the "work" done by my coming out story, and we began to articulate what might be called "genre conventions" for the story. Then, I described those same "genre conventions" as they have been articulated by Judith Roof in her 1996 text, *Come As you Are*.

The narrative structure of these stories, according to Roof, is demonstrated quite clearly by the 14 coming out stories in *What a Lesbian Looks Like* (1992), from which Roof draws her analysis:

> Each features a protagonist who somehow feels that she does not fit into the role typically assigned to women in the larger heterosexual cultural story. Sensing the disparity between her narrative and that which culture has written for her (an inner/outer dichotomy), the coming out protagonist locates herself in the place of difference (both within herself and between herself and patriarchal culture). The lesbian protagonist experiences an internalized struggle between her discomfiture with the known heterosexual part and an unknown, but intuited correct identity. She pretends to be straight, affects an unfelt stereotypical femininity, and feigns an

interest in boys. Solving the conflict between inner and outer by aligning the inner lesbian with the ultimate truth of lesbian identity finally expressed in self-affirmation and visible "lesbian" behavior, the lesbian protagonist's assertion of lesbian difference becomes the victorious truth of lesbian identity and the end of the story. (1996, pp. 104-105)

The description resonates with my students; they see how it matches the narrative that I have already provided about my own life. For many of the straight-identified students, I have confirmed that "this is what it's like for lesbians," and for the bisexual- or lesbian-identified students, I have provided a neat linear model that they could, if they wanted, fold their experiences into. By the end of the first class session, I know the claimed sexual identity labels of twenty-two of the twenty-eight students. And of course, in my head and in this essay I'm calling them identity-labels, and I'm referring to lesbian-identified and straight-identified students, though the students themselves are not using this terminology, though they may well be thinking about the inadequacy of whatever labels they have chosen.

"This 'I' does not wear its lesbianism as a role." So stated Judith Butler (1993, p. 311) in her landmark essay, "Imitation and Gender Insubordination"–a statement that might well be the first exit sign in the "contested terrain" where Queer Theory meets LGBT Studies. Turning left off the exit ramp, we would likely find a commuter parking lot filled with young LGBT students, eager to find themselves represented in the curriculum of the university and in the texts of its scholars, but just as eager to find representations that affirm their hard fought identities, or that give them rhetorical fodder for the arguments they continue to have daily with their parents, dorm-mates, and friends. "Reading Lillian Faderman was a revelation to me," wrote one of my students in a Lesbian Studies seminar in Spring 2003. "I never knew there was this rich history of lesbian life in the U.S., and Faderman showed me how I fit into that tradition."

When that same student hits Monique Wittig (1989) in week 6 of the course, can we really blame her for being angry? Wittig's argument, that a lesbian is "beyond the categories of sex (woman and man), because the designated subject (lesbian) is *not* a woman, either economically, or politically, or ideologically" complicates the coming out narrative (p. 120). "Not a woman? Who does this Wittig think she is?" my students asked. "I'm proud to be a woman," one said, "and I think it's insulting for Wittig to call lesbians 'subjects in the making.'"

My initial response to such reactions from my students was less thoughtful, perhaps, than the one I have today. "You need to re-read Wittig," was probably what I said to my students. "They just don't get it," what I complained to my colleagues. My frustration with students' "mis-reading" of important texts in Queer Theory was short-lived, however, because such readings were so predictable and, ultimately, productive. I don't mean to imply that my students have it right, and that my reading of Wittig–one where "subjects in the making" seems like a productive and interesting way to rend gender loose from sexuality and in the process cast lesbians as the new heroes of a queer revolution–is wrong. But I do mean to imply that a queer pedagogy requires teachers to question such responses from students–to ask what "work" they do. My own work with coming out stories argues that narratives provide both fetter and freedom. We write our way into existing narrative structures, because we need those structures to understand who we are, but we contest those structures, and in the process our identities, in the very process of narrating them. If I ask my students to read both "with" and "against" the texts of the classroom, then the least I can do is apply that same ethic to the texts they produce for me.

This is the contested terrain where Queer Theory meets LGBT Studies most frequently in my classroom. For my students, many of them 19 and 20 years old, away from their suburban Pennsylvania homes for the first time in their lives, finding a space to be "queer" at college is a liberating experience. They are meeting other LGBT students, some for the first time, and dealing with the consequences of being "out"–dealing with the complexities of dating and studying and finding a voice in campus politics. So imagine, then, the thrill of finding courses in the curriculum that promise to reflect that experience. "Lesbian Studies," the course I offer, must seem a beacon in the wilderness to those students brave enough to have it on their transcripts.

Walking into that class the first day, and finding me at the front of the room must also provide some sort of definitional coherence for them–because I "read" as queer–and in the act of doing so confirm their need to see lesbianism "modeled" as a safe and valid professional role. I hardly have to "come out" at that point, because it's lesbian studies. Like heteronormativity outside the bounds of my classroom, homonormativity provides an assumptive glaze here that casts anyone in the room as potentially queer. But queer is a word that I use differently from my students at this particular pedagogical moment, because they are looking for allies–allies with real identities–who can help to shoulder the burden of coming out, and coming into, identities of their own.

Brenda Jo Brueggemann and Debra Moddelmog (2002) write about this mismatch of ideas in their article in *Pedagogy* titled "Coming-Out Pedagogy: Risking Identity in Language and Literature Classrooms." "Without a coherent, foundational, permanent sense of identity, how does one come out?" they ask. "What exactly does one come out as?" (p. 312). In a classroom where LGBT Studies is already part of the course content, this "coming out" issue is further complicated by student expectations around identity. "In these classes students typically have a vested interest in promoting their own sense of identity. . ." perceiving the class "as a place where they can 'be themselves,' read about others like them, and acquire increased self worth" (p. 318).

In the LGBT classroom, they might just get what they're looking for. But in the queer classroom, this can be more difficult. Being a queer teacher involves a performance that might actually work against students' agendas in the classroom, write Brueggemann and Moddelmog. "[O]ur presentation of our identities as provisional and fluid disrupts almost everyone's expectations . . . [our identities] become overdetermined texts on which students project their anxieties and desires" (p. 319). In my classroom, I begin the semester presenting an identity that is static. I tell a coming out story. I inhabit, and perform, a lesbian body. But as the course continues, the provisional and fluid identities of which Brueggemann and Moddelmog write are going to appear, and it's my job to make that overt and explicit for my students.

So, I tell alternate versions of my coming out story as the semester progresses:

"My parents were feminists, and I think I'm probably a lesbian because they always treated my brother and me as equals."

"I was raised in the 80s, and when David Bowie and Boy George are your role models, how can you not consider bisexuality to be a potential inside us all?"

"I was speaking to a group of high school students, answering questions about what it's like to be a lesbian, when I realized that all of the "right" answers were lies."

"I almost never think of myself as a lesbian. I think of myself as a gender bender and sexual non-conformist, but those aren't terms in the vernacular, so I get stuck with lesbian."

It's always the straight-identified students who get it first, and this is a source of both frustration and revelation for me. When my Lesbian Studies students read about the exclusion of bisexual women by lesbians–they react in ways that draw lines in the classroom. The lesbian-identified students pay lip service to the idea that social justice demands inclusivity from queers, but they also tend to give voice to some deep-seated fears about bisexuality–fears that by and large have my students arguing that they wouldn't date a bisexual woman, because it would double the chances that you might get dumped. The straight-identified students throw all of their collective weight behind the inclusivity argument, with "How could a group that is discriminated against turn around and discriminate against others?" as their rallying cry.

Not unusual, this argument, in any classroom, but probably a mainstay of Women's Studies discussions, and a tough one for teachers to manage. If I chime in here and agree, "You're right, exclusion doesn't make sense. A queer world demands we work toward inclusivity in all arenas of sexual expression," then I alienate half the class. If I disagree, "There are some valid reasons for questioning the inclusion of bisexuality for lesbians and gays," I risk the same. If I historicize, which is what I tend to do, I tread a very tenuous course through the contested terrain: "We've all read Faderman, so we know that the tension around bisexuality is not a new phenomenon. Instead of asking whether bisexual identities are valid or invalid, can we ask how it is that this particular issue has played out in different moments, and why it is that we're still having a heated discussion about it today?"

Using this one particular issue, bisexuality, as an example, the strategy works like this:

Teacher: Why might lesbians, in 2003, distrust bisexual women?

Students: They can't make up their minds.

T: About what?

S: About what they want?

T: Because they want, potentially, both men and women?

S: Right.

T: But what if a bisexual woman is totally clear about that–she HAS made up her mind–that she's capable of loving both men and women. Why is that a threat?

S: Because then she might leave you for a man?

T: And why is that different or worse than if she leaves you for a woman?

S: Because you can't compete with a man.

Ahhh. In helping them "get" it, they've helped me "get it" as well. You CAN'T compete with a man. Not because of the penis–Cathy Griggers' (1994) essay, "Lesbian Bodies in the Age of (Post)Mechanical Reproduction," makes that clear. But because of the privilege. The "I can't give her what he gives her" argument that seems to rely for its logical coherence on some sort of sexual difference between men and women is actually a beautiful articulation of the "real" tension bisexual women face. No lesbian can give the bisexual woman what a man can give her in a culture that is already organized around heterosexism, because social acceptance, the rule of law, and civil rights are all on his side. The lesbian can provide, as queer rockers Bitch and Animal (2001) put it, "the best cock on the block," but she can't marry you, visit you in the hospital, or give you health insurance. So you're competing on a terrain that is not only contested, it's un-level.

T: So, the lesbian can't compete with the man in a culture that so thoroughly privileges heterosexuality. Are bisexuals to blame for this?

S: No.

This conversation continues over weeks, of course, not minutes, because these questions of exclusivity and inclusivity, as framed by the tension over bisexuality, are the same questions of exclusivity and inclusivity that frame the tension between LGBT Studies and Queer Theory. To the extent that lesbians refuse to date bisexual women because such women can more easily tap into heterosexual privilege, lesbian identity is being carved out and roped off as something much more "real" than social construction really allows. To the extent that identities are contingent and fluid, and that the potential for queer sexual expression exists in us all, exclusions on the basis of her access to privilege should glom together around normalcy, not deviance. What we should worry about, as queers, is the potential, in all of us, to slip on occasion and find ourselves normal.

By the end of the class, I didn't so much want to convert the straight women into lesbianism; I wanted to recruit them all–and the lesbians were the tough ones–into the world of the queer. Or at least that's my take. I'm not so sure that's what the Women's Studies department was after when they gave me this gig.

IF YOU CAN'T BEAT THEM, JOIN THEM?

Having returned recently from a trip to Mongolia, I have begun to rethink some of my assumptions about the ascendancy of the queer. How do Mongolians feel about homosexuality? Well, the ones I asked seemed to think it's pretty funny, funny in the way that lots of things "Americans" do might be conceived of as funny–like being a vegetarian, or keeping a live animal in your house as a pet. It doesn't hurt anyone, so it shouldn't be judged or banned, but it also just doesn't make a whole lot of practical sense. Homosexuality–whether male or female–may just be a harmless jamboree to cultures for which lesbian and gay "identity" categories have little meaning, and for whom the privilege of recreational sex seems like the sort of leisure activity that you can't take for granted, and so certainly shouldn't judge–because you've got more important things to worry about, like food.

None of this, of course, is to say that lesbian and gay identities aren't important, or that the theoretical questions surrounding those identities and their performances aren't important ones to be engaging. But if Queer Theory has taught us anything at all, then certainly we must admit that context matters, and that identities, whether essential or constructed, occur in wildly different forms in different cultures. Judith Butler, Michael Warner and Eve Sedgwick–among others–had some time on their hands when they began the process of interrogating drag, or normality, or the metaphor of the closet. And I'm grateful for it–the jamboree–the carnival–the parodic performance–these are all playful and useful ways for thinking about the consequences of identity, and how those consequences vary across the imaginaries that validate and invalidate different behaviors at different times. But we live our lives, most of us anyway, with identities that feel more coherent than not, and we have an obligation to our students to bear that coherence, even as we push them to question it.

What all of these minor, and major, incidents at West Chester University have in common is that they reveal the clash of ideas that I am attributing to, or at least aligning with, to a theoretical tension between LGBT Studies and Queer Theory. That tension is, in part, a tension that we all deal with in our classrooms, curricula, and institutions everyday, because it is a tension that resides within each and every one of us. We all rely on identity, and yet we are troubled by it. We all want inclusion, and yet we sometimes find ourselves feeling exclusive. We all want to challenge heterosexist and homophobic ideas, structures, and discourses when we find them, and yet we sometimes find ourselves wanting to be normal. Our students want to be normal too, because it is a measure of privilege to be able to shun the normal–to queer the categories of our lives for the delight of pushing our politics further than our bodies might readily go, and they are in the process of acquiring that privilege.

Queer Theory can offer many things to our students. As literary criticism, it might offer a compelling interpretation of *Fight Club*. As post-structural critique of the normal, it might offer a way for deviance to seem less deviant, and normal to seem less enticing. In the process, it might also offer way for students to engage deeply-rooted belief systems, like the binary gender system, or the ubiquity of structural inequality. As a teacher whose pedagogy bounces along on the contested terrain between LGBT Studies and Queer Theory, it warms me inside to see my students contesting that terrain themselves–seeing its tensions as the necessary fertilizer to a more just form of knowledge dissemination.

In my friend's "Queer Theory" seminar, while his students are bubbling in their course evaluations, it does my female, lesbian body good to overhear them arguing among themselves about whether it's a good idea or a bad idea to answer the question that asks, simply, GENDER, because they know it is not a simple question. In my own course, when I suggest that students might earn extra credit for coming to class in drag, I can only be thrilled when the women who take on this assignment come to class dressed as *women*, arguing that "all gender is drag" and earning much more than extra credit from me in the process.

Queer Theory might also offer a compelling model for curricular and institutional reform at the University, but we will have to be vigilant about the ways that identities and categories are not only important for students, but for programs, and institutions, with rich histories and complicated politics. "Sexuality Studies" may be a queerer minor–but it might also "read" as an act of assimilation to a conservative university system that seeks to deny the queer. And if quiet incrementalism doesn't seem like a particularly queer strategy–then we are obligated to find a way to make it loud, or to call attention to the ways that "business as usual" can co-opt queers into a normal way of thinking. What are at stake here are the identities and rationales for those identities that get forged in the process of teaching, curriculum planning, and institutional reform. Also at stake are the theoretical debates about sexuality as a critical characteristic of 'personhood,' and about "identity" as a sometimes unifying, sometimes divisive signifier.

For my stake in it, this has been an incredibly rewarding journey. It took me 18 hours to travel 400 miles on a jeep-ride in Mongolia, but that terrain was not nearly so contested as this. I spent the better portion of that journey laughing, because the ridiculousness of the situation I was in left me with a set of choices I could stomach even less than the ride. Bang my head against the door? Sulk in my privileged status as an American and whine until someone else takes responsibility for my comfort? Bury my head in the sand (and there is an abundance of sand in Mongolia)? Too normal. You can think of rough terrain as a miserable

minefield to cross–or you can think of rough terrain as an amuse-
ment-park-ride to be ridden. You need to think both, all of the time, to
the extent that you can. See the minefield, so that you can avoid the
deepest of the craters, but find ways to turn the craters you do hit into
opportunities for learning, laughing, and selling lemonade.

NOTES

1. By "lifestyle" here, I do not mean to imply that lesbian and gay identities can be accurately categorized as "lifestyles"–a position often aligned with right-wing maligning
of the "gay agenda." Instead, I am using the term "lifestyle" to describe a common
praxis among students who choose to perform their identities in ways that resist norms.
In this sense, a heterosexually identified student who chooses to wear clothing, jew-
elry, or other identifying markers that "read" as gay or lesbian could be said to be living
a "queer" lifestyle.

2. Until 1927, West Chester University was known as West Chester Normal School,
Pennsylvania's leading preparatory school in teacher training. At that time, it was re-
named West Chester State Teacher's College, and in 1983 it became West Chester University and joined the State System of Higher Education in the Commonwealth of
Pennsylvania. More than 70% of the 13,000 students who attend WCU come from, and
return to, a 5-county region in the Southeast corner of Pennsylvania, and many are from
Chester County, the richest county in Pennsylvania (where registered Republicans out-
number Democrats 2 to 1). Over 88% of the students are white.

3. Quinlivan and Town (1995) summarize this debate, from Sedgwick, writing "the
operation of binary systems of thinking around male/female, masculine/feminine, het-
erosexual/homosexual have operated to mutually reinforce the normality of heterosexuality and the abnormality of same-sex desire . . . the normality of heterosexuality is
maintained in relation to the abnormality of same-sex desire and conversely homosexuality is framed as abnormal in relation to the heterosexual norm" (p. 511).

4. The student handbook states: "West Chester University recognizes the rights of
students and other persons under the Constitution of the United States and the Commonwealth of Pennsylvania to assemble peacefully, exercise free speech rights, and
demonstrate concerns. All members of the University community are challenged to
think critically, engage in discussion, and seek out opportunities to learn and express
differing and similar viewpoints. In order to manage these events and support its mission of teaching, research, and public service, the University may regulate the time,
place, and manner of these activities to the extent it is constitutionally permitted to do
so. This policy has been developed under that principle." The policy in question, developed in part by the LGB Concerns committee in order to address the problem of homophobic speakers on campus, provides for the following time, place, and manner
restrictions: (1) Activities must not "substantially interfere with the orderly operation
of the campus. (2) Individuals wishing to engage in non-sponsored presentations must
"register with the associate vice president for student affairs/dean of students and complete the appropriate request form at least two hours prior to the time they wish to speak
and/or distribute literature." (3) Presentations may take place "in all public areas on the

campus, but must occur without amplified sound and be at least 50 feet away from any classroom building; activities proximate to classroom buildings create a high potential for disruption to class activities and other essential operations of the University. Any activities that are determined to be disruptive to classes or other essential operations of the University will need to cease." (4) Presentations may occur "during the hours of noon to 5 p.m. on all days of the week."

5. It is unfortunate, but the University response to sexism, racism, homophobia, and heterosexism has been profoundly normal. Even as I write this article, the University is embattled over the issue of Domestic Partner Benefits, which the University President, in private conversations, would seem to support. Asked to respond publicly, however, the President comments that it would be "inappropriate" to comment. And when the preacher who screams "Fags burn in Hell" stands on the Quad, the response is similar: "the views of such individuals do not necessarily reflect the views of the university."

6. Project Lemonade is the name given to our local effort to discourage hate speech on campus. Borrowed from a similar effort to discourage KKK activity in other parts of the country, the Project Lemonade concept is "taking something bitter and turning it into something sweet." According to the Project Lemonade website, the mission is to "promote tolerance." Allies do this by pledging to donate money to a tolerant cause as a response to a racist act or presentation (or in our case, a homophobic presentation). Pledges of even five cents a minute for every minute that a hate-speaker stays on campus can generate substantial revenue. The speaker, therefore, realizes that the longer he/she speaks, the more money he/she raises for the LGBT cause on campus.

7. The bribe, I suspect now, was actually an attempt to get more institutional support for our work, rather than to undermine it. But at the time, given the reactions from administrators, faculty, and students, I interpreted it as a knee-jerk reaction–invested in keeping these debates out of women's studies.

8. Sedgwick (1990) reminds us, in her analysis of the Book of Esther that "coming out" into a ready-made identity category has consequences that cannot be controlled. Coming out, writes Sedgwick, can "bring about the revelation of a powerful unknowing as unknowing" (p. 77). The danger, then, in such alignment with identity is that we "have too much cause to know how limited a leverage any individual revelation can exercise over collectively scaled and institutionally embodied oppressions (p. 78).

9. In characterizing my pedagogy this way, of course, I am both self-effacing and smug. I did want students thinking about, and questioning, the "compactness" of identity categories from the very beginning. I did expect that I could use my own subject position to achieve that end, and I did, ultimately, undermine that identity over the course of the next 15 weeks. I am neither as compact, nor as friendly, smart, and funny as I allowed myself to seem that day.

REFERENCES

Abelove, H., Barale, M., & Halperin, D. (Eds.). (1993). Introduction. *The lesbian and gay studies reader* (pp. xv-xvii). New York: Routledge.

Bitch & Animal (2001). Best cock on the block. *Eternally Hard* [CD Recording]. Buffalo, NY: Righteous Babe Records.

Britzman, D. (1995). Is there a queer pedagogy? Or, stop reading straight. *Educational Theory, 45*(2), 151-165.

Brueggemann, B., & Moddelmog, D. (Fall 2002). Coming out pedagogy: Risking identity in language and literature classrooms. *Pedagogy: Critical Approaches to Teaching Literature, Language, Composition, and Culture, 2*, 311-336.

Butler, J. (2002). Capacity. In S. Barber & D. Clark (Eds.), *Regarding Sedgwick: Essays on queer culture and critical theory* (pp. 109-120). New York: Routledge.

Butler, J. (Spring 2002). Is kinship always already heterosexual? *differences: A Journal of Feminist Cultural Studies, 13*, 14-44.

Butler, J. (1993). Imitation and gender insubordination. In H. Abelove, M. A. Barale, & D. M. Halperin (Eds.), *The lesbian and gay studies reader* (pp. 307-320). New York: Routledge.

DeLauretis, T. (1993). Sexual indifference and lesbian representation. In H. Abelove, M. A. Barale, & D. M. Halperin (Eds.), *The lesbian and gay studies reader* (pp. 141-158). New York: Routledge.

Faderman, L. (1991). *Odd girls and twilight lovers: A history of lesbian life in twentieth century America*. New York: Columbia University Press.

Faderman, L. (1999). *To believe in women: What lesbians have done for America–a history*. New York: Houghton Mifflin.

Gatto, J.T. (2003, September). Against school: How public education cripples our kids, and why. *Harper's Magazine, 307*, 33-38.

Griggers, C. (1994). Lesbian bodies in the age of (post)mechanical reproduction. In L. Doan (Ed.), *The lesbian postmodern* (pp. 118-133). New York: Columbia University Press.

Martin, B. (1993). Lesbian identity and autobiographical difference[s]. In H. Abelove, M. A. Barale, & D. M. Halperin (Eds.), *The lesbian and gay studies reader* (pp. 274-293). New York: Routledge.

National Gay and Lesbian Survey (1992). *What a lesbian looks like*. London: Routledge.

Quinlivan, K. & Town, S. (1999). Queer pedagogy, educational practice and lesbian and gay youth. *Qualitative Studies in Education, 12*(5), 509-524.

Roof, J. (1996). *Come as you are: Sexuality and narrative*. New York: Columbia University Press.

Sedgwick, E. (1990). *Epistemology of the closet*. Berkeley: University of California Press.

Sedgwick, E. (2003). *Touching feeling: Affect, pedagogy, performativity*. Durham: Duke University Press.

Taylor, J. (1994). Performing the (lesbian) self: Teacher as text. In R. J. Ringer (Ed.), *Queer words, queer images: Communication and the construction of homosexuality* (pp. 289-295). New York: New York University Press.

Wittig, M. (Fall 1989). One is not born a woman. *differences: A Journal of Feminist Cultural Studies, 1*, 101-24.

Younger, J. (2003). University LGBT/Queer programs: Lesbian, gay, bisexual, transgender, transsexual queer studies in the USA and Canada. Retrieved May 28, 2003 from http:// www.whatever.com.

doi:10.1300/J082v52n01_11

Containing Uncertainty:
Sexual Values and Citizenship

Claudia Schippert, PhD

University of Central Florida

SUMMARY. This essay reflects on one dimension of the challenge of being a queer ethicist. Can we have norms/values without liberal assumptions that might undo the important contributions of queer theory? The reemergence of appeals to "citizenship" in lbgt and queer debates serves as illustrations of this question. Reading Weeks's *Invented Moralities: Sexual Values in an Age of Uncertainty* (1995), while considering various scholars who have engaged the issue of sexual citizenship since, enables me to illustrate some of the issues that emerge around ethics and queerness at this particular moment. My argument is that attempts to offer constructive ethical engagement in the end often *contain* challenges rather than successfully address them. Critically examining Weeks's intervention into what he sees as our "loss" of moral authority and ethical concerns to the right wing is helpful for queer ethical conversations that consider available theoretical and philosophical models of claiming citizenship as a way of claiming values in uncertain times. Weeks (1995; 1998), Richardson (2000), Bell and Binnie (2000), and

---

Correspondence may be addressed: Assistant Professor of Humanities, Director, Religious Studies Program, Department of Philosophy, University of Central Florida, 411 G Colbourn Hall, Orlando, FL 32816-1352 (E-mail: cschippe@mail.ucf.edu).

[Haworth co-indexing entry note]: "Containing Uncertainty: Sexual Values and Citizenship." Schippert, Claudia. Co-published simultaneously in *Journal of Homosexuality* (Harrington Park Press, an imprint of The Haworth Press, Inc.) Vol. 52, No. 1/2, 2006, pp. 285-307; and: *LGBT Studies and Queer Theory: New Conflicts, Collaborations, and Contested Terrain* (ed: Karen E. Lovaas, John P. Elia, and Gust A. Yep) Harrington Park Press, an imprint of The Haworth Press, Inc., 2006, pp. 285-307. Single or multiple copies of this article are available for a fee from The Haworth Document Delivery Service [1-800-HAWORTH, 9:00 a.m. - 5:00 p.m. (EST). E-mail address: docdelivery@haworthpress.com].

Available online at http://jh.haworthpress.com
doi:10.1300/J082v52n01_12

Phelan (2001) provides helpful guides to the struggle with tensions that faces us in lbgt/queer debates of citizenship. doi:10.1300/J082v52n01_12 *[Article copies available for a fee from The Haworth Document Delivery Service: 1-800-HAWORTH. E-mail address: <docdelivery@haworthpress.com> Website: <http://www.HaworthPress. com> © 2006 by The Haworth Press, Inc. All rights reserved.]*

KEYWORDS. Sexual values, queer ethics, citizenship, transgression, Jeffrey Weeks

ALL GROWN UP?

Most queer theoretical work adopts Foucault's skeptical stance toward the modern organization of power and seeks to construct interventions (in texts or practices) that might resist the pervasive influence of normalizing power operations. While at this point it is not contested that queer theory provides useful suggestions for developing strategies of resistance to specific normativities, a larger set of important questions still remains at issue: Can there be ethics that are not implicated in normativity or effect domination? Are there norms, or constellations of norms, that do not produce or require abjection of others? Can we describe ethics that can formulate value (and thereby produce valuable bodies) without at the same time producing or requiring deviants who must be disciplined? How are we to formulate such ethics and what would its embodiment or political manifestations look like, what would it *do*?

For me, as someone who works in queer theory and in ethics, these are pressing questions: Does a queer theoretical view of power and resistance to identity prevent queers from having an ethics (with values and norms), concrete political agency, and a practical theory of "sexual liberation" that can respond to the contemporary political climate? In sum: Is queer theory a merely academic discipline forgetful of its activist roots? Or, does struggling for liberation and proposing specific rights automatically implicate us in normalizing power operations?

Like most questions, these arise in relation to a specific context. During the 1990s, parallel to the diversification in feminist/lbgt discourse and the formation of queer theory as academic discipline, an urgency became noticeable on the part of liberals or left-of liberal thinkers to (re-)claim language and discourse of morality and ethics from conservative and right wing institutions and ideologies. Yet, at the same time, critical discourses addressing postmodernity had made it even more difficult to formulate such an ethics. One area in which these issues have been discussed–and an area that can serve as example to illustrate the tensions or differences at the lbgt-queer border–is citizenship. Turning to citizenship, itself a contested term, opens up both possibilities and problems: Can the idea, term, or political concept of citizenship be rehabilitated and used (Patton & Caserio, 2000)? Are debates about sexual citizenship a sign that queer theory has "grown up" and matured to discuss issues of social and political theory and public policy? And, if so, would that be a good thing? Within lbgt and queer movement the meaning of sexual citizenship has been both appropriated and redefined. However, the relationship between queer politics and a politics based on citizenship remains a highly ambivalent one. By appealing to sexual citizenship, do lesbian and gay communities increasingly self-integrate into heteronormativity, as Seidman (2001) argues?

A rich discussion of ethical and political concerns surfaced within the reemergence of terminology of "citizenship" and particularly "sexual citizenship." In an early study of the conditions of emergence of sexual minority claims to citizenship status and rights, Evans (1993) places these debates within an analysis of consumer culture and explores various kinds of material citizenship (also see Clarke, 1996). Debates of lbgt identity vs. queer are reflected in the ongoing political and social theoretical discussion of dynamics of exclusion and inclusion in late modernity. In an influential essay in which he raises questions about existing accounts and understandings of exclusion and inclusion in lbgt (and queer) groups, on which the political appeal to citizenship is built, Gamson (1997) examines the significance of communication contexts in processes of inclusion and exclusion in gender/sexual-identity social movement formation and shows that symbolic public communications were/are often more important than actual participation or exclusion. Urging greater consideration of the gendered nature of collective identity construction, Gamson proposes a shift in how social and political accounts of group identity formation are contextualized. Relating this discussion explicitly to political appeals to citizenship, Gamson (1997) argues that the meaning of citizenship within the changing conditions of late modernity remains largely unclear. Examining how different understandings of citizenship (state-centered, pluralist, and poststructuralist) might enable response to the fragmented conditions of late modernity, he suggests that we rather consider citizenship as a "reflexive condition of defensive engagement." Similar engagement of the challenge of struggling with this tension between, on the one hand, identity-focused appeals to group inclusion or rights and, on the other hand, a queer impulse to resist the (necessarily hetero-) normativity of identity, can also be found in Rankin's (2000) examination of the failure of queer nationalism and her suggestion that queer theoretical and feminist theoretical accounts that consider lesbian experience/identity can and must lead to new important libratory strategies for queers (in the Canadian context, in her case).

Discussing sexual citizenship thus clearly engages social and political realms. Taking this site of citizenship as example for issues of morality, ethics, and sexual agency, my essay additionally keeps in mind the larger concerns and challenge of being a queer ethicist. Can we have norms/values without liberal assumptions that might undo the important contributions of queer theory? I focus on the influential work by Jeffrey Weeks, the British sociologist and gay scholar who has written about the production of sexuality for many years. Indeed, some of his work explored the "construction" of sexuality through historically specific discourses even prior to the emergence of Foucault's work. Weeks has thus made substantive contributions toward shaping some of the current field of lbgt/sexuality-scholarship.

As I will argue, Weeks's *Invented Moralities: Sexual Values in an Age of Uncertainty* (1995) is an excellent example of a serious attempt to wrestle with some foundational challenges at the lbgt/queer border–and is exemplary for current debates of sexual citizenship. As recently as November 2003 (in a plenary address at the conference *Sexuality* After *Foucault* in Manchester, England), Weeks explored issues of citizenship and democratic discourse he had begun to outline in *Invented Moralities* (1995) and "The sexual citizen" (1998). My essay argues that Weeks's approach serves as a window into the theoretical sticking points we face when trying to describe (or even overcome) problems posed at the intersection of queer theoretical and lbgt scholarship. Indeed, Weeks's work is symptomatic for the different directions and strategies "LBGT" and "queer" might stand for. (He does not himself position his work in this way, but its reception demonstrates such a position.) Thus reading Weeks's text alongside various scholars who engage the issue of sexual citizenship enables me to illustrate some key issues that emerge around ethics and queerness at this particular moment.

I hasten to add that I do not turn to Weeks's work because it offers a "solution" to the many issues we face when attempting to write, think, or *do* a postmodern or "queer" ethics. Indeed, my argument is that *In-*

vented Moralities can serve as window into subsequent lbgt discussions of sexual citizenship, as it attempts to offer constructive ethical engagement, but in the end often *contains* challenges rather than successfully address them. This is not something necessarily avoided by moving into queer theoretical realms. Critically examining Weeks's intervention into what he sees as our "loss" of moral authority and ethical concerns to the right wing continues to be helpful for queer ethical conversations that consider available theoretical and philosophical models of claiming citizenship as way of claiming values in uncertain times. Weeks (1995; 1998), Richardson (2000), Bell and Binnie (2000), and Phelan (2001) provide helpful guides to the struggle with tensions that faces us in lbgt/queer debates of citizenship.

WRITING VALUES IN AN AGE OF UNCERTAINTY

Jeffrey Weeks positions *Invented Moralities: Sexual Values in an Age of Uncertainty* (1995) within the problematic tension between conservative anti-sex moralism on the one hand and libertarian radicalism on the other. Weeks does not want to leave the field of sexuality either to the moralist right wing or unprincipled libertarianism. He recounts that when he began writing the book, many of his friends and colleagues suggested that values, specifically sexual values, are the domain of the right. Weeks does not deny that to talk about values and morality in the contemporary context often seems to imply a conservative moralism or right wing politics that is characterized by "hostility toward the advances made by women during the past generations, fear and loathing of homosexuality, and a deep anxiety caused by the growing diversity both of public life and our private arrangements" (ix). However, Weeks claims that this need not be the case and that it is important not to cede the terrain of values to the right. In his work he attempts to investigate the ethical dilemmas we currently face, specifically as they involve sexuality, and to explore possibilities to formulate, hold, and act with a set of values that inform an ethics or a morality that is *unlike* right wing moralism.

In this regard, *Invented Moralities* is symptomatic: most of the influential texts engaging and developing sexual citizenship emerged in reaction to, or in conversation with, the neo-conservative/neo-liberal political debates in the U.S. and U.K. in the 1990s (Evans, 1993; Berlant, 1997; Sullivan, 1996). Like Giddens (1992) and Bauman (1993), Weeks suggests that our current situation is characterized by an ever-increasing diversity of identities, choices, and values, which are accompanied by "uncertainty" or lack clear guidance. This quintessentially postmodern situation correlates with the disappearance of religion and its absolutist guidance for individual and social morality and values. To be sure, secular sociologist Weeks does not suggest that we return to religious guidelines for appropriate conduct. Religion figures in Weeks's text mostly as the source of

> "old verities, . . . narrative comforts" (p. 25) that provide "value-laden arguments–largely from the political and moral right, but also from popes and preachers, ayatollahs, religious revivalists and fundamentalists of various hues–which instruct us how to live and whose moral entrepreneurs do their best to make us conform to *their* values." (p. 10)

Consequently, Weeks is not invested in religious discourse nor does he seek to re-formulate ethics or morality with reference to any religious tradition. He does acknowledge, however, that such traditions provided "certainties" and guidelines that, although problematic in many specific ways, provided a sense of orientation for the actor who had to decide or choose an action. As he sees it, in the postmodern decline of master narratives, such confidence and certainty disappeared and left us in a society characterized by uncertainty.[1]

In Weeks's analysis, the postmodern situation is one of unlimited choices given to unstable selves in a world of constant flux. The resulting postmodern ethical paradox restores full moral choice and responsibility while depriving agents of the universal guidance upon which modern self-confidence relied. Weeks here agrees with and draws on the contention of Bauman (1993) that "moral responsibility comes together with the loneliness of moral choice," or, as Giddens (1992) writes, that we are "faced by a cacophony of options . . . day-to-day-decisions" (Weeks, 1995, pp. 12, 28, 33).

Despite his commitment to such an analysis of the postmodern "situation," Weeks limits the validity of descriptions such as "we have no choice but to choose" to "those who have the freedom to choose" (p. 33, 27). The foregrounding of material differences in the "ability to choose" is a noteworthy aspect of this stance vis-à-vis postmodernism, and is indicative of Weeks's conversation between and across several disciplinary fields; in this way his gay scholarship inflects his liberal discourse.

Nevertheless, Weeks agrees with the analysis that a troubling situation of "uncertainty" is related to an ever expanding diversity of choices, identities, conceptions of life or actions, and a multiplicity of meanings and values. What or who one *is*, decisions of how to act, and how to find or make meaning out of one's life and actions, all are no longer guided by a few universally applicable sets of norms, but have become unstable, fluctuating, and in some ways confusing. Weeks does not seek to resolve or "fix" this problem of instability and uncertainty. On the contrary, he foregrounds the fact that moralities and values, much like conceptions of identities, are "invented," i.e., they are constructed by actors within historically, politically distinct contexts.

At the same time, Weeks refuses to accept that uncertainty *necessarily results* in moral relativism or total subjectivism (where every option within an indefinite multiplicity would be interchangeable or equally valid). Instead, he proposes to struggle with the difficult question of how to make values, how to create or find meaning, how to answer the question "how shall I/we live?" in a way that is morally responsible and can enter into conversation with other claims, meanings, and lives for the purpose of exchange, communication, and democratic process. Taking on this challenge, his goal is a morality that emerges out of a struggle with uncertainty yet does not need to embrace universal doctrine and does not attempt to prescribe or dictate what shall constitute moral value for others or all.

Promise

The promise of Weeks's approach is that it corresponds to the complexity of challenges we face when thinking about norms and normativity. These challenges are important to both queer theoretical analysis of contemporary social and political thought as well as liberationist work on gender and sexuality in lbgt studies. Weeks clearly wants to resist a prescriptive formulation of values that everyone has to follow. On the other hand, he finds it imperative that "we" be able to formulate a framework (however narrow or minimal) to compare, adjudicate and distinguish between different values in order to agree on some common standards (that may again be minimal).[2] The strength of this approach is the way Weeks attempts to avoid liberal and prescriptive gestures that would simply locate a particular value or norm that might resolve the problems. Rather, Weeks throughout his work is thinking about the ways in which *valuing* happens, and argues that valuing should be required. His is a methodological, or "meta-ethical" engagement, rather than a proposition of a particular libratory norm or value; his work is therefore useful to explore in the context of the questions about 'queer ethics' with which I began this essay.

It is Weeks's *insistence* on engaging questions of norms and values that is useful and that is crucial to address when trying to engage questions of values and democracy at the lbgt/queer ethics intersection. Is a framework necessary? Can we do (or have an) ethics that does not in some way require the setting of boundaries and limits that leave some real bodies outside the realm of the viable, the possible, the good? Do "good gays" always produce "bad queers"–as Stychin (1998) suggests in the context of gay rights claims and their appeal to ideals of "respectability." Can a recognizable, and recognizably queer, ethics emerge once we take seriously Foucault's radically challenging conceptions of power and bodies?

The challenge Weeks sees in uncertainty is "to find ways of living, and loving, together, in a world without intrinsic meaning or foundational givens, which are securely rooted in our common humanity and our care and responsibility for each other" (p. xi). Following Laclau's description of a radically democratic society Weeks does not want to search for a single foundation but rather accepts the "contingent and open character of all its values" (p. 44). However, writes Weeks, "that does not mean that we should abandon the effort to articulate and clarify the values that do inform our behavior. There can be an agreement on the importance of valuing, even if the conclusions we come to are different" (p. 44).

In positing the need for a thorough reflection on values, Weeks's approach need not contradict his earlier assertion that morality should not be prescriptive. Nevertheless, the posited necessity of frameworks for values deserves examination.

The Problem with Containing

Despite Weeks's focus on the dynamic processes of valuing, he assumes that an ethics that is "securely rooted in our common humanity" and connected to "care and responsibility" also and necessarily has to *rank* values and needs to provide means to (hierarchically) *differentiate* between them. Yet Weeks does not consider how his own assumption in this regard is as equally invented as are the other moral frameworks he had briefly discussed.[3] It seems to be obvious, or implied as a given, that "we" should want to be able to rank, compare, and discuss the differences of values.

Weeks posits that the situation of uncertainty is the irrevocable condition of living in postmodernity and should be viewed as a challenge rather than as an unsolvable problem. While this evaluation is promising because of its ability to address uncertainty or ambiguity, I have found Weeks's larger argument to be less appreciative of the challenge than he initially claims. Indeed, he adopts positions that elide the challenge of the continuously ambiguous place that queers have in contemporary culture. Consequently, his positions often *contain* (the threat of) uncertainty.

Rather than impose artificial order, Weeks wants to "chart principles . . . which might enable us to steer through the ethical dilemma posed by sexual diversity" (p. 49) and to "learn to negotiate hazards of social complexity" (p. 12). "The contemporary sexual landscape," according to Weeks, "is *haunted* by a double headed spectre: the *irredeemable* diversity of sexualities, the fact of otherness confronting us in all our dealings with individuals and collectives; and the necessity of choice" (p. 58, my emphasis). To the extent that these terms are negative, frightening, certainly undesirable, they render the situation described as something other than a welcome challenge or productive site of postmodern complexity. I am not suggesting that a more pollyannaish portrayal of "the postmodern condition" or even a celebration of its lack of guidance would be a more accurate description of the contemporary moral landscape. Nevertheless, as I will argue below, it is a problem to neglect to note how disciplinary operations of modern power re-produce tight networks of norms that function as a kind of "guidance" in that they compel particular behavior, action, practice.

It is obvious to Weeks, as a secular sociologist, that we *make* values. Values, moralities, as well as our sexualities and identities are "invented" or produced by us. However, rather than assert an accidental or random character, Weeks posits that "we need to be clear why we are making the decisions we do make, what values inform our practices" (p. 50). Weeks argues that we need values. Only if we can answer the question "how shall I live?" for ourselves, can we be in conversation about different values; only then can we communicate with each other about our choices, ways in which we ourselves (individually and collectively) make sense of what we do; only then can we clarify, think though, evaluate which choices we (want to) make. At the center of Weeks's project is this commitment to thinking through how we make values and to imagining ways of doing so that avoid replicating right wing moralism.

Weeks's struggle with this ambiguity is challenging and important: placed between voluntary agency and radical constructivism, the question of values and of who acts according to which criteria needs to be asked in new terms that can account for the insights and commitments of lbgt/queer scholars since Foucault.

Affirming the variety and validity of different values and moral claims that can be observed in different communities and practices, Weeks also wants to establish a means of comparison:

> The challenge is to endorse the value of diversity without surrendering to absolute relativism, a relativism which abandons any attempt to achieve certain agreed minimum standards of human value and conduct. . . . The key issue becomes: what are the norms by which ways of life can be ranked? (pp. 59, 64)

This is an important discursive move that begins to demonstrate the tension in Weeks's approach that is so symptomatic of more recent lbgt approaches to citizenship: Calling for rankings *contains* uncertainty rather than enable us to deal with ambiguities and complexities. To Weeks, the fact that we "need" values means that we need them in a specifically differential way, i.e., what we really need are not values so much as the ability to distinguish and rank values and norms within a *comparative* framework. Any uncertainty resulting from the complicated relationship between choices, necessities, and possible actions in a highly complex world will need to be placed in a hierarchical (ranking) structure or at least it should potentially be able to be placed and contained therein. In my view, the "challenge" that uncertainty was supposed to provide is evaded by briefly acknowledging its existence while immediately channeling it into differential and hierarchical frameworks.[4]

Weeks's approach to the contemporary situation as one of uncertainty strikes me as unlike what one would take from Foucault or queer theory, which might foreground the normalizing incentives that are at work even in multiplicities of choices within a highly disciplinary organization of power. Similarly, more Foucaultian readings of this deployment of, or desire for, rankings and patterns to contain order, would assert the typical disciplinary and normalizing operation of power in modern society, pointing to the establishment of precisely such comparisons and hierarchies.

TRANSGRESSION VS. CITIZENSHIP

Weeks contains uncertainty within the necessity of having a specific value-framework. Such an approach points to some of the differences that are characteristic for the liberal-queer-intersection and that I am engaging here as well: in struggling with the tensions that characterize postmodern multiplicities of meanings, haunted and irredeemable as Weeks states they are, a turn to the notion of citizenship provides if not redemption then at least a reason to insist on ranking values. The specific framework that enables containing uncertainty is thus intimately connected to (the appeal to) a particular notion of citizenship (see also Seidman, 2003, for another account that demonstrates how arguments regarding values are "haunted" by the desire for citizenship).

Weeks names "two distinct political 'moments' in contemporary sexual politics" that point to both possibilities and dangers (p. 107). He describes these two important sites as "the moment of transgression" and "the moment of citizenship" although his juxtaposition of the concepts of transgression and of citizenship could also be paraphrased as "transgression is good, citizenship is better."[5]

Transgression is Good (but Gets Old)

Unlike some lbgt discussions, Weeks does not discuss the sexual politics of a particular group or community (like the gay community or sadomasochists or other specifically identified communities). By thus attempting to resist a particular identity-based lbgt discourse, Weeks's approach parallels the impulse in queer theoretical work to foreground the operations of sexuality as a discourse rather than rely on sexual identities as discreet categories or analytical tools. His critical explication of the *invention* of identities provides the background for his discursive strategy. Rather than evaluate a particular movement or context, Weeks tries to locate and discuss the *moments of challenge and inclusion* which he detects in various sites, movements, and communities and which seem to share certain characteristics.

Weeks defines transgression as "the breaching of boundaries, the pushing of experience to the limits, the challenge to the Law, whatever it is . . . a crucial moment in any radical sexual project" (p. 108). Boundaries are flexible and constantly changing (much like a Foucaultian description of transgression as a spiral would also suggest; Foucault, 1987, pp. 44-45). Weeks's critical assertion that "it is difficult to believe that any individual act in itself will shock" (p. 109) is well taken. Nevertheless, he finds reasons why transgressions matter. They are "the critical elements and the various possibilities spelt out in the transgressive transaction, the new niches of possibility that appear, and these depend on the changing social geography of sexuality" (p. 109). It is not surprising, given his description and valuing of transgression, that Weeks turned to the new "queer politics" as his example of the transgressive moment in contemporary sexual politics.

However, Weeks places the queer theoretical or queer activist project in a framework that ultimately requires its integration into more "constructive" politics and ethics of citizenship/inclusion. He qualifies his presentation in the following way:

> In the long perspective of history, queer politics may well prove to be an ephemeral ripple rather than a refreshing wave. Queer politics has all the defects of a transgressive style, elevating confrontation over the content of alternatives. Although it seeks to deconstruct old rigidities, it creates new boundaries; although it is deliberately transgressive, it enacts its dissidence through the adoption of a descriptive label which many lesbians and gays find offensive, often seeking enemies within as much as enemies without (. . .) Despite this it is an interesting phenomenon not only because of what it says or does, but because it is a reminder of the perpetual inventiveness of a collective sexual politics which stretches toward different ways of being. (Weeks, 1995, p. 115)

After this (not entirely enthusiastic) sketch of queer politics as a moment of transgression, Weeks turns to the second site he observes in contemporary sexual politics, the moment of citizenship, by quoting Elizabeth Wilson (1993):

> We transgress in order to insist that we are there, that we exist, and to place a distance between ourselves and the dominant culture. But we have to go further–we have to have an idea of how things could be different, otherwise transgression ends in mere posturing. (qtd. in Weeks, 1995, p. 116)

Weeks uses this quote by Wilson to authorize his turn to citizenship as a supersessional moment in sexual politics.

Such a turn to citizenship–and especially sexual citizenship, paired with its potential for lbgt and queer movement in terms of political rights claims–has been discussed in many sites and from multiple directions by both activists and scholars around issues of public culture and sex, the effects of AIDS and AIDS activism, questions of class, and public-private sphere debates (Dangerous Bedfellows, 1996; Berlant, 1997; Cohen, 1997; Patton & Caserio, 2000). More recently, Phelan (2001) engages the figure of the "stranger" in the context of citizenship and sexuality, although she comes to more radical conclusions than Weeks. She might be joined by Bell and Binnie whose polemical but thorough *The Sexual Citizen* (2000) also expands on Weeks's approach.[6]

Is Citizenship Better?

Weeks suggests that "the concept of citizenship has been seen as one possible way of expressing how, in response to Wilson's appeal, 'things could be different'" (p. 116f). At the same time, he reminds us that the concept of citizenship is filled with problems, for example "that historically, aspiration to citizenship has encoded a particular version of sexual behaviour and private life into its central discourse" (p. 117). Many thus remain skeptical of the idea of sexual citizenship. Nevertheless, Weeks argues that the concept and claim to full citizenship and campaigns for rights have been important elements of sexual politics since the 1970s: "If the discourse of transgression as a road to emancipation or liberation is one pole of recent sexual politics, the discourse of rights is the other, and they are complexly intertwined." However, the relationship between these two poles is less balanced than it appears initially.

In a more recent discussion of "the sexual citizen" (1998), Weeks seems to shift some of the definitions even while he reiterates the significance of both, the moments of transgression and the moments of citizenship. They are, he writes, "both necessary to each other" (Weeks, 1998, p. 37). However, explicating their relationship further, he writes, "transgression appears necessary to face the status quo with its inequities, to hold a mirror up to its prejudices and fears. . . . But without the claim to full citizenship, difference can never find a proper home" (p. 37).

Given the prominence of citizenship discourse in recent lbgt/queer conversations, Weeks's privileging of citizenship over transgression may not seem remarkable. Indeed, appeals to citizenship are visible in many realms. Consider how ongoing political struggles over gay marriage, or the successful election of a queer Anglican bishop, or the visibility of queer characters in various media, most notably the success of *Queer Eye for the Straight Guy* are based on such a move to citizenship as "next step." Problematically, in a case like *Queer Eye for the Straight Guy*, potentially transgressive queerness finds itself integrated into (and defused by) productive and constructive support of heterosexual masculinity.

Nevertheless, I find an interesting and instructive tension in the temporal linking of the moments of transgression and citizenship, as one succeeding the other (see also Bell & Binnie, 2000). It is interesting to me that several approaches have focused on the tone of the argument that is criticized and that is taken as indication for a larger discursive and political argument–but maybe that is one way to examine the lbgt/queer border as well: differences and departures in political agenda begin in intonations and style, yet carry with them significant political consequence. Regarding Weeks's approach to citizenship, Bell and Binnie write,

> [Weeks] argues that the 'moment of citizenship' represents the only way that 'difference can [ever] find a proper home'–we think that is an especially telling phrase: who defines what a 'proper home' is for sexual citizens? What happens to those who refuse to be confined to 'home', or to living in the 'proper' way? (2000, p. 3)

One of the troubles with citizenship (or "the trouble with normal," as Warner, 1999, would likely put it) is that in this approach, moments of transgression are important and valid primarily if they are part of a "larger" strategy of transformation or emancipation. There is a call for a "wider politics" which de-values (individual or social) transgression, practices of defiance, or even unintentionally invoked or effected resistances to specific normative constellations that may shift, disrupt, or alter the discursive situation without relying on a social movement or wider political plan.

In my own work, when focusing on transgressive or queer body-practices, I certainly do not seek to avoid social significance. However, I would not agree that transgressive body-practices are "mere posturing" if the actors do not formulate "how things could be different" in terms related to a discourse of citizenship or rights. Knowing that things need to be different, i.e., that one does not want a particular discursive configuration, is important (and not always easy in contemporary highly normalized US culture). Formulating a "constructive" alternative may not be possible (or desirable) without substantial cumulative disruption of the larger vocabulary. I would claim, for example, transgressive gender-practices as important and valid, even in the absence of an alternative gender-model.

Balancing/Framing Transgression

When examining the de-valuing of transgression compared to citizenship, what raises my interest (or suspicion) is the evaluation of what "counts" as a framework or context. It is here that my earlier point–that Weeks seeks to contain uncertainty–reenters my exploration of appeals to citizenship. This is a discursive feature that, far beyond Weeks's work, is characteristic of much lbgt writing on citizenship. While I agree with Weeks's claim that isolated acts of transgression may not be the only possible way to effect shifts in sexual politics (or politics that can challenge sexual normativities), an insistence on thinking transgression necessarily together with, and as preceding, the more important moment of citizenship is problematic. Such a move narrows the significance of transgressive actions to something akin to "foreplay."

After all, there are different kinds of transgressions and the same act may have very different effects in different contexts. A successive (supersessional) pairing of transgression with citizenship narrows productive political actions (and moral or ethical decisions) to a limited set of possibilities that are recognizable (a priori?) as such. As I read it, Weeks fails to see the "productive" side of transgression: how transgression or dissent can constitute productive discursive moments and interventions that can enable new networks, without being describable in terms of a democratic process or concept of citizenship (however modified as sexual citizenship). These limiting effects of privileging citizenship parallel other critical perspectives on this issue: In his argument for keeping sexual specificity even within a move to queer politics, Leo Bersani (1995) warns about the dangers of replicating liberal versions of sexual identity/community in a shift to queer, and suggests that "[t]here are glorious precedents for thinking of homosexuality as truly disruptive–as a *force* not limited to the modest goal of tolerance for diverse lifestyles, but in fact mandating the politically unacceptable and politically indispensable choice of an outlaw existence" (p. 76). Such a critical perspective on the appeal of social and political normality is also reflected in Phelan (2001).

Others critical of a sequencing that produces citizenship as more mature version of transgression or dissent have suggested different approaches to (the importance of) dissent. Highlighting the value and significance of dissent for democratic processes that are cognizant of race, gender, class, and sexuality, Sparks (1997) draws on the historical example of Rosa Parks to illustrate the significance of dissent in the context of what she calls an ethic of political courage within democratic processes. Exploring the issue of sexual citizenship from within a similarly complex consideration of social, political, and geographic space, geographer Bell (1995) proposes to take the figure of the "citizen-pervert" as lens through which to examine the spatial relationship between what I have here called transgression and citizenship, and highlights that the "paradoxical geography" of the citizen-pervert raises questions about both the promises and limits of sexual citizenship.

Extending what "queering the state" (Duggan, 1995) might look like, Bonnie Honig discusses instances where citizenship has been used to subvert the very project of national citizenship (Patton & Caserio, 2000, p. 6). A discussion predetermined on balancing transgression and citizenship (especially in a temporal succession) also will miss more complicated considerations of the place of identity formation vis-à-vis national narratives that Povinelli (2002) explores.

Diane Richardson (2000) argues that within emerging debates over sexual or intimate citizenship distinctions can be made between "[a]nalyses which place greater emphasis on the discussion of rights *per se* and struggles for rights acquisitions, and those which are concerned with wider social and theoretical implications" (p. 87). I agree with her evaluation that Weeks (and many of the scholars he is in conversation with or draws on, such as Anthony Giddens or Ken Plummer) are part of this latter strand of citizenship-debates. However, it is by declaring that transgression and citizenship are–or maybe it is rather, that they should be–part of the same project that Weeks sets the stage for promoting citizenship over transgression in a way that enables him to substitute this appeal to "constructive ethics" for the empty space of the never defined "same project." While successful or "constructive" sexual politics need not provide a written party platform, a desire to contain uncertainty by producing constructive values that have to go *beyond* transgressive actions gestures in such a direction. I thus return one more time to Weeks's text to consider another description of the relationship of citizenship and transgression:

> The aim of such carnivalesque displays [examples of transgression] whether conscious or not, is to challenge the status quo and various forms of social exclusion by exotic manifestations of difference. Yet contained within these moments is also the claim to inclusion . . . this is the moment of citizenship. (1989, p. 37)

Again citizenship is the more that transgression needs–and indeed here citizenship, and specifically a rights-based conception of citizenship is always already part of, "contained" within, transgressive moments. This seems to describe the dependency in other terms: citizenship is always already part of (valid) transgression, is its enabling condition and goal. Transgression is always already framed by citizenship.

Transgression contains citizenship–but also the reverse: the moment of transgression has to be contained by, and integrated into, wider politics of inclusion and citizenship. Indeed, I find this reverse to be the stronger and the more problematic move in the argument: Transgression is good, but not good enough. Putting this more strongly, Bell and Binnie (2000) state that in Weeks's approach, "a notion like 'queer citizenship' would be oxymoronic . . . 'queer' is the opposite of 'citizen'" (p. 143). Seidman (2001) raises similar question about a perception that queer and citizen are somehow necessarily incompatible opposites.

What I am arguing is that the specific (circular) positioning of moments of transgression and citizenship speak of a desire for belonging, or for grown-up-status, within democratic discourse that corresponds with configurations of valuing normative strategies in ethics. Another way to say this is that "constructive ethics" are defined in a way that replicates the discursive moves I have described above and that seem to be familiar feature in many areas of ethics. To risk over-generalizing, but in order to make clear the stakes, at times it seem that no matter how radical or subversive the intent, a challenge to "ethics as we know it" often runs into the requirement of having to be "constructive," i.e., having to be *more* than "mere" transgression (or, to read this with and across the issues explored above, transgression is good, but not good enough; dissent and transgressive sexual enactment are useful, but only within the larger, constructive framework of citizenship).

This is an important issue to consider at the intersection of lbgt and queer approaches because such criticism has been used to discredit earlier feminist, antiracist, and also lbgt interventions into dominant discourse (which were often called too limited because of their focus on only certain people's experiences and therefore not universally valid, which supposedly rendered them irrelevant). Similar "disqualifications" have been leveled against other innovative ways of reading texts, viewing society, or approaching politics. Some defenses or reverse criticisms, although often taking some time to emerge, have been able to shift paradigms by successfully demonstrating that what was initially viewed as "not constructive" or "mere transgression" constituted specific interventions in aspects of the dominant paradigm that could not be approached, seen, or described from within that paradigm.

Placing these larger phenomena again directly at the lbgt/queer border, I read a prescriptive insistence on citizenship to parallel some of the gay and lesbian strategies of de-legitimization (in the political and the academic realm) that have been frustrating to many queers or sexual radicals. While appealing to mainstream, liberal, or otherwise constructive political and ethical norms, those who could or would not fit into constructive norms were abjected and 'othered' within the newly acceptable community. Consider how ILGA excluded NAMBLA in a symbolic expulsion aimed at establishing and maintaining proper and respectable status. Gamson (1997) offers a compelling account for the importance of such symbolic communication in the formation of identity and group definitions that involve processes of inclusion/exclusion and (symbolic) expulsion of (too) deviant others. (Besides the exclusion of NAMBLA from ILGA Gamson also shows how place and fate of 'Camp Trans' in the context of the Michigan Women's Music Festival suggests the significance of gendered negotiations of acceptability and group identity especially when the struggle occurs in a quasi-public realm with stakes akin to normative discourse.) Dividing homosexuals into good gays and bad queers, as discussed by Stychin (1998), mirrors the position Phelan (2001) suggests is occupied by bi and trans people who are often ignored, as they are threatening to, or "stranger within," the inclusive naming of "lbgt." Weeks (1995; 1997) perhaps unintentionally replicates these problematic moves in a continuous insistence on ranking values, which I believe to be aimed at shedding the immaturity of transgressive queerness and an embrace of citizen adulthood.

Watching the tensions that characterize such moves toward constructive political engagement and related versions/visions of moral agency allows us to raise further questions: Given the prevalence of appeals to the normal, even within lbgt or queer approaches, is there something about norms, or ethics in general, that automatically requires ethics to be constructive, to appeal to a 'larger picture' or constructive inclusion (in citizenship) as both beginning and end of (the temporary strategy of) transgression? Do norms always "contain" and do they have to, finally, prescriptively circumscribe behavior, values, and actions in hierarchical or at least strictly differential ways? Can sexual or intimate citizenship be thought and lived as also queer? Is there value in transgression, or to restate Wilson (1993) "is transgression transgressive?"

Queering Citizenship

While raising important questions about strategies to use difference for change, approaches like Weeks's illustrate that *containing* uncertainty and ambiguity is easily justified by invoking the "necessity" to have constructive values and ethics. In the end, transgressive moments, or radical shifts in paradigms, will confront the claim that they are "mere" transgression and require a second step. What counts as recognizably a value or a sexual norm (or liberationist or "good") is often *pre-determined* by a set of interacting networks and normative relations.

In trying to formulate alternatives to such reinscription into normativities, Phelan (2001) points out that

> the question . . . is not 'queer or not,' or 'how to make citizenship queer,' but how to queer citizenship– how to continue the subversion of a category that is nonetheless both crucial and beneficial for millions of people around the world. (pp. 140-141)

The earlier mentioned examples like *Queer Eye for the Straight Guy* point to the ongoing appeal of citizenship and political inclusion and suggest the necessity to continue to raise questions about how to shift to queering citizenship rather than merely buying into its (redemptive?) appeal.

The significance of dissent (and the experience of citizenship having a hard time accommodating dissent, something we can observe in recent popular political culture) as formulated by Duggan's (1995) project of queering the state have lead to further insightful discussion of the ambivalent political dynamics around sexual regulation and queer politics in Jakobsen and Pellegrini (2003); or as Phelan (2001) suggests, "a thorough queering of public culture is needed" (p. 8). Such work is helpful amidst continuing discussions about sexual citizenship that explore its potential to subvert normative sexualities and to account for radically altered political and sexual lives.[7]

Questioning the assumed public-private split and the sequencing into transgressive foreplay and citizenship as 'the real thing,' and insisting on a wider range of possibilities for transformative action, we could appropriate the conception of queer as verb (Jakobsen, 1998), as political and ethical activity that draws on ambiguity and difference without an 'underlying' foundation of constructive ethical frames. Jakobsen illustrates such a concept by exploring how when acting in alliance, those who join in dissenting or counter-normative activity need not share (all) values and need not be able to formulate how they are similar (or, I would add, how values are ranked or ordered within a larger framework). Rather, being an ally becomes *the effect of being in alliance* and can thus transgress and go beyond the social-movement-definitions currently available. Jakobsen's (1998) proposal that a politics of "working alliances" are a way to enact dissent politically without predetermined (or ranked) values that would (pre-)determine commonalities can be effective even given (or maybe precisely because of) an absence of common values or norms, i.e. without a moment of citizenship that is always already contained within transgression. Such an approach is further explored in *Love the Sin* (2003) where Jakobsen and Pellegrini intervene in political debates about sexual morality and argue for the value(ing) of sex in rights-debates, but attempt to do so without relying on a notion of constructive citizenship that needs to produce, or pretends to be, 'grown up' normality.

As lbgt and queer scholarship continues to grapple with challenges of sexual values and uncertainty, citizenship will likely continue to be an important notion and marker of difference within and across scholarly and intellectual commitments and communities. The scholarly debates discussed in this essay indicate that political morality and sexual ethics need not be conceptualized according to a particular constructive engagement of citizenship in order to 'count' as politically effective. In continuing to explore these insights and applying them to theoretical discussions and activist politics around citizenship, we will hopefully continue to develop ways to queer citizenship that go beyond merely asking for inclusion for specific groups of people.

NOTES

1. Today, and especially in the U.S., it seems less likely that an argument about the decline of religious values and normative claims would be made in the same way. Far from offering the kind of *helpful* guidance Weeks imagines, religious discourse has become, and perhaps always was, available as guiding master narrative in "secular" U.S. culture. See also Phelan (2000).

2. Generally, Weeks does not consider subjectivism or relativism to be a real problem. He attempts to approach the postmodern condition of uncertainty from what he takes to be a radical and liberal direction, with an interest in democracy much like that of Laclau and Mouffe (1989) or Benhabib (1992). Weeks is one of several scholars who are interested in precisely the questions of how to create meaning and value without implementing universal and imperialistic doctrines of good behavior. Also see Squires (1993).

3. This aspect of Weeks's argument, and my critical reading of it, also provides parallels to discussions in feminist theory and ethics, where debates about values and meta-ethical theories have been ongoing; see Benhabib (1992), Fraser (1997), Jakobsen (1998; 1999).

4. For more explicit reflections and a defense of normative theorizing see Fraser (1997).

5. The supersessional character at which such a formulation gestures is discussed further below; it parallels what I had asked in my initial question if queer theory is 'all grown up': If queer theory is all grown up does it mean that such an 'adult' theory has to play within a certain (constructive) public square?

6. The transgressive potential of queer sex(uality)–or what Berlant discusses as 'sex acts on the live margins' (1997, p. 62)–threatens the conception of the appropriateness of privacy and the assumed protection of a common version of national rights. Transgressions of this sort re-orient queer intervention to one refusing privacy as protective norm, even while remaining aware of the dangers and risk of such an approach, as Bell and Binnie (2000) point out. Nevertheless, the coupling of citizenship with privacy has had the effect that tolerance and assimilation seem to be a necessary part of current appeals to citizenship–no matter if those wanting citizenship rights aim to assimilate or wish for the dubious benefits of being tolerated (see Richardson, 1997, for an extensive delineation of this issue).

Weeks's approach takes these critical approaches to a place where he can re-think privacy as newly politicized in a move to intimate citizenship. Such an approach shifts our attention away from compelled choices between, on the one hand, privacy without rights and, on the other hand, rights without interference in our intimate lives. Despite the value of accounting for the socio-political influence of new sexual identities (and the differences among various sexual citizenships, see Evans, 1993), such a reorienting move from public deliberation to the shifts in more complex individual and private negotiations can leave out of consideration the changing sexual political landscape–and strategies of transgression vis-à-vis public policy and rights debate around citizenship. I claim that an opposition (however supersessional) of transgression and citizenship maintains and further contributes to this move.

7. Other ways to approach the issue are available in some recent scholarship that offers promising approaches to sexual citizenship, and further refines political ethics for lbgt/queer struggles (Bell, 1995; Sparks, 1997). Further connections, such as appeals to the market and consumer culture, have been explored for example by Cohen (1997).

REFERENCES

Bauman, Z. (1993). *Postmodern ethics.* Cambridge, MA: Blackwell.

Bell, D. (1995). Pleasure and danger: The paradoxical spaces of sexual citizenship. *Political Geography, 14*(2), 139-153.

Bell, D., & Binnie, J. (2000). *The sexual citizen: Queer politics and beyond.* Cambridge: Polity.

Benhabib, S. (1992). *Situating the self: Gender, community and postmodernism in contemporary ethics.* New York: Routledge.

Berlant, L. (1997). *The queen of America goes to Washington City: Essays on sex and citizenship.* Durham, NC: Duke University Press.

Bersani, L. (1995). *Homos.* Cambridge, MA: Harvard University Press.

Clarke, P. (1996). *Deep citizenship.* London: Pluto Press.

Cohen, P. (1997). 'All they needed': AIDS, consumption, and the politics of class. *Journal of the History of Sexuality, 8,* 86-115.

Dangerous Bedfellows. (Eds.). (1996). *Policing public sex: Queer politics and the future of AIDS activism.* Boston: South End Press.

Duggan, L., & Hunter, N. D. (1995). *Sex wars: Sexual dissent and political culture.* New York: Routledge.

Ellison, N. (1997). Toward a new social politics: Citizenship and reflexivity in late modernity. *Sociology, 31,* 697-717.

Evans, D. (1993). *Sexual citizenship: The material construction of sexualities.* London: Routledge.

Foucault, M. (1978). *The history of sexuality, vol. I: An introduction.* New York: Random House.

Fraser, N. (1997). *Justice interruptus: Critical reflections on the "postsocialist" condition.* New York: Routledge.

Gamson, J. (1997). Messages of exclusion. Gender, movements, and symbolic boundaries. *Gender & Society 11*(2). 178-199.

Giddens, A. (1992). *The transformation of intimacy.* Cambridge: Polity Press.

Jakobsen, J. R. (1999). *Working alliances and the politics of difference.* Bloomington, IN: Indiana University Press.

Jakobsen, J. R. (1998). Queer is? Queer does? Normativity and the problem of resistance. *GLQ, 4*(4), 551-536.

Jakobsen, J. R., & Pellegrini, A. (2003). *Love the sin: Sexual regulation and the limits of religious tolerance.* New York: New York University Press.

Laclau, E., & Mouffe, C. (1985). *Hegemony and socialist strategy: Towards a radical democratic politics.* London: Verso.

Patton, C., & Caserio, R. L. (2000). Introduction: Citizenship 2000. *Cultural Studies, 14*(1), 1-14.

Phelan, S. (2000). Queer liberalism? *The American Political Science Review, 94*(2), 431-442.

Phelan, S. (2001). *Sexual strangers: Gays, lesbians, and the dilemmas of citizenship.* Philadelphia: Temple University Press.

Povinelli, E. (2002). *The cunning of recognition. Indigenous alterities and the making of Australian multiculturalism.* Durham, NC: Duke University Press.

Rankin, P. (2000). Sexualities and national identities: Re-imagining queer nationalism. *Journal of Canadian Studies, 35*(2), 176-96.

Richardson, D. (2000). *Rethinking sexuality.* London: Sage.

Seidman, S. (1998). Are we all in the closet? Notes toward a sociological and cultural turn in queer theory. *European Journal of Cultural Studies, 1,* 177-192.

Seidman, S. (2001). From identity to queer politics: shifts in normative heterosexuality and the meaning of citizenship. *Citizenship Studies, 5*(3), 321-328.

Seidman, S. (2002). *Beyond the closet: The transformation of gay and lesbian life.* New York: Routledge.

Sparks, H. (1997). Dissident citizenship: Democratic theory, political courage, and activist women. *Hypatia, 12*, 74-110.

Stychin, C. (1998). *A Nation by rights: National cultures, sexual identity politics, and the discourse of rights.* Philadelphia: Temple University Press.

Squires, J. (Ed.). (1993). *Principled positions: Postmodernism and the rediscovery of value.* London: Lawrence and Wishart.

Sullivan, A. (1996). *Virtually normal: An argument about homosexuality.* London: Picador.

Warner, M. (1999). *The trouble with normal: Sex, politics, and the ethics of queer life.* New York: Free Press.

Wilson, E. (1993). Is transgression transgressive? In J. Bristow, & A. R. Wilson (Eds.), *Activating theory: Lesbian, gay, and bisexual politics* (pp. 107-117). London: Lawrence and Wishart.

Weeks, J. (1995). *Invented moralities: Sexual values in an age of uncertainty.* New York: Columbia University Press.

Weeks, J. (1998). The sexual citizen. *Theory, Culture, Society, 15*(3-4), 35–52.

doi:10.1300/J082v52n01_12

Ferment in LGBT Studies and Queer Theory: Personal Ruminations on Contested Terrain

R. Anthony Slagle, PhD

University of Puerto Rico, Río Piedras

SUMMARY. The tensions between queer and gay rights theorists, not surprisingly, have grown as queer theory has developed and matured. In this self-reflexive essay, the "contested terrain" between these distinct perspectives is explored, particularly within the discipline of communication studies. The assumptions of queer theory are summarized briefly, and the author takes an autoethnographic approach to demonstrate the constant interplay between lived experience and the basic assumptions of queer theory. The author challenges both LGBT theorists and queer

---

Some portions of this essay were presented at the conventions of the National Communication Association in November 2001 and November 2002.

The author wishes to thank John Elia, Karen Lovaas, and Gust Yep for their helpful insights and their willingness to listen to him go on *ad nauseam* about these issues. The author is indebted to Derick Grundyson who, although not academically trained, listens to his (often bizarre) lines of thought, and pushes him to think about issues in ways that he couldn't have without his help. The author also wishes to thank two anonymous reviewers for their insightful comments on the proposal for this essay.

Correspondence may be addressed: English Department, College of Humanities, University of Puerto Rico, P.O. Box 23356, San Juan, PR 00931- 3356.

[Haworth co-indexing entry note]: "Ferment in LGBT Studies and Queer Theory: Personal Ruminations on Contested Terrain." Slagle, R. Anthony. Co-published simultaneously in *Journal of Homosexuality* (Harrington Park Press, an imprint of The Haworth Press, Inc.) Vol. 52, No. 1/2, 2006, pp. 309-328; and: *LGBT Studies and Queer Theory: New Conflicts, Collaborations, and Contested Terrain* (ed: Karen E. Lovaas, John P. Elia, and Gust A. Yep) Harrington Park Press, an imprint of The Haworth Press, Inc., 2006, pp. 309-328. Single or multiple copies of this article are available for a fee from The Haworth Document Delivery Service [1-800-HAWORTH, 9:00 a.m. - 5:00 p.m. (EST). E-mail address: docdelivery@haworthpress.com].

theorists to always consider the implications of their theories and practices. doi:10.1300/J082v52n01_13 *[Article copies available for a fee from The Haworth Document Delivery Service: 1-800-HAWORTH. E-mail address: <docdelivery@haworthpress. com> Website: <http://www.HaworthPress.com> © 2006 by The Haworth Press, Inc. All rights reserved.]*

KEYWORDS. Queer theory, gay rights theory, assimilation, essentialism, heteronormativity, privacy, experience, autoethnography, personal ethnography

We have to be there at the *birth of ideas*, the bursting outward of their force: not in books expressing them, but in *events* manifesting this force, in *struggles* carried on around ideas, for or against them. Ideas do not rule the world. But it is because the world has ideas (and because it constantly produces them) that it is not passively ruled by those who are its leaders or those who would like *to teach it, once and for all, what it must think.* (Foucault as cited in Eribon, 1992, p. 282)

AN INVITATION AND A CONFESSION

This essay has been exceptionally difficult for me to write. As a queer theorist, I have prided myself on being a scholar who has never hesitated to push the envelope and to challenge traditional ways of thinking, yet I have really struggled with this piece. I believe, with all my heart, that queer theory poses significant epistemological and ontological challenges to both mainstream (heteronormative) and LGBT studies. That is, queer theory poses significant challenges to our understandings of how knowledge is acquired and how we understand the nature of reality. Consistent with these questions, although not often pursued by theorists, are alternative ways of writing, or, perhaps more appropriately, at times, *performing* queer theories. My writing here is decidedly non-normative and anti-canonical. I am sure that some will contend that it is "non academic" in the sense that I am not sufficiently "detached" from my subject. While I have long believed that the ways in which we think, conduct research, and come to understand the world in which we live–that is, our actions–are primarily a function of our experience–social, political, economic, cultural, etc., it has not always been easy for me to break free of the academic canon that values "objectivity" and "detachment" in research.

I am trying to just "let the words flow," without carefully choosing my every word with the realization that this is an "academic" essay, intended for an "academic" audience, that will be reviewed by academics. This is difficult for me because I can't help feeling like I've made some kind of "commitment" when particular words, sentences, and ideas appear on my computer monitor. I know that I run the risk of over-personalizing and over-internalizing my story. But, I also realize that queer theory demands new ways of looking at the world, creative ways of presenting information, and the recognition that our ways of knowing about the world in which we live come from many points of our history and experience. So, I am simply trying to say, "fuck it," and write this story, personal though it may be, because these experiences have helped to shape the particular ways in which I work and think as a theorist.

In this essay, I explore the tensions–the contested terrain–between LGBT studies and queer theory, specifically in the field of communication studies. Even though the characters and scenarios are obviously different, I know that the tensions in other disciplines are similar. As I was thinking about this essay, I realized that the best way for me to explore these tensions was to reflect on my experiences in my own field.

To be sure, writing an essay that is highly self-reflexive is risky business for many reasons. First, as I have already mentioned, the essay is likely to be criticized for being "non academic." That problem is the one that poses the least concern for me personally. I recognize that those who will disagree with the stylistic choices I have made in terms of writing are the same people who will likely disagree with me on a theoretical level as well. I can live with that. Second, I realize that referring to actual events that have occurred over the last several years might not be the best thing for my popularity. I have wavered back on forth on this particular issue, but I ultimately find myself returning to the fact that these issues are simply too important to be left unsaid, and I am really only responding to criticism that was leveled at me, directly or indirectly. Besides, my point is not to "sling mud," but to demonstrate the tensions that exist, and to advance queer theory by theorizing these experiences. Third, and perhaps most importantly, I realize that putting myself at the center of the essay is likely to be viewed as self indulgent. I hope that isn't the case. By centering myself in this essay, I have strived, as Middleton (1996) points out, to do better theorizing "by making visible to the reader the processes which are hidden beneath the mask of disembodied uninvolvement which traditional accounts have required"

(p. 14). To the extent that my personal experience seems to be directly related to queer theory, and to the contested terrain between LGBT and queer scholars, bringing in the personal voice seems particularly appropriate at this point in history. The best theories, after all, directly bear on the "real world." Finally, by writing from this particular subject position, I run the risk of self-disclosing more about myself than I should. I'm not likely to do that simply because there are aspects of my life, like anyone else's, that are intensely personal and it shouldn't be too difficult to refrain from committing these things to paper. This is not to say that I fail recognize the potential risks involved with disclosing my experiences, thoughts, and feelings.

Roughly twenty years ago, the *Journal of Communication* (1983), published a special issue entitled, "Ferment in the Field" which described the current state of affairs in communication studies. I have to confess that I have always been somewhat confused when I have seen the word *ferment* used in the context of research. As a noun, *The Oxford American Desk Dictionary and Thesaurus* defines the noun *ferment* as "agitation; excitement; tumult" (Jewell, 2001, p. 293). However, the definition of the verb is also instructive: "[to] leaven, brew; stir up, simmer, seethe; bubble, foam, froth; boil; agitate, inflame, rouse; foment, insight, instigate" (Jewell, 2001, p. 293). However, I can't get out of my mind the idea that something that has fermented has "spoiled," or "gone bad," like a fruit juice that has been in the refrigerator for too long. I believe that all of these definitions bear on the tensions between LGBT studies and queer theories. There is no doubt that "agitation," "excitement," and "tumult" are fitting adjectives to describe the tensions between LGBT studies and queer theory. The verbs also seem to accurately describe what has been happening, not only in my field, but in other fields as well. Sadly, though, the fact that these issues have "spoiled" or "gone bad" is also true as I hope to demonstrate in this essay. This isn't to say that I am going to "throw out" (as I would with the juice) or abandon my project–I wouldn't be writing this essay if that were the case. Instead, by pointing out the very real ways in which the "contested terrain" has played out, I can only hope that, while gay rights and queer theorists might disagree with one another, we can find a place where our discourses about one another can be more civil and open- minded.

In both my academic and personal lives, I have always wanted to make a difference. I don't think that's particularly unusual among academics, at least not among those I know. We all hope that we will one day our work will be able to "change the world," even if only ever so slightly. The funny thing is that, although we all hope to change the world, every academic I know also spends a lot of time questioning her/himself. We are all waiting for the day, and we are sure that it is coming, when someone is going to "figure out" that we are a bunch of frauds–that we've been faking it all along, that we're not "smart enough," and that somehow we all got through graduate programs and found jobs. It's a tenuous line that we walk, and the intrapersonal conversations and arguments are intense, disturbing, and difficult to reflect upon for any length of time.

QUEER THEORY MEETS COMMUNICATION STUDIES

In 1995, while a doctoral student, I wrote an article on queer theory in communication (Slagle, 1995). When I wrote this article, I was deeply concerned about a number of issues. These issues ranged from questions about methodologies and questions about privilege in our research designs, to fundamental questions about a gay[1] rights movement that has primarily represented the concerns of a rather select group of mostly white, mostly wealthy, mostly gay men at the expense of other members of our communities.[2] This is a group that one of my queer activist friends refers to as the "A-Gays."

In that initial article, as well as elsewhere, I laid out a number of queer challenges to both mainstream (heteronormative) theory and gay rights theory. I certainly don't claim to be the first person to write about these issues; queer theorists in other fields have done so beautifully. Neither do I claim to be the first to write about issues of sexual identity in communication; again, other scholars in my own field have been writing about these issues since not long after I was born.[3] My article, however, was the first to propose queer theory as a potential way out of some of the problems that I believed were inherent in gay and lesbian studies in communication. Because I have written about these challenges elsewhere I am providing only a brief summary of these challenges here.

Queer theorists challenge the notion of *heteronormativity*. This challenge is made against the assumption that heterosexuality is the only "normal" or "valid" sexual identity. As problematic as I believe traditional identity political theory to be in general, and gay rights theory in particular, this challenge applies primarily to "mainstream" theories. In this essay, since my focus is the contested terrain between "traditional" LGBT studies and queer theory, I don't focus much on this particular issue.[4] However, the other three challenges apply directly to gay rights theory.

Specifically, queer theorists challenge the assumptions that (1) the purpose of activism is the *assimilation* of LGBT people into an otherwise unchanged mainstream, (2) that LGBT people share an *essential* identity, and (3) that sexuality is ultimately a privacy issue that bears little relevance to public life. I discuss these issues, or tensions, in greater detail below. In addition, queer theory challenges the notion of hierarchy–the idea that one difference is any better than any other difference. I also believe that queer theory is activist oriented, or at least it should be. I am personally concerned that, as academics, we spend far too much of our time pontificating from the comfort of the ivory tower, writing in language that only a few of us can even understand, and we spend far too little time producing work that is useful in effecting any real change. I wish that there was more effort to draw connections between theory and praxis.

When I published that article in 1995, I remember being particularly nervous about how these issues would be perceived in my discipline. I knew that as a Ph.D. candidate, I would eventually need to find a job, and I had fears that my "extremist" views might hinder that process. Whereas a publication would normally be perceived as a positive indication of future productivity, I was concerned that this particular publication would be viewed, instead, as an indication of future trouble making. It didn't take me long to realize that my nervousness was justified, although the criticism has come from a much different source than I had anticipated. I thoroughly expected members of what I viewed as the "mainstream," who were determined to maintain the status quo, to be either loudly critical of the position that I was advancing, or worse to remain silent on the issue thereby symbolically denying what I had said. On the other hand, I expected LGBT scholars to embrace this approach because it presents some solutions to the problems that are inherent in the gay rights model. I thought that these problems were obvious, and yet what I perceived as "problematic" were, indeed, ideals embraced by many of my colleagues in LGBT studies. I was naïve.

THE INTERPLAY OF THEORY AND LIVED EXPERIENCE

A Disclaimer

One of the risks that I take in writing a highly reflexive essay, is that my memory of events may not be completely reliable. Human beings in general, I believe, have a tendency to see events as more significant, or more dramatic, than they really are, particularly those events that are extremely positive or extremely negative. I am not an exception to that; I am not immune to bouts of "drama queendom." In cases where I have been concerned that my perception of events might have been inaccurate, I have "checked" my perception with others who were present. Even with this in mind, I am, by no means, claiming an objective subject position. The perception checks were helpful in confirming things that were said, but I own my personal interpretations and responses. These were critical turning points in my professional life, as a queer theorist, that have shaped not only my beliefs as a queer scholar, but my career as an academic in general. Unlike a traditional essay, I cannot, or will not, dismiss my personal experiences as significant periods of learning. I agree with Sams (1994) who argues that

> [t]o doubt the wisdom of one's own experience is to reduce the rivers of life to an arid desert. To give away the validity and authority of personal experience by deferring to a self-proclaimed expert, is to dehydrate the flows of creation that naturally course through all people who honor their personal feelings and truth. (p. 47)

A Former "Role Model" Attacks

The criticisms that have been leveled at queer theory in general have been received loud and clear. Indeed, it has been hard to miss them. I have attended the National Communication Association (NCA) convention every year since I started graduate school. I have been asked on several occasions over the last decade to participate in discussions of "future directions" in gay/lesbian/bisexual/transgender/queer/and so on research in the discipline of communication. I remember one of those panels as clearly as if it happened yesterday, even though it was several years ago. On the panel were some of the biggest names not only in gay and lesbian studies, but in communication studies in general. I was also aware that, present in the audience, were members of the search committee for a job for which I had applied. I was nervous about this particular presentation because I was, at this point, well aware of the feelings of some of the panelists when it comes to queer theory. I walked into the room, which later filled with an audience that overflowed the seating capacity of the small conference room. I sat down behind the long table at the front of the room, and struck up a friendly conversation with a good friend, colleague, and ally who was chairing the session. Since not all of the panelists had arrived, the seat to my left was empty. Just as the session was about to begin, the final panelist walked into the room and took a seat in the front row of the audience, rather than taking the open seat next to me. I've known this particular man for years, and although I knew him to be a critic of my work, I understand the importance of being polite in professional settings:

"You can sit here if you like. I won't bite . . . unless you want me to," I teased. Humor is, I guess, one of my defenses that kicks in when I am under stress.

"I'm actually more concerned that you might hit me," he replied as he reluctantly moved to the open chair. Apparently, he wasn't amused by my attempt to relieve the tension.

The moderator decided that we would proceed alphabetically by last name. Since my last name is toward the end of alphabet, this meant that I would present last, but it certainly didn't mean that I would have the last word.

Most of the session was tame and, frankly, self-congratulatory. "We've come such a long way." "The quality of our work has really improved." "Studies about gay and lesbian communication are being published with greater frequency than ever before." What I remember most clearly about this particular session were the comments made by the first presenter (the man who didn't want to sit next to me), my mixed emotions while I waited my turn, and my presentation at the end. We were like unmatched bookends.

"Queer theory will mark the death of gay and lesbian studies," divined this scholar who, incidentally, had published a fair number of articles on the gay liberation/rights movement. He went on to say that "young people engaged in this line of research not only don't deserve to be granted tenure, but they probably don't deserve jobs in the first place." Let me add that not only was I actively seeking a permanent job at the time, but this man was the chair of a search committee in a department where I had applied.

While I am perfectly willing to accept criticism on the merits of research and rational argument, it was difficult to stomach criticism that was clearly mean-spirited, intellectually vacuous, and, undeniably, personal. The fact that this criticism was leveled at queer theorists in general, and at me in particular, by a scholar well-known in rhetorical studies, seemed particularly ironic. I would have expected that a scholar of rhetoric would be familiar with the basic fallacies of argument, and that he would realize that attacking me personally did not strengthen his position. Rather than confronting the substance of the arguments that queer theorists have made, he was more interested in developing his case against queer theory by making *ad hominem* attacks. Upon returning home, I should have withdrawn my application from the search he was chairing, but I did not. I wasn't invited for an interview.

My own comments, which had been prepared in advance, were fairly conciliatory given what had been said earlier in the session. In some social contexts, I am prone to saying things without carefully thinking them through. I was careful, though, in this professional context not to give a "knee jerk" reaction to the personal attack. I attempted, instead, to recognize the contributions of LGBT studies scholars that had made it possible for queer theorists to do the research that we do. I emphasized, however, that we need to be critically self-reflexive about the implications of the gay rights approach. I also commented that I believed that there was plenty of room in our discipline for a wide range of perspectives on these issues.

One of my favorite films is *Broadcast News*. In the film, Jane, a news producer, is arguing with one of her supervisors, Paul, about an editorial decision that has to be made. She tells him that he is wrong, and he responds: "You're just absolutely right, and I'm absolutely wrong. It must be nice to always believe that you know better, to always think you're the smartest person in the room." Jane replies, "No, it's awful" (Brooks, 1987). While I find this dialogue amusing, it reminds me of this colleague–he appears to believe that he is the smartest person in the room, and that because he has been around for a long time he, therefore, knows what is best for all of us. The difference is that he doesn't seem to think it's awful at all.

Although this criticism was painful at the time, and still bothers me today, I bring this up not to relive a difficult moment in my life rather, because it draws the theoretical tensions between LGBT studies and queer theory clearly into view. While the gay rights theorists and activists have sought equal protection for gay men and lesbians in the workplace and other areas, the reality is that this has worked well for individuals who are not too deviant, not too radical, and not too open about their relationships. In other words, this strategy has worked well for those who are willing (or able) to *assimilate* into the mainstream. When this individual argued that queer theorists should be denied a livelihood, while he probably did not intend to make such a profound theoretical statement, he made it perfectly clear that (great) difference is not something that should be valued or rewarded. Gay rights theorists strive to make sexual identity something that ultimately should not be a major factor in determining who is allowed to participate in society.[5] In some ways, this sounds appealing, but the risk of such an approach is that queer identities completely vanish from public life. Furthermore, this approach has really only been successful for those who do not deviate too far from the heteronormative mainstream to begin with. Queer theorists argue that sexuality is significant in *all* aspects of our life, and that difference (sexual or otherwise) should be celebrated, encouraged, and welcomed. In other words, for queers the purpose of challenging an oppressive political and social structure is not to simply be granted the right to participate in the system.[6]

Moreover, this criticism draws another of the tensions between LGBT studies and queer theory into clear view–the challenge of *essentialism*. Queer theorists reject any approaches to the construction of identities from a universal perspective. Queer theorists argue that individual identities and differences are constantly being (re)constructed, that identities are not stable, and that identity categories are, therefore, a myth. Indeed, queer theory argues for what Seidman (1993) refers to as a "postidentity politic" (p. 111), or what I have called a "politics of difference" (Slagle, 1995). My interpretation of the comments was that those of us who refuse to conform to this scholar's view of what it means to be gay, don't deserve a place at the table. In other words, some of us "young scholars"[7] are too deviant and too radical to be of any use–in fact, we are perceived as a threat to the advances that have been made in the past.

Because this person's criticism of queer theory was primarily a criticism of the rhetorical strategies employed by queer activists, the issue of privacy is also at stake. He was concerned that queer theorists, because we necessarily bring queer differences into plain view, would so enrage the heteronormative sensibilities of the mainstream, that the dubious gains that have been made in gay rights (that have really benefit only a select few), would be in jeopardy. Apparently, queers are too public about our issues; or, perhaps, we are public about them in ways in which the more "traditional" among us can't, or won't, accept.

Another concern of queer theory and activism relates to issues of power and the hierarchies within particular systems. Although clearly idealistic, because hierarchies will always exist, queer theorists and activists are interested in dismantling hierarchies as much as possible. In other words, queers are interested in a world in which particular differences (we *all* have them) are not inherently valued over other differences. I can't help but think that when this criticism, couched in "intellectual" language, was leveled at queer theorists in general, and at me in particular, that the critic was fundamentally concerned about losing his particular status as one of the "top dogs" in LGBT studies. A bright, well educated, generation of theorists has arrived on the scene.

Some Job "Advice"

Several years before this particularly contentious conference session, I was involved in a pre-conference session at the NCA convention that brought together members of the various caucuses. Our goal for the session was to work on strategies for giving greater voice to issues of diversity within our discipline. I remember one graduate student, a member of the Women's Caucus, who asked what we can do as scholars to encourage our graduate students–future members of the professoriate–to engage in more research that is aimed at issues of diversity. In a particularly skeptical moment, and perhaps willing to take the role of devil's advocate, I replied that perhaps we should not be so quick to encourage our students to follow such a path because being perceived as "nonconformist" or "activist" might make it more challenging for our students to find positions–particularly in a time when the ratio of Ph.D.s being earned far exceeds the actual number of open positions on a yearly basis. I was immediately questioned about my comment. I explained that, at the risk of tooting my own horn, I had done everything that I *thought* I would have to in order to find a permanent position. I had published an article in a respected journal in my field, I had two book chapters in press (not related to queer theory), I had actively participated in conferences every year by presenting my work, and I had taken on a position of leadership in the national association by co-chairing the Caucus on Gay and Lesbian Concerns.

Another scholar responded to my comments in a way that both surprised me and bothered me. "Well, Tony, no communication program is interested in hiring someone who only specializes in gay and lesbian studies." This comment particularly was stinging given that my training is in rhetorical theory generally, and that my research agenda is, in fact, no more specialized than anyone else's in the discipline. It seems to me that most scholars are broadly trained, and yet they choose a clearly defined line of research to pursue. Interestingly, although this particular comment was painful to hear, it supported the argument that I had made in the first place. From a pragmatic standpoint, at least in my field, perhaps only the permanently employed or even the tenured and fully promoted can afford the risk of pushing the envelope when it comes to sensitive issues. And issues of sexuality are, if nothing else, sensitive issues in U.S. cultures.

This incident was interesting to me, in part because the criticism was coming from a scholar with a strong commitment to issues of diversity as evidenced not only by his activism within the NCA, but also by his active (and, I might add, "specialized") research agenda. Because of his own history, I can't be sure if he was being critical of my approach personally, or if he was making an observation about our discipline that has not had a strong record when it comes to bringing issues of sexuality into the fold.

Regardless of his intentions, I took away from this the idea that I had not sufficiently positioned myself as a scholar with a broad training/understanding of rhetorical theory. In other words, I have not done an adequate job of *assimilating* into the mainstream of the discipline. I should add that my "generalist" background was evident from my curriculum vita which not only described my coursework, but also the very traditional (read: not queer) courses that I had taught (e.g., public speaking, argumentation, rhetorical criticism, etc.).[8] Apparently, I was perceived by this particular critic as being too "in your face" about my personal (and political) research agenda; I wasn't being "private" enough about issues that challenge the system and my research, obviously, makes some people very uncomfortable. Queer theorists reject the notion that sexuality is something that must be kept private. Sexuality, like any other individual characteristic of identity (and identity is *always* individual), plays a significant role in shaping our understandings of the world and our interactions with others. Implicit in this assumption is the idea that sexuality is far more than sexual behavior–what we do to/with each other in the bedroom (or other places). Though I have never been particularly interested in discussing my sex life with students, colleagues, or friends, I refuse to hide the fact that I am attracted to men in general, and that I am in a committed relationship with one man, in particular. These aspects of my life affect every other aspect of my life, and the expectation that I should keep this private is, without a doubt, restrictive and oppressive.[9]

Incidentally, I didn't follow this "advice," although doing so might have made my life easier, at least at the time. I have done the work that I wanted to do, that I felt passionate about, that moved and excited me. I did this because I really believed, and I continue to believe, that the best research is research that we care deeply about. If I didn't care about what I was doing, I would have pursued a career that involved choices that are less risky. I've never been one to shy away from pushing a few buttons, particularly when I feel passionately about something, and I continue(d) to push. I can only hope that by doing so, I have cleared the road a bit for others who will follow.

Where Have All The Women Gone? (with Apologies to Pete Seeger)

One of the ongoing problems that has been faced by LGBTQ scholars in the NCA has been the absence of women in our interest groups. The Caucus on Gay and Lesbian Concerns as well as the Gay/Lesbian/Bisexual/Transgender Communication Studies Division have a tradition that has made this virtually impossible to miss. Although it is not written into the by-laws of either group, the tradition is to alternate elections of officers by sex. This practice is intended to make certain that the groups are as inclusive as possible. The difficulty that both groups have faced has been finding women who are willing to take on positions of leadership. In fact, the primary reason that this has been a problem is that there are very few women who attend the business meetings of either group. When this issue has been raised, as it is from time to time (but not often enough), the assumption has been that the "absent" women are focusing their attentions on the academic and activist agendas of the Women's Caucus and the Feminist and Women's Studies Division of the association, and the discussion is often left at that. I can't help wonder why we have not done a better job making women feel included in the rooms where we discuss issues of sexuality. Why is there such a division, a fracture, between issues of sexuality and gender in our discipline?

There are two particular issues that I believe are evidence of the fact that we have done a horrendous job creating a climate that is welcoming to those who feel marginalized within our interest groups. First, despite several efforts to change this, to this day the caucus still includes only gay men and lesbians in the name. Second, in the eight years that the caucus has presented the Randy Majors Memorial award, designed to honor a person who has made outstanding contributions to LGBT issues in our discipline, the award has, only once, been given to a woman.

A variety of arguments have been made against changing the name, perhaps the most dubious has been invoking the argument of "tradition" (i.e., "this has always been the name and to change it would be an insult to the founders of the caucus."). I can't help but think that the real issue is that some members aren't really interested in changing the "boy's club" nature of our group. Another argument, while still problematic, makes more sense to me as a rhetorical strategy. "If we change the name to the Gay/Lesbian/Bisexual/Transgender/Queer Caucus," one of the most recent proposals, "we will so offend people in the mainstream that it will be impossible to achieve anything politically." There is a significant need for us, according to opponents of the name change, to delineate a "clearly defined constituency" represented by the caucus, and we need to do whatever we can to "fit in" (read: assimilate) within the structure of the association. Of course, by clearly defining a "constituency," we have made it abundantly clear that there are others who are not included. Each time this issue is raised, the membership votes, and the proposal fails.[10] I personally find the essential categories to be highly problematic, but I also recognize the very pragmatic issue of working within, and simultaneously against, the current political structure, or, as Butler (1991) points out, "there remains a political imperative to use these necessary errors or category mistakes . . . to rally and represent an oppressed political constituency" (p. 16).[11] We must, nevertheless, make a stronger effort to include those who feel excluded by the very symbolic act of naming.

New (Not Improved) Uses of Queer

A few years ago, I arrived at the national convention the night before the beginning of the "official" conference. That particular day had been devoted to preconference sessions and seminars on specific topics. I was looking forward to this particular conference because, for the first time in my career, I was employed in a permanent, tenure-track position. I would not have to spend the conference attempting to impress potential employers. Upon entering the hotel lobby, I ran into a friend who invited me to dinner with the group he had spent the day with in one of the seminars. Anxious to catch up with this friend, I accepted the invitation although I was to spend the next several hours with my mind reeling about the latest trend in gay and lesbian studies. As I looked around the table at a rather upscale restaurant, I looked at some of the most traditional scholars in LGBT studies that I know. Noticeably absent from this group, who had participated in the "by invitation only" seminar to plan a book on "queer" rhetoric, were any of the people I know who "do" queer theory in the discipline. It seems that while many scholars in LGBT studies are less than happy about the emergence of queer theory, they have become less hesitant to use the term themselves. In an odd, yet equally brilliant, rhetorical move, many scholars are now beginning to produce work and labeling it "queer," when the reality is that this work has nothing to do with queer theory, and is consistent with the traditional assimilationist approach that queer theorists have been criticizing all along. If queer theorists and activists have "taken back" the term *queer* from the "hetero swine" (Patton, 1993), the assimilationists are now, with increasing frequency, claiming the word for themselves, re-defining it again, and using it to advance their own agendas. Specifically, I am concerned about the increased use of the label to refer to work that adds sexual identity to the mix, but while it may challenge notions of heteronormativity, isn't consistent with the other significant challenges raised by queer theorists, particularly the challenges of *assimilation* and *essentialism*.

For some of these scholars, particularly the relatively "new" academics (i.e., graduate students), this is probably unintentional. I have a hunch that many young scholars are using the term *queer* to label their work, and they aren't really familiar with the debates and tensions between two distinct schools of thought. In this case, the use of the term is "trendy" and "cool" (not to mention the fact that the term is far less cumbersome than using the always growing list of initials used to describe assimilation studies). However, for some of these scholars I contend that they know *exactly* what they're doing–take the word back (again), re-define it (again), and use it to describe more traditional, and more importantly (in their view), "acceptable" work. They realize that *queer* isn't going away, so they are now using it for their own purposes. The result, of course, is that if they are successful, queer theory will lose much of its critical force in the process.

POSTSCRIPT

I can't resist the temptation to reflect back on what has happened during my relatively brief academic life from the perspective of where I now stand. After finishing my Ph.D. in 1998, I was hired by St. Cloud State University in central Minnesota. My "temporary" visiting position in Minnesota, that lasted over three years, was beginning to feel permanent. In Minnesota, while I had many friends and I very much enjoyed working with my colleagues there, I was frustrated by living in small town with little diversity of any kind, but I had begun the process of building a life there.[12]

I had just signed a contract with St. Cloud State for another year when I was offered a tenure track position in the most unlikely of places–San Juan, Puerto Rico. Although I had signed a contract already for one more year at St. Cloud State, the members of my department and my dean understood the importance of me finding a permanent job. I will be forever grateful to the university for allowing me to renege on my contract. The position I now hold at the University of Puerto Rico is a faculty line teaching communication and rhetorical studies, although it is within the Department of English. The irony of finding employment in an English department does not escape me, nor does it particularly surprise me. The discipline of English has a much better record when it comes to queer issues than does my own field. My research agenda has never been questioned in my new department; in fact, it has been encouraged. For example, I have been encouraged to propose a new graduate courses for students in literature and linguistics entitled "Gender and Sexuality Discourses" and "Queer Theories and Film." In addition, I have proposed an undergraduate course entitled "Queer Sexualities in Film." With the exception of a handful of forward thinking communication programs, I can't imagine that courses of this nature would be embraced in my own discipline. In a very real sense, I can't imagine a more comfortable situation.

On the other hand, I am one of only three communication professors in a department of about thirty faculty. The majority of my colleagues specialize in literature, and they are closely followed in number by linguists. So, in some ways, I am more marginalized than ever before and I have been, at times, put in the position of defending communication studies. Nevertheless, I have worked hard to draw links between my own interests and those of the other areas of my department. Recently, one of my colleagues remarked that I have become one of the "gender experts" in the department.

Aside from the potential of being marginalized in my work life because my academic training is distinct from most of my colleagues, living in Puerto Rico couldn't possibly be more different than living in central Minnesota. As a non-Spanish speaking *gringo*[13] living in Puerto Rico, I have certainly had experiences that help me to better understand what it means to be "different." I am also a queer-identified man, living with a partner, in a culture that can be less than hospitable to non-normative relationships. I realize that I run the risk of sounding like I am complaining about my cultural position–nothing could be further from the truth. First, I realize that the choice to move to Puerto Rico was mine and I viewed it then, as I do now, as a learning opportunity that was simply too attractive to pass up.[14] Second, I believe that in my cultural position(s), I have learned more about being queer and the implications of queer theory than years of reading, writing, and talking about it has ever taught me. I am in a position where I am, in many ways, more queer than ever before; or, at least, my queer status is more apparent. If *queer* is about difference from the mainstream, I have certainly realized, from my own lived experience, that queer potentially extends far beyond sexual differences into other differences in location.

As I was working on this essay, my partner asked: "How queer are you really?" This is a question that I have struggled with, at least internally, for quite some time. I recognize the many ways in which my life is not queer at all. I have been in a committed relationship with one person for over four years, we have a joint checking account, we have taken the necessary legal steps that we can to protect one another in case of emergencies, and I make a respectable salary by Puerto Rico standards. In many ways, I can be accused of the assimilationist strategy of which I have been so critical. I do not deny that I have benefited directly from gay rights theory and activism, although I have opposed these approaches and will continue to do so. Instead, I will continue to think critically, and voice my concerns, about the implications of such an approach for those who continue to feel outside of the gay rights movement. I have never fought for such dubious goals as gay marriage or gays in the military which are all about assimilating seamlessly into a largely unchanged, heteronormative, mainstream; what seems to be ignored is the fact that for many of us we can't easily fit in among such an unchanged system because the essential categories used to describe us are simply not accurate. Furthermore, many of us are simply not interested in merely being "tolerated" by the heteronormative mainstream; instead, we are interested in radical social changes in the ways that difference is perceived. For me, the real question is an ethical one: how can we continue to fight for simple inclusion and ask to be simply tolerated when the costs are so high for so many? Queer theory, while perhaps not the panacea that we all hope for, is our best chance to overcome the problems that currently ail us.

NOTES

1. The omission of the word *lesbian* here is intentional. Likewise, other groups have been intentionally omitted here as well–*bisexual, transgender,* etc. While the gay rights theorists and activists have tried to be more inclusive in recent years, the primary action has been to add more "letters" to the name (e.g., "LG," "LGB," "LGBT," etc.). The interesting thing to me here is that while the names may have changed, the theory has not. Let's call it what it is rather than continually adding to the alphabet soup in an effort to appear inclusive. Ultimately, these theories cannot be truly inclusive without adopting, at least to some degree, the ideas put forward by queer theorists.

2. I have referred to this movement elsewhere as the "liberation" movement, but this is really not an accurate term. In one article, I argued that the liberation movement, at some point changed from a movement that sought freedom from the constraints of a heteronormative system, but that the movement mutated later into one that focused on social assimilation as a primary goal (Slagle, 1995). This new movement, which I am

now calling the "gay rights movement," appealed primarily to (white) gay men, although there were some lesbians involved. This movement has been called different things by different theorists: *liberalism* (Ball, 2001; Sullivan, 1995; West, 1998), *ethnic nationalist/ethnic* models in which (primarily) "gay men represented themselves as an ethnic group oriented toward assimilation" (Seidman, 1993, p. 117; cf. Epstein, 1987; Seidman, 1995), or simply *assimilationist* (Seidman, 1993; Seidman, 1995; Warner, 1993). Whatever one chooses to call the changed liberation movement, the goal is equal rights and social assimilation. I regret that I haven't been clearer about this terminology in the past, and I hope that the "new" terminology is more clear.

3. I mention this in defense of a comment made about me at the 1995 Speech Communication Association (now the National Communication Association) convention in San Antonio. In a presentation celebrating the anniversary of the Caucus on Gay and Lesbian Concerns of the association, one presenter argued: "Gay and lesbian studies in communication have been around long before queer theory was an apple in Tony Slagle's eye. In fact, gay and lesbian studies in communication have been around long before Tony Slagle was an apple in his mother's eye."

4. For a more detailed discussion of *heteronormativity*, see Seidman (1993), Slagle (1995), Slagle (2003), Warner (1993), and Yep (2003).

5. Gay rights theorists have pointed to the ways that gay men, lesbians, and, supposedly, bisexuals can fit in neatly among the mainstream. Queer theorists reject the notion that the goal of theory and activism is for queer people to assimilate seamlessly into a relatively unchanged "mainstream." Gay rights theorists and activists have argued that gay men (and lesbians, and bisexuals) are essentially no different from heterosexuals except for the erotic activities in which we engage. To put this in Andrew Sullivan's (1995) terms, gay men and lesbians are "virtually normal." Queer theorists and activists, on the other hand, aim to challenge and destroy traditional notions of what it means to be "normal."

6. Don't misunderstand me. Many of us are interested in the same "special rights" granted to non-queers, but we are not interested in giving up our individual identities in the process.

7. My "youth" (which is quickly fading) seems to be an on-going concern for this particular scholar. This was the same scholar who, just a few years earlier, made the comment that he and gay and lesbian studies had "been around" long before me (see Note 3).

8. It's also hard to miss the irony of the comment. If no communication program offers such a specialization, under the assumption that this was my only training, how in the world did I get through my coursework? I didn't, after all, attend Queer U.

9. Ironically, this "insistence" on privacy really only applies to non-heteronormative relationships. For those in heteronormative relationships, there is little thought about public displays of affection, placing pictures of spouses on one's desk, or the announcement of engagements or marriages in the newspaper.

10. Because the bylaws of the caucus require that any amendment–which would include a name change–must be submitted in writing no later than fifteen days before the annual business meeting, when a proposal fails, the discussion is over for another year. While the bylaws might be overlooked when it comes to other issues, rest assured that those opposed to changing the name (in any form) are quick to point out this parliamentary rule.

11. I also agree with Butler (1991) when she argues that we must be very cautious about our use of "strategic essentialism":

[I]dentity categories tend to be instruments of regulatory regimes, whether as the normalizing categories of oppressive structures or as the rallying points for a liberatory contestation of that very oppression. This is not to say that I won't appear at political occasions under the sign of lesbian, but I would like to have it permanently unclear what precisely that sign signifies. (p. 13-14)

12. Others living in St. Cloud with concerns about issues of diversity in general used to disparagingly refer to the town as "White Cloud." I was often frustrated in my courses trying to convince students of the importance of thinking about what it means to live in a multicultural world when I was looking at a sea of white faces.

13. The term *gringo/a* is often used to describe a foreigner in Latin America. Most definitions of *gringo* contend that the word is intended as an insult. My experience, however, is that gringo is not necessarily derogatory. I have found the word is particularly common in describing persons from the 50 states living in Puerto Rico. The word "American" is not an appropriate moniker, although it commonly used by people from the U.S. to describe their national identity, because anyone living in North, Central, or South America, as well as parts of the Caribbean, are indeed "Americans." *Estadounidense*, which doesn't have a direct translation in English (roughly "United Statesian") is another possibility, but doesn't really distinguish Puerto Ricans from persons originally from the 50 states; Puerto Rico is a U.S. Commonwealth, and Puerto Ricans are, after all, U.S. citizens.

14. O.K., I have a confession. There was also something undeniably attractive about living on a tropical island where the average temperature *every* month is 85 degrees. Seasonal Affective Disorder has not been an issue for me since I moved to San Juan.

REFERENCES

Ball, C. A. (2001). Essentialism and universalism in gay rights philosophy: Liberalism meets queer theory. *Law and Social Inquiry, 26*, 271-294.

Brooks, J. L. (Producer/Director). (1987). *Broadcast news* [Motion picture]. United States: Twentieth Century Fox.

Butler, J. (1991). Imitation and gender insubordination. In D. Fuss (Ed.), *Inside/out: Lesbian theories, gay theories* (pp. 13-31). New York: Routledge.

Epstein, S. (1987). Gay politics/ethnic identity: The limits of social constructionism. *Socialist Review, 17*(3/4), 9-54.

Eribon, D. (1992). *Michel Foucault* (B. Wing, Trans.). Cambridge, MA: Harvard University Press.

Jewell, E. J. (Managing Ed.). (2001). *The Oxford American desk dictionary and the-saurus* (2nd ed.). New York: Berkeley Books.

Middleton, S. (1996). Doing qualitative educational research in the mid-1990s: Issues, contexts and practicalities. *Waikato Journal of Education, 2*, 1-18.

Patton, C. (1993). Tremble, hetero swine! In M. Warner (Ed.), *Fear of a queer planet: Queer politics and social theory* (pp. 143-177). Minneapolis, MN: University of Minnesota Press.

Sams, J. (1994). *Earth medicine: Ancestors' ways of harmony for many moons*. San Francisco: Harper.

Seidman, S. (1993). Identity and politics in a "postmodern" gay culture: Some historical and conceptual notes. In M. Warner (Ed.), *Fear of a queer planet: Queer politics
and social theory* (pp. 105-142). Minneapolis, MN: University of Minnesota Press.

Seidman, S. (1995). Deconstructing queer theory or the under-theorization of the social
and the ethical. In L. Nicholson & S. Seidman (Eds.), *Social postmodernism: Beyond identity politics* (pp. 116-141). New York: Oxford University Press.

Slagle, R. A. (1995). In defense of Queer Nation: From identity politics to a politics of
difference. *Western Journal of Communication, 59,* 85-102.

Slagle, R. A. (2003). Queer criticism and sexual normativity: The case of Pee-wee
Herman. *Journal of Homosexuality, 45* (2/3/4), 129-146.

Sullivan, A. (1995). *Virtually normal: An argument about homosexuality.* New York:
Alfred A. Knopf.

Warner, M. (1993). Introduction. In M. Warner (Ed.), *Fear of a queer planet: Queer
politics and social theory* (pp. vii-xxxi). Minneapolis, MN: University of Minnesota
Press.

West, R. (1998). Universalism, liberal theory, and the problem of gay marriage.
Florida State Law Review, 25, 705-730.

Yep, G. A. (2003). The violence of heteronormativity in communication studies: Notes
on injury, healing, and queer world-making. *Journal of Homosexuality, 45* (2/3/4),
1-60.

doi:10.1300/J082v52n01_13

Index

A Gay Synagogue in New York, 84
AAR. See American Academy of
        Religion (AAR)
Abelove, H., 24,263
Abu-Lughod, L., 191
Ace of Spades, 197,205
Affirmation, 74
"A-Gays," 313
AIDS epidemic, 62
Ailen, L.S., 37,38
"All man Friday," 194
Alpert, R., 88
Althaus-Reid, M., 91
Altman, D., 244
"Always historicize!," 151
American Academy of Religion
        (AAR), 87,94
American Historical Association, 186
Amoroso, D.M., 52
Analysis of a Phobia in a
        Five-Year-Old Boy, 219
Anderson, M., 120
Andrews, C., 206
Angelides, S., 10,125,165,175-177
Anti-homosexual attitudes
    social constructionism and, 48-50
    social psychology of, queer theory
        and, 47-71
Anti-homosexual prejudice, 47-71
    defined, 47
    measuring of
        gay liberation and universalizing
            models, 50-54
        social reform and minoritizing
            models, 54-57
Anxiety, queer, 101-123. See also
        Relax . . . It's Just Sex,

assimilation politics and
        cinematic hedonics in
Archeology of Knowledge, 26
Assimilation politics, cinematic
        hedonics and, in Relax . . .
        It's Just Sex, 101-123. See
        also Relax . . . It's Just Sex,
        assimilation politics and
        cinematic hedonics in
Atlantic House, 195,197
ATLG scale. See Attitudes Toward
        Lesbians and Gay Men
        (ATLG) scale
Attitude(s)
    anti-homosexual
        social constructionism and,
            48-50
        social psychology of, queer
            theory and, 47-71
    behaviors and, linking of, 57-59
Attitudes research, queer theory and,
        59-64
Attitudes Toward Lesbians and Gay
        Men (ATLG) scale, 55,56
Ault, A., 173,175

Babbit, J., 117-118
Bacon, J., 11,257
Bailey, J.M., 165
Baoine, P., 196,201-202
Barale, M.A., 24,263
Barnett, F., 201
Barthes, R., 25,29
Baudrillard, J., 25-27
Bauman, Z., 289,290
Bay Area Bisexual Network, 163

Beautiful Thing, 107
Beck, E.T., 79
Behavior(s), attitudes and, linking of,
    57-59
Bell, D., 12,285,289,297,300,301
Bennett, J., 10,101
Bergler, E., 134
Bersani, L., 299
Betsky, A., 27
Between Men, 27
Bhaba, H., 216,219-221,225
Bi Any Other Name, 163-164
Bi Women, 163
"Bi-curious," 241
Billy's Hollywood Screen Kiss, 105,
    107,119
BiNet USA, 163
Binnie, J., 12,285,289,297,301
BiPol, West Coast, 163
Bisexual activist narratives, 162-165
Bisexual epistemology, queer theory
    and, 174-175
Bisexual theorizing, historical review
    of, 161-170
Bisexualities, 129
Bisexuality, 134
    concurrent, 166
    erasure of, queer theory and,
        136-143
    forms of, 166
    historicizing of, 125-158
    history of, rereading of, 127-136
    invention of, 130-136
    politics and, identification of,
        175-177
    queer theory and, 159-184
        described, 170-177
        GLBT/queer scholarship,
            170-172
        psychological research related
            to, 165-167
        social sciences/humanities
            accounts, 167-170
    serial, 166
    simultaneous, 166

Bisexuality: A Critical Reader, 127
Bitch & Animal, 278
Blackwood, E., 83
Blasius, M., 12-13
Blessing of the Fleet, 206
Blockbuster Video, 120
Bloomfield, E., 194
Blumstein, P., 161
Boatwright, K.J., 38
Bodenhausen, G.V., 63
Boston Bisexual Women's Network,
    163
Boswell, J., 80-81
Bowie, D., 162,276
Boyarin, D., 81,92,214,216-220,225
Boyd, M., 78
Boys Don't Cry, 102,105
Broadcast News, 317
Brodkin, K., 224
Brookey, J., 105
Brown, M., 52
Brueggemann, B., 276
Bryant, A., 54
Buchbinder, D., 240
But I'm a Cheerleader, 117-118
Butler, J., 14-15,27,33,34,36-38,
    58-59,63,105,113,133,145,
    146,150,164,188,213,214,
    216,225-227,229-232,258,
    263,271,274,279,322

Cagle, C., 128
'Camp Trans,' 302
Cantarella, E., 127
Cape Queer, 185-212. *See also*
    Provincetown, Massachusetts
Cape Queer? A Case Study of
    Provincetown,
    Masssachusetts, 11
Cape Tip, 201
Capitalism, late
    mirroring of, in queer theory, 21
    queer theory and, 28-39
Carlos, A., 193

Carpenter, R.C., 200,201
Carriage Room, 197
Carson, T.C., 111,116
Carver, C.S., 38
Cass, 37
Castellaneta, P.J., 101,104,110,
    116,119
Castells, M., 22-23,40
Caucus on Gay and Lesbian Concerns,
    319,321
Center for Lesbian and Gay Studies in
    Religion and Ministry, 87
Cesco, 194
Chamber of Commerce, in
    Provincetown,
    Massachusetts, 199,205
Chauncey, G., Jr., 129,188,190
Cherry Grove, 188
Christian Century, 86
*Christianity, Social Tolerance, and
    Homosexuality,* 80
Churchill, W., 52,53
Cinema of Outsiders, 103
Cinematic hedonics, assimilation
    politics and, in *Relax . . . It's
    Just Sex,* 101-123. *See also
    Relax . . . It's Just Sex,*
    assimilation politics and
    cinematic hedonics in
Citizenship
    queering, 303-304
    sexual values and, 285-307
    transgression vs., 295-304
Clarke, J., 198
Clarke, L., 51
Classroom(s), *normal,* contested
    territory of sexual identity in,
    270-278
Clem and Ursies Seafood Restaurant,
    206
Clinton, K., 206
*Closer to Home: Bisexuality and
    Feminism,* 164
Closet, bringing back, 248-251
CNN, 105

Coad, D., 239
Coble, M., 205
Cohen, C.J., 3
Cohen, D., 108
Come As You Are, 273
Coming out, injury of, 244-246
"Coming-Out Pegagogy: Risking
    Identity in Language and
    Literature Classrooms," 276
Commercial Street, 199
Communication studies, queer theory
    meets, 313-314
Community(ies)
    emotional, 30
    geographic, 30
Comstock, G.D., 74,85,86,89,90
Concurrent bisexuality, 166
Condon, B., 107
Constructionism, social,
    anti-homosexual attitudes
    and, 48-50
Containing, problem with, 292-294
Cornell, D.P., 63
Costa, M., 196
Costa, N., 196
Countryman, L.W., 79
Coyle, A., 61
Creet, J., 248
Critcher, C., 198
Crown and Anchor Hotel, 197
Cryobank's artificial insemination
    clinics, 272
"Culture-ideology," 30
Curriculum reform, queering, 263-270
Cushing, Archbishop, 201
Cutright, J.D., 63

"Dark Continent" metaphor, 217
Darwin, C., 131
Däumer, E., 174
Davis, M.C., 37,38
De Cecco, J., 166
de Lauretis, T., 27,75,172,263
Deaux, K., 57

DeGeneres, E., 102
Deleuze, 25
Delft Haven Cottages, 194,200
D'Emilio, J., 207
Demuth, C., 194
Derrida, 25
Derridean deconstruction, 126,138
Desiring mates, 237-255
    described, 251-252
Deviancy, ensnared into, 241-243
Dewey, J.C., 63
"Dick dock," 197
Difference, performativity of,
    "Parenthetical Jews" and,
    223-233
Dignity, 74,83
Doane, M.A., 217
Doty, A., 103
du Plessis, M., 139,147,168
Duberman, M., 40-41
Dufour, L.R., 95
Duggan, L., 129,144,173,188,303
Dunbar, J., 52
Dundee, C., 240
Durber, D., 11,237
Dyer, R., 108

Eadie, J., 127,162,179
Eagleton, T., 28,33
Edelman, L., 126,141-144,149,150,218
Edelson, S., 88
Edgar, D., 239
Edwards, A., 192
Eilberg-Schwartz, H., 91
Elia, J.P., 1
Ellis, A., 51
Ellis, H., 131-133,165
Elwell, S.L., 88
Emotional communities, 30
Entertainment Weekly, 102
Epistemology, bisexual, queer theory
    and, 174-175
Epistemology of the Closet, 27,137,
    146,228,263-265

Evans, A., 51
Evans, D., 287
Everett, R., 102
Experience, lived, queer theory of,
    interplay of, 314-323

Faderman, L., 271
Fanon, F., 216,219-221
Female Desires, 83
Feminist and Women's Studies
    Division, of Women's
    Caucus, 321
"Ferment in the Field," 312
"Fetishism of labor," 26
Fight Club, 279
Fisher, D., 249
Flagship Bar and Restaurant, 196
Forrest, L., 38
Foucauldian theory, 126
Foucault, M., 23-26,32,59-60,62,
    137,150,217,241-242,244,
    286,288,292,294,295
Frable, D.E.S., 37
Freedom of speech/the freeing of
    speech, 260-278
Freud, S., 51,132-135,215-223,
    225,231-233
Furey, P., 79
Fuss, D., 126,138-140,142,148-150,
    249-250

Gallipoli, 240
Games, R.G., 52
Gammon, M.A., 10-11,159
Gamson, J., 5,176,287,302
Garber, L., 76
Garber, M., 127-128,167-168
Gay, 51
Gay, defined, 75-76
Gay Activist Alliance of New York, 51
Gay and Lesbian Liberation
    Movement, 163
Gay liberation, universalizing models
    and, 50-54

Gay Men's Issues in Religion, 87
Gay New York, 188
Gay studies. *See also* Lesbian; LGBT
    development of, 23-24
Gay Sunshine Press, 88
Gay/Lesbian/Bisexual/Transgender
        Communication Studies
        Division, 321
Gender
    construction of, Jewish
        disappearing acts and,
        213-236
    race and, in "the invention of
        heterosexuality,"
        interarticulation of, 216-223
Gender Trouble, 27
Gender trouble, in queer theory,
    144-150
Geographic communities, 30
George, B., 276
Gergen, K.J., 61
Get Real, 107
Giddens, A., 289,290,300
Gilbert, M.S., 38
Gilman, S., 216-219
Glaser, C., 78
GLBT/queer scholarship, 170-172
*GLQ: A Journal of Gay and Lesbian
        Studies,* 59
Go Fish, 102,105,268
*God's Phallus and Other Problems for
        Men and Monotheism,* 91
Gonsierek, J., 60
Goodman, J., 102
Goss, R.E., 79,91
Gramick, J., 79
Gray, E.R., 85
Great Depression, 193
Griggers, C., 277
Grosz, E., 245

Haeberle, E., 129
Hall, D.E., 169
Hall, S., 121,198

Halperin, D.M., 7,24,27,263
Hamer, D., 153
Hand, P., 193
Haraway, D., 33
Hartley, M., 194
Hawley, J.C., 3,93
Hawthorne, C., 186
Haynes, T., 106
Heath, S., 148
Hedonics, cinematic, assimilation
        politics and, in *Relax . . . It's
        Just Sex,* 101-123. *See also
        Relax . . . It's Just Sex,*
        assimilation politics and
        cinematic hedonics in
Hegarty, P., 9,47,63
Heisenberg uncertainty principle, 231
Hemmings, C., 168-169,175
Henking, S.E., 74,90
Hennessy, R., 7,40,209
Herek, G.M., 55-57,62
Herman, D., 86
Herring Cove, 195
Herring Cove Beach, 205
Heteronormativity, 313
History of Sexuality, 24,244
History of Sexuality: Volume I, 59
Hogan, 27
Homographies, 141
Homophobia, 51
    institutional, queer responses to,
        260-278
    internalized
        politics and, 35-39
        queer theory and, 35-39
Homosexual League of New York, 51
Homosexual Threat Inventory, 54
Homosexuality and World Religions,
    82
Homosexuality Attitude Scale, 54
"Homosexuality debates," 84-85
Homosexuality in Modern Catholicism,
    88
Honig, B., 300
Howell, J.L., 63

H-Scale, 54
Hudson, 27
Huebner, D.M., 37,38
Huggins, J., 52
Human Rights Campaign, 260
Human Rights Resolution Working
        Group, 208
Hump Inn, 197
Hunt, P., 194,195
Hutchins, L., 163-164
Hyannisport, 195

Identity
    experimenting with, linking
        attitudes to behaviors, 57-59
    sexual, contexted territory of, in
        normal classroom, 270-278
ILGA, 302
"Imitation and Gender
        Insubordination," 226,
        263,274
Incitement, libratory, 243-244
"Incitement to Discourse," 244
*Inside/Out: Lesbian Theories, Gay
        Theories,* 138,148,149
Institutional homophobia, queer
        responses to, 260-278
Intrinsically Catholic, 83
*Invented Moralities: Sexual Values in
        an Age of Uncertainty,*
        285,288-289
Isgro, K.L., 10-11,159
Ivans, I., 194

Jackson, S., 7
Jagose, A., 23,27,62,171
Jakobsen, J.R., 86,92-93,303,304
Jameson, F., 31,33,151
Jefferson, T., 198
Jeffrey, 102
Jeffreys, S., 7
Jesus Acted Up, 79

Jewish American Princess, 224
Jewish disappearing acts, construction
        of gender and, 213-236
Jewish Mother, 224
John, E., 162
Johnson, B., 126
Johnston, R.D., 11,213
*Jokes and Their Relation to the
        Unconscious,* 215
Jordan, M., 81,88,89,92,94
Joseph, J., 37
Journal of Communication, 312
Journal of Homosexuality, 259

Ka'ahumanu, L., 163-164
Kameny, F., 51
Kelley, R.D.G., 198
Kellogg, R., 54
Kelly, N., 240
Kent, R., 196
Ketzenberger, K., 38
King, A., 196
Kinsey, A., 165
Kirsch, M.H., 7,9,19
Kite, M.E., 57
Kitzinger, C., 49,60,61
Klein, F., 166
Krafft-Ebing, R., 131
Krahulik, K.C., 11,185
Kramer, L., 104
Kudrow, L., 118

Lacan, 25
Lacanian psychoanalysis, 126
Laclau, E., 292
Land's End, 194,195,198,200-204,
        206,208
LaRonde, 106
Late capitalism
    mirroring of, in queer theory, 21
    queer theory and, 28-39. *See also*
        Queer theory, late capitalism
        and

Lawson, H., 240
Lemieux, A., 63
Lesbian, gay, bisexual, and transgender
    (LGBT) studies, queer theory
    and. *See* LGBT studies and
    queer theory
  contested terrain of, surveying of,
    1-18
Lesbian and gay studies
  development of, 23-24
  goal of, 4
  queer theory and, crossroads of,
    21-23
*Lesbian and Gay Studies: A Critical
    Introduction,* 7
Lesbian and Gay Studies Reader, 21
"Lesbian Bodies in the Age of
    (Post)Mechanical
    Reproduction," 277
Lesbian Feminist Issues in Religion,
    87
Lesbian Rabbis, 88
Lesbian/gay, defined, 75-76
Lesbian/gay/bisexual, defined, 75-76
Levy, E., 103
Lewis, O., 35
LGBT, defined, 75-76
LGBT studies
  ferment in, queer theory and,
    309-328
  queer theory and
    contested terrain of
      productive possibilities on,
        12-15
      surveying of, 1-18
    enduring tensions related to, 5-8
    historical notes on, 4-5
    objectives for, 8-9
    rationale for, 8-9
    religious studies and, 73-100
    study of religion and, 77-86
  religion and, 86-90
Libratory incitement, 243-244
Lilies, 120
Lincoln, B., 95

"Little Hans," 219-221,231
Lived experience, queer theory of,
    interplay of, 314-323
Livingston, J., 226
Long Nook Beach, 200
Longtime Companion, 119
Lorde, A., 89
Lovaas, K.E., 1
Love the Sin, 86,92,304
Lughod, L.A., 190
Lyotard, J.F., 25,31

Macara, J.E., 199
MacDonald, A.P., 52,165
MacKinnon, C., 148
Madeira Room, 197
Mahaffy, K.A., 84
Malcolm, J.P., 37
Mandel, E., 29
Mars, E., 194
Martha's Vineyard, 195
Martin, B., 145-146,272
Marvin, F., 194
Marx, K., 25,32
Marxism, 25-26
Mary Sphaghetti's place, 197
Massey, S., 9,47
Mate(s)
  defining of, 239-241
  desiring of, 237-255
    described, 251-252
"Mateship," 239
Mayflower, 186,198
McGregor, B.A., 38
McNeill, J.J., 78,79
McWhorter, L., 242
Medhurst, A., 7
Mehlman, J., 215
Melton, J.G., 82
"Men who have sex with men
    (MSM)," 241
Metropolitan Community Church, 85
Michigan Women's Music Festival,
    302

Middleton, S., 311
Millet, K., 115
Millham, J., 54
Minoritizing models, social reform
        and, 54-57
Mirror of Production, 26
Moddelmog, D., 276
Mollenkkott, V.R., 79
Moors Restaurant, 195
Moreno, K.N., 63
Morton, D., 7
Mosher, D.L., 53,54,56
MSM. *See* "Men who have sex with
        men (MSM)"
Munt, S.R., 7
Mutchnick, M., 102

"Nachträglichkeit," 221
Namaste, V.K., 7
NAMBLA, 302
Narrative(s), bisexual activist, 162-165
National Communication Association
        (NCA), 315,320,321
National Organization of Women
        (NOW), 55
NCA. *See* National Communication
        Association (NCA)
Nemeroff, C.J., 37,38
New Beach, 195,199
New York University, 187
Newsweek, 102,162
Nice Jewish Girls, 79
Nichols, J., 51
1987 March on Washington for Gay
        and Lesbian Rights, 163
No Skin Off My Ass, 105
Noors Bar and Restaurant, 196
Normal classroom, contested territory
        of sexual identity in, 270-278
Normal school, teaching queer theory
        at, 257-283
North American Multicultural
        Bisexual Network, 163

NOW. *See* National Organization of
        Women (NOW)
Nugent, R., 79

O'Brien, J., 74
Odd Girls and Twilight Lovers, 271
Oedipus complex, 214,215,218,223
O'Grady, K.E., 53,54,56
O'Haver, T., 105
O'Laughlin, B., 40
Old Colony Tap, 197

"Parenthetical Jews," performativity of
        difference and, 223-233
Paris is Burning, 226
Parks, R., 300
Parnaby, J., 2,7
Parting Glances, 102
Pattanaik, D., 94
PBG. *See* Provincetown Business
        Guild (PBG)
Pedagogy, 276
Pellegrini, A., 86,92-93,216,303,304
Perry, T., 78
Phelan, S., 12,286,289,297,299,
        302,303
Philadelphia, 104,105
Pied Piper, 197
Pierce, K., 105
Pilgrim Club, 197
Pilgrim House, 194,195,197
Pilgrim Monument, 197
Plain and Fancy Restaurant, 196
Plummer, K., 5,300
Poison, 102
Policing the Crisis, 198
Political organizing, queer,
        identification of, 175-177
Politics
    assimilation, cinematic hedonics
        and, in *Relax . . . It's Just Sex,*
        101-123. *See also Relax . . .*

It's Just Sex, assimilation
politics and cinematic
hedonics in
bisexuality and, identification of,
175-177
of "queer," 172-174
queer theory and, internalized
homophobia and, 35-39
Postmodernist theory, critique of, 32
Poststructuralism, 126
Pramaggiore, M., 162
Pratto, F., 63
Prejudice, anti-homosexual, 47-71. *See
also* Anti-homosexual
prejudice
Primiano, L.N., 83
"Project for a Scientific Psychology,"
215,221,223
Promise, 291-292
Proton pseudos, 221
Provincetown, Massachusetts
case study of, 185-212
displacements, 203-209
Chamber of Commerce in, 199,205
Provincetown Advocate, 186,200,202
"Provincetown 'Boys' A Problem,"
198,199
Provincetown Business Guild (PBG),
205
Provincetown Players, 186
Psychoanalysis, Lacanian, 126

Queer
clash of, 238
defined, 75-76
described, 2-3
new uses of, 322-323
politics of, 172-174
principle of, 27-28
terminology of, 172-174
theory of, 28
Queer anxiety, 101-123. *See also
Relax . . . It's Just Sex,*

assimilation politics and
cinematic hedonics in
Queer Dharma, 88,90
Queer dilemma, 176
Queer Eye for the Straight Guy,
297-298,303
Queer interruption, 246-247
Queer Jews, 90
Queer Nation, 4,173
Queer political organizing,
identification of, 175-177
"Queer" Question, 200
Queer theory, 19-45
attitudes research and, 59-64
bisexual epistemology and, 174-175
bisexuality and, 159-184. *See also*
Bisexuality, queer theory and
communication studies and,
313-314
comparative collections about,
82-83
consequences of, 33-35
described, 4-7,20-21,28
erasure of bisexuality and, 136-143
ferment in LGBT studies and,
309-328
gender trouble in, 144-150
history of, 24-28,80-82
late capitalism and, 28-39
lesbian and gay studies and,
crossroads of, 21-23
LGBT studies and,
1-18,73-100,309-328. *See
also* LGBT studies, queer
theory and
lived experience and, interplay of,
314-323
making of, 24-28
mirroring of late capitalism in, 21
politics and, internalized
homophobia and, 35-39
religion and, 90-96
social psychology of
anti-homosexual attitudes
and, 47-71

teaching of, at *normal* school,
          257-283
Queer Theory and Communication:
          From Disciplining Queers to
          Queering the Discipline(s), 8
"Queer wars," 14
Queering Christ, 91
Queering citizenship, 303-304
Queering curriculum reform, 263-270
"Queersville, U.S.A.," 190
Que(e)rying Religion, 74,90

Race, gender and, in "the invention of
          heterosexuality,"
          interarticulation of, 216-223
Rado, S., 134
Randy Majors Memorial award, 321
Rankin, P., 288
Reading Week, 285
Reform, social, minoritizing models
          and, 54-57
Relax . . . It's Just Sex, 10
          assimilation politics and cinematic
                    hedonics in, 101-123
          "no more films about
                    homosexuality," 104-106
          representation in, 106-114
          utopia and its discontents,
                    114-120
Religion
          LGBT studies and, 86-90
          queer theory and, 90-96
          study of, queer theory, LGBT
                    studies and, 77-86
Religion is a Queer Thing, 90-91
Religious studies
          defined, 76-77
          LGBT studies and, 73-100
          queer theory and, 73-100
Research, attitudes, queer theory and,
          59-64
Reynolds, R., 248
Rich, B.R., 121,271
Richardson, D., 12,285,289,300

Richtman, J., 196,197
Robert, B., 198
Robinson, P., 14
Rogers, W.N., 199
Rogin, M., 223
Roof, J., 273
Rorty, R., 33
Ross, L., 194,196
Rowen, C.J., 37
Rubin, G.S., 55,91,145,148,203
Rudy, K., 91
Russo, V., 104,121
Rust, P., 161,164,168
Ryan, P.C., 198-199

Sacred texts, theology and, 78-80
Same-Sex Unions in Premodern
          Europe, 80
Sams, J., 315
San Miguel, C.L., 54
Sapphic Slashers, 188
Savoy, E., 214,232,233
Scanzoni, L., 79
Schippert, C., 12,285
School(s), *normal,* teaching queer
          theory at, 257-283
Schwartz, P., 161
Sedgwick, E.K., 9,27,50,58,62,126,
          136-138,141,146-148,150,
          188,213,216,217,228-231,
          239,263-265,279
Seidman, N., 216,225-227,229-231,
          287
Seidman, S., xxvi, 5,171,173,176,178,
          301,318
Serial bisexuality, 166
Sex and Character, 220
Sexual identity, contested territory of,
          in *normal* classroom,
          270-278
"Sexual Indifference and Lesbian
          Representation," 263
Sexual Inversion, 131

Sexual values, citizenship and,
    285-307
"Sexualities Without Genders and
    Other Queer Utopias,"
    145-146
Shallenberger, D., 86
Shively, M., 166
Shokeid, M., 84
Shultz, P., 194,196
Sigelman, C.K., 63
Silva, C.A., 192,206
Silva, D., 206
Simultaneous bisexuality, 166
Sisters of Perpetual Indulgence, 94-95
Slagle, R.A., 12,309
Smith, K.T., 52,54
Social constructionism,
    anti-homosexual attitudes
    and, 48-50
Social reform, minoritizing models
    and, 54-57
Social scientific studies, 83-86
"Socialism," of Soviet bloc, 25
Society and the Healthy Homosexual,
    51,52
Sparks, H., 300
Spelling, T., 118
Spencer, B., 194
Sphaghetti, M., 197
Squires, M., 194
St. Cloud State University, 323
Stabile, C.A., 32
Stallybrass, P., 197
Stein, A., 109
Stein, M., 188,208
Stonewall, 40
Storr, M., 127,169-170
Stratton, J., 216,221,223-225,227,
    229,230
Stuart, E., 90-91
Students for Democratic Society, 22
Stychin, C., 292,302
Sulloway, F., 131
Swanson, R.A., 52
Swidler, A., 82

"Texts of terror," 79
The Anti-Gay Agenda, 86
The Broken Heart's Club, 107,119
The Celluloid Closet, 104
The Church and the Homosexual,
    78,79
"The Gospel Hour," 85
*The Incredibly True Adventure of Two
    Girls in Love*, 102
"The invention of heterosexuality,"
    race and gender in,
    interarticulation of, 216-223
The Jazz Singer, 223
The Lesbian and Gay Studies Reader,
    144,145,263
The Opposite of Sex, 102,107,118,119
*The Oxford American Desk Dictionary
    and Thesaurus*, 312
The Queer God, 91
"The 'Queer' Question," 186
The Sexual Citizen, 288,297
The Silence of Sodom, 81,88,92
"The Trouble with Harry Thaw," 189
Theology, sacred texts and, 78-80
"Thinking Sex," 145
"Third Space," 250
*Three Essays on the Theory of
    Sexuality*, 215
Thumma, S.L., 85
Tierny, W., 74
Tilly, J., 118
Time, 162
*To Believe in Women: What Lesbians
    Have Done for America–a
    History*, 271
Tobin, K., 51
Town House Restaurant and Lounge,
    197
Townhouse, 195
Transgression
    balancing/framing of, 299-302
    benefits of, 295-297
    citizenship vs., 295-304
Treichler, P.A., 61,62,64
Trick, 107,118

Umphrey, M., 188-189
Uncertainty
    age of, writing values in, 289-294
    containing of, 285-307
Unheroic Conduct, 92
United Church of Christ, 85
United Methodist Church, 85
United States Navy, 186
Universalizing models, gay liberation
        and, 50-54
University at Albany, xxvi
"University LGBT/Queer Program,"
        264
University of California–Santa Cruz,
        27
University of Puerto Rico, 323

Valocchi, S., 174
Value(s)
    sexual, citizenship and, 285-307
    writing of, in age of uncertainty,
        289-294
Veblen, T., 203
*Vice Versa: Bisexuality and the
        Eroticism of Everyday Life,*
        167
von Krafft-Ebing, R., 165

Walton, T.J., 205
Warner, M., 60,104,176,278,298
"Wash-ashores," 194
Weathering Heights Club,
        195,196,201,202
"Weathering Knights," 196,202
Weeks, J., 12,35,128,285,288-303
Weinberg, G., 51-53,231
Weise, E.R., 164
Weninger, O., 220
West Chester University,
        257-263,265-267,270,279
What a Lesbian Looks Like, 273
White, A., 197

White, M., 78
White, W., 201
Wicker, R., 51
Wieringa, S.E., 83
Wilcox, M.M., 9-10,73
Will and Grace, 102
Williams, P., 35
Williams, T., 194
Williamson, I.R., 37-38
Wilson, E., 296,297,302
Winchell, B., 102
WIP. *See* Women Innkeepers of
        Provincetown (WIP)
Wittig, M., 271,274
Wolf, E., 23
Women Innkeepers of Provincetown
        (WIP), 205
Women's Caucus, 319,321
    Feminist and Women's Studies
        Division of, 321
Women's Week, 205
Wood, E., 32
Worcester Telegram, 198
World War II, xxiii, 51,194,223
Wortman, C., 37

Yep, G.A., 1
Yip, A.K.T., 85
Young, S., 52,168,169,176
Younger, J., 264

Zinik, G., 166
Zita, J.N., 3

BOOK ORDER FORM!

Order a copy of this book with this form or online at:
http://www.HaworthPress.com/store/product.asp?sku= 5979

LGBT Studies and Queer Theory
New Conflicts, Collaborations, and Contested Terrain

—— in softbound at $32.00 ISBN-13: 978-1-56023-317-6 / ISBN-10: 1-56023-317-6.
—— in hardbound at $92.00 ISBN-13: 978-1-56023-316-9 / ISBN-10: 1-56023-316-8.

COST OF BOOKS _____

POSTAGE & HANDLING _____
US: $4.00 for first book & $1.50
for each additional book
Outside US: $5.00 for first book
& $2.00 for each additional book.

SUBTOTAL _____
In Canada: add 6% GST. _____

STATE TAX _____
CA, IL, IN, MN, NJ, NY, OH, PA & SD residents
please add appropriate local sales tax.

FINAL TOTAL _____
If paying in Canadian funds, convert
using the current exchange rate,
UNESCO coupons welcome.

❏ **BILL ME LATER:**
Bill-me option is good on US/Canada/
Mexico orders only; not good to jobbers,
wholesalers, or subscription agencies.

❏ **Signature** _____

❏ **Payment Enclosed: $**_____

❏ **PLEASE CHARGE TO MY CREDIT CARD:**
❏ Visa ❏ MasterCard ❏ AmEx ❏ Discover
❏ Diner's Club ❏ Eurocard ❏ JCB

Account #_____

Exp Date_____

Signature_____
(Prices in US dollars and subject to change without notice.)

PLEASE PRINT ALL INFORMATION OR ATTACH YOUR BUSINESS CARD

Name

Address

City   State/Province   Zip/Postal Code

Country

Tel   Fax

E-Mail

May we use your e-mail address for confirmations and other types of information? ❏Yes ❏No We appreciate receiving
your e-mail address. Haworth would like to e-mail special discount offers to you, as a preferred customer.
We will never share, rent, or exchange your e-mail address. We regard such actions as an invasion of your privacy.

Order from your **local bookstore** or directly from
The Haworth Press, Inc. 10 Alice Street, Binghamton, New York 13904-1580 • USA
Call our toll-free number (1-800-429-6784) / Outside US/Canada: (607) 722-5857
Fax: 1-800-895-0582 / Outside US/Canada: (607) 771-0012
E-mail your order to us: orders@HaworthPress.com

For orders outside US and Canada, you may wish to order through your local
sales representative, distributor, or bookseller.
For information, see http://HaworthPress.com/distributors

(Discounts are available for individual orders in US and Canada only, not booksellers/distributors.)

Please photocopy this form for your personal use.
www.HaworthPress.com

BOF07